D1230695

The United States of India

In the series *Asian American History and Culture*, edited by Cathy Schlund-Vials, Shelley Sang-Hee Lee, and Rick Bonus. Founding editor, Sucheng Chan; editors emeriti, David Palumbo-Liu, Michael Omi, K. Scott Wong, and Linda Trinh Võ.

Also in this series:

A list of additional titles in this series appears at the back of this book

MANAN DESAI

The United States of India

Anticolonial Literature and Transnational Refraction

TEMPLE UNIVERSITY PRESS
Philadelphia • *Rome* • *Tokyo*

TEMPLE UNIVERSITY PRESS
Philadelphia, Pennsylvania 19122
tupress.temple.edu

Library of Congress Cataloging-in-Publication Data

Names: Desai, Manan, 1980- author.
Title: The United States of India : anticolonial literature and
   transnational refraction / Manan Desai.
Description: Philadelphia : Temple University Press, 2020. | Series: Asian
   American history and culture | Includes bibliographical references and
   index. | Summary: "Reconstructs exchanges and interactions among
   networks of expatriate Indian and American authors as they struggled in
   similar yet distinct ways for an anticolonial future, attempting to
   reimagine and reshape the relationship between the U.S. and India during
   and immediately following World War I"— Provided by publisher.
Identifiers: LCCN 2019024305 (print) | LCCN 2019024306 (ebook) | ISBN
   9781439918890 (cloth) | ISBN 9781439918906 (paperback) | ISBN
   9781439918913 (pdf)
Subjects: LCSH: East Indian Americans—Politics and government—20th
   century. | East Indians—Political activity—United States. |
   Racism—United States—History—20th century. | Anti-imperialist
   movements—United States—History—20th century. |
   India—History—Autonomy and independence movements. | Radicalism. |
   American literature—East Indian authors—History and criticism. |
   Imperialism in literature.
Classification: LCC E184.E2 D38 2020 (print) | LCC E184.E2 (ebook) | DDC
   305.89/1411073—dc23
LC record available at https://lccn.loc.gov/2019024305
LC ebook record available at https://lccn.loc.gov/2019024306

Printed in the United States of America

9 8 7 6 5 4 3 2 1

Contents

Acknowledgments

This book would not have been possible without the support and labor of many friends, family members, colleagues, and teachers over the years. This project began as a dissertation at the University of Michigan, where I received critical guidance from the faculty in the English Department. I owe a debt of gratitude to Jennifer Wenzel for her sage advice as I first navigated academia and for her continued support ever since. My committee members Alan Wald, Susan Najita, and Christi Merrill each encouraged me to persevere as the project moved in unexpected directions, and it has been a great privilege to continue to benefit from their wisdom now as colleagues. I am also grateful for the mentorship and support from my wonderful colleagues at Syracuse University: Crystal Bartolovich, Susan Edmunds, Carol Fadda-Conrey, Mike Goode, Chris Hanson, Coran Klaver, Prema Kurien, Patty Roylance, and Silvio Torres-Saillant.

I had the great fortune of returning to Michigan to work at the Department of American Culture and the Program in Asian/Pacific Islander American Studies, where I have been supported by my colleagues in innumerable ways. I would like to thank my Michigan network: Charlotte Karem Albrecht, Paul Barron, Melissa Borja, William Calvo Quiros, John Cheney-Lippold, Matthew Countryman, Clare Croft, Greg Dowd, Jatin Dua, Frieda Ekotto, Julie Ellison, Jesse Hoffnung-Garskof, Sandra Gunning, Colin Gunckel, Bethany Hughes, Brandi Hughes, Roland Hwang, Aswin Punathambekar, Larry La Fountain-Stokes, Leila Kawar, Mary Kelley, Su'ad Abdul Khabeer, S.E. Kile, Scott Larson, Allan Lumba, Scott Lyons, Victor Mendoza, Anthony Mora, Susan Najita, Lisa Nakamura, Silvia Pedraza, Yeidy Rivero, Ian Shin,

Balbir Singh, Alex Stern, Matt Stiffler, Keith Taylor, Antoine Traisnel, Penny Von Eschen, Michael Witgen, Magdalena Zaborowska, and the late Dick Meisler. I would like to express my gratitude to graduate students—Stephanie Fajardo, Ai Binh Ho, Meryem Kamil, Mika Kennedy, Michael Pascual, Jasleen Singh, Vivian Truong, and Joo Young Lee—who have helped build the vibrant intellectual community of A/PIA Studies. Thank you also to the incredible administrators in American Culture, who have helped me in many ways throughout the years: Abbie Dykstra, Mary Freiman, Judy Gray, Kate Klemm, Marlene Moore, Andrew Reiter, Hannah Yung, and the late Tammy Zill.

I would especially like to thank Toy Basu, Stephen Berrey, Varuni Bhatia, Maria Cotera, Gaurav Desai, Anna Watkins Fisher, Jonathan Freedman, Kris Klein Hernandez, Madhumita Lahiri, Christi Merrill, Supriya Nair, Ava Purkiss, Amy Stillman, and Alan Wald, whose valuable comments during my manuscript workshop and third-year review helped shape the project during a critical period in the writing process. Thank you to June Howard for skillfully chairing the workshop, and to Sidonie Smith and Meg Sweeney for being such gracious and insightful readers. I am also deeply grateful to Dohra Ahmad for her generosity and her substantial feedback, which helped me reformulate key questions of the book. Madhumita Lahiri has constantly encouraged me throughout this project, and her insights into this history have been immensely helpful. Anna Watkins Fisher has been hugely supportive and her careful feedback during the revision process helped clarify and advance several key ideas in the book. Victor Mendoza has been an invaluable mentor, helping me navigate multiple stages of the profession. Ever since I joined the department, Evelyn Alsultany has been a tremendous mentor and has modeled what it means to be a committed and compassionate scholar, teacher, and colleague.

Many librarians and archivists have assisted my research on the project over the years. I would like to especially thank Jyothi Luthra at the Jawaharlal Nehru Memorial Museum and Library, Eri Mizukane at the Kislak Center at University of Pennsylvania, Isabel Planton at the Lilly Library at Indiana University, Blake Spitz at the Special Collections & University Archives at University of Massachusetts–Amherst, Marisa Louie at the National Archives at San Bruno, Eric Van Slander at the National Archives at College Park, and the staff at the Special Collections at Syracuse University and Bancroft Library at the University of California–Berkeley. Jeffrey Martin at the University of Michigan has been helpful at every turn. Patrick Williams at Syracuse rescued me, on more than one occasion, by finding an obscure reference that I thought was lost in the stacks.

I have benefited immensely from the mentorship, camaraderie, and inspiring scholarship of my colleagues in Asian American Studies over the years. I had the privilege to attend the East of California Junior Faculty Mentoring Workshop sponsored by the Association for Asian American Studies and hosted at the University of Illinois–Chicago. Mark Chiang, Tina Chen, Judy Wu, Loan Dao, Ronak Kapadia, Lori Lopez, Nitasha Sharma, John Cheng, and Zelideth Rivas all provided valuable feedback during an earlier stage in this project. I would also like to thank the National Center for Faculty Development and Diversity, in particular Melissa Braaten and Chu Kim-Prieto for helping me reach the finish line. I am grateful to Daniel Elam for graciously reading portions of this manuscript. Tamara Bhalla has been a wonderful interlocutor and friend since graduate school, who encouraged me early on to see my work as a part of Asian American Studies.

I am enormously indebted to Samip Mallick, who asked me to be a part of the South Asian American Digital Archive just as I was finishing graduate school. Samip and everyone involved in SAADA have supported this project in countless ways, consistently renewing my interest in this material whenever I had doubts about my own writing. Thank you to Kritika Agarwal, Michelle Caswell, Jennifer Dolfus Ford, Tina Bhaga, Sindya Bhanoo, Pawan Dhingra, and Rabia Syed. I think often about the camaraderie we shared and the lessons we learned about what it means to represent these histories.

Sara Cohen has been an incredibly generous, responsive, and supportive editor throughout the process of seeing this book to publication. I am also very grateful to series editor Cathy Schlund-Vials for her sharp editorial eye, and to the two anonymous readers for their valuable comments. I owe a great thanks to Shelley Lee and Rick Baldoz for all their help and encouragement along the way. Thank you to Aaron Javsicas, Nikki Miller, Kate Nichols, Ann-Marie Anderson, Ashley Petrucci, Jamie Armstrong, Gary Kramer, and Sarah Munroe for all their help in getting the book through its final stages. Thanks also to Kim Greenwell, whose editing helped strengthen earlier drafts of this manuscript.

I am lucky to have a community of dear friends (including many above) who have encouraged and supported me throughout the years: Asim Akhtar, Alex Beringer, Brian Chung, Sean Conrey, Sri Craven, Sally Curran, Kelly Delevan, Dan Fargo, Chris Fraga, Sugi Ganeshananthan, Kate Hanson, Adil Haq, Cooper Holoweski, Darcy Holoweski, Rory Loughnane, Adam Machado, Navaneetha Mokkil, Tessa Murphy, Cynthia Nagendra, Fabiola Ortiz, Anshuman Pandey, Fiza Quraishi, Dipankar Rai, Ratheesh Radhakrishnan, Kiri Sailiata, Adam Schubel, Stephanie Schubel, Eric Shih, Richard Shin, Farha Ternikar, Sheel Upadhyay, Travis Vande Berg, Lee Ann Wang, Alisa Weinstein, and Kathy Zarur. Ever since our first seminar together at UM, Brian Chung has been a consistent source of advice and laughter. Chris Fraga has been my most important interlocutor since middle school, and without his encouragement over the years, I am not sure where I would be. I wrote the opening passage of this book when I stayed with Adil and Fiza in Oakland years ago. The two of them have encouraged me every step of the way, and I only wish I could share news of this book finally coming out with Fiza.

Thank you: To my family in Kathmandu, Mumbai, Ahmedabad, Navsari, London, Los Angeles, Chicago, Toronto, the Bay Area, and all points in between. To all my cousins, aunts, and uncles, who have shared their homes with me during research trips, picked me up from conferences, and reminded me not to take myself too seriously. To Abhay Desai and Mandaben Parikh, who encouraged me to pursue this path early on and have cheered me on from afar ever since. To Kavita and Justin—for being there at the most critical moments—and to Isla and Hudson, for reminding me that a PhD isn't nearly as impressive as solving a Rubik's Cube. To my parents, Smita and Ramchandra, for their boundless love and support. And finally, to Retika, who has lived and labored with me through every stage of this process, and whose patience and care carried me through.

The United States of India

Introduction

An Indian in Washington

India and America are located on opposite sides of the
earth; therefore it is natural for America to think that we
walk upside down, and for us to think that Americans walk
upside down.

—Pandita Ramabai,
  The Peoples of the United States (1889)

The Sufferance of the Foreigner

In late September 1905, the Indian nationalist Lajpat Rai had gathered with
a group of tourists in the rotunda of the U.S. Capitol, when a guide directed
their attention to the works of art surrounding them. Plastered on the ceil-
ing was *The Apotheosis of Washington*, a fresco featuring the first U.S. president on a celestial throne, flanked on each side by figures from classical
Greco-Roman and nouveau American mythology (Figure I.1). Just below,
The Frieze of American History encircled the rotunda with its selective timeline, and at eye level were enormous neoclassical canvases depicting scenes
from the American Revolution and the conquest of the Americas. From ceil-
ing to floor, the artwork of the Capitol presented a set of interwoven images
that moved seamlessly from the mythological to the historical, containing
within it, it would seem, a visual argument: The United States was the heir
apparent of Western empire. At the dawn of the new century, as America
extended its imperial reach across the globe, who would have thought to see
otherwise?

In Washington, DC, during a three-week tour of the East Coast, Lajpat
Rai discussed his visit in an editorial for the *Panjabee*, an English-language
weekly based out of Lahore. The Capitol was indeed a "picture [that] tells
volumes of history," he told his readers, but Rai paid little attention to its
classical influences and imperial overtures.[1] Instead, he called attention to
the images of the British, who, by the turn of the century, were viewed more
as American allies than as historical adversaries. Throughout his editorial,

FIGURE I.1 Detail from *The Apotheosis of Washington* (1865). (Architect of the Capitol)

Rai added details and subtle quips that emphasized that American independence was an act of opposition against the very same British from whom India was currently wresting its freedom. When describing John Trumbull's painting *Surrender of Lord Cornwallis*, Rai cast George Washington with a kind of personal defiance ("Washington declines to accept overtures from Lord Cornwallis"), knowing that readers of the *Panjabee* would remember the latter as governor-general of India rather than as a redcoat general in the American Revolution. Rai appended the title of Trumbull's *Surrender of General Burgoyne* with the note "by the British," as if to make the sides of the battle unmistakably clear.[2] He especially relished that, for the British, the Capitol was full of "humiliating themes." When the tour guide pointed out that the floor beneath the party's feet was "paved by beautiful tiles imported from England" and that "it was a matter of great satisfaction that the only English material used for [. . .] this national edifice was one which was always underfoot," Rai noted that the audience, barring the few Englishmen in attendance, erupted into cheers.[3]

By the end of his tour, however, Rai's mood had changed. When he traveled down the Potomac to George Washington's Mount Vernon estate, his prose grew more maudlin and he confessed that the "visit saddened [him]."[4] He remembered the plight of India under British rule and described his shame at remaining a colonial subject while in the home of Atlantic patriots:

> Reader! Can I tell you what thoughts arose in my mind in the course of my itinerary through Washington and what feelings and sentiments were born and stifled in the course of two brief days I stayed in this city. No! I cannot. I dare not. Bonded slave as I am, how can I give utterance or thoughts which though noble in themselves cannot be uttered with freedom and impunity in the land of the mighty Aryans—in the land of Pratap and Shivaji—in the land which is mine by birth and by birth of my forefathers but where I now live only by the sufferance of the foreigner.[5]

Rai's address to the reader turned what may have first appeared as dispassionate description into overwrought testimony. His "itinerary through Washington" provided an occasion to voice a form of Indian nationalism that reflected his and, by proxy, his readers' status as colonized subjects. But critically, in his editorial, Rai's Indian imaginary was viewed through the lens of American history: George Washington rubbed shoulders with figures from India's past, while the British appeared as a common enemy of liberty in both the New World and Old. To walk through the hallways of American history was to confront the "feelings and sentiments" of being an Indian on the cusp of the twentieth century—not only to bear the indignity of remaining colonized but also to imagine the "freedom and impunity" that could come with national sovereignty.

I begin with this moment in Rai's itinerary less for the merits of his comparison and more because it captures how expatriate Indians who came to the United States in the early twentieth century engaged in deeply self-reflexive ways of seeing. For figures such as Rai, the social and historical landscape of America acted as a reflective surface that provided glimpses of recognition and comparison—a means of seeing oneself in the transnational other. But if "reflection" describes the mirror image returned to a viewer, then "refraction" describes the distorted and often transformed image that appears when glancing from "a comparative angle of vision."[6] From the vantage point of the U.S. capital, Rai glimpsed the Indian anticolonial cause through what I call a "transnational refraction," a political optic and discursive strategy that allowed him to reframe his cause from the local to the international, from a single nationalist struggle into the latest episode in a string of liberal revolutions that included the United States. Through such refractions, the walls of the Capitol and Mount Vernon provided a prism that opened up analogies, encouraged new interpretive frames, and offered ways to imagine how American history could shed light on an anticolonial Indian future.

While transnational refractions were generative to Rai's anticolonial imaginary, they also led to distortions, which obscured as often as they revealed. To give one example, while Rai spent time in DC, scenes of the U.S. colonization of Native American lands also appeared in his peripheral vision, suggesting unseemly comparisons that did not map so neatly onto his Indian–American analogy. He had observed the recurring "pathos"-filled images of Native Americans throughout the National Mall, noting "a pioneer in desperate conflict with a savage" painted in the portico and a "dejected chieftain and Indian (Red) mother" etched in the *Frieze*.[7] Yet Rai abstained from evoking the obvious comparison between British colonialism in India and settler colonialism in the Americas, even if the appellative twins of Indians and "Indians (Red)" shared the common narrative of societies subjugated by the European outsider.

The reflections and distortions that emerged from Lajpat Rai's refracted encounter with the United States—the analogies he saw and the ones he did not—raise a series of questions: What did it mean for an Indian nationalist to compare his cause to the conservative revolution of white settlers? What was the effect of describing India as a "land of Aryans" when such a word conjured different racial connotations in the United States? How did his allusions to religiously Hindu figures Pratap Singh and Shivaji expose his communal, rather than secular, vision of Indian nationhood? The comparisons Rai articulated and the details he fixated on reveal as much about his image of America as they do about his image of India. But comparisons—whether used as sustained analogies or fleeting metaphors—are often unpredictable, slipping easily into directions unintended by their writer. When Rai described himself as a "bonded slave," for instance, how could his readers not also draw a link to the history of African Americans, who had gained emancipation only one generation earlier? In 1905, the stories of Native American dispossession, of Black inequality—and more broadly, the histories of race in the United States—continued to lurk in his periphery, never fully erased, always threatening to unsettle Rai's tidy Indian–American analogy of national, anticolonial revolution. The very presence of, and discrimination against, Indians (or Hindus, as they were called) in the United States disrupted the analogies that Rai so readily sought.[8]

After Rai returned to the United States in November 1914, where he resided in exile for the four years that marked World War I, he eventually came to understand America differently, reckoning with the issues of race, immigration, and empire head-on. As he worked for the cause of Indian independence from an office in Manhattan, Rai developed a network of friendships and acquaintances with American liberals and radicals, through whom he began to understand the complexities of life for immigrants, the working classes, and racialized communities in the United States. For the Americans who formed alliances with Rai and other Indian expatriates, this engagement with the Indian cause led to their own transnational refractions, dramatically shifting their perspective. Agnes Smedley, a working-class radical from Missouri who was mentored by Rai, later wrote that her work with the Indian expatriate scene led her to apprehend world events "through the eyes of men from Asia—eyes that watched and were cynical about the phrases of democracy."[9] Rai's friend W.E.B. Du Bois, one of the period's leading African American intellectuals and theorists of race, held on to the promise of Indian decolonization for decades to come, declaring in 1947 that India's independence was "the greatest historical date of the nineteenth and twentieth centuries."[10] By engaging one another, these writers gleaned insights into the unlikely ways that the conditions of British India were mirrored in a postwar America dominated by racism, capitalism, and the ongoing project of empire. They forced themselves to see "through the eyes of" their American and Indian others, in the process unsettling their own entrenched understandings of race, caste, nation, empire, and, no less importantly, themselves.

The United States of India argues that these transnational ways of seeing, and the refractions they enabled, played a key role in the development of anticolonial thought in the years during and immediately following World War I. In print journals, monthly organs, works of fiction, and pages of propaganda, this network of expatriate Indian and American authors attempted to reimagine and reshape the relationship between the United States and India during a critical period that witnessed not only wide-scale global and domestic transformations wrought by the war, but also a series of legislative measures restricting immigration and stripping Indian migrants in the United States of naturalization rights. As the American state was building borders and closing off its relationship with India, writers such as Rai, Smedley, and Du Bois, as well as less-heralded figures such as Dhan Gopal Mukerji and Saint Nihal Singh, actively challenged such decisions by rallying American support for the cause of Indian independence, attempting to free Indian political prisoners in the United States, challenging racist immigration laws, and—especially important for this study—developing new forms of writing that imaginatively aligned people and populations facing various forms of subjugation in the United States and India. The result was a sophisticated yet imperfect project of anticolonialism, which imagined a new world that sometimes recast, but often reproduced, the social and political structures of dominance that came before it.

India in America

By the turn of the century, the United States had come to mean a number of things for the Indians who endured the journey. For Rai, the alabaster monuments of Washington may have conjured dreams of freedom, but for most the United States simply meant work. Hundreds of men from Punjab—primarily Sikhs—left colonial India and found work in the lumberyards, canneries, and railroads along the Pacific Coast of the United States and Canada. Those who ventured farther south settled in the central and southern valleys of California, a landscape that resembled the irrigated farmlands of Punjab that they had left after the British enacted wide-scale changes in land tenure policy.[11] As Vivek Bald has documented, a number of Muslim men from East Bengal had arrived as peddlers of Oriental wares in the late nineteenth century, where they fed a growing consumer market for all things "Indian" while integrating into communities of color in port cities, such as New Orleans.[12] For their more well-heeled countrymen, the United States had become a desirable destination for higher education; American colleges promised degrees for those interested in industrial education, science, and agriculture. These early twentieth-century migrants and sojourners were mostly men, for whom certain pathways of travel were accessible, but a few women also arrived during this period to study and work. In 1883, for example, Anandi Joshi came to Philadelphia, where she earned a degree at the Women's Medical College of Pennsylvania. Even earlier, in 1880, scholar Priya Srinivasan explains, four teenage women, whose names were recorded in the local papers as Sahebjan, Vagoirba, Ala Bundi, and Oondabai, arrived in New York on a contract visa as part of a troupe of dancers hired to perform during interludes of a local opera.[13]

In the early part of the twentieth century, the United States also became a political refuge for Indians targeted by an increasingly paranoid and powerful British colonial government, which had passed legislation to restrict free speech, imprison "subversives" without trial, and enact preventive detention.[14] Many radicals and nationalists who successfully evaded colonial authorities and imprisonment in India fled to outposts such as the United States, where they redoubled their revolutionary efforts. Given its official diplomatic position of neutrality, America had become a popular destination for revolutionaries across the world who sought a base of operations abroad. In 1911, Sun Yat-sen toured across the United States, raising funds and building organizations to support the Chinese Revolution.[15] The Bolshevik leader Mikhail Borodin, who would later cross paths with Bengali revolutionary Manabendra Nath (M. N.) Roy, resided in Indiana in the 1910s, before the October Revolution of 1917 lured him back to Russia.[16] Irish republican organizations such as the Friends of Irish Freedom, a natural ally to anti-British Indian expatriates, promoted independence and raised funds for the Easter Rebellion of 1916.[17] Indian activists who arrived in the period before the war may have believed the United States to be remote enough to escape the watchful eye of the British.

As it turns out, they were mistaken. World War I and the decade after marked a shift in British and American relations, which changed from a phase of "rapprochement" to strong interimperial alliance.[18] This alliance was reinforced both culturally and politically. Culturally, an emergent racial discourse of Anglo-Saxonism encouraged "British and American elites to think themselves as the twin vanguards of modernity."[19] Such sentiments were famously captured in Rudyard Kipling's poetry, the American author Lothrop Stoddard's paranoid volumes on the end of "white world-supremacy," and journals such as the *English Speaking World* that published editorials on "Anglo-Saxon solidarity."[20] Politically, the period saw a new phase of cooperation between British and American intelligence, which kept tabs on the activities of Indian migrants and expatriates, monitoring their mail, countering anticolonial propaganda with colonial apologia, censoring books, and enacting deportations.[21] The British Foreign Office had long been concerned with North America as a den of Indian radicalism and anticolonial sedition, and attempted to coax the U.S. government into preventing the naturalization of Indian "seditionists" who migrated to America.[22] Each of the figures I discuss in this book, from the radical Agnes Smedley to the nationalist Lajpat Rai, even the popular children's author Dhan Gopal Mukerji, appeared in the reports of U.S. and British agents, who feared a conspiracy of "Hindus and radical elements."[23]

These regimes of surveillance and repression notwithstanding, the 1910s saw the emergence of two powerful organizations of Indian expatriates agitating against British rule in India, both of which served as important nodes in the interconnected and transnational network of writers this book examines: the Gadar Party on the West Coast and the India Home Rule League of America (IHRLA) on the East Coast. The latter was formed under the leadership of Lajpat Rai. After his arrival in New York in 1914, Rai toured the country and developed friendships with a number of prominent American progressive leaders, including Margaret Sanger, W.E.B. Du Bois, Booker T. Washington, Oswald Garrison Villard, Walter Lippmann, and Jabez Thomas (J. T.) Sunderland. Many of these leaders opened important doors for Rai by providing audiences for lectures and venues for publication. By 1917, Rai had established the IHRLA, operating it from an office on Broadway. The league published a number of political pamphlets and newsletters, including a monthly journal, *Young India*, that featured news stories and editorials denouncing British rule, alongside eclectic works of art criticism and poetry. In accordance with Rai's position and as its name suggested, the IHRLA advocated for "home rule," not total decolonization. Under home rule, India would remain a part of the British Empire but would gain some measure of autonomy over its internal management, including establishing its own parliament.

Just a few years earlier, in 1913, a more radical anticolonial organization known as the Gadar Party had formed on the West Coast and had called for the complete overthrow of British rule through armed revolution. Led by itinerant radicals Har Dayal, Taraknath Das, and Sohan Singh Bhakna, the group first formed in Oregon as the Pacific Coast Hindustan Association, with a membership that included a cadre of laborers, students, and revolutionaries who had been involved in anticolonial activities back home.[24] The Gadar Party soon established an office in San Francisco, ran a printing press, and published a newspaper in English, Urdu, Gurmukhi, and Gujarati editions.[25] Its reach would eventually extend far beyond the national borders of the United States and Canada and throughout the diaspora, with agents and actors in Europe, East Asia, South Asia, and Central America. With the political and financial backing of Germany, in 1917 the Gadar Party hatched a plan to send two shipments of arms to India to incite an insurrection. The plan was thwarted, however, by U.S. and British intelligence, and eighteen Gadar Party members, along with nearly twenty German and American citizens, were arrested on charges of conspiring to violate the wartime "neutrality laws."[26] The subsequent court case, which the press dubbed the "Hindu–German conspiracy trial," was at the time one of the longest and most expensive trials in American history.[27]

Between these bicoastal associations, a number of smaller institutions created by Indian expatriates, migrants, and their American allies flourished, including the Friends of Freedom for India and the Hindustani Progressive Association of New York, each of which produced its own periodicals, pamphlets, and books. Other publications printed outside of the United States, such as the Calcutta-based *Modern Review* and Canada's *Hindustanee*, also became critical venues for circulating information about the Indian diaspora, the independence movements in India, and the struggle for immigrant rights in Canada. In college towns such as Urbana, Berkeley, and Ann Arbor, university organizations such as the Hindusthan Association of America and the Nalanda Club became spaces for intellectual exchange among students across the country, many of whom would go on to become politically active in the struggle for Indian independence upon returning home. Friendships and acquaintances were fostered in spaces such as Manhattan's Civic Club, where progressive leaders congregated for speeches on pressing issues of the day. Other political friendships were forged more covertly, in spaces such as the Yugantar Ashram in San Francisco and the Bakunin Institute in Oakland, and in watering holes such as the Taj Mahal Hindu Restaurant and Ceylon Inn in New York City. Within this network of diasporic Indians and Americans, writing was a shared means of fighting for the cause of Indian freedom abroad and petitioning for the rights of Indian migrants in the United States. Print and publishing connected U.S. and Indian authors, providing, as Brent Hayes Edwards has argued in the case of

Black internationalist print culture, "spaces of independent thinking [and] alternative modes of expression and dissemination, articulating transnational groupings."[28] Publications such as the IHRLA's *Young India* and the Gadar Party's newspaper not only served as means of disseminating information; they also became sites of imagining colonial India as an independent nation, or print manifestations of what Benedict Anderson once described as "long-distance nationalism."[29]

The forms of long-distance nationalism that Indian expatriates and immigrants in the United States expressed were often shaped by their firsthand experiences with racism, experiences that often fostered transnational affinities with communities of color. For writers such as the journalist Saint Nihal Singh, the sting of racism in America provided occasion for recognizing the shared fate of "coloured peoples" around the world, as he would describe in the *Modern Review*: "The white man metes out the same treatment to coloured people in India and out of India. It makes little difference whether the coloured man is an Indian, a Chinese, a Japanese or an Afro-American."[30] This was especially true for Indian laborers, who were directly subjected to instances of racial and xenophobic violence stoked by anti-Asiatic labor organizations and an American public riven with anxieties over threats against white labor. West Coast publications such as the *Survey* and the *World's Work*, as well as local newspapers, exacerbated fears of the "Hindu" as a menace, threat, and foreign invasion. These fears occasionally exploded into acts of violence, as they did in Bellingham, Washington, in 1907, when a mob of white men assaulted a group of Sikh laborers and forced them out of town. For some expatriate Indians, seeing or hearing about such events reinforced their second-class citizenship as both colonial subjects at home and racial subjects in the United States. Gadar Party leader Sohan Singh Bhakna, for instance, described how the experience of racial subjection was refracted through the colonial question: "It dawned upon us Indians that since we were slaves in our homeland nobody cared for us, and there could be no redressal to the situation unless we became free as a people."[31]

But even as experiences in the United States led some Indians to recognize how racism shaped their experiences both as migrants and as colonial subjects, many continued to proclaim their racial identity as "Aryan" or "Indo-Aryan," a category partially synonymous with "whiteness" and endorsed by philologists and ethnologists of the day. The path to American citizenship depended on proving oneself to be the "free, white person" eligible for citizenship under the Naturalization Act of 1790. Not surprisingly, then, Indian migrants who sought to naturalize would often claim "Aryan" identity as a means to citizenship. For the nationalist-minded, claiming "Aryan" identity was also a means of closing what Partha Chatterjee has termed the "rule of colonial difference" and arguing against the injustice of colonial rule by deploying racial categories.[32] To live in the United States was to be caught in someone else's translation. Part of what this book seeks to explore is how Indian expatriates responded to this aspect of transnational life. Which mistranslations would they instrumentalize and to what end? Which would they challenge?

For Americans in the early twentieth century, India conjured a wide spectrum of images. The subcontinent still evoked a cluster of exotic ideas inherited from sources low-brow to high, from pulp tales to the transcendentalists, Hindu holy men to *The Jungle Book*. The editors of *Young India* commented on this fascination, and its fickle nature, in their inaugural issue:

> for the man in the street, the only thing he knew about India was that it was painted red on a map, or that it was the land of the snake-charmer, or at the best that it was inhabited by heathens. Sometimes the India brand of tea on the breakfast table aroused his curiosity and he felt inclined to know what kind of *tree* "India" was, but discovering that nobody at the table knew better than he, he closed the topic once for all.[33]

For a certain group of liberal and radical Americans, however, the Indian independence movement had greater significance. W.E.B. Du Bois believed that an independent India would be a blow against white supremacy and benefit the broad struggle of the color line both globally and locally. Others still saw the draconian measures taken by the U.S. government against Indian radicals as a threat to American democracy.

In challenging the new Anglo-American imperial terrain, Indian expatriates and American allies alike continued to rely on analogies such as Rai's, highlighting the symbolic parallels that linked the American Revolution and the Indian Independence movement. For the American allies who supported the Indian cause, such analogies were more than mere gestures of solidarity or attempts to arouse patriotic sentiment. The comparisons evoked and called to account the core values of American democracy: namely, a tradition of political refuge and a commitment to struggles for self-determination—ideas contradicted by America's tacit support of British empire. Friends of Freedom for India secretary Agnes Smedley and president Robert Morss Lovett invoked such historical metaphors in an appeal letter on behalf of imprisoned Indian radicals in the United States who had been arrested and faced deportation: "In British eyes, these Hindus are guilty of treason (just as were Benjamin Franklin, Jefferson and Adams), and death will be their reward for love of their country. Can you rest while America is sending back to their executioners men who have come to America seeking refuge, men whose crime was working for the freedom of their native land?"[34] This was more an appeal to emotion than any kind of sustained historical comparison; nevertheless, Smedley and Lovett's analogy attempted to convince their audience that the Indian question raised deeper questions about the state of the union.

The stakes of such analogies were even higher for Ram Chandra and the seventeen other Gadar Party members who stood trial in a San Francisco courthouse in November 1917 on charges of violating the neutrality laws when, as mentioned, they collaborated with the Germans to ship arms to India. A skilled propagandist, Chandra had become the editor of the *Gadar* newspaper in 1914, and eventually rose to become head of the party after key associates from the organization fled the country.[35] Under his leadership, Gadar Party pamphlets continued to connect the struggles of immigration to the colonial condition of Indians. In one pamphlet titled *Exclusion of Hindus from America Due to British Influence*, Chandra warned of efforts by the U.S. Congress for an "Oriental exclusion law" targeting Indians.[36] Whereas Japanese immigrants could appeal to their government, Chandra quipped that the British, fearful that Indians were "becom[ing] imbued with pestiferous ideas of political freedom" in the United States, would never come to their aid.[37] Other Gadar Party pamphlets characterized the United States as a nation that had always supported causes for self-determination. The party reprinted an old 1906 editorial in which former secretary of state William Jennings Bryan denounced British rule in India (and, according to Bryan, deliberately excised statements in which he spoke favorably about Britain).[38] By the time of their trial in 1917, Chandra and the other Indian defendants were left with very few strategies to protest their innocence: one was to minimize their connections to Germany, the other was to assert the same Indian–American analogy they had promoted repeatedly in their propaganda.[39]

A pamphlet titled *The Appeal of India to the President of the United States*, published by the Gadar Party office, included three open letters that Chandra had written to Woodrow Wilson. In his third and last letter to the head of state, dated February 26, 1918, as the trial was raging on, Chandra drew on the nationalist history of the United States to plead the defendants' (and India's) cause:

> Mr. President: Your own dear country, the United States of America, became a free nation by an act of rebellion against the British. And the [. . .] tyranny inflicted by the British upon the Americans in 1776 is far exceeded by the indescribable things which have been perpetrated upon the devoted Hindus.[40]

Deeming Wilson the "noble successor" of Washington and Lincoln, Chandra recast the cause of war as a moral struggle, fought in order that the "weaker nations be saved and the 'world made safe for democracy.'"[41] Referring to Wilson's "Fourteen Points" speech, Chandra underscored the American president's demand for a "free, open-minded, and absolutely impartial adjustment of all colonial claims," one that weighed the interests of "populations concerned" against the "equitable claims" of the colonial government.[42] Only then, Chandra wrote, would India "be ready to live up to the very principles which you have laid down better than any other people in the world."[43]

Chandra's rhetorical strategy, like Rai's nearly a decade before, sought to frame an independent India as but another project inspired by and in keeping with the United States' own history. It deliberately overlooked, of course, the contradictions of the analogy—namely, that the United States was, and continued to be, a settler colonial project that differed from India's colonial experience even before the Revolutionary War, or that it was invested in its own forms of racialized colonization. Facing imprisonment and caught at the mercy of the state, Chandra nonetheless leaned on such nationalist metaphors to change the tenor of the trial, which branded the Hindu–German alliance as a foreign threat and wartime adversary requiring swift removal.

At the trial, defense attorney George McGowan presented the court with pamphlets by Chandra and other excerpts from the *Gadar* newspaper that quoted from Washington, Lincoln, and Wilson. In his opening statement, McGowan denounced British rule in India and its role in censoring dissent in the United States: "We will show [. . .] that the British government has suppressed newspapers, imprisoned editors and closed the shores of its self-governing possessions against the Indians."[44] McGowan then quoted from Patrick Henry's iconic speech at the 1775 Second Virginia Convention, reciting the famous lines "give me liberty or give me death" as if to stoke the judge and jury's nationalist sympathies. Upon hearing all this, the U.S. district attorney protested that McGowan's comments were "scurrilous, unpatriotic, and almost treasonable," and petitioned for the entire statement to be scratched from the record.[45]

The Indian–American analogy was perhaps doomed from the start, and as it turned out, so was Ram Chandra. On April 23, Chandra was walking across the courtroom when he was gunned down by Ram Singh, another Gadar Party member standing trial. Singh seemed to have several motives for Chandra's murder: the proceedings revealed that Chandra had used Gadar Party funds for personal use, and Singh's loyalties were with a rival leader from the organization. Whatever the exact cause, the event became an early, sensational moment in South Asian American history, and newspapers nationwide offered several dramatic and gory accounts. The *San Francisco Chronicle*, for its part, played up tropes of Indian exoticism by describing the courtroom murder as the "Climax of Hindoo Romance" (Figure I.2). By the end of the trial, eight of the Gadar Party defendants had been found guilty and served sentences from sixty days to twenty-two months.

In retrospect, it is a particularly bitter irony that the freedom of those Indian defendants was partially staked on whether or not the court was con-

WHERE MURDER CAPPED CLIMAX OF HINDOO ROMANCE

The first murder in a Federal courtroom on the Pacific Coast came as a climax to the German-Hindoo revolt trial yesterday noon after United States District Attorney John W. Preston had concluded his closing argument to the jury. The upper left photograph is that of Ram Singh, who shot and killed Ram Chandra (upper right photograph), and was in turn killed by United States Marshal James B. Holohan. The diagram shows the scene as Holohan shot Chandra's murderer, and the Federal courtroom where the double tragedy was enacted is shown below.

RAM CHANDRA

RAM SINGH

U.S. MARSHAL J.B. HOLOHAN

Ram Singh Slays Ram Chandra; Holohan Kills the Murderer

FIGURE 1.2 Illustration from the April 24, 1918, edition of *San Francisco Chronicle* diagramming the deaths of Ram Chandra and his assassin Ram Singh. (*San Francisco Chronicle*)

vinced by a historical analogy linking Indian independence with American liberty, on whether or not Americans could see something of themselves in the eighteen Indian men standing trial. Whereas the Gadar Party and its defense framed the trial as a question of freedom, the *Chronicle* cast it as the tragic conclusion of an ill-fated "Hindoo Romance." Yet, in spite of its obvious failure in the Hindu–German conspiracy trial, imagining the Indian nation through U.S. history—and attempting to persuade American readers (or juries) to do the same—continued as a common strategy among expatriate Indians and American allies well into the next decade. One of this book's concerns is investigating these authors' investment in this tactic and how they handled its more unwieldy implications. As discussed, there were obvious drawbacks to the rhetorical move. It often produced awkward and untenable comparisons, drawing equivalences between the colonized Indian and the white settler colonialist, collapsing distinctions between radically different forms of colonialism, and tacitly endorsing American democracy without critically engaging the country's own stratification along racial lines. To mobilize American nationalist history was also to mobilize American nationalism itself, a discourse that, by the early twentieth century, had already demonstrated its power—even if that power was just as easily used to exclude migrants, trumpet white supremacy, and suppress dissent. In using this strategy, Indian and American authors advocating for Indian independence hoped to evoke identification and empathy, while avoiding the more complicated questions that could come from a more careful comparison. As a piece of rhetorical architecture, analogy served as a bridge between two continents, however uneven its foundation.

One particularly unwieldy transnational analogy makes up the title of this book. "The United States of India" was a phrase used by several Indian writers and political actors to facilitate the imagining of an independent Indian nation-state in the years before Indian and Pakistani independence. Ram Chandra's widow Padmavati would later describe how her husband spoke with Gadar Party members about the dawn of a "United States of India" free from British rule.[46] When the remaining members of the Gadar Party reassembled after the Hindu–German conspiracy trial as the Pacific Coast Hindustani Association in the 1920s, the phrase found a second life, with the *United States of India* (*USI*) eventually replacing the title of the organization's monthly print journal the *Independent Hindustan* in 1923.[47] Its inaugural editorial announced:

> It is true that "Every Day and in Every Way . . . Is India Becoming More and More United and Democratic." She is coming fast to her political goal, The United States of India, modeled after The United States of America.[48]

In drawing parallels between the United States and India, the editorial took imaginative leaps, going so far as to claim that the Indian National Congress had named itself after the U.S. Congress. The editorial embellished the American rhetoric by announcing the organization's ultimate goal of achieving a "free, independent, republican national state in India [. . .] of the people, for the people, by the people."[49] The cover image of the inaugural issue (Figure I.3) featured an illustration of "Mother India" towering over a globe, her sari billowing out from the South Asian landmass and over the west coast of North America, as if to symbolize a transpacific bridge connecting the United States and India (with Britain conspicuously absent). The February 1926 issue went one step further, presenting a dollar-bill portrait of George Washington with the text "Our Ideal and Inspiration" printed above, and below, an injunction to "Champions of Liberty in all lands," to "be strong in hope."[50] The quote was drawn from a message that Washington had written to "Patriots of Ireland" in 1788, and was regularly used by Irish leader Éamon de Valera during his 1920 visit to the United States, including in his addresses to groups such as the Friends of Freedom for India.[51] In recirculating and decontextualizing the quote, the *USI* editors creatively reassembled the iconography of American nationalism for their own ends.

The term "The United States of India" continued to appear throughout political science reports as the name for a hypothetical independent Indian republic.[52] Bhagat Singh Thind, an immigrant from Punjab and U.S. Army veteran, whose case for citizenship would reach the U.S. Supreme Court, used the term in a political broadside. "India will be fully free to evolve according to her own ideals, her destiny, unfettered from within, unmolested from without," Thind wrote, concluding optimistically that "Burma will voluntarily join the United States of India."[53] The phrase also appeared in an essay by expatriate intellectual Taraknath Das (one of the men arrested during the Hindu–German conspiracy trial), who wrote in 1923 that "responsible Indian nationalists are working for a Federated Republic of the United States of India."[54] In a similar vein, some decades later, Dalit leader and chairman of the Constitution Drafting Committee, Dr. Bhimrao Ramji Ambedkar, who studied at Columbia University between 1913 and 1916, used the term in the proposed preamble to the Indian constitution:

> We the people of the territories of British India [. . .] with a view to form a more perfect union of these territories do—*ordain* that the Provinces and the Centrally Administered Areas (to be hereafter designated as States) and the Indian States shall be joined together into a Body Politic for Legislative, Executive and Administrative purposes under the style *The United States of India* [. . .].[55]

The language of "We the people" and "a more perfect union" clearly echo the Constitution of the United States, suggesting the powerful influence that ideas of American democracy, from broad ideals to details about governance, had on Ambedkar as a visiting student. The scrambling of "The United States of America" for the purpose of imagining an independent India was itself a deliberate political strategy. For Ambedkar and Das, it was a direct call for India to adopt a federalist style of government in the model of the United States. For the editors of *USI*, to name an independent India "the United States" was also a strategic, rhetorical cutting of India's umbilical tie to the British Empire and an appeal to their American readers to recognize the political affinities connecting these seemingly disparate places.

For the purposes of this book, the phrase "United States of India" evokes the complex and cross-cultural ways of seeing and strategies of writing that

AUG 21 1923
The UNITED STATES OF INDIA
INDEPENDENCE
A Monthly Review of Political, Economic, Social and Intellectual Independence of India
Vol. 1.
JULY, 1923
No. 1
Editorial: India Becoming More Democratic; The United States of India
India Progressing Toward Unity
Fighting Spirit Needed
There Is a Difference Between Independence and Independence
Poisoning the World Monopolized by England
The Irish Situation
The Salt Tax in India
News and Notes
No. 5 Wood Street
SAN FRANCISCO, U. S. A.
One Dollar the Year
Published Monthly by the Pacific Coast Hindustani Association
Ten Cents the Copy
169

FIGURE I.3 (a) *The United States of India* (July 1923), and facing page (b) *The United States of India* (February 1926). (South Asian American Digital Archive)

I described as transnational refraction. The "United States of India" tracks a way of viewing America from the perspective of India—"India's United States," as it were—while also marking the unsettling and self-reflexive way by which that image of the United States could turn back onto its viewer and reveal a reflection that was slightly different, distorted, refracted. One might argue that for Das and Ambedkar, imagining a "United States of India" was simply filling an American frame with Indian content, something akin to

The United States of India

A Monthly Review of Political, Economic, Social, and Intellectual Independence of India Published by the Pacific Coast Hindustani Association at No. 5 Wood Street, San Francisco. Calif., U.S.A.

Vol. III   FEBRUARY, 1926   No. 8

George Washington

Our Ideal and Inspiration

"CHAMPIONS OF LIBERTY IN ALL LANDS, BE STRONG IN HOPE. YOU ARE CALUMNIATED IN YOUR DAY. I WAS MISREPRESENTED BY THE LOYALISTS OF MY DAY. HAD I FAILED THE SCAFFOLD WOULD HAVE BEEN MY DOOM. HAD I FAILED, I WOULD HAVE DESERVED THE SAME HONOR. I STOOD TRUE TO MY CAUSE, EVEN WHEN VICTORY WAS FLED. IN THAT I MERITED SUCCESS. YOU MUST ACT LIKEWISE."

what Partha Chatterjee has described as the "derivative discourse" of nationalism.[56] But this overlooks the productive, unsettling function of the term. The "United States of India" denaturalizes a name we have heard thousands of times. It appears first as a typo, a slip of the tongue, an act of mimicry. But like an act of mimicry, "The United States of India" is similar but not quite the same, an implicit analogic argument that disturbs the very notion of American exceptionalism.

For each of the figures mentioned—Ambedkar, Das, Rai, and Chandra—to see the United States was also to see oneself differently, to imagine India not just as it was or as it appeared to others, but as it ought to be. Pandita Ramabai's observation that serves as this chapter's epigraph exemplifies this kind of refraction. After visiting the United States at the end of the nineteenth century, Ramabai penned a Marathi travelogue, using an ethnographic eye to detail her experience of the culture and institutions of the United States. "It is natural for us to think Americans walk upside down," Ramabai wrote, in a rare moment of jest, describing the subcontinent's inverted perspective on America.[57] As the book's English translator Meera Kosambi writes, Ramabai "subjected the American continent and culture to an Indian—albeit internationalized and eclectic—gaze."[58] Yet there is another gaze, twinned but hidden, in Ramabai's quip—one that afforded a view of India from the vantage point of the United States. As if caught in a transnational camera obscura, Ramabai's perspective from America also turned her image of India upside down, and in so doing, unsettled her entrenched understanding of its practices, structures, and narratives. In this way, Ramabai's travelogue from the late nineteenth century was an earlier iteration of what the Indian American writer Amitava Kumar would later observe in the twenty-first: "to come to America means to discover anew what had till now been home."[59]

Transnational Refraction

Literally speaking, refraction describes the optical phenomenon in which light passes through a medium, changing direction and speed, and thereby appears transformed in some critical way: a straw in a glass of water appears bent; a face viewed through a marble appears inverted. As a metaphor for cross-cultural encounter, the term captures the assemblage of transnational gazes, reflections, distortions, and perspectives that were enabled by authors who literally or figuratively crossed national boundaries and engaged with new cultural, social, and historical mediums. For someone such as Rai or Ramabai, to experience the United States as an exile or visitor was also to engage with themselves and to see themselves differently after. Put another way, their view of India was refracted through the mediating narratives of the United States, and in the process it no longer appeared as it once had.

As a cultural concept, refraction has been theorized by a handful of scholars, each of whom has applied the term to a wide array of contexts, describing shifts in visual perspective, the appropriation of foreign discourses, or the transformation of social practices as they migrate from one "cultural medium" to another.[60] Yuko Kikuchi, for example, develops the term "refracted modernity" to describe how the discourses of Euro-American colonialism were absorbed by imperial Japan and further transformed as they were applied to its colonial possessions. Daniel Coleman coins "cross-cultural refraction" to illustrate how gendered practices travel and transform through "international, intercultural, [and] interracial migration."[61] Present in each of these definitions of refraction are its defamiliarizing effects, how movements across place, media, or time often lead to renewed understandings of both home and away, the self and the other. In their study of intertextuality in postmodernist literature, Susana Onega and Christian Gutleben deploy the term to describe how a "refracting" postmodern text leads not only to new readings but also to "renovations" of the canonical text.[62] Refraction, then, describes not a one-directional optic but a "double process" or dialectic interplay, "affecting the result as well as the source, the new text as well as the old."[63] To draw on this textual schema, we might characterize the Indian American network of authors in this book as similarly reflecting on both text and hypotext—they rethought the United States as they set their sights on India, and India as they interrogated the United States. It was through this dialectical process that such writers could puncture the discourse of American exceptionalism as they drew comparisons to India, destabilizing the myths of U.S. nationhood while simultaneously undermining the racial justifications of British rule in India. Transnational refraction thus describes a set of optics that enabled American and Indian writers in this network to actively think and write about each other's political struggles. For the sake of clarity, in the remainder of this introduction I focus on just three effects of refraction: comparison, identification, and disruption.

As we have already seen, comparisons abounded within this network, and each of the writers I examine in this book engaged in comparisons to different ends, both directly and indirectly through straightforward analogies and more inchoate correlations. In his 1916 volume *The United States of America: A Hindu's Impressions and a Study*, Rai, for instance, directly argued that there was "some analogy between the Negro problem in the United States of America and the problem of the depressed classes in India," to describe how the structures of racism in the United States could provide insights into the oppressive caste hierarchies at home.[64] Such comparisons drew these places momentarily together, offering a glimpse of cross-cultural recognition. But at times these analogies could also render the social relations of race and caste as "discrete and comparable," a method that Grace Hong and Roderick Ferguson have argued is limiting, insofar as it presumes commonalities without tending to crucial historical differences. In contrast, Hong and Ferguson outline what they call modes of "heterotopic comparison" that refuse "to maintain that objects of comparison are static, unchanging, and empirically observable," instead sitting with, and thinking through, objects that exist in "unstable interrelation to each other" without drawing direct equivalences.[65]

In the case studies of this book, both simple analogies and heterotopic comparisons were enabled through a refractive optic, which allowed writers to do more than simply compare and contrast different social systems—to simply claim that the problems of India and the United States were the same, for instance—but to understand the interconnectedness of modern systems of power and to draw out the links between them. Through comparison, writers began to connect the structures of colonialism to racialized governance or understand the overlaps between gender, caste-based, and racial oppression, all the while tending to how such systems unevenly "value and devalue" different communities.[66] To give an example, in her autobiographical novel *Daughter of Earth* (1929), Agnes Smedley's protagonist explains that as she spent more time with a network of Indian radicals in New York, she began to recognize in them traces of her working-class father and her brother. Such affinities helped her imagine the links between the conditions of the American proletariat and the colonized Indian. Both communities were subjugated under an exploitative system wrought by capitalist interest, yet this did not lead Smedley to the clumsy formulation that class in the United States and race in British India were coeval. This constitutively different mode of comparison instead laid bare what Lisa Lowe has described as the continental "intimacies" that underwrote the liberal project through the conditions of "colonialism, slavery, capitalism, and empire."[67] Comparison thus provided a form of anticolonial rhetoric that forged connections between the struggles of subjected peoples across continents without reducing each struggle as identical.[68]

As Indian and American writers in this network came to recognize the interconnectedness of their political struggles, they also began to identify with those across racial and cultural lines. While we have already seen how political leaders such as Rai and Chandra deployed strategic identifications with historical figures like George Washington as a means to prop up the cause of anticolonial Indian nationalism, more often these forms of identification took the shape of more complex affinities and attachments. In his novel *Dark Princess* (1928), W.E.B. Du Bois linked his protagonist, an African American exile, with the Indian leader of an anticolonial network, using the tropes of romance and a clever rewriting of *A Midsummer Night's Dream* to imagine a Black–Indian alliance against a world divided by the color line. These practices of identification resembled what Shu-mei Shih and Françoise Lionnet call the lateral networks of "minor transnationalism," the networks of affiliation formed among minoritized subjects that negotiate and transgress "national, ethnic, and cultural boundaries."[69] In the process, these authors grasped at forms of solidarity and coalition that expanded understandings of their own political subjectivity: to be Black in the United States was to be the subject of a broader imperialist project undergirded by white supremacy; for Smedley, to be a working-class woman in America was to be intertwined, as both victim and perpetrator, in Euro-American empire. That said, identification did not always serve progressive ends, nor were they always cross-racial. In stark contrast to Smedley's feminist anticolonialism, the American journalist Katherine Mayo was an ideologue of imperialist feminism, whose "muckraking" work *Mother India* (1927) discredited the independence movement by focusing on the social ills of India. For Mayo, India served as a mirror for her anxieties about racial mixture, immigration, and threats to white patriarchal order in her native United States and shored up feelings of a shared Anglo-Saxon racial identity between Americans and the British. Put another way, her racial identification with British imperial rule refracted her view of American national identity.

In each of these examples, refraction had the potential to produce what I describe as acts of disruption—means of challenging, recoding, disturbing, or at times parodying dominant discourses of nationalism, immigration, and Orientalism. Several writers actively sought to undermine the entrenched understandings of their readers, to rethink their own perceptions of the United States and India. A case in point was the writer Dhan Gopal Mukerji, who first made a splash in American literary circles in the early 1920s with his nonfiction books and children's literature. Mukerji's writings often navigated a terrain of American representations that reduced India to a panoply of distant, exotic, and unmistakably Orientalist images. At times, Mukerji attempted to challenge such images directly through his fiction; at other times, he simply tried to make Americans aware that their understanding of India was itself a refraction, a distortion peered from "imperial eyes," as Mary Louise Pratt famously describes it.[70] But beyond contesting Orientalist discourse— whether it came through Mukerji who "revised" the works of Rudyard Kipling, or Du Bois, whose *Dark Princess* resignified elements of Shakespeare, or Smedley, who challenged Americans to identify with the cause of Indian independence—transnational refraction engendered forms of estrangement that disrupted prevailing understandings of both India and the United States.

Of course, the effects of transnational refraction that I have described— comparison, identification, and disruption—overlap and interact: comparisons lead to disruptions, identifications lead to analogies. What linked these different processes among the authors examined here was the way they prompted a rethinking of one's own conditions through the perspective of the other, a recognition of oneself in a strange yet strangely familiar context, and an imagination of new possibilities in a postwar future. As I explain in the chapters that follow, I especially pay close attention to the ways that form—rhetorical, literary, and social—served as the medium that shaped these refractions, that bent comparisons in one direction as opposed to another, allowing for some visions while obscuring others.

While this book does trace various expatriate Indian political movements, legislative restrictions against South Asian migrants, and moments of political collaboration during the period of the mid-1910s to the late 1920s, it is less an exhaustive account of this history and more an examination into the modes of seeing and writing enabled by this Indian American milieu. In recent years, new scholarship in the field of American studies has helped recover an earlier history of South Asians in the United States, long preceding the wide-scale migrations that were inaugurated by the 1965 Immigration Act. The publication of Nayan Shah's *Stranger Intimacy* (2011) and Vivek Bald's *Bengali Harlem* (2013) have both provided detailed accounts of the rich and complex lives of early South Asian settlers in the United States, describing the interracial and "queer" social intimacies that shaped these largely working-class migrations. Maia Ramnath's *From Haj to Utopia* (2011) and Seema Sohi's *Echoes of Mutiny* (2014) have focused on the rise of the West Coast-based Gadar Party, examining the political genealogies that shaped the group as well as how its political radicalism led to the racialization of South Asians as both an economic and political "menace." While each of these books has enriched our understanding of early South Asian America, they are grounded in historiographical methodologies that use primary texts—namely immigration files, court cases, political pamphlets, and correspondence—as evidence to reconstruct this past. In contrast, *The United States of India* draws on literary methods, closely reading an expansive archive of texts that includes literary novels, children's books, travelogues, political illustrations, and newsletters to examine both the discursive forms of racism that these writers navigated as well as the forms of anticolonial rhetoric they developed. In its emphasis on the writings of novelists, intellectuals, and journalists who played a central role in the development of early South Asian American politics, the book also provides new readings of works by canonical figures such as Rai, Smedley, and Du Bois, as well as accounts from lesser-known writers such as Sudhindra Bose, Saint Nihal Singh, and Dhan Gopal Mukerji. Mukerji alone, a prolific poet, essayist, and children's author, was the first successful Indian American writer in the twentieth century and yet has been mostly overlooked in accounts of South Asian American history.

Another set of scholarship has recently brought attention to the networks forged between Indian and American intellectuals during this period and after. Studies such as Nico Slate's *Colored Cosmopolitanism* (2012), Gerald Horne's *The End of Empires* (2008), and Bill Mullen's *Un-American* (2015) have provided rich accounts of the exchanges between transnational intellectuals, often emphasizing terms such as "solidarity" and "cosmopolitanism" to describe these historical moments of connection, identification, and comparison. Slate, for instance, coins the term "colored cosmopolitanism" as a means to describe the way that Indian social reformers and nationalists identified with African Americans, and vice versa, as groups subjugated under a global system of racism.[71] Such approaches, however, present these histories as a series of political and ideological choices made by actors, and often overlook how they were deeply structured by the very literary, rhetorical, and social forms through which they were imagined and articulated. As Yogita Goyal reminds us, "the form of anti-colonialism is as important as its content, as literary form shapes and makes concrete the body of thought that makes up anti-colonialism, [. . .] mak[ing] certain statements possible, and others impossible."[72] The writers in this Indian American network were well aware of the power of rhetorical and literary form, deploying an arsenal of genres, from travelogues to muckraking journalism, children's books to the romance novel, each in an effort to articulate appeals to their anticolonial project. While these forms often enabled complex and unique political visions of freedom, they could also be limiting.

To give a simple example, the rhetorical form of the historical Indian–American analogy, as we have discussed in the case of Rai's 1905 visit to Washington, DC, directly drew on comparison to make appeals to American audiences at the risk of foreclosing complexity. The structure of the one-to-one comparison left little room to address the multiple contradictions that analogy opened up. To draw on an example of literary form, we might consider Ram Chandra's letters to Woodrow Wilson. The form of the open letter provided Chandra the opportunity to address President Wilson as an equal, engaging in a dialogue (however one-sided) that sought to transform the "Hindu" problem from a faceless abstraction into a plea from a speaking subject. Chandra's language, his deference and flattery of Wilson, which cast the president in the same light as Lincoln and Washington, softened whatever critiques of American hypocrisy Chandra may have felt and reworked them into a call for empathy. By engaging with the letter, readers were pulled in as objects of address, encouraged to express American benevolence through a moral identification with Indians.

By social form, I refer to terms such as nation, caste, race, gender, and empire, which designate categories of relations, identities, polities. For these writers, both social and literary form worked like a pair of interlocking lenses, constraining, expanding, and bringing into focus what they envisioned as the relationship between the United States and India. It meant, for writers such as Rai, that the imagining of an independent India would be articulated through the national form of the United States. For Smedley and Du Bois, domestic questions about race and class in America were reformulated within a broader framework of imperialism. The literary forms they used—for Smedley, the proletarian novel and political pamphlet, for Du Bois, a hybrid "realist and romance" novel—served as a kind of second prism, through which these political questions passed and were reimagined.[73]

The term "United States of India" itself points to limitations and the way that many of these cross-cultural linkages were refracted through the social form of the nation-state, as opposed to other more imaginative political forms and alliances. As Erez Manela explains, the postwar period "established the self-determining nation-state as the only legitimate political form throughout the globe, as colonized and marginalized peoples demanded and eventually attained recognition as sovereign, independent actors in international society."[74] However, as we discuss in Chapter 1, attempts to draw analogies between colony and nation, to imagine a "free India" as refracted through the "United States," also produced counternarratives that undermined the idea that nationhood could ensure that all its subjects were universally equal and free. In its attention to form and close reading, *The United States of India* both adds to our historical knowledge of this period of Asian American history and argues for the value of literary methods to understand the complex modes of anticolonialism that emerged in this important but overlooked historical moment of transnational exchange.

Each chapter of this book examines a key figure within this network of Indian and American writers. By closely tending to the genres and social questions that these writers negotiated, each chapter also examines a different facet of transnational refraction. We begin by returning to Lajpat Rai's activities during his period of exile in the United States during World War I. With particular attention to his book *The United States of America: A Hindu's Impressions and a Study* (*USAHIS*, 1916), Chapter 1 looks at how Rai and other U.S.-based Indian writers adopted the travelogue as a tool to illustrate the barriers that restricted their free movement in the United States and a comparative text to work through the meanings and distinctions of racial difference. Just as the European travel book produced what Mary Louise Pratt called the "domestic subject of empire," the travel narrative allowed Indian writers to articulate what it meant to be a colonial subject of empire, not only in the colony and the metropole but across the vast geopolitical terrain of the globe.[75] Central to that articulation was the unstable racial classification of Indians, who were at times categorized as "white" and at other times as "colored." In *USAHIS*, Rai claimed that the "problems" of the United States were similar to India, but, indeed, no problem seemed to interest him as much as the problem of race and color, which he wrote about with particular attention to three social groups: African Americans, Indian migrants in North America, and the colonized subjects of the Philippines. Chapter 1 asks: In what ways did these American forms of subjugation shape Rai's understanding of power and hierarchy within colonial India? What kind of Indian national subject arose through such comparative visions?

As Rai continued his efforts with the India Home Rule League in New York, he met and mentored the American radical Agnes Smedley, who would eventually become a central figure in the history of expatriate Indian nationalism in the United States. Chapter 2 begins by tracing Smedley's identification with the Indian anticolonial network in the United States, starting with her initial encounters with the Gadar Party as a reporter in California and later with her work with the Friends of Freedom for India. In her wide-ranging political work, Smedley constantly presented the case for Indian freedom in terms that were legible to American liberals and radicals. This entailed a rhetorical practice that refracted the cause of Indian freedom through the language of American nationalism, evoking the discourse of U.S. history, national ideals, and sovereignty. In the second half of the chapter, I turn to Smedley's autobiographical novel *Daughter of Earth* (1929), which has been described as the "Ur-text of women's proletarian fiction."[76] In contrast to her journalistic and propaganda work, *Daughter of Earth* de-centered the United States, casting the domestic autobiography onto the global terrain of empire. Throughout, I show how Smedley's engagement with the Indian freedom struggle hinged on complex forms of identification. Whether through her propaganda work, in which she attempted to domesticate the Indian cause by rendering it internal to the values of American nationalism, or whether through her novel, in which she used the proletarian genre to imagine the intimate even familial bonds forged between working-class whites and colonized "men of color," Smedley's larger project was to dramatically reconsider the relationship possible between America and India.[77]

In Chapter 3, I turn to the writings of Dhan Gopal Mukerji. Born into a family of prominent upper-caste Bengali revolutionaries, Mukerji migrated to the United States in 1910 as a student, where he became a prolific writer, publishing a variety of books that ranged from children's fiction to autobiography and travelogues. The chapter examines Mukerji's attempts to represent India to an American audience and disrupt the unconscious Orientalist gaze through which American readers often understood India. A key contributor to that gaze was Rudyard Kipling, whose popular works had largely shaped the middlebrow discourse of India for American readers. I examine the many ways that Mukerji challenged Kipling, not only through veiled critiques of the latter's casual imperialism but also by offering a form of fiction that encouraged American readers to learn about India without mastering it. These critiques appeared in his nonfiction works such as the travelogue *Visit India with Me* (1929), in which he wrote from the perspective of a "typical" American narrator, and his memoir *Caste and Outcast* (1923), where he challenged prevailing views of Indian migrants. Even in his children's novels and short stories, which were often published in Boy Scout magazines, Mukerji found ways to remind readers that their experience of India through fiction was always a mediated one. In effect, Mukerji's writing attempted to challenge his American readership to imagine a relationship to India that was not predetermined by the hierarchies of empire.

Not all forms of Orientalism were imperialist, however, and Chapter 4 examines the paradoxically anti-imperialist Orientalism of W.E.B. Du Bois. From the 1910s onward, Du Bois had become an important member in this network of Indian expatriates. He was acquainted with Rai, Smedley, and Mukerji and wrote several editorials in support of Indian decolonization. His longest treatise on India was also his most bewildering: the novel *Dark Princess* (1928), a self-described "romance" between an exiled African American surgeon and an Indian princess who leads a clandestine anticolonial society composed of leaders of the "dark nations." Combining several genres, including gritty social realism and Orientalist fantasy, *Dark Princess* served as a political and aesthetic experiment to imagine African American political subjectivity beyond the borders of the U.S. nation-state—even, indeed, as the vanguard of global anticolonialism. The chapter examines how Du Bois reworked the concept of "double consciousness" in concert with his involvement with Indian expatriate nationalism. If "double consciousness" describes how African American subjectivity was structured through the "sense of always looking at one's self through the eyes of others," the chapter asks how Du Bois refracted that concept through an anti-imperialist framework: What did it look like to see one's self through the eyes of the anticolonial Indian?[78]

The final chapter examines Katherine Mayo's best-selling *Mother India* (1927), a thinly veiled work of propaganda masquerading as "muckraking" journalism that set off an international media circus and the publication of more than fifty book-length responses of both praise and rebuttal. Central to Mayo's text was a "racial triangulation" framework that justified the project of imperialism in British India (as well as U.S.-administered Philippines and Dutch Guiana) by positing Euro-American governance as the only mechanism to protect a native subaltern class from native elites. This chapter argues that the controversy surrounding *Mother India* opened up new ways for Indian writers to articulate the relations of caste and race at both global and national scales. Books such as K. L. Gauba's *Uncle Sham* (1929) and Dinshah Ghadiali's *American Sex Problems* (1929) developed forms of anticolonial parody that engaged Mayo's racial triangulation and underscored a racialized geopolitical imaginary that pitted the white West against a unified colonized identity. Because such works did not challenge Mayo's basic framework, they reinforced the upper-caste character of the Indian nation that ignored and erased lower-caste and Dalit critiques of the nationalist project.

In all, the decade between World War I and the Great Depression marked a significant but largely overlooked period of anticolonialism in the United States, which momentarily brought together authors from a motley crew of communities—from expatriate Indian nationalists to Irish republicans, working-class radicals to laboring immigrants from Asia, liberal social reformers to African American intellectuals—each striving to define freedom in the wake of the Great War. *The United States of India* recreates the intimate dialogue formed by these writers and activists, as they pondered the political meanings of India and the United States in the early twentieth century. By tracing their stories, we can glimpse an emergent literary and historical moment of American anticolonialism, produced through the cumulative and strategic interactions between and among this diverse set of writers.

To trace this history is also to catalog how the writers within this network evolved, how solidarities were nurtured as other ideological rifts were exposed, how writers such as Rai or Smedley would begin to reassess positions they once held firmly. The Lajpat Rai that begins this book and the Lajpat Rai of 1928, when this study ends, for instance, held vastly different views of the United States. In his 1928 tome *Unhappy India*, Rai forsook the hagiography of George Washington in order to call out the hypocrisies of America, describing the United States as one of the focal points of "white imperialism" and the "greatest world menace known to history."[79] Such sentiments were a far cry from the reverence he had experienced that September day in 1905, when he stood in the Capitol admiring *The Apotheosis of Washington*. But that gets us ahead of the story. We pick up nine years later: Rai is aboard the S.S. *Philadelphia* crossing the Atlantic from England to the New World, from the metropole of the British Empire to a place he was only beginning to understand.

1

Race across Empires

Lajpat Rai's The United States of America

America had had a pronounced effect upon Lalaji. He had
acquired the Yankee twang. He delighted in employing
slang. His point of view, too, had changed.
—SAINT NIHAL SINGH, "Lala Lajpat Rai as I Knew Him" (1928)

[The United States] is truly "the melting pot" of the
different nations of the world, of its social, political, and
economic problems.
—LAJPAT RAI, *The United States of America: A Hindu's Impressions
and a Study* (1916)

n 1914, the voyage from Liverpool to New York City lasted a week, enough
time for the passengers on the S.S. *Philadelphia* to befriend Lajpat Rai and
his fellow Indian travelers. The scientist Jagdish Chandra Bose impressed
fellow passengers with his lab equipment and theories of radio waves and
plant physiology. A young woman from Europe fell in love with one of Rai's
aloof compatriots, a point that troubled Rai enough that he devoted several
pages in his journal to her. Also on board were several prominent Indian
internationalists—Shiva Prasad Gupta, who later represented the Indian National Congress at the second conference of the League Against Imperialism,
and Benoy Kumar Sarkar, the prominent ideologue and poet of the Bengali
swadeshi movement. It was during this journey that Rai had an early glimpse
of the xenophobic fears that shaped American immigration and that would
color his experience in the United States. Once docked in New York harbor,
Rai and his companions stood in a line that in many ways organized the
racial hierarchy of immigrants at the time: "The American citizens get off
legally by stating the place of their birth and the date of their birth; next
come the white people; the Asiatics are examined most searchingly, spe-
cially the Indians and the Japs."[1] As they disembarked, Rai noted that "Indians, Syrians, Egyptians and people from south-east Europe" were singled
out and inspected twice as possible contagions for trachoma, an infectious
eye disease that, if diagnosed, led to deportation.[2] While Rai elaborated no
further, the inspection marked an early moment of experiencing firsthand

the scrutiny that migrants from India endured when arriving in North America.

For Indian travelers who came to the United States in the early twentieth century, experiencing American forms of racism was both disquieting and estranging. As colonial subjects in British India, the racial line that divided the Indian from the English—"the rule of colonial difference"—was a familiar one.[3] Yet the United States had its own idiosyncratic systems of racial hierarchy that interpellated Indian migrants and travelers in ways that would have felt unfamiliar. The racial status of Indians in America was unstable, shifting between terms like "Asiatic," "Hindu," "Colored," and "Aryan." When migrant laborers from Punjab and Bengal began to settle in North America, they found themselves written into the discourse of the "Yellow Peril," which portrayed Chinese and Japanese laborers as a swarm poised to take over the white workforce. Indian travelers—including dignitaries such as Rai and English-speaking students, who had arrived from upper-class and upper-caste families in India—also found themselves as targets of racism and xenophobia. For some, being labeled as "colored" would be occasion to distance themselves from East Asian migrants, African Americans, and other working-class populations, and assert their own sense of superiority; for others, these moments of racial interpellation and misidentification served as occasions to pledge solidarity as "colored" subjects victimized by racial hierarchies in the United States and in colonial India. More often, however, these travelers' engagement involved more than just simple rejections or affirmations of their newfound racial status, but instead entailed a dynamic negotiation. As they traversed the American social landscape, Indian travelers compared themselves with American others, mapping their native forms of social hierarchy—the relations of caste, religion, and colony—onto the American forms of class, race, and nation. This act of transnational comparison, by which the terms of race in the United States were refracted through the lens of native social forms, destabilized entrenched understandings of social identity such as caste and race, occasionally leading to new understandings of themselves.

Travel writing—including travelogues, essays, and editorials published in the United States and India—was a particularly powerful literary form for recording these comparisons, and serves as a complex archive of expatriate Indian ways of seeing. While Inderpal Grewal has argued that travel writing often "consolidated assumptions [. . .] of stable unitary identities of nation, class, sexuality, or gender," the form's constant wrestling with difference also meant it could unsettle those very assumptions.[4] Such was the case for the exiled Lajpat Rai, for whom experiences with race in the United States often reinforced his national identity as a colonized Indian, but on occasion destabilized his own sense of nationalism, forcing him to reckon with the internal stratifications of Indian society. Rai's fullest statement on the country was

The United States of America: A Hindu's Impressions and a Study (1916), which he penned after a tour that took him to New York, Chicago, Atlanta, New Orleans, Los Angeles, and Berkeley from November 1914 to June 1915. By the end of his tour, Rai was in the East Bay, developing the monograph's central thesis that "the problems of the United States are very similar to those that face us in India." No "problem" in America captured Rai's attention like the problem of race and color. Until that point, Rai's thoughts on race were at best rudimentary. If he evoked race at all in his earlier writing, it appeared in vague phrases like the "ruling races" and "subject races," or in notions of Indian nationhood being constituted by "Aryans," a relic from his religious background as part of the Hindu reformist Arya Samaj. This identity was further complicated in the United States because the term "Aryan" had been absorbed into the racial formation of whiteness, which had important consequences for perceptions of racial identity and legal rulings on citizenship.

This chapter examines how Rai's exilic writings from, and about, the United States shaped and reshaped his thinking about the global role of race in the early twentieth century. Rai's encounters with forms of American racial hierarchy entailed a series of transnational comparisons, in which his experience of race in the United States were both refracted through and onto the Indian social landscape. I demonstrate this by examining how Rai wrote about three social groups entangled in the American racial project—African Americans, Indian migrants, and the colonial Filipino subject—each of which represented a different form of how race operated, through enslavement and segregation, through xenophobia and exclusion, and through colonialism. Rai's encounter with what was then termed the "Negro problem" raised both productive and uneasy comparisons; when he and other Indian intellectuals in the United States engaged the issue of Black inequality, they often articulated a double analogy in which the legal, social, and political subjugation of African Americans was compared to the oppression of both the colonized and the lower castes in India.[5] As an Indian migrant in North America, Rai had become interested in the rise of "American prejudice against Hindu immigration,"[6] and these discussions dovetailed into debates about the unstable racial classification of Indians. Through Indian migrants, who by the late 1910s were the subject of congressional debates on immigration, Rai also perceived the second-class status of Indians on the global stage. The chapter concludes with Rai's assessment of American colonial rule of the Philippines, whose presence underscored the history of U.S. imperialism and forced Rai to reckon with his own internalized racial and cultural chauvinism.

Reading Rai's treatment and analysis of these racialized figures in America raises several questions: In what ways did these figures, whose relationship to the United States was defined by legacies of slavery, racial disenfranchisement, xenophobia, and colonialism, shape how Rai understood the concepts of race, the color line, and caste? What was the racial logic behind Rai's brand of anti-imperialism, which he was developing during his period of exile? And finally, what kind of Indian subject arose out of these comparisons? As I argue, Rai's encounter with the racial formations of the United States opened up new insights, allowing him to see Indian decolonization as what Du Bois famously described as a "local phase" of a global problem.[7] Yet his own ideological commitments to an Indo-Aryan identity—undergirded by his position as an upper-caste Hindu nationalist—prevented him from imagining a more expansive anticolonial politics.

In Exile

Much had changed in the nine years that elapsed between Rai's first visit to the United States in 1905 and his second visit, which began in November 1914. In 1905, Rai was forty years old, a young nationalist leader from Punjab. His tour had covered New York, Buffalo, Chicago, Philadelphia, and Boston, where he lectured as much on Hinduism as he did on the nationalist movement. In his observations of the United States, captured in interviews with the *Boston Globe*, editorials in the *New York Post* and the *New York Republican*, and Indian publications such as the *Panjabee*, Rai emphasized the differences between Americans and the British, characterizing the former as amiable and welcoming in contrast to the latter. In England, Rai wrote, "hospitality [. . .] is an exception while in America it is the rule."[8] Rai did not fully ignore the problems in American society—he noted, for instance, that "whites have a great prejudice against what are here known as the coloured people"—but also wrote with optimism about the non-European heterogeneity of the United States. "There are Filipinos, Cubans, Indians (both Red and East), Arabs, Syrians, Chinese, Japanese," he explained, adding that "almost every nationality in fairly good strength publishes its own organs."[9] Among the Indians he met during his short stay, Rai mentioned a meeting with Maulana Barkatullah, president of the newly established Hindustani Progressive Association of New York.[10] He also made acquaintance with Moorfield Storey and the Anti-Imperialist League, an ideologically eclectic group opposed to the American annexation of the Philippines and whose membership once included Mark Twain, Andrew Carnegie, Ambrose Bierce, and William Jennings Bryan.[11] An interview during the week of Rai's departure from the United States to England in 1905 was published in the *New York Evening Post* under the headline "The Lesson that Indians Should Learn from the United States." What Indians could glean most, Rai remarked, was "the spirit of unity and nationality that obtains in [the United States] among a mixed population composed of all nations of the earth."[12] Colonial India, with its myriad religions, regions, and castes played against each other under British rule, could learn the unity of nationhood from the United States, Rai seemed to imply, however fragile that unity was in the tumultuous years of the Gilded Age.

When Rai returned to the United States in 1914, his stature in the Indian nationalist movement had risen considerably. In 1907, after being arrested for sedition and jailed at Mandalay Fort Prison without a trial, Rai discussed the episode in the pamphlet "The Story of My Deportation," quickly becoming a public symbol of the colonial government's punitive excess. That same year, he, alongside fellow Congress leaders Bal Gangadhar Tilak and Bipin Chandra Pal, became known across the colony as the trifecta "Lal-Bal-Pal." For their incisive commentary and protests, the trio were turned into nationalist icons of resistance against the partition of Bengal. Rai's notoriety quickly traversed national borders, reaching the small diasporic communities in North America. N. S. Hardikar, a medical student at the University of Michigan and leader of the Hindusthan Association of America (HAA), noted, "Before leaving India for America, I had read of the 'Lal-Bal-Pal' Trio and young as we were in 1907, we [the HAA] had the utmost regard and respect for them."[13]

During his period of exile in the United States in the late 1910s, Rai had left behind the monuments he had visited during his first trip in 1905. In New York, he had become a regular member of the Civic Club, working alongside the club's "India Group," where he met figures such as the bohemian feminist Henrietta Rodman and radical Agnes Smedley, with whom he would collaborate for the next half decade. He began to move in circles of American liberals and progressives, actively recruiting them to support the cause of Indian home rule. Figures such as Storey, the leader of the American Anti-Imperialist League; Margaret Sanger, the birth control advocate and eugenic feminist;[14] J. T. Sunderland, the Unitarian minister and Civil War veteran who later became the president of Rai's IHRLA; and African American leaders as ideologically opposed as W.E.B. Du Bois and Booker T. Washington—all lent their support and contacts to Rai. Along the way, an eclectic cast of secondary characters from the early South Asian diaspora appeared on his itinerary, including Indian students and laborers on East and West Coasts, as well as a number of Gadar Party revolutionaries with whom he formed sharp rivalries. As Rai was defining and advocating his home rule version of Indian nationalism in a text such as *Young India* (1916), which he started writing in Boston in December 1914, he was also defining and contending with the complexities of life in the United States.

Indeed, Rai's stay in the United States from 1914 to 1919 marked an extremely productive period of exile. During those years, he tirelessly worked to spread propaganda for Indian home rule to American audiences, lecturing across the country and associating with a wide range of Americans from various ideological positions on the Left. As Dohra Ahmad explains, Rai's audience was as broad as it was eclectic; he lectured to "labor unions, Unitarian congregations, Theosophical lodges, Irish home-rulers, and anyone else who would listen."[15] Some of those listeners were, in fact, agents of the U.S. Bureau of Investigation, who had begun to intercept Rai's letters, planting informants at his speeches and cooperating with the British to suppress his publications and provide information on his activities in the United States.[16] In March 1918, for example, Rai was reported to have given a speech on the cruelties of British rule at the Open Forum in Detroit, which led to a series of memos passed between the U.S. Army and the Bureau of Investigation, and sworn affidavits from the event organizer requested by British intelligence.[17] In a report entitled "Connection between Hindus and Radical Elements," Rai's name was placed at the very top. "Lajpat Rai," the report read, "has formed close associations among many prominent radicals whose names figure in the radical press and he appears with them on radical platforms."[18] Another report described him simply as "a very dangerous Hindu conspirator."[19]

In spite of being labeled a radical in the United States, Rai was drawn to conservative and communalist tendencies within the Indian struggle for independence, separating him from the far more revolutionary Gadar Party on the West Coast. Rai's political thought was shaped by a form of Hindu nationalism that he had inherited from his commitments to the Arya Samaj.[20] Formed in the late nineteenth century, the Arya Samaj was a revivalist Hindu movement with aims that were both reformist (simplifying Hinduism and discarding forms of idol worship) and militant (imagining India as a Hindu nation).[21] In one of its most controversial and aggressively Hindu supremacist actions, the Arya Samaj led conversion drives under the auspices of *shuddi* or "purification," a means to convert (or in their terms, "reconvert") Muslims, Sikhs, and Christians to Hinduism. While members of the Arya Samaj also supported the abolition of caste hierarchy—some proposing a caste system based on "worth" instead of "birth"—critics such as B. R. Ambedkar distrusted the sincerity of such reforms.[22] With their investments in imagining a premodern "Hindu" nation, the Arya Samaj held, unsurprisingly, deeply Islamophobic and Hindu nationalist beliefs. Over the course of his life, Rai offered more secular visions of an Indian future—describing India as "neither Hindu nor Muslim, not even both [but] one"—but his leadership in the All-India Hindu Mahasabha in the mid-1920s and comments on Hindus as being "a nation in themselves" have also been interpreted as "gestatory" for the more radical right-wing Hindu nationalism that began to flourish after his passing in 1928.[23] Indeed, even in his earlier writings, Rai invoked the figure of the Muslim through a form of cultural ressentiment.[24] "It is futile to think of bringing about a complete political union of Hindus and Mohamedans," Rai commented in 1907, adding that the "Mohamedans think that they belong to a race of rulers, and their fellow-subjects, the Hindu, [. . .] cannot claim an equality with them in the scale of nations."[25] As Babli Sinha argues, "communal thinking was a perpetual limit to Rai's pluralism."[26] This communalism not only shaped his views on Muslims, it inflected his understanding of race and racial identity.

By 1917, Rai had become a fixture among the coterie of American liberals, institutionalizing his propaganda efforts by forming the India Home Rule League of America (IHRLA) in an office on Broadway, and publishing the monthly journal *Young India* from 1918 to 1920.[27] First issued in January 1918, *Young India* outlined its mission and that of the IHRLA in its inaugural edition, characterizing its purpose as partially educational. "In India we suspected that the outside world knew little about our country, her past or present, and cared even less for her future," the editors of the journal announced, citing the "knowledge" of India that most Americans could name: "that it was painted red on the map," "it was the land of the snake-charmer," that there was an "India brand of tea."[28] The editorial argued that the sources that Americans had used to gain knowledge about India were, in fact, colonial in form—"from British sources, or from their own globe-trotters, or from the Reverend Fathers [who have been] sent to convert and comfort the heathen."[29] *Young India* would serve as a corrective, providing a perspective from Indians and allies, contesting the "received image of India as fractious and fragmented."[30] The stated intention of the IHRLA was to promote the cause of Indian home rule within the British Empire, much like that of Canada, South Africa, and Australia.[31] But more than a source of information or polemics, *Young India* itself served as an argument for India as a unified nation, replete with its own traditions, political aspirations, arts, and culture. The journal soon transformed into what Dohra Ahmad has called "a periodical nation: a pluralist entity, at once theoretical and actual, that appeared every month."[32] Drawing on Benedict Anderson's formulation of the nation as imagined community brought to life through the processes of print capitalism, Ahmad carefully demonstrates how *Young India* inculcated a type of anticolonial nationalist subjectivity through the very form of the periodical. Filling its pages with news from India, examples and discussions of Indian art, and poetry from the likes of Rabindranath Tagore and Sarojini Naidu, Rai's *Young India* was itself a metonymic performance of Indian national unity. "India is young again," the February 1918 edition announced, telling its readers, "Every time her life was threatened she managed to revive, become young again, to play her part in the final destiny of humanity."[33] Through the form of the periodical, *Young India* presented itself not only as an argument against colonial subjection and home rule but as a cohesive political project, a nation that had existed since antiquity and, after achieving home rule, would once again be restored. This argument was presented visually on each issue's cover (Figure 1.1). A hand-drawn image of the Indian subcontinent radiates beams of light outward to the title "Young India," while below a Sanskrit verse reads "Mother and the motherland are greater than the heavens" (*janani janmabhoomishcha svargadyapi gariyasi*).[34] Through such symbols, *Young India* formulated the image of a nation not

BANDE MATARAM.

Published by the INDIA HOME RULE LEAGUE of America
1465 Broadway, New York City

Vol. I.   JANUARY 1918   No. 1.

MESSAGE TO PRESIDENT WILSON

Commander Wedgwood and Montagu ·
on Indian Government

TAGORE'S LATEST POEM

To Members, Yearly $1.00   15c. a Copy   To others, Yearly $1.50

FIGURE 1.1 The inaugural issue of *Young India* (July 1918). (South Asian American Digital Archive)

only rooted deeply in the past but, in its use of Sanskrit, drawn on an image shaped by the league and Rai's own Hindu-centric imaginary.

In *Landscapes of Hope* (2009), Dohra Ahmad provides a powerful illustration of how literary analysis can offer a method to think about the connection between the aesthetic and political project of expatriate anticolonial writing. Her argument draws on "utopianism" and "utopian fiction" as formal categories to understand the anticolonial work of figures such as Rai and Du Bois, and the contours of solidarity that allowed them to imagine the "emancipation for the colored peoples of the world."[35] But what if we consider how Rai's time abroad in exile, and the kind of writing that it facilitated, unintentionally developed cracks and aporias in the reified form of the nation? Rai's other major writing projects in the United States, after all, opened up different type of questions, which disrupted the idea of the nation as the most cohesive form of social and political organization. His book *The United States of America* (*USAHIS*, 1916), especially, while always connected to a nationalist project also attended to the fissures of the national form. As mentioned, the key argument of the book was that "the problems of the United States are very similar to those that face us in India."[36] If, in his propaganda work—written primarily for sympathetic Americans and Indians in the United States—Rai consistently maintained the party line of Indian home rule, his writings on and about the United States rendered the nation as a problematic, a negotiation, which came up against other forms of social organization and hierarchy. Thus, while the comparison between the United States and India solidified national aspirations by proposing that the forms of nation-state and colonial state were "similar" and that the latter would lead to the former, Rai's emphasis on "problems" opened up a series of counter-narratives, each pointing to fragments that challenged the form of nationhood as natural, settled, orderly. These fissures, by extension, were as operative in India as they were in the United States.

With *USAHIS*, Rai assembled a book that drew upon various forms of writing—including reportage, sociological report, history, and travelogue—and that, perhaps inadvertently, challenged the identification with the United States that he so eagerly drew upon in his propaganda work. Divided into thirteen chapters, the book ranged from the textbook-like chapters "Outlines of the History of the United States" and "Education in the United States," to inquiries into "The Negro in American Politics" and "Caste in America." Du Bois later praised the book for "not simply [writing] a conventional history of white America [. . .] but giv[ing] a quarter of his space and intelligent interpretation to the Negro Problem in the United States."[37] *The New York Times*, for its part, described *USAHIS* as "a strange novelty, written by a Hindu for Hindus" that had much to teach American readers.[38] In truth, Rai's book was neither that strange nor novel. It shared qualities with a number of similarly themed (even similarly titled) books and essays written by

Indian male travelers and migrants during the 1910s and 1920s. A few years after the publication of Rai's *USAHIS*, Indu Bhushan De Majumdar, a graduate student at Cornell, published *America through Hindu Eyes* (1918) with presses in London and Calcutta. Sudhindra Bose, a lecturer at the University of Iowa who had come to the United States in 1903, published *Fifteen Years in America* (1920), compiling his many essays for the *Modern Review*. The journalist Saint Nihal Singh, who wrote extensively about the United States during his time in the country, contributed a series of essays titled "As an Indian Sees America" to the *Hindustan Review* in 1909. Mostly published in Calcutta, these writings were a sharp contrast to the colonial travelogue produced by white Europeans and Americans as they ventured abroad to colonies in Asia and the rest of the non-Western world. As scholars such as Javed Majeed have argued, the nineteenth- and twentieth-century Euro-American travelogue was a genre intimately tied to the project of empire building, "encod[ing] and legitimiz[ing] the aspirations of empire."[39] Indian travelogues about the West, however, posed a different kind of project. For colonized subjects, travel provided "modes of knowing" and "epistemological strategy," but they also served as a reminder of the "global extent of British power."[40] "The further they travelled," Majeed explains, "the more disempowered they sensed themselves to be in relation to the empire."[41] Indian writers such as Rai, Bose, and Singh may very well have assumed that the United States could serve as a temporary respite from the panoptic eye of empire, but, as they quickly learned, that was not the case. Their travels to and through the United States often entailed barriers restricting their free movement, encounters with British agents and spies, and other conditions that characterized the experience of a colonial subject in the late 1910s and 1920s. Moreover, while traveling they encountered the racial discourses present in various regions of the United States and were just as soon interpellated by them. If the European travel book produced what Mary Louise Pratt calls the "domestic subject of empire," these travelogues began to illustrate what it meant to be a colonial subject of empire, not only in the colony or metropole, but across the vast geopolitical terrain of the world.[42] Rai had begun to sense this even before he had made it to New York.

In May 1914, Rai was in London as an Indian National Congress delegate. While his major preoccupation involved the colonial–metropole relations between Britain and India, he had become aware of a story that was unfolding on the western coast of Canada. That month, the *Komagata Maru*, a steamship with nearly four hundred Indian (and mostly Sikh) passengers aboard, sought entry into Canada, having traveled from Hong Kong to the Port of Vancouver in a grueling month-long transpacific journey.[43] For years, the Canadian government had created measures to restrict immigration from Asia, including the infamous "Continuous Passage Act," which ordered that "immigrants may be prohibited from landing or coming into Canada unless they come from the country of their birth, or citizenship, by a continuous journey."[44] Given that no direct line from India to Canada existed, the act had effectively prohibited all immigration from India through a sly work-around. Defying the regulation, the passengers of the *Komagata Maru* challenged the Canadian government, seeking entry on the basis of their rights as subjects of the British Empire. The Canadian government refused, and after a protracted battle that entailed South Asian migrants in Vancouver creating a "shore committee" to legally challenge the Canadian government, the ship eventually returned to India. News of the incident traveled across the globe, stirring outrage in India and throughout the diaspora. In England at the time, Rai was invited by a Sikh leader to visit Canada, but with the war underway Rai postponed his visit.[45] Nevertheless, he seized the opportunity for commentary and on June 7, Rai wrote a letter to the editor of the India-based *Tribune*. The *Komagata Maru* incident had exemplified the rule of colonial difference, Rai argued, for the British Government

> want[s] the Indians to believe that they are the equal subjects of the King, but when the former claim their rights as such, they behave as if they have neither the power nor the desire to secure the same for them. Perhaps, it is not so much the fault of the Government of India as of those statesmen who have to reconcile their professions and principles of liberalism with their policy of subjection.[46]

While Javed Majeed and Inderpal Grewal have described travel as a "mode of knowing" for the colonized, the *Komagata Maru* incident adds a new wrinkle to that idea. For colonial subjects, travel underscored the restrictions imposed on their movement across the globe, and for the colonial government it was a reminder of, as Rey Chow describes it, "the discomforting fact that the natives [were] no longer staying in their frames."[47] The story of the 376 passengers of the *Komagata Maru* served to point out the façade of imperial citizenship, in which one's status as "equal subjects of the King" was dismissed whenever one attempted to gain access to other settler colonial dominions within the empire. Imperial citizenship was a position marked by borders, regulations, and "subjection" for those who existed on the wrong side of the color line. Rai had been made aware of this the moment he stepped off of the S.S. *Philadelphia* onto New York in the fall of 1914, queued through customs inspections and noting the differential treatment of "whites and coloured."

By the time he wrote his monograph *The United States of America* the following spring, American race relations had become a growing interest for Rai. Before that point, if Rai had written about race, he used the word in a civilizational sense, deploying phrases such as subject, dominant, or ruling races.[48] "Race" was a shorthand to describe ethno-national communities caught in a struggle for power, and racial characteristics were marked by cultural generalities rather than the complicated language of modern scientific racism. If there was any critical content in Rai's use of race, it came in the form of quotations from House of Commons member J. G. Godard, whose polemic *Racial Supremacy* defined imperialism as "the rule of one race of people by another race of people involving—of course, the subjection of the former to the latter."[49] Yet the notion of a multiracial society or even an intranational racism, for that matter, was largely absent from Rai's writings.

In *USAHIS*, race, and particularly what was then known as the "Negro Problem," had become a new site for Rai to interrogate various structures of power, from the hierarchies of caste to the dynamics of class and nation. The metaphors in *USAHIS*, however, quickly became entangled. If at times Rai saw the position of African Americans in the United States as analogous to the material and symbolic violence faced by lower-caste communities (then described as "Untouchables") at the hands of upper-caste Indians, at other times he saw such a position as analogous to the indignity faced by Indians (and metonymically, the entire Indian nation) at the hands of the British. At other times, Rai turned the direction of the analogy, using caste as an analytical category for the various racial struggles in the United States as well as a metaphor for class struggle in the industrialized West.

Armed with letters from his New York acquaintances W.E.B. Du Bois and Mary White Ovington, co-founders of the NAACP, Rai traveled to the deep South in the winter of 1915. He first visited Alabama, where Booker T. Washington gave him a tour of the Tuskegee Institute. From there, he traveled to Georgia, where he visited Morehouse College and met John Hope, the first African American president of the school. Along the way, Rai also witnessed the overt racism of Jim Crow America. Attending a screening of D. W. Griffith's *Birth of a Nation*, Rai was shocked to find a frenzied audience reaching what he called "the highest pitch of race hatred."[50] Twice during dinner conversations with his otherwise "charming" white hostesses, Rai asked about the unequal treatment of Blacks in the nation, only to receive angry responses about the "new generation" of "modern Negroes.[51] One of the hosts confessed to Rai,

> Oh, Mr. Rai . . . you do not know how wicked the modern Negroes in this country are. The old generation was very good, even lovable. They knew their place and were very faithful servants. My father had a Negro gardener, and he was a dear. We used to love him; but the new generation are so wicked that every time I went out for a ride in Virginia, my father armed me with a revolver lest a Negro might assault me.[52]

Rai expressed dismay at the racist reactions from his hosts, who he said were all personally kind and even expressed "admiration for Hindus and Hinduism."[53] Their responses betrayed what Rai described as a deeply entrenched "caste feeling" in the United States, one that he suspected would not disappear in the near future. Race had basis not in reality but in affect, Rai argued, quoting Josiah Royce, who had written that "our so-called race problems are merely the problems caused by our antipathies."[54] That Rai attempted to explain racism through the metaphor of "caste feeling" is deeply telling—it suggested not only similar structures of disenfranchisement and violence, but how race and caste worked on the psyche, dredging up feelings of sexualized fear ("lest a Negro might assault me") and paternal superiority ("They knew their place"). Describing racism as "caste feeling" echoes Ambedkar's description of untouchability as "an aspect of social psychology . . . a sort of social nausea of one group against the other."[55]

Rai's readings and experiences with racial prejudice against African Americans culminated in three chapters in *USAHIS*: "The Education of the Negro," "The Negro in American Politics," and the more provocative and analytic "Caste in America." Studying the "Negro Problem on the spot" was "one of the things that prompted me to pay a second visit to the United States," Rai wrote at the onset.[56] As in the other chapters in his book, Rai quoted extensively, filling pages with statistics, verbatim passages of local law, and the paraphrased arguments of national leaders. One downside of this method of writing is that it is sometimes difficult to extract Rai's own position from the long passages he excerpted from the likes of Booker T. Washington, Du Bois, and Kelly Miller, the dean of Howard University.

Only when Rai began to draw comparisons between the United States and India did he stake any sort of claim on the subject. Projecting the issue of India's caste system onto racial hierarchy in the United States, Rai declared, "The Negro is the PARIAH of America."[57] Lest the caste origins of the word "pariah" be lost on American readers, he clarified, "There is some analogy between the Negro problem in the United States of America and the problem of the depressed classes in India."[58] While Rai maintained that the "two cases are not on all fours with each other," one major thread that tied the "Pariah" and "Negro" together was the way in which social segregation became a means of maintaining the boundaries and hierarchies of race and caste.[59]

When Rai discussed the discrimination against "people of a different color [and] (between the *Varnas* of the Hindus)," he noted that when it came to inter-dining and intermarriage, caste and racial segregation played out in the same way in the United States as it did in India.[60] Rai drew on two examples he had heard about in his first months of his stay to make his point. A Harvard professor of economics had told Rai that after a conference that both he and W.E.B. Du Bois attended, they wished to continue the conversation over dinner; "Dr. Du Bois remarked that the only eating place open to him was the refreshment room of the railway station, and how eventually all of them had to go there in order to have the pleasures of Dr. Du Bois's company."[61] John Hope, the president of Morehouse College, later explained that he was forced to sit in the back of a streetcar and, in Rai's words, "give up the front seats to the most ignorant, dark-colored white scoundrel."[62] Neither Hope's "education and learning" nor his light complexion could save him from the indignities of the color line.[63]

While comparing racism in the United States to the caste system in India, however, Rai continued to defend Hinduism by downplaying the realities of caste discrimination. In one passage, he discussed the hypocrisy of Christian America, which proclaimed the "doctrine of the equality of men and of universal brotherhood" while also sanctioning segregation and policing against miscegenation. Rather than use this as an opportunity to further address the forms of segregation that restricted the social mobility of lower-caste communities in "Hindu India," his language had the effect of minimizing, even defending, caste as the lesser of two social evils:

> To me it seems that the Hindu Aryans of India never applied the color bar so rigidly as the Christian whites of the United States of America are doing today [. . .] yet Christian writers who dare not raise their voice against the color line in the U.S.A., have no hesitation in sitting in judgment on Hindus and denouncing them and their religious system for the institution of caste.[64]

Rai's critique underscored the hypocrisy of white Americans who were quick to point to the inhumanity of the caste system but "dare not raise their voice" against the racism in their backyard. Such a critique resembled the *tu quoque* or "you too" argument; as Nico Slate points out, such responses led to troubling forms of "transnational justification," wherein Indians downplayed the atrocities of caste by pointing toward racism in the United States. Nevertheless, in reading against Rai's intent, perhaps we see how his analogy forced him to conceive of the caste system as a racialized "color line" or "color bar" that existed within the borders of the Indian nation, upheld by the religio-racial "Hindu Aryans" in much the same way that it was maintained by "Christian whites."

During the period in which Rai wrote *USAHIS*, fellow Indian writers also drew similar comparisons between racism and caste discrimination. One of these figures was Sudhindra Bose, an immigrant from Bengal who arrived in the United States in 1904 and would eventually earn his PhD at the State University of Iowa in political science, where he continued to lecture throughout his life.[65] In 1920, Bose published *Fifteen Years in America*, a book that detailed his experiences in the United States, compiling and revising various essays that had originally been printed in the *Modern Review*. Like Rai, Bose pointed out the hypocrisy of calling out caste in India without addressing race in the United States. Unlike Rai, however, he did not defend

Hinduism but rather used the caste metaphor to better understand the workings of racism. In one section, Bose described examples of racial segregation in the American South, from separate facilities to forms of racialized menial labor, before imploring his readers to "let Indian reformers and professional uplifters who still cling to the notion that there is no caste outside of India take note."[66] In a chapter titled "Life in the Southern States," Bose, in fact, described racial segregation through the terms of the caste system:

> Negroes are considered by the white Brahmans, the American 'caste people,' as unspeakable, untouchable 'outcasts,' the scum of the earth. Their lot is the most pitiable of any I have ever seen. And yet these despised downtrodden blacks are the foundation of the southern economic structure. They carry the load, and if they ever take a notion to falter, there is no doubt in the minds of those who have made a careful study, that the southern economic structure will topple.[67]

Bose did not extend the caste–race analogy much further. Nevertheless, his linking of "white" racial identity to "Brahman" caste identity, of "Negro" to "untouchable," offered a quick comparison for his Indian readers to consider the ways that caste hierarchy resembled racial hierarchy in the United States. The resemblances, he argued, were the product of two particular dynamics: First, the contradictory way by which the entire Southern economy was dependent on, but disdainful, of Black labor, in much the same way that lower-caste and Dalit labor was a necessity to Indian society. And secondly, the practice of "untouchability" functioned in ways similar to the persistent racial violence and stigmatization of Blackness in a white supremacist nation.

In describing the racialization of labor in the South he had witnessed during his travels, Bose pointed out that "all manual work is looked upon by the southern whites as degrading."[68] Compared to the American North, the Southerner was obsessed with titles and nobility, crafting a "home-spun" gentility to create new hierarchies. The reason the Southerner did this, Bose explained, was because of what he describes as their "secret reverence for rank and caste."[69] As it did for Rai, caste feeling provided an explanatory framework for Bose's anecdotes about traveling through the South. He recalled noticing that all common laborers were Black, before providing a run-down of occupations, ranging from "the porters, the waiters, the janitors, the drivers, the barbers, the farm hands, [to] the house servants."[70] In providing a detailed list of these occupations, Bose may very well have been drawing attention to the way that racialized labor in the United States resembled the kinds of labor practiced by lower castes in India. Bose wrote, for instance, that while such forms of Black labor were completely integral to the maintenance and operation of Southern society, these were also forms of work that whites, like the upper castes, had a disdain, even disgust, for. Bose related an anecdote in which his landlady in the South refused to do any menial work. She told him, "I would rather die of hunger than work in the kitchen. The kitchen is for the darkies, the niggers."[71] By framing the story more broadly through the framework of "white 'Brahmans'" and "Negro untouchables," we might tease out an implicit commentary on the inequalities wrought by caste in India. Centering race and caste on an economic system, Bose seemed to imply that lower-caste and "untouchable" labor was similarly central to the entire workings of the Indian economy, even while that labor reproduced the lower-caste subjects' stigmatization.

When discussing racialized violence and the stigma of Black racial identity, Bose drew even stronger comparisons between the relations of caste and race, elaborating further on his characterization of "Negroes" as the "unspeakable, untouchable 'outcasts'" of the United States. He described how he was reprimanded by Southern friends for using the term "colored person," which he had learned was "much preferred by the self-respecting negroes themselves."[72] Through a quick series of juxtapositions, Bose described the hypocrisy of a nation in which African Americans were indispensable laborers, contributors to U.S. military, "eminent doctors, editors, preachers, and . . . professors," while also the subjects of daily denigration through language and, more severely, through acts of violence. Drawing on reports by the NAACP to describe the lynchings, Bose concluded that such forms of racial violence have become a "part of the routine history" of the United States.[73] Much of Bose's discussion of anti-Black racism in the United States is relegated to his chapter on the American South, but he briefly mentions how such practices continued in the North. In one of the opening chapters of *Fifteen Years in America*, titled "Traveling through the Country," Bose described a train ride where one passenger openly and joyously discussed a lynching he had witnessed:

> "Did you hear," asked one of my neighbors, "about that lynching in our town in Illinois?" Without waiting for a reply he continued, "Jolly, we had the biggest time ever. We strung up the nigger from the tallest tree in the town and I tell you we had some practice in shooting."[74]

Beneath the veneer of the United States as a moral giant and exemplar of democracy, Bose described a society abounding with spectacles of racial violence and buoyed by racial (caste) feeling. This feeling was maintained through an elaborate system of social segregation, developed in order to "keep the negroes in their proper places," including segregated waiting rooms, theater sections, churches, and "Jim Crow Cars."[75] Bose also hinted at how these laws of segregation affected property, citing a recent law passed in Baltimore that prevented African Americans from moving into areas occupied by whites.[76] All of these forms of social segregation, Bose described, were either tacitly or explicitly endorsed by the church.[77]

Another of Rai's acquaintances, Saint Nihal Singh—an Indian journalist based in the United States for some time and a regular contributor to the *Modern Review*—also wrote a series of articles on African American life for the Calcutta-based journal. Rather than connect the forms of racism experienced by African Americans to caste hierarchy, Singh connected American racism to the same "crime of colour" that had been used to justify the colonization of Indians under British rule. Through examples of African Americans resisting and progressing in spite of the "difficulties and handicaps" in their way, Indian readers could find "practical suggestions" for resistance and better understand the ways that racism operated.[78] In his lengthy profile of Booker T. Washington and the Tuskegee Institute, Singh even mentioned that industrial and practical education could serve as an example to "those patriotic Indians who are anxious to add their mite (*sic*) to the uplift of the Indian masses."[79]

Singh's grasp of the racism in the United States hinged on his understanding of the "colour line," a line that he maintained was reinforced by law, segregation, and violence:

> The Afro-American's equal rights merely exist on government documents. Despite the professions to the contrary, the pall of slavery, of inferiority, still hangs over the coloured man and in the year of Christ nineteen hundred and eight the Africander in America, no matter what his education, what his attainments or even how singularly successful he may have been in amassing the riches of this world, is still a mere "nigger"—liable to be hated, despised, maltreated, and molested—even done to death—by the wretched specimen of humanity, ill-mannered, boorish, without education, without refinement, without much money, Christian only in name, his only claim to superiority lying in his white hide.[80]

Singh's rhetorical barrage of descriptors—"wretched specimen," "ill-mannered," "boorish"—served to underscore the power and privilege of whiteness. A "white hide" could erase all shortcomings, much in the same way that dark skin undermined all achievements, success, and access to basic human dignity. The color line, in other words, was the racial base upon which American society had founded its system of hierarchy. Singh's claim, of course, was not without legal basis, given the racial prerequisite for citizenship in the United States for "free, white persons." While racial prerequisites for citizenship were amended after the Civil War to include people of African descent, that citizenship was at best second class and "merely exist[ed] in government documents," as Singh put it—in name, and not in action.

Singh extended that narrative and applied it to the treatment of Indians under British rule, drawing a connection between the racism that undergirded white supremacy in the United States and colonial rule in India. The power afforded to whites in the United States, he explained, is what allows "the white man [to] mete out the same treatment to coloured people in India and out of India."[81] Moreover, any claims to "equal rights" by Blacks in the United States and Indians in British India were false. Singh later described how African Americans' "equal rights" were comparable to those enjoyed by Indian subjects, who are "unable to secure even-handed justice from the law-courts," unable to enjoy freedom of press and speech, and unable to find any positions within government "except through a small, dismal-looking postern gate."[82]

In language similar to Du Bois's famous statement about the "color line [that] belts the world," Singh's essay for the *Modern Review* was a sharply worded indictment of the power of white supremacy and its extensive reach. For Singh, the color line not only disenfranchised African Americans and colonized Indians but, he noted, it also affected Asian migrants, who had been systematically discriminated against on the basis of racial difference. "It makes little difference whether the coloured man is an Indian, a Chinese, a Japanese or an Afro-American, the Anglo Saxon [. . .] arrogates to himself superiority on the score of 'colour.'"[83] Using disparaging and classist language, Singh further ridiculed the alleged racial superiority of European migrants over Asian migrants, writing that "the coloured laborer, in my mind, certainly is far superior to the scum that the American immigration companies are importing into North America."[84] In his bifurcation of the world into white and "coloured" people, Saint Nihal Singh's polemical essay offered a vision of racial solidarities (at the expense of class solidarities), drawing a link between the Asian migrant laborer, the African American subject, and the colonized Indian, each connected to the other by the sheer fact of being on the wrong side of the color line.

Singh's formulation was anything but commonplace during his time. For Indian migrants in the United States, who faced enormous amounts of discrimination because of their racial difference, the hazy categories of racial classification had nevertheless allowed, even encouraged, identifications with whiteness. This was dramatically played out in citizenship cases in the early decades of the twentieth century, in which Indian migrants claimed whiteness as their racial identity. This strange racial logic, by which Indian migrants could be classified as white, inflected the kind of arguments that Rai and others made, as they contested the discrimination that was fomenting around migrants from colonial India.

Contesting the "Hindu Threat"

By the 1910s, an argument had developed regarding the racial stock shared between Americans (who were implicitly "white") and Hindus (who were classified as "Caucasian"). Life on the ground, however, revealed another story altogether. As early as 1907, the Chinese and Korean Exclusion League, based in San Francisco, contested Indian immigration along the Pacific Coast, displaying an ironically inclusive spirit by renaming themselves the Asiatic Exclusion League in order to bring Hindus into the fold.[85] That year, the league played a role in the Bellingham riots in Washington state, organizing a mob that gathered to assault and displace hundreds of Sikh laborers who had arrived in the logging town months earlier. Soon thereafter, copycat actions followed along the coast—in Everett, Washington, that November; in Live Oak, California, in 1908; and in St. John, Oregon, in 1910.[86] Formed as a consortium of labor organizations and supported by American Federation of Labor (AFL) president Samuel Gompers, the Exclusion League kept a watchful eye on the number of Indian migrants who worked in the orchards, lumberyards, and sawmills on the West Coast. In a report on "The Hindoo Question in California" presented during a February 1908 meeting, the question was raised whether "the Hindoos [were] here in sufficient numbers to constitute a menace to the American laborer?" The report enumerated the "undesirability" of Indians, citing "their lack of cleanliness, disregard of sanitary laws, petty pilfering [. . .] of chickens, [their] insolence of women," but concluded they were "more sinned against than sinning," blaming specifically the Canadian Pacific Railway and lieutenant governor of British Columbia for importing Indian labor in order to reduce wages."[87]

In the years that followed, the Hindu Question, as it was called, continued to be a fraught topic of debate. In January 1909, the league again raised concerns about Indian migration into California. "Who are these Hindus and what are their antecedents?" one report asked. "What evidence is there that they are seeking to come to the United States to acquire homes and participate in the institutions that have builded (sic) here by citizens of the white race?"[88] Dichotomies between the Indian and white laborer became increasingly racialized. While the league framed their opposition to migrants in terms of labor (the Asian migrants lived in such poor conditions, they lowered wages for white workers, etc.), their underlying ideology always hinted at a broader formation of white supremacy. Their opposition toward Chinese, Koreans, and Japanese, for instance, had often invoked an essentialized racial difference, supported by the then-ethnology-sanctioned categories of "Caucasoid" and "Mongoloid," and at times invoking hackneyed historical narratives of Genghis Khan, Timur the Lame, and Babar to feed conspiracies of an eminent Asian takeover of the Pacific.[89] But even if the league and the supporting press argued against Indian immigration and naturalization, legally the Hindu's rights to citizenship could not be contested, at least on the grounds of racial classification. In an editorial published in the *New York Call*, U.S. Commissioner of Immigration Hart H. North stated, "The Hindus are not governed by an exclusion law such as we have respecting Chinese, Japanese, and Koreans; they have the same legal standing that any European immigrant has, and I cannot treat them otherwise."[90] As a solution, North proposed a hypothetical "general Asiatic law" to avoid discriminating between the different "Asiatics" who turned up on the Pacific shore for work, in order to discriminate against them all.

The "legal standing" that North referred to was the imprecise definition of "white" that shaped the racial prerequisites to American citizenship. In 1790, the U.S. government ruled that in order to become a naturalized citizen of the Union, one must be a "free white person," a requirement that lasted until the Civil War.[91] What "white" actually meant, however, was still a contentious issue, which played out in citizenship cases across the late nineteenth and early twentieth century. Race-based arguments forwarded by Indians suggested that the terms "white" and "Caucasian" were equivalent, and the latter category was derived by a racial classification system that gained traction in succeeding decades. According to Augustus Henry Keane's ethnological study, *The World's People* (1908), the human family could be divided into four main categories: "Negroes or Blacks," "Mongoloid or Yellow," "Amerind (Red or Brown)," or the "Caucasian (White and also Dark)" who resided across a vast area, including "North Africa, Europe, Irania, India, Western Asia, and Polynesia."[92] Drawing from the racial theory of Indian civilization, which hypothesized that Aryan settlers migrated (from the region now known as Iran) to the Indian subcontinent and constituted the ancestry of Northern Indians, many South Asians applying for citizenship in the 1910s and 1920s presented evidence of their eligibility for citizenship on grounds that they were "Aryan," and therefore also "Caucasian" and "white." Depending on the judges and clerks making the decision, this argument would or would not hold: For Abdullah Dolla (1909), Bhicaji Framji Balsara (1909), Akshay Kumar Mozumdar (1913), Taraknath Das (1914), Mohan Singh (1919) it did, but for Sadar Bhagwab Singh (1917) and a younger Taraknath Das (1911) it did not.[93] For those early decades in South Asian American history, rights to citizenship effectively hinged on the whims of state courts.

While the racial classification of Indians in citizenship cases pointed to the instability of racial categories, these classifications were further interrogated during a 1914 congressional hearing on the restriction of immigration of Hindu laborers. The argument about the racial classification of Indians as white "Aryans" was a familiar one to the congressmen, but the hearings also indicate the various ways that the racial categorization of Hindus was enmeshed with categories of class, caste, and religion. Among the two Indian migrant representatives at the congressional hearing one was none other than Sudhindra Bose, who fielded a number of questions from congressmen from Pennsylvania, Minnesota, and California. The committee pressed Bose to explain whether the racial classification of the Hindu as Aryan applied to Indian laborers. Minnesota representative James Manahan, for instance, asked for a clarification, mentioning that while it is "pretty generally conceded" that the "high-class Hindu is Caucasian [. . .] I have heard it said that the so-called coolie laborers, what might be called common laborers of India, are not of the same race, that they are a sort of a mongrel mixture, possibly part Caucasian and part Mongolian."[94] California representative John Raker continued that line of questioning, referencing a Spokane judge who argued that the Hindu was eligible for naturalization, holding that "the applicant was a high-caste Hindu." "Now," Raker asked, "what does he mean by that as compared with the ordinary laboring Hindu that comes to this country?"[95]

The congressmen's discussion, in which they described the laborer as "mongrel," "part Mongolian," and antithetical to the "high-caste Hindu" reveals both the slippage between racial, class, and caste categories and the formulation of high-caste as coeval to "whiteness," an idea further exploited in the 1923 *US v. Bhagat Singh Thind* U.S. Supreme Court case.[96] At stake in the congressional hearing was not a sociological examination of the validity of racial categories. As Ian Haney López argues, the courts never had "substantive disagreements about the nature of race itself."[97] Similarly, government officials never seemed particularly interested in debating whether or not the Hindu *ought* to be excluded from immigration and naturalization, but mainly concerned themselves with what the most effective way was *to* exclude them. To that end, they mobilized a variety of arguments about class and caste not to investigate whether the Indian migrant was truly "white" or not, but rather to posit that the Hindu was undesirable, regardless.

By 1916, while Rai was addressing audiences along the coasts, Congress debated a bill to further secure legislation that would prevent the migration of Indians to the United States. The bill, which would eventually become the 1917 Immigration Act (or the "Asiatic Barred Zone" Act) was the first in a series of successful legislative and judicial decisions that would prevent immigration from India to the United States until the mid-century. In June 1916, Rai sent a letter to Senator Ellison Smith of South Carolina, petitioning the bill. His means of arguing against it relied on deploying Hindu claims to "whiteness," exemplifying what Sucheta Mazumdar has described as "racist responses to racism."[98]

> That it is a gross injustice and, if I may be permitted to say, an outrageous reflection on the Hindus, to be selected as the only people on God's earth who are to be excluded from entry into the United States as a race. It has been acknowledged by the highest scholastic authority in the world, that the Hindus are from the Aryan stock, that their ancient language, Sanskrit, and many of their present spoken languages belong to the Indo-European branch of languages, and that they are the inheritors of a great and noble literature and civilization. In fact, of all the people inhabiting the continent of Asia, they are

with the Persians and Caucasians, the nearest of kin to the majority of the inhabitants of the United States. Their exclusion as a race is not only an undeserved and unjustifiable reflection on their national honour but is equally unworthy of the high-mindedness of this great nation which stands for equal opportunity and open door for the meanest of God's creatures on earth.[99]

Rai's use of the Aryan narrative to define Hindu racial identity was not simply a passive acceptance of racial typologies, but was shaped by his own ideological grounding as an Arya Samajist who believed that "Hindus today are descendants of the Aryans."[100] In describing the bill as an affront to "national honour," Rai reframed exclusion into a belligerent and wholly unfitting act between two equals—a "great nation which stands for equal opportunity" and "inheritors of a great and noble [. . .] civilization."

Such uses of the Aryan narrative were commonplace among Indian expatriates and nationalists, who deployed it to challenge exclusionary policies while simultaneously affecting a racial fraternity between Indians and white Americans. In April 1911, Har Dayal—Punjabi anarchist, part-time Stanford lecturer, co-founder of the Gadar Party, and "idealist of a strange type," as Rai described him—penned an essay, "India in America," published in the *Modern Review* that drew on similar language.[101] In his essay, Dayal cathected onto the symbol of the American flag, almost to the point of religious zealotry. "No one can breathe beneath the Stars and Stripes without being lifted to a higher level of thought and action," he explained, adding that the flag stands for "unity, liberty, tolerance, and individual progress and not for racial self-assertion and bitter memories of the past."[102] The assertion that the American flag represented "unity, liberty, tolerance" and the lack of "racial self-assertion" contradicted the actual experience of Dayal and the laboring Indians along the Pacific Coast. By March 1914, Dayal's name had already turned up in the national press when he was arrested by U.S. immigration authorities and faced deportation charges, to which he responded by claiming that his arrest was further proof of "the despicable pro-British subservence of the United States government" under Woodrow Wilson.[103] Three years earlier, however, Dayal had gone as far as describing how the American frontier had renewed all Indian subjects, from "Hindu laborers" to students to "swamis," each of whom embody the spirit of "the old Aryans who colonized [India]." "All that life is being lived over again here," he commented, "[with] the Sikhs representing the sturdy Aryan settlers."[104] Dayal's choice of words is curious, to say the least. His gushing description of the process of Aryan colonization reveals the racial contradictions of his anticolonial critique, which skewered British rule while also lauding narratives of settler colonialism.

Lajpat Rai devoted one chapter of his *USAHIS* to the subject of Indians residing in the United States, and for the most part he used those chapters to contest the discourse of the "Hindu threat" of migration. He had explained that part of his desire to come to the United States was, in fact, to better understand "why the American prejudice against Hindu immigration had developed so strongly in recent years."[105] In the chapter "India in America," Rai described the Indian diaspora across the Americas, noting the presence of populations in Alaska, Brazil, Mexico, British Guiana, Canada, Panama, and "Argentine and Chili." In the United States, he noted, the populations consisted of primarily "religious preachers," "students," and "laborers," but most of his attention was paid to the latter two groups. It was through his discussion of Indian students and workers in the United States that Rai disarticulated the language of race and color, albeit inconsistently.

Rai described laborers from India with a degree of paternalism, commenting on their "honest" and "warmhearted" character, while also pointing to the various ways in which poor working conditions and discrimination had shaped their experiences. Rai explained that the laborers' efficient work habits had made the group particularly sought after for agricultural labor, but also underscored the difficulties they faced:

> Judged from the output or from the standard of efficiency, he is very much sought after, particularly by the employers of agricultural labor. But for his race and color, he would never be out of employment and there would be room enough for hundreds and thousands more. Ten or fifteen years ago, there was no prejudice against him, but during this period the volume of prejudice has grown thick and fast.[106]

Rai argued that "race and color" were the main reasons behind anti-Indian discrimination and the uneven treatment between the Indian and white laborer. While Indian migrants had low literacy rates and "unclean" living standards, he pointed out that European immigrants were no different in that regard. Rai also mentioned how the common complaint that Indian laborers were regularly arrested for drunken disorder was also a product of race and color prejudice, explaining that "the Sikh has the disadvantage of being immediately identified," which led to more arrests. The real objection to the Indian laborer could be explained by white antipathy toward racialized labor: "The Hindu is [. . .] Caucasian by race, it is true, but then his color and his habits and manners are so different that the Europeans are not prepared to acknowledge that his racial origin is the same as theirs."[107] Compared to the Chinese and Japanese, Rai contended that Indian laborers—and primarily Sikhs—had faced the most prejudice. The Chinese drew American pity because "China is America's protégé," and the Japanese were reviled but tolerated by Americans because of the political power of the Japanese empire. In contrast, the Indian drew the most scorn, due to the Sikh's unassimilated appearance, namely his "pagri (turban)" and long hair, two markers of racialized difference.[108] It bears mentioning that unlike other Indian commentators at the time who used the example of the Sikh laborer as an object of derision, Rai went as far as praising the laborer for "this trait of his character," maintaining tradition in the face of xenophobia.[109]

Rai described Indian students as a group that by-and-large came from sites of social privilege, but, facing adversities and a lack of resources in the United States, had transformed into "prodig[ies] of enterprise and industry and resourcefulness."[110] Over the course of several pages, Rai added one anecdote after another, describing the struggles of students as they paid their way through school—a Punjabi engineering student "slept on roadsides" and earned his food by working where he could, an "Aggarwal" worked as a domestic servant for a family in Los Angeles, while others worked in asparagus fields, or "roll[ed] wheel chairs" at the 1915 Panama Pacific Expo.[111] These stories produced a transformational narrative about the Indian student abroad, who discovers a masculine spirit of "self-reliance" through manual labor and loses his attachments to caste identity. In "The Hindu in America" published in *Overland Monthly* in 1908, Girindra Mukerji similarly described how experiences abroad transformed students, forcing them to dispense with their beliefs in caste and social distinction. "Here are the students of the highest caste, as well as from the lowest, living in amity," he wrote, repeating a similar sentiment in a caption under a staged photograph of six Indian students, each outfitted in a Western-style suit.[112] In making this claim, Mukerji was also writing against a familiar script, which pointed to caste difference as a barrier to both Indian self-rule as well as South Asian assimilation into the United States[113] Caste, along with customs of diet and religion, were markers of the "otherness" of the South Asian, which only reinforced the notion that the "Hindu" would be unable to conform to the culture of the United States. But the persistence of caste was also perceived as antithetical to the democratic ideology of the United States, a logic that was conveniently exploited by exclusionists.

Whether students and laborers of this early migration actually began to repudiate caste difference is a more complicated question, with the historical record leaving unclear answers. Student narratives often described how the shared experience of being racialized as "colored" in the United States helped dissipate markers of caste difference. In an article from the *Modern Review*, Sarangadhar Das viewed the United States as a space of politicization, and for that reason alone asserted that Indians ought to go to the United States, the "Land of Liberty, Equality, and Fraternity." Das discussed the regularity with which he was mistaken for "Negroes at the first sight" and regularly confronted anti-"Asiatic" prejudice, but at the same time, claimed that "in a railway train no American comes forward and says to a Hindu, 'Get out of here, you dog of an Indian,' or 'Get out of here, you nigger,'" a statement that would not have held true for colonial India, let alone En-

FIGURE 1.2 Image from Girindra Mukerji's "The Hindu in America." The caption reads, "A group of the Indian students on the Pacific Coast. One may easily judge the high character and intelligence of the race by five castes presented here. These students, however, represent no caste, and do not recognize the same." (South Asian American Digital Archive)

gland.[114] Working at the Western Sugar Refinery Company of San Francisco had made Das acutely aware of "the fight between Capital and Labor," and he claimed that the few encounters with "race hatred knocks out all our caste, religious and provincial prejudices and reminds us of our inhuman treatment of our 'untouchables' and pariahs."[115]

The testimony of Premanand Valji Vaishya, a migrant from Gujarat, on the other hand, tells another story about the treatment of expatriates who hailed from non-Brahmin backgrounds. Arriving in the United States around 1910, Vaishya first worked and studied on the West Coast, attending the University of California in Berkeley and eventually settling in the college town for nearly six years. Military intelligence believed that during this time he had become an active supporter of the Gadar Party and was involved in producing the Gujarati edition of the *Gadar* newspaper, although he denied it.[116] After his time on the West Coast, Vaishya crisscrossed the country, living in New York, Pittsburgh, and Washington, DC, where he attended Howard University. Vaishya eventually relocated to Harlem, working as a door-to-door peddler of wares, including jewelry, cream, perfumes, and powder in primarily Black neighborhoods. During this time, he attracted the unwanted attention of British agents, who believed that his peddling was actually a ruse to disseminate anticolonial propaganda among African Americans. In March 1918, Vaishya had been coaxed into selling his goods to a federal agent, who reported that the peddling was a "mere sham": "He began to discuss the race situation in the United States and from that he branched off into the condition of India. He said that if the colored race would stand together as the white race did, they could dominate the world."[117] Such a vision of Indian–Black unity echoed the opinions of figures such as Rai, Saint Nihal Singh, and Du Bois, each of whom characterized the position of the colonized Asian as akin to African Americans in the segregated United States. But Vaishya also insisted that caste hierarchies had fractured the unities among immigrant Indians in America.

In October 1918, Vaishya had applied for a passport in order to relocate to British Guiana, when he was interrogated by a British control officer, to whom he explained: "I know very few Indians in this country and none of them intimately . . . I lived with colored people and associate with them. I belong to the Lohana Caste, which is a Sudra Caste. The Indians in New York belong to higher castes and would not care to associate with me."[118] Vaishya denied having any connection to the Gadar Party or that he had ever met with *Gadar* editor Ram Chandra. Besides, he explained, "owing to class prejudice they would not have cared to have me. [. . .] We of the lower castes do not uphold such [Indian revolutionary] notions."[119] How truthful Vaishya's testimony was about either his experience or his own caste status is not entirely clear, given that he may have made such remarks to placate a British control officer in order to receive his passport. Nevertheless, Vaishya's story offers a glimpse into the complexities of race, class, and caste among Indian expatriates. His movement within African American spaces from Howard to Harlem reveal the way that migration had also compounded certain ideas of caste difference, leading to different arrangements of solidarity.

Perhaps no student felt the sting of caste prejudice as sharply as did B. R. Ambedkar, who in 1916 was studying at Columbia University, only blocks away from Harlem at the cusp of its cultural renaissance. Born into the Mahar caste (an "untouchable" caste, or what he would later term "Dalit"), Ambedkar would return to India to become one of the most important anticaste leaders and intellectuals in the twentieth century and the chairman of the Constitution Drafting Committee. Ambedkar's early writing also tried to distinguish the social relations of caste and race. In "Castes in India," written for an anthropology seminar at Columbia University, Ambedkar suggested that endogamy ultimately gave rise to the Indian caste system. While other noncaste endogamous groups such as "Negroes and Whites [. . .] in the United States" existed, Ambedkar dismissed the comparison—perhaps preemptively—concluding that "in India the situation is different."[120] Nevertheless, in the decades to come Ambedkar turned to the "Negro question" again, once in responding to Lajpat Rai, and another time in 1946 when reaching out to W.E.B. Du Bois. Ambedkar explained that he had been a "student of the Negro problem," and that "there is so much similarity between the position of the Untouchables in India and of the position of the Negroes in America that the study of the latter is not only natural but necessary."[121] While there has been much scholarly speculation about whether or not Ambedkar had made close acquaintances with African Americans when he studied in New York, very little personal writing exists from his time at Columbia to confirm or deny such claims.[122]

Most Indian students who came to the United States described the way they were often identified as "colored," and how they navigated that racial interpellation. According to one *Modern Review* article, the India Society of Detroit, whose membership primarily consisted of "high-caste" Indian male students and white women benefactors, assisted and supported Indian students at the University of Michigan, organized lectures, and described their objective as "strictly educational."[123] The article mentioned that the society had advised Hindus to wear turbans in order to "preserve their nationality" and not be mistaken for African Americans.[124] Chandra Gooneratne, a graduate student at the University of Chicago in the 1920s, told a similar story. Years later, after returning to Ceylon, Gooneratne documented his experiences traveling through the Jim Crow South, in which his ambiguous racial identity was often treated with confusion. "Any Asiatic [. . .] can evade the whole issue of color in America by winding a few yards of linen around his head. A turban makes anyone an Indian," the article explained.[125] Gooneratne, however, distanced himself from this strategy, explaining that by wearing a turban "you miss [. . .] the whole point of this game, which is to make the American know you and leave him as your friend for life."[126] If the turban served as a marker of ethnic and racial identification, then it could thwart the Indian student's interpellation into the black–white racial logic of the United States.

Other Indian students, however, insisted that they faced little racial prejudice. Sudhindra Bose was quick to add that students were not afflicted by the same forms of "race prejudice" as were African Americans in either the North or the South. Bose described his various experiences in American universities—in Park College, Missouri, Illinois, and Iowa—where he received "sympathetic appreciation" from fellow students and professors. He contrasted his experience in the United States with that of Indian students in England, where, "the vicious color line has been so tightly drawn that even in the Inns of Court [. . .] Indian and native English students seldom eat together."[127]

Rai, too, had considered these issues as they pertained to the Indian student in America. In an address to the faculty of the University of California in February 1916, Rai had acknowledged that "even in democratic America

[Indian students] have to face a certain amount of race and colour prejudice."[128] Yet, drawing on a familiar transformational narrative, he added that
while some students "succumb and wreck themselves," others thrive and
"learn a lesson which is the most precious for them personally and for the
country of their birth."[129] These lessons included a new discovery of self-
reliance, an interaction with "all the representatives of the races of mankind,"
and a chance to build character without charity or patronage.[130] These shared
hardships, experienced abroad due to "race and colour prejudice," would
transform the Indian student into an idealized national subject. As Rai explained in a message published in the *Hindusthanee Student*, the experience
of being abroad in the United States was forcing students to begin "thinking
nationally," ridding themselves of the "provincialism and sectarianism" that
was so detrimental to the nationalist cause, and solely identifying with the
Indian nation.[131] In the figure of the Indian student abroad, Rai found a symbol of an idealized national subject, one whose provincial identifications—be
that caste, region, religion, or language—would melt away to reveal the sin-
gular identity of the Indian. The transformational narrative, thus, was as
much about the actual experience of students as it was a metaphor for the
anticolonial nation, whose hardships in the face of racism—a feature faced
not only by the Indian subject abroad but at "home" where Indians lived as
second-class citizens—would lead to a newfound self-reliance. All roads, as it
were, lead to the independent Indian nation.

Yet, as much as Rai drew on the analogical and metaphorical in his writing, rendering historical figures into national allegories, turning "impressions
and studies" of the United States into metaphors for Indian independence,
there still existed contradictions between Rai's democratic ideals and his
interpretations of America. This was most explicit in his treatment of the
American occupation of the Philippines.

"Making India Like Philippines"

Rai made the Philippines an object of study during his second visit to the
United States, but, perhaps surprisingly, he used the American colony as a
model to describe how the British ought to rule India. While Rai counted
several members of the American Anti-Imperialist League as acquaintances,
his account of the Philippines was, as historian Paul Kramer explains, largely "based on interviews with Frank McIntyre of the Bureau of Insular Affairs."[132] Kramer points out, for instance, how Rai "affirmatively quoted a
letter from McIntyre to the colonial secretary in England [. . .] that stated
Filipinos had been given more power in his government than is exercised by
oriental people."[133] In February 1916, Rai pitched an article to his acquaintance Walter Lippmann, provisionally titled "Political Conditions in Philippines and India: A Contrast." Though Lippmann found no space for the

article in his magazine *The New Republic,* eventually a version of the essay turned up in the *Boston Evening Transcript* and the *Los Angeles Times* under the more commanding title, "Making India Like Philippines." Throughout the essay, Rai pointed out the differences between British rule in India and American rule in the Philippines, praising the latter for its effectiveness in preparing its subjects for democracy.

For a leader who had spent much of his life deconstructing imperialist arguments about democratic "fitness," Rai strangely recognized little subterfuge—at least publicly—in President William McKinley's proclamation that "the preparation of the Filipino peoples for popular self-government in their own interest and not in the interest of the United States."[134] On the contrary, he pointed out that the British government's sole objective was the "continuance and the perpetuation of British rule by British agency."[135] Rai further underscored the difference between the two imperial powers by writing that "after twenty years of American rule the administration of the islands is more democratic than that of British India today after over a century and half of British rule in Bengal."[136]

In his chapter titled "The Philippine Islands" from *USAHIS,* Rai argued more or less the same thing, only adding detailed notes about the improvements to the Philippines that came after the transition from Spanish to American rule. Nowhere did Rai provide room for arguments for independence made by Filipino nationalists or mention the Philippine Revolution (1896–1898). The effect was to render the United States into a paradoxical object: a benevolent, anti-imperialist empire, a temporary but necessary aberration to American liberalism that would pave the path for an independent Philippines. He characterized American political opinion on the Philippines, between both Republicans and Democrats, as unanimously opposed to permanent annexation of the colonies. "The only difference that existed among the political parties of the United States was to the fixing of the time when the United States should withdraw from the islands," Rai wrote, explaining that the Democrats favored an early withdrawal while the Republicans opposed such a timeline.[137] Absent from the discussion was, in fact, the very complicated racial logic that fueled both Republican and Democratic opposition toward empire. Some members of the Anti-Imperialist League, such as Erving Winslow, Moorfield Storey, and Oswald Garrison Villard, had criticized American rule over the Philippines as essentially a racist project that continued the legacy of slavery. Villard went so far as describing Philippines president Emilio Aguinaldo as fighting in the "same cause as John Brown."[138] But most anti-imperialist arguments that came from Republican and Democratic parties were tepid, stemming from a pragmatic if not exclusively racist point of view.

While in form the anti-imperialist goals of both Southern Democrats and Northern Republicans seemed broadly liberal, both positions were built on ideas of racial Darwinism. As Christopher Lasch has explained, Southern Democrats unanimously opposed the cause of imperialism "on the grounds that Asiatics, like Negroes, were innately inferior and could not be assimilated to American life."[139] The Northern Republicans, on the other hand, argued that if the Filipinos became citizens, they would migrate to the United States and compete with American labor. In agreement was labor leader Samuel Gompers, a key member of the Anti-Asiatic League who was also a member of the Anti-Imperialist League. In terms compatible to his stance against Asian migrant labor, Gompers asked, "If the Philippines are annexed what is to prevent the Chinese, the Negritos, and the Malays coming to our own country?"[140] The resistance to American imperialism in the Philippines from both Republican and Democrat parties was not grounded in "broad humanitarian principles," as Rai had argued, but in the unwillingness to incorporate more non-Whites into the Union.[141]

Recent scholars have been perplexed by what seems to be Rai's equivocal position on the American occupation of the Philippines. Historian Erez Manela attributes Rai's wariness to British censorship, arguing that he "avoided explicit comparison to British rule in India, but his discussion of the details of United States rule in the Philippines left little doubt as to what he had in mind."[142] Manela implies that Rai restrained himself from offering a more critical view of the United States colonial project in the Philippines, but I am not so sure. It is certainly true that the United States, working in cooperation with British intelligence, had kept Indian nationalists under surveillance, which Rai was keenly aware of. In intelligence reports, Rai was described as a dangerous radical in spite of his moderate stances, and agents were particularly concerned about the way that he, and other Indian activists, were using the press as a means of conveying information about British rule in India. One memo warned that the "radical press is bestowing increasing attention to Indian affairs in general," identifying socialist papers such as the *New York Call, Nation,* the *New Majority,* the *World Tomorrow,* the *Dial,* the *Survey, Gale's Magazine,* and "the revolutionary Negro paper" the *Messenger* as spaces that publicized opinions from "such Indian agitators" like Rai and others.[143]

In order to counter the propaganda work of Rai, British intelligence worked within Indian diasporic circles and paid counter-propagandists, who published direct rebuttals to Indian nationalist arguments for independence in newspapers. A case in point was Rustom Rustomjee, the former editor of the *Oriental Review* in Bombay, who immigrated to the United States in 1912. Living in a hotel room in Boston, Rustomjee and his wife were first introduced to Rai in January 1915, when he happened to be staying in the same hotel during a visit to New England. Rai later came to learn that Rustomjee had been discreetly put on the British payroll for propaganda work, when he published one colonial apologia after another in U.S. newspapers.[144] A week after a June 1916 *New York Times* editorial, in which Rai argued that the majority of governing posts in India were taken up by British citizens, Rustomjee immediately fired back. "I fear that Lajpat Rai has only told half of the truth, which is almost worse than to utter falsehood, about the administration of India," Rustomjee wrote, adding his wide-eyed approval of British rule: "I venture to say that [the British administration's] motives are unimpeachable and their intentions bona fide. They mean well to India. And without them there would be anarchy and bloodshed."[145] *Gadar* editor Ram Chandra faced a similar response when his editorial warning of an impending revolt in India was countered by Rustomjee's enthusiastic assertion that "the evidence of India's loyalty to the British throne is so overwhelming and [. . .] so enthusiastic, spontaneous, and unanimous that it seems almost a work of supererogation to contend and confute the assertions of Mr. Ram Chandra."[146] Like clockwork, letters of opposition appeared in the American newspapers the moment the British were criticized for their rule in India.[147]

There may have been ample reason to believe that Rai, who had already been charged with sedition without seeing trial, was cautious of any direct criticism of the United States while residing there. Between 1917 and 1918, Rai had been questioned a half dozen times by the police, military intelligence, and agents of the Justice Department,[148] and among the files that British intelligence had created for expatriate nationalists, Rai's was the largest.[149] Rai was clearly cautious about what his American liberal readership would tolerate and what they would not. His opposition to the West Coast-based radical Gadar Party, for instance, which had drawn financial support from Germany in order to foment an insurrection against the British, was partly a matter of political ideology but also a question about audience. Rai had once told his acquaintance Henrietta Rodman that "no matter whether what [the Gadar Party] are doing is legal or not legal, public opinion in this country at this time will not tolerate it, and they are utterly unreasonable to attempt anything of the sort."[150]

Dohra Ahmad attributes the lack of solidarity toward the Philippines as a practical decision, an effort to avoid alienating American readers. Two articles from the IHRLA's *Young India*, which were published anonymously in 1920, for instance, cited the United States' governance of the Philippines with uncritical approval.[151] But even in a December 1916 pamphlet published on the distant shores of Japan, at least partially out of the purview of American readers, Rai still wrote of U.S. and French empire in a positive light compared to the British dominion of India. "Indians travelling abroad have seen American rule in the Philippines and the Hawaii islands and the French rule in Indo-China," Rai observed, "and the superiority which in their eyes British rule in this respect possessed, as compared with other foreign administrations in the world, has at least dwindled if not disappeared."[152] His distinction between Britain's bad imperialism and the United States' good imperialism, then, does not appear to be simply an aberration or an act of self-censorship.

A case could be made that Rai's approval of American colonial govern-ance was in step with arguments he made for Indian home rule within the British Empire. As opposed to the Gadar Party, which endorsed complete independence from British rule and the birth of an independent republic of India, Rai took a more evolutionary approach to the issue of Indian indepen-dence. In a May 1916 letter to the editor of the New York Times, Rai argued that the "Indian nationalist wants the Government of India to be free and unfet-tered, which would be best served if the colony was in a position similar to one occupied by Canada or South Africa."[153] If Rai could support the home rule solution for India—that is, a representative Indian democracy still under the dominion of the British empire—then arguably a more democratic Philip-pines still under American rule would not have been such a contradictory idea. Acknowledging the disastrous economic and political consequences of British rule, Rai wrote that the unexpected outcome of imperialism was that India is "awakening to its possibilities and a remarkable renaissance."[154] Per-haps Rai saw another version of this dialectic between colonization and na-tionalism as a potential outgrowth of American rule in the Philippines.

More likely, however, Rai's wholesale support for American rule in the Philippines translated to a belief in the benevolent role of American colo-nial institutions at the time. Throughout the chapter in USAHIS, Rai discussed the effectiveness that the United States displayed in regulating and disciplin-ing its colonial subjects. The chapter is filled with photographs from the Bureau of Education, Manila, displaying Filipinos in highly organized ar-rangements, with captions that read "Kitchen and Cooking Class," "Sewing Class at Work," "Interior of Machine Shop," "Manila School Garden." In Visualizing American Empire (2010), David Brody argues that such photo-graphs were a convenient medium to justify empire, as images in the press circulated in American homes, disseminating a healthy, non-coercive pic-ture of empire to an American public.[155] Moreover, the photographs' empha-sis on heteropatriarchal order—displaying, for instance, feminized domestic labor and masculine industrialized labor—also fit conveniently into an im-perialist script. Rai's recirculation of images of American empire served as evidence of the progress made under imperial rule: this, USAHIS seemed to say, was colonialism done well.

What distinguished the Philippines from India for Rai was racial differ-ence, based on the racism and chauvinism that shaped his understanding of the "Hindu." "Every student of history knows what a gifted race the Hindus are," Rai wrote, describing the advances of Indian civilization while Europe was still "immersed in primitive methods of life."[156] In comparison to the state of India during British occupation, "the Filipinos had not a vestige of democratic institutions and ignorance and illiteracy reigned supreme" be-fore American occupation. He concluded with a disclaimer that no insult was intended, but added that "neither in character nor in culture nor yet in intelligence and personal valor can there be any comparison between the Hindus and the Filipinos."[157]

Therein lay the limits of Rai's racial politics and the limits of his refractive anti-imperialist vision in 1916. In *USAHIS*, Rai articulated an anti-imperialism that was still largely shaped by his belief in an existing racial hierarchy. During the period of Rai's exile in the United States, he held tightly to a racialized logic for Indian independence. Such logic was present in his 1905 statement about Pratap Singh and Shivaji, patriots from the "land of Aryans," and it was present when he finished *USAHIS*, maintaining that Indians were from the same "stock as Europeans."[158] In other words, claims to Indian self-governance were based on proving that colonial difference was a fallacy, whereas in the context of the Philippines the colonial difference was an unbridgeable gap created by racial difference.

Nevertheless, the very act of investigating social divisions in the United States opened up a series of comparison that nudged Rai—and others, such as Sudhindra Bose and Saint Nihal Singh—to consider the ways in which the hierarchies forged by racial difference organized life not only in the United States but in India, more generally. Through his investigations of the social conditions of African American life, Rai had at least partially begun to grasp that race was, above all else, a social form that stratified communities into positions of power and disempowerment. It was a form analogous to caste in India, even if, as he maintained, it was not a perfect comparison. Race could also explain the subordination of the colonized by the colonizer, the Indian by the British. Through this analogical mode of thinking, Rai understood race as a social form that could explain the operation of power, even if, when it came to his own sense of racial identification, his positions were ambivalent. It would take another decade after his return to India before Rai would write so intently about the United States again. In *Unhappy India*, a monograph that he penned in 1928, just a year before his death, Rai reconceptualized his understandings of the global relations of postwar America. The symbol of anti-British revolution that Washington had emblematized had been tarnished, as Rai lumped the country into a larger formation that included Europe: "When we say Europe, we mean the white races of the world—Europe and America, for America is only a child of Europe." The occasion for this reformulation of race would come with the publication of Katherine Mayo's *Mother India* in 1927, which we turn to in Chapter 5.

"A Wandering Beggar"

Rai left the United States in November 1919 and until his last days in the United States he continued to advocate publicly for the cause of home rule in India. One of his farewell dinners was sponsored by the League of Oppressed Peoples and held at New York's Hotel des Artistes, where a host of figures who had intersected with Rai—including Dudley Field Malone, Oswald Garrison Villard, Soumay Tcheng, Frederick William Pethick-Lawrence, B.S. Kamat, Arthur Upham Pope, and Norman Thomas—each took turns to speak about him, expressing their sorrow that he was leaving the United States but optimistic about what his return to India might herald for the independence struggle.[159] Rai also spoke, recounting his past five years in the United States, the work he and his colleagues had achieved, and the path that still lay ahead. In private correspondence, however, he expressed his dismay over the ineffectiveness of his strategies, asking whether anyone was listening. In a letter to his friend Frieda Hauswirth, a Stanford graduate and Gadar Party associate, who had contributed two chapters to *USAHIS*, Rai confessed:[160]

> At this time I almost despise myself and wish I had been dead before I left India. I am more than ever convinced that no one will ever help India in her struggle however fine may be the language in which people might profess to sympathise with our cause. And why should they? [. . .] I feel that I am a wandering beggar, who at times bores people, at times excites their pity but hardly ever arouses their active and earnest sympathy. Yet this is probably going to be my future career.[161]

There is something at once disarming and uncharacteristic about Rai's private confession. Toggling between different expressions of self-pity ("I almost despise myself") and resigned commitment ("this is probably going to be my future career"), the letter also reveals the primary reason why Rai believed he could not leave any impact on his American audience. His propaganda work and speeches at best "excited pity" but ultimately, could not arouse "earnest sympathy." The distinction between pity and sympathy is slight but revealing. Pity suggests a process of externalization: One witnesses suffering, but also views that suffering as disconnected from oneself. Sympathy suggests identification with that suffering, a connection to pain. Rai felt pity toward the "Indians (Red)" in 1905, but very well may have lacked sympathy, never fully identifying with the subjects of America's settler colonial history. Ironically, it was sympathy that Rai felt he could never quite arouse in his American audiences and allies. The speeches and the writing that attempted to convince Americans that the Indian anticolonial cause was a part of the legacy of 1776 was never convincing, and Rai, it appeared, knew it.

Nevertheless, at least one of Rai's American acquaintances was drawn to this form of appeal. While Rai was in New York, he had gotten to know a young white woman from Missouri who had found her way to the liberal and radical political activists in Manhattan in the 1910s. During a speech Rai delivered at the Civic Club, Agnes Smedley was in attendance, and would later describe Rai's address as a turning point in her interest in the movement for Indian decolonization. For Smedley, however, the key to her engagement with the movement was that it was not a matter of pity, but rather sympathy, in which she had envisioned the movement as a part of her own struggle for liberation. This was a matter of reframing the Indian struggle as part and parcel of an American struggle, one she felt as the daughter of a poor white laborer in Colorado and Missouri. As she would describe years later in her autobiographical novel, to feel sympathy was a matter of fully adopting the vision of the Indian expatriate, to see the world "through the eyes of men from Asia."[162]

In the next chapter, we look more closely at the story of Agnes Smedley, to investigate what this vision meant. If Rai's project in *USAHIS* and in his other writings in the United States was to see how the conditions in the United States could teach a few lessons to Indians, then in Smedley's oeuvre, we witness how the Indian struggle could inform the larger socialist struggle taking place in the United States during and after the Great War.

2

The Indian Plot

Agnes Smedley and American Anticolonialism

The War was always before our eyes in that house, and I
came to see it through the eyes of men from Asia—eyes that
watched and were cynical about the phrases of democracy.
Sad eyes, eyes filled with despair at times.
—AGNES SMEDLEY, *Daughter of Earth* (1929)

In British eyes, these Hindus are guilty of treason (just as
were Benjamin Franklin, Jefferson and Adams), and death
will be their reward for love of their country.
—FRIENDS OF FREEDOM FOR INDIA (July 21, 1919)

American Girl, India Plotter

On Easter 1918, Agnes Smedley was locked in The Tombs. Arrested for
her involvement in an alleged conspiracy hatched against the British,
Smedley had been detained in Manhattan City Prison since the middle
of March. For the past few years, she had turned her attention away from the
socialist circles she'd traveled in, focusing almost exclusively on the expatriate and migrant Indian communities in the United States that were agitating
for independence from abroad. Most recently, she had worked alongside
Bengali radicals to draw support for the nationalist movement. As secretary
to Pulin Behari Bose—"the special representative of the Indian Nationalist
Party in the United States"—Smedley issued letters of appeal to ambassadors
of Europe, Asia, and South America in Washington, DC.[1] Even Woodrow
Wilson and Leon Trotsky, strange political bedfellows to say the least, received messages with an appeal "that Indian people should not continue to
exist as a slave of alien autocratic masters."[2]

As it turned out, the Indian Nationalist Party's headquarters, listed on the
letterhead as the imposing "Tagore castle" in Calcutta, was actually Smedley's
small apartment in Greenwich Village. There was no one named Pulin Behari
Bose, either.[3] American and British agents, who had been intercepting and
reading letters exchanged between Smedley and her Indian comrades, were
onto the ruse. On March 19, 1918, Smedley and her co-conspirators were ar-

rested for violating the Espionage Act, with charges of "unlawfully, willfully, and knowingly [. . .] pretend[ing] to be officials of a foreign government" and "defraud[ing] the President of the United States."[4] Such a draconian measure for what essentially entailed mailing out letters indicates the degree of hysteria that surrounded the activities of Indian revolutionaries and other forms of political radicalism in the United States during this period. The *New York Times* added its own sensationalist spin to the story the next day in a headline that described Smedley as an "American Girl" turned "India Plotter."[5]

How and why Agnes Smedley—the daughter of a white working-class family from middle America, who described her childhood as reared in "intellectual poverty"—had come to identify with the fight against the British rule of India serves as the historical entry point of this chapter. Everyone among the expatriate Indian community in the United States seemed to know Smedley. When Lajpat Rai was an exile in New York in the late 1910s, he brought Smedley under his wing, enlisting her as secretary for his India Home Rule League organization and preparing her to teach in India. The Communist Amir Haider Khan met Smedley during his travels through New York, describing how her unceasing work on behalf of Indian anticolonialism inspired and "intensified [his] vaguely awakened patriotic feelings."[6] Radical activists such as Taraknath Das and Sailendranath Ghose were close associates, relying on her as she galvanized support for them during their imprisonment. The stack of paperwork on Smedley generated by U.S. and British intelligence was its own testament to how important a figure she had become to Indian revolutionaries abroad.

This chapter opens by tracing Smedley's engagement with the multifarious Indian anticolonial movement in the United States, beginning with her initial encounters with the Gadar Party as a reporter in California and her work with Lajpat Rai's IHRLA in New York, leading up to her arrest in 1918. After her release from prison, Smedley continued to work on behalf of Indian political prisoners in the United States with the Friends of Freedom for India, an advocacy organization she helped form in New York.[7] In examining why India mattered so much to Smedley, this chapter considers the strategies by which she attempted to make India matter to Americans. In her wide-ranging political work—which involved penning articles for the American and Indian press, composing appeal letters, circulating pamphlets, organizing lectures, and generally serving as a "communication center," as she described herself— Smedley presented the case for Indian freedom within terms that were legible to American liberals and radicals alike.[8] This was, in part, a rhetorical practice that entailed reframing and refracting the cause of Indian freedom through the language of American liberalism, evoking the discourse of U.S. history, national character, and sovereignty. To be concerned with Indian freedom was, the logic went, to be concerned with maintaining the very character of the U.S. nation—a line of thinking that led to strategic and at times uncanny forms of ahistoricism.

In the second half of the chapter, we turn to Smedley's autobiographical novel *Daughter of Earth*, published in 1929. In contrast to her journalistic and propaganda work, which attempted to "domesticate" the Indian cause, the novel inverted that relationship, decentering the United States and casting the domestic autobiography—"born of American soil," as one reviewer put it—onto the terrain of global empire.[9] In that way, *Daughter of Earth* was more than the thinly veiled autobiography that it has been often read as. On one hand it was a work of fiction about fiction, examining the relationship between revolutionary subjectivity and literature, and on the other it was an attempt to show how the intersecting experiences of subjugation for working-class whites through capitalism, and white women through patriarchy, was connected to the relations of colonialism. The result was an ambitious, if also strange, proletarian novel, which sought a politics that merged anticapitalist critique with anticolonial imperative. If, as some critics have maintained, Smedley's novel was a foundational text for women's proletarian fiction, then this chapter asks, how do we reckon with the centrality of Indian decolonization to the book's politics?[10] In other words, what does it tell us about American proletarian culture that one of its earliest examples was so invested in the cause of India's decolonization?

As this chapter examines these two facets of Smedley's engagement with the Indian freedom struggle, it builds upon the concept of transnational refraction we have discussed. Chapter 1 introduced the way that refractions enabled Indian expatriates to develop comparisons between systems of social hierarchy in the United States and colonial India; this chapter points to the complex forms of identification that were enabled by these transnational encounters. However uneven and at times unstable, such forms of identification allowed Smedley to tenuously grasp the connections between anticolonial revolution and world revolution, and to dramatically reconsider the relationship possible between the United States and India in the twentieth century. In doing so, she urged her readers on the American Left to envisage what each place could symbolically and politically mean to one another in the postwar period.

Anticolonial Beginnings

Agnes Smedley described her childhood as a life lived on the wrong side of the Gilded Age. Born in 1892, Smedley grew up under the roof of an abusive mother and a wandering father who eked out a living as a cattle farmer, a miner, and eventually a laborer for Rockefeller's Colorado Fuel & Iron. All she knew of "culture," she would later recall, was Scottish and English folk songs, and ballads about Jesse James. Shifting frequently between homes in Missouri and Colorado and faced with the uncertainty of steady income, Smedley was put to work at a young age. Those experiences had a profound effect on her politicization and worldview, as she would later recount: "The poverty and ignorance of my youth were the tribute which I, like millions of others, paid to 'private interests.'"[11]

Her entry into a life of political activism stemmed not only from her acute experiences with class disparity but as a woman navigating a number of alienating social institutions, including family life, school, and marriage at an early age. In 1912, she married a young socialist named Ernest Brundin. Though their relationship quickly ended in divorce, she credited it for both introducing her to American socialist circles and for providing her with fodder for her long-standing critique of the institution of marriage, which, at best, she called an "economic investment," and at "its worst, a relic of human slavery."[12] Soon after, Smedley turned to journalism as a student at the Territorial Normal School at Tempe (later, Arizona State University), contributing short essays on a range of topics, including at least one sympathetic sketch of San Francisco's Chinatown, which according to biographers Janice and Stephen MacKinnon, "tried to counter the racial prejudices against the Chinese."[13] After a move to California, Smedley joined the Socialist Party of America, living by day as a journalist for the *Fresno Morning Republican.*

It was as a reporter that Smedley first encountered the vibrant scene of Indian activism taking root along the Pacific Coast. In September 1916, Smedley had been assigned to cover a mass meeting of Indians in Fresno.[14] By the middle of the decade, California had seen an influx of Indian agricultural laborers, mostly Sikhs from Punjab, who concentrated in areas around the San Joaquin, Sacramento, and Imperial Valleys.[15] As the influx of Punjabi agricultural labor grew, so too did the anticolonial movement on the West Coast of the United States and Canada, spearheaded by Indian radicals, intellectuals, and laborers who had sought to overthrow British rule in India. In 1913, a group of Indian activists, including Sohan Singh Bhakna, Har Dayal, and Taraknath Das had formed the Pacific Coast Hindustan Association, the organization which eventually became the Gadar Party.[16] The Gadar Party coordinated outreach to farming communities, developing a broad base of support among Sikh agricultural workers and radicalized laborers, who had faced hardships as an exploited and discriminated population in North America.[17] Smedley, whose familiarity with radical politics to that point had been mainly framed by domestic concerns, made the trip to Fresno, documenting her observations in a story titled "All India Revolts against Rule of Briton."

Smedley reported that five hundred Hindus from the farming town and surrounding areas had pledged their "financial support to the anti-British revolutionary movement."[18] Speaking at the event was Ram Chandra, the fiery editor of *Gadar*, who told the gathered crowd that the money collected would be forwarded to "revolutionists" and be used to arm rebels to revolt against "Britain's murderous career of aggression and exploitation."[19] Chandra also attacked the British censorship of news in the United States, which kept neutral nations "in ignorance of the true state of affairs in India."[20] Smedley was alarmed by the sheer number of police present, describing a detail of officers who forcibly searched the attendees at the rally. In hindsight, it seems significant that her introduction to the Indian cause came from a scene that tied together anticolonial aims with a working-class community. The attendees of the rally were not the nationalist students that came from elite classes in their native India, but agricultural laborers in the Sacramento Valley who, despite the hardships they faced as "undesirable" immigrants, had nevertheless pledged their meager earnings to the cause.

If the political rally in California piqued her interest in India, then Smedley's move to New York City in 1917 transformed her from a passive observer to a committed traveler. In Greenwich Village, she befriended fellow supporters of India, including Henrietta Rodman, a schoolteacher and bohemian feminist who had thrown her weight behind a number of causes, including dress reform, women's suffrage, and Indian decolonization.[21] Rodman was a charter member of the New York Civic Club in Manhattan, an interracial group formed in 1916 that included liberals, radicals, and bohemians with the express purpose of facilitating the "opportunity for social intercourse for people actively interested in civic affairs."[22] Among the list of prominent members were W.E.B. Du Bois, James Weldon Johnson, Walter Lippmann, and publisher Benjamin W. Huebsch.[23]

Smedley first saw Lajpat Rai speak at the Civic Club,[24] and soon thereafter became the secretary for the club's "India Group," which was devoted to the study of the colony.[25] She would later recall how at this time Rai began to tutor her in Indian history, and in her fictionalized account in *Daughter of Earth* described this period of study as a kind of political and quasi-intimate courtship: "The hours passed and we studied. Heavy things at times, made beautiful by the man who loved them."[26] Smedley continued to work for Rai, first by doing secretarial work for the IHRLA and its monthly publication *Young India*. According to Naeem Rathore, Smedley also helped arrange classes for Indian workers in New York during this time, tutoring them in English as well as teaching them about American institutions in an effort to assist them acclimate and eventually gain citizenship in the United States.[27]

Although there were significant overlaps in interest between the "India Group" and Rai's IHRLA, not all of the former subscribed to the political goals of home rule. Herambalal Gupta, a young activist involved with the more radical strain of Indian expatriates, had gotten into a heated exchange with Rai at the Civic Club, precisely on this matter.[28] Like the Bay Area, New York in the 1910s had become an important center for Indian nationalist activity, including a diverse set of actors with vastly different approaches to the colonial question. The city played host to a number of expatriate organizations, including the short-lived United India League, the Hindustan Association of America, and the Hindu Workers Union of America.[29] It also housed social gathering spaces, such as boarding homes and restaurants across the city, which, as Vivek Bald has shown, played an important role in fostering new networks among expatriates, activists, and laborers from different walks of life.[30] One such restaurant—regularly advertised in *Young India* and closely surveilled by U.S. and British authorities—was the Taj Mahal Hindu Restaurant in Manhattan, where Rai, Smedley, and Rodman were all recorded to have met.[31] Several Indian activists were based in or passed through New York, Bald writes, including pro-independence writers such as Syud Hossain, J. J. Singh, and Kumar Goshal, Bengali radicals such as Gupta, Chandra Chakravarty, and Taraknath Das, and future Dalit leader B. R. Ambedkar, who studied uptown at Columbia.[32] While many of these figures were divided along ideological lines, they were all part of an interconnected network of activists. It was through this web of actors that Smedley met many of the radicals with whom she would later become closely associated, as she began to reject the more conservative anticolonial politics of Lajpat Rai.

Sailendranath Ghose was one such radical. An upper-caste Bengali, Ghose lived something of a double-life, like many other student-revolutionaries in India at the time. He was both a promising student of science, who had been awarded scholarships for his work in chemistry and physics, as well as a young radical in the making, influenced by the revolutionary ferment and government repression in Calcutta. Years later, Ghose would explain that his political radicalism also shaped his investments in science, that he studied chemistry to learn "the business of making bombs" and physics to build a "device by which bombs could be exploded."[33] Over the course of his studies at the University of Calcutta, Ghose was mentored by Jatin Mukherjee (cousin of Indian American writer Dhan Gopal Mukerji), who had cautioned him that the English would only ever respond to violence, and soon entrusted the young student to store arms and ammunition.[34] Ghose received a scholarship to study physics at Harvard, but as he was preparing to leave the country, a police official stripped him of his passport and told him that he was not permitted to leave India. Not long after, he received a notice to report to the police commissioner and "be ready for deportation to [the penal colony in] Andaman islands."[35] Apparently unaware of the reasons behind the warrant for his arrest, Ghose fled the country disguised as a Muslim maritime worker, arriving in Philadelphia in January 1917 on "a mission to provide an easier means of communication" between radicals in India and the United States.[36] Ghose claimed to have discovered the reasons for his fugitive status only years later, when he learned that his name was listed in the Hindu–German conspiracy trial, a failed plot that entailed Gadar Party operatives smuggling arms from the United States by way of Java, eventually to be hidden in Balasore, the Sundarbans, and Karachi.[37] This effectively meant that when he arrived in Philadelphia in 1917, Ghose was already wanted for arrest in the United States for his involvement in the conspiracy.[38] Along with M. N. Roy—who would later found the Mexican Socialist Workers' Party (*Partido Socialista Obrero*)—Ghose fled to Mexico as a fugitive, but not before going to New York, where he established contact with Agnes Smedley.

In spite of her early attachments to Lajpat Rai, Smedley found herself drawn to the more radical politics of "his younger countrymen," including Ghose, Taraknath Das, and others in New York.[39] Her association and collaboration with them on two particular plots also led to her arrest in the spring of 1918. In an effort to gain more visibility, Smedley and Ghose, along with Das and Gadar Party leader Bhai Bhagwan Singh, conspired to create something called the Indian Nationalist Party (INP) in hopes of gaining recognition among diplomatic leaders.[40] As historian Maia Ramnath explains, the INP—in spite of listing Rash Behari Bose as provisional president and Jadu Gopal Mukherjee as chairman of the Foreign Relations Committee— was little more than "an impressive letterhead."[41] In fact, it was the stationery that eventually foiled their plans. American agents had established that the petition, which was supposed to have been written from India, was marked with a wax seal that was sold to Ghose and Das at a San Francisco stationery shop.[42] The fact that these letters were sent to diplomats may have constituted a case of fraud, but the larger danger, according to the Intelligence Office was they were sent to Trotsky, thus signaling a new radical alliance.[43] Rounding out the charges, Smedley was also accused of overseeing the publication of *The Isolation of Japan in World Politics*, a book deemed "seditious" for discouraging U.S. military recruitment, and credited to an "Asiatic Statesman" who turned out to be Taraknath Das.[44] During her interrogation, Smedley remained steadfast in refusing to answer questions—"particularly those dealing with Indian affairs," an officer reported—but all for naught, since police had found multiple copies of Das's book and the INP letters in her apartment.[45] For both violations, Ghose and Smedley were arrested in New York City that March and indicted under the Espionage Act.[46] After a protracted legal battle, which entailed being released on bail one month and being re-indicted the next, Smedley was finally released in December 1918.[47]

The arrest and indictments show just how much Smedley had drifted away from her mentor Lajpat Rai. By 1919, she counted several Indian radicals as comrades, each of whom was tied up with plots in Germany, Russia, and Mexico, and almost all of whom criticized Lajpat Rai's home rule nationalism in favor of total freedom "by revolution."[48] In 1919, while imprisoned at Fort Leavenworth for his involvement in the Hindu–German conspiracy, for instance, Taraknath Das wrote to Smedley, providing details about his latest readings, including the most recent edition of *Young India* issued by the IHRLA. While he remained hopeful that Rai was "thinking on progressive lines," he nevertheless considered Rai "inconsistent" and admonished him for his reluctance to speak out. "The work of stopping of exploitation of the Indian people by [the] master-class," Das wrote in one letter, "will not be carried out by his preaching Home Rule."[49]

British intelligence agents, who were eavesdropping on their intercepted letters, also noticed Smedley's break from Rai and her newfound interest in the tenets and tactics of the Gadar Party. In one memo, an agent named J. P. commented: "You will see that [Ghose and Smedley] are very down on Lajpat Rai and his crowd and their idea is to join forces with the P.C.H.A. [Pacific Coast Hindustan Association]."[50] In another memo, he noted that Ghose and Smedley were planning to start "an organization like the I.H.R.L. but which will stand for the complete independence of India."[51]

Rai had long been troubled by his mentee's growing attraction to the Gadar Party, even threatening that he would no longer be affiliated with her if she continued to associate with them. In her testimony to a grand jury, Rodman recalled a conversation at the Taj Mahal Hindu Restaurant, where Rai was forthright in his disapproval. He warned Smedley that "no matter how legitimate their activities might be, [. . .] American public opinion would not stand it at the present time, that the alliance with Great Britain was so strong emotionally that anything tending to reflect against Great Britain would get in trouble."[52] Whether Rai's disagreement was tactical, ideological, or a combination of both, it points to the pervasive Anglo–American bond—a bond that was political, racial, and affective—during the period.

By March, just a few months after her release from prison, Smedley helped launch the Friends of Freedom for India (FFI), an organization run from an office in the Rand School of Social Sciences and created to defend the numerous Indian expatriates who were being arrested and imprisoned on grounds of sedition.[53] Smedley and her colleagues in the FFI seemed keenly aware of America's Anglophilic attachments and one way to read their appeals is to recognize them as rhetorical strategies to destabilize that alliance. They did this in two distinct ways: First, they framed the repression of Indian anticolonialists, including the arrests of key activists, as a matter of American national sovereignty. The British were encroaching on national borders by interfering with the governance of the United States, their argument went. Second, they drew analogies between Indian anticolonialism and U.S. history. This entailed not only using the by-then familiar analogies of the American Revolution that writers such as Lajpat Rai regularly used, but also repurposing essays from the U.S. anti-imperialist movement that had first been written after the 1898 Spanish–American war. Using these two tactics, the group translated the terms of "India's Freedom" into an American nationalist register. What was at stake for their American audience, Smedley and the FFI argued, was not solidarity with a distant cause or a form of political cosmopolitanism, but, in fact, the very idea of the United States as an independent nation-state. In other words, the FFI attempted to domesticize the terms of anticolonial solidarity. At the center of this question were not the dozen or so Indian radicals on trial and marked for deportation, but rather, the tradition of political refuge and the belief in national sovereignty that they argued were core values of the American state.

The timing of the FFI's argument was particularly striking given the rising xenophobic sentiment in the federal government. With the passing of the 1917 Immigration Act, the United States had drastically tightened its national borders, inaugurating a period of increased political oppression and racial gatekeeping. The FFI, however, recoded the threat to American national sovereignty as coming not from Asian bodies but from British agents. In fact, in an elaborately staged mass meeting on March 20, 1921, at the Lexington Theatre—which, according to intelligence agents, featured men outfitted in turbans and one Indian man in full military regalia—the FFI decried threats of a "British Peril" in a clever reworking of the language of anti-Asian xenophobia (Figure 2.1a and 2.1b).[54] Adopting the discourse of the anti-Chinese and anti-Japanese "Yellow Peril" and the South Asian "Dusky Peril," the FFI described the British Peril as a "menace to the safety and security of the American Sovereignty," calling on Americans to "crush the British peril" that was interfering with the "social, political and economic life of the United States."[55] As we will see, the activists in the FFI, including Smedley, adapted the language of anti-Asian xenophobia and redirected it toward the British, slyly recoding Anglo–American cooperation into a threat against national autonomy.

Indian Freedom, American Sovereignty

By the time the Friends of Freedom for India was launched in the spring of 1919, Agnes Smedley had, in the space of a few short years, become a masterful organizer.[56] In early FFI meetings, the group had recruited activists of different stripes, including Sinn Féin nationalists, Bolshevik sympathizers, birth control advocates, and prominent liberals.[57] Even while Smedley privately confessed to a Gadar Party member that she felt "a very strong dislike for [American] liberals," she sensed that they were politically valuable for the FFI cause and continued to work closely with them.[58] By the late 1910s and early 1920s, the organization began to produce propaganda and regularly host dinners and speeches in New York that publicized and raised funds for a number of impending deportation cases of Indian radicals. While formally named the secretary of the organization, Smedley had, for all intents and purposes, become the de facto center of the FFI.[59] When the Communist activist Amir Haider Khan visited New York City in 1920, he described

HAVE WE A DUSKY PERIL

HINDU HORDES INVADING THE STATE

BELLINGHAM workmen are becoming excited over the arrival of East Indians in numbers across the Canadian border, and fear that the dusky Asiatics with their turbans will prove a worse menace to the working classes than the "Yellow Peril" that has so long threatened the Pacific Coast.

FIGURE 2.1 (a) "Have We a Dusky Peril?" *Puget Sound American* (September 16, 1906), 16; facing page (b) "British Peril," Friends of Freedom for India Mass Meeting, March 20, 1921. (South Asian American Digital Archive and National Archives at College Park, Maryland)

Smedley as the organization's "originator, founder, and moving spirit," and was particularly impressed by her flare for orchestrating theatrical protests against the actions of the British government. On one occasion, Smedley led a group of young American women to the British Consulate in New York, instructing them to wear placards inscribed in bold letters with accounts of the Jallianwala Bagh massacre.[60] A large crowd of spectators joined the gath-

INDIA IN ACTIVE REVOLT!

INDIA!   AMERICA!   IRELAND!

BRITISH PERIL

The British Control of the Trade Routes, the Potential Oil Resources, the Cable Systems of the World and her unwarranted interference in the social, political and economic life of the United States has made the British Peril the greatest menace to the safety and security of the American Sovereignty.

A British Peril Mass Meeting

Will be held on

Sunday Afternoon, March 20, 1921, at 1:30

At the

LEXINGTON THEATRE—51st St. and Lexington Ave.

New York City

Speakers

MAJOR EUGENE F. KINKEAD of the General Staff
CAPTAIN JOHN F. McAREE of the 69th Regiment
CAPTAIN THOMAS KISSANE of the Signal Corps, American
    Expeditionary Forces attached to the General Staff
GENERAL S. PEARSON famous commander of the Transvaal
    Army of the Boer War

CRUSH THE BRITISH PERIL

HELP INDIA!   HELP AMERICA!   HELP IRELAND!

JOIN FORCES TO DESTROY THE BRITISH PERIL, THE MENACE TO HUMAN CIVILIZATION.

Auspices of

THE FRIENDS OF FREEDOM FOR INDIA
799 Broadway, New York City

Help India to liberty and independence. The British Empire can alone be destroyed by separating India from it. Only INDEPENDENT INDIA can save America, Ireland, Egypt and the whole world from the BRITISH PERIL. Register your support for an INDEPENDENT INDIA by joining the Friends of Freedom for India, membership of which is only $1.00 per year.

ering, until police were summoned by consulate officials to disperse the crowd. Another time, Khan recalled that at a FFI gathering that November, Smedley had arranged saris to be worn by American women and red turbans for Indian male attendees. Khan explained, "the colours of the turbans and the saris combined to give the meeting an Indo-American appearance, which was exactly what Agnes Smedley wanted to attract the attention of the American public toward the gathering."[61] By the time the organizers had made it to the venue, a crowd of bystanders had joined the event, which was already overflowing with guests. Smedley well understood the theatrics of protest and used them often in her work with the FFI.

By spring of 1919, Smedley and Ghose were putting the dramatic tale of their arrest and detainment in The Tombs to use in the FFI's pamphlets. "India's Freedom in American Courts," a twelve-page booklet published that April, narrated their imprisonment, describing the two charges brought against them—falsely acting as representatives of a foreign government, and publishing a book that was suspected of "containing false statements and reports"—in such a way that they seemed like the outburst of an ever-paranoid government rather than a radical global conspiracy.[62] The booklet's real effectiveness, however, came in connecting Smedley and Ghose's arrest with two other cases against Indian radicals, Taraknath Das and Gopal Singh, whose arrests the previous year illustrated the repressive tactics of a U.S. government that was working at the behest of the British. For their activities in the Hindu–German conspiracy trial, Das, who was naturalized in 1914, had been threatened with being stripped of his U.S. citizenship, while Gopal Singh faced deportation, a sentence that Smedley and Ghose argued would certainly "mean his death."[63]

Through a series of rhetorical maneuvers, the booklet cleverly reformulated the British, and not the Indians, as "foreign" intruders, effectively flipping the story of the arrests on its head. First, the arrests were portrayed as counter to American practices of refuge, which in the past had been extended to "Cuban revolutionists, who prepared [. . .] for armed insurrection against Spain" and the Irish who "publicly challenged" English rule.[64] Secondly, and more critically, the booklet argued that the trials were examples of foreign meddling, explaining how "by deporting the offenders [America plays] into the hands of the British authorities, [and] make ourselves the agents of punishment for a foreign power."[65] British power and influence had not only threatened to insert itself into the U.S. courtroom, but it had effectively made its way into the interrogation room. The FFI described the "hands of British secret police" all over a case in New York, "coerc[ing] American citizens" and sussing out each witness's "loyalty to, the British Empire."[66] At stake, then, were not only traditions of political refuge, but the history of America itself: to deport Indian radicals was to concede the sovereignty of the United States to the nation's historical masters, thereby undoing the legacies of the American Revolution altogether. A similar refrain marked many of the pamphlets issued by the FFI on behalf of Indian prisoners. "For them," the pamphlets read, "deportation means death. For America, it means the surrender of *our sovereignty* to the British Empire."[67]

The arrest and imminent deportation of Das, Singh, and others like them was critically linked to what historian Seema Sohi calls the "mutually constitutive anti-Asian and antiradical discourse of the era," which found its apotheosis in the 1917 Immigration Act.[68] Among its restrictions on "idiots, imbeciles, epileptics, alcoholics" and other undesirables, the 1917 Act also included a provision that prevented the entry of aliens from the "Asiatic Barred Zone," stretching from West Asia to Eastern China and encompassing all of South Asia. A second relevant detail, Sohi explains, was that it "increased the statute of limitations for deportation from three to five years for 'any alien [. . .] advocating or teaching the unlawful destruction of property, or advocating or teaching anarchy or the overthrow by force or violence of the Government of the United States or all forms of law or assassination of public officials.'"[69] As Sohi argues, the 1917 Act effectively illustrated that the federal government used immigrant exclusion and deportation as "the quickest and most effective methods of suppressing political radicalism in the United States."[70] The imminent deportation of Gopal Singh and denaturalization of Das were case in point, the FFI pamphlet explained. Such actions "will mean that we in America [. . .] are submissive tools of a foreign government."[71]

The FFI was well aware of the effects that the 1917 Act would have on Indian laborers. As historian Kritika Agarwal explains, the Act led to mass arrests and deportations of undocumented Indian workers by immigration authorities, including one well-publicized case involving the round-up and deportation of thirty-nine Indian workers at Bethlehem Steel Industry in Pennsylvania.[72] In an essay published in the *Independent Hindustan*, Basanta Kumar Roy of the FFI pointed out that in a similar case, the immigration inspector admitted that since June 1919, nearly "one hundred East Indians have been impressed into the British service by the action of the Immigration Department." Roy concludes, "England seeks to hurt the American trade by creating an animosity between India and America."[73] America was effectively doing "England's Dirty Work."[74]

Such rhetorical reframings by the FFI illustrate how the organization attempted to redirect the question of Indian activism onto a broader field of questions pertaining to liberal American ideals in the twentieth century. This may explain how and why it received support from people otherwise unsympathetic to Indian migrant labor, such as AFL president Samuel Gompers, who at the 1919 Pan-American Federation of Labor Conference told his crowd:

The American Labor movement has always stood for the right of asylum for political offenders. It is true of Mexican refugees, of Irish refugees, and of Polish refugees. Permit me to remind you that only a few days ago the Federation of Labor officially protested against the deportation of Hindus to India, where they would most certainly be shot by the English authorities.[75]

Gompers's statement was a far cry from the position he, along with other labor leaders and organizations, had consistently taken regarding Chinese, Japanese, and Indian migrant workers in the United States. Even in the years that followed, Gompers would continue to pursue exclusionary policies; for instance, the AFL supported the 1924 Immigration Act that restricted immigration to those eligible for citizenship, a category that put an end to nearly all migration from Asia. Yet, when reframed as a question of "American asylum," the AFL provided support, even promising to present these matters to the Secretary of the U.S. Department of Labor. In a private letter to Santokh Singh, Smedley wrote (a little too optimistically, in hindsight) that "we shall from now on depend upon labor for justice."[76]

As she tirelessly organized events, mailed letters, and published pamphlets with the FFI, Smedley continued her day job as a correspondent for the socialist New York Call,[77] regularly reporting on the British Empire, on domestic labor issues, as well as contributing shorter editorial pieces on subjects such as Indian revolutionary poetry and the role of women in India.[78] At times, she would also write about the activities of FFI. In a headline that read "Gompers to Lay Petition before Wilson for Hindus Facing Exile and Death," Smedley related the stance taken by the AFL in supporting the broader cause against political deportation. The New York Call, thus, had become another venue to continue her propaganda work, informing her socialist readership about stories of the ongoing atrocities of colonial rule.

In a report titled "Trinity of Starvation, Disease and Executions Bringing 'Peace' to India," Smedley excoriated British rule in India, calling it "rule by violence and savagery [. . .] a powerful foreign people over another," by which logic, she fancifully suggested, Britain could conquer the United States.[79] In several ways, Smedley attempted to connect the story of Indian freedom to the United States, using the familiar metaphor of Indian anticolonialism to the American Revolution. In a caption for one of the images in the article, which featured a lineup of emaciated Indians, Smedley wrote, "The starving natives are guilty of the same crime that the founders of the United States committed when they took up arms against British tyranny in the American Revolution."[80] At once, Smedley drew on the moral outrage of the readers, using "atrocity photographs" of starving natives, who were described as victims of a "slow murder" by British authorities.[81] The starving bodies most obviously represent the symbolic metonym of the suffering colonial body, but other appeals are at work in this text. The "sovereignty" argument appears once again in the form of Smedley's assertion that "India's fight has extended to America, and American citizens have been bought or prostituted to do Britain's dirty work." Smedley further drew comparisons between the nationalist histories of the U.S. and the struggle by Indian expatriates in the United States. In one appeal letter written on behalf of the FFI, she wrote: "In British eyes, these Hindus are guilty of treason (just as were Benjamin Franklin, Jefferson and Adams), and death will be their reward for the love of their country."[82]

Drawing on analogies between American history and the movement for Indian freedom was a common strategy used by both the IHRLA and by the Gadar Party in its many English-language pamphlets, leaflets, and other print materials. One such Gadar Party broadsheet quoted from Lincoln—"A country cannot live half slave and half free"—before including an excerpt from the Fireside poet James Russell Lowell's "Stanzas on Freedom," originally written as a plea for abolitionist and women's suffrage causes. Deploying American historical analogies and recirculating quotes, poems, and phrases from an American nationalist canon—flawed or superficial as they seem to us now—was a well-worn and effective textual strategy for anticolonialists in the United States. Lowell's "Stanzas of Freedom" was printed, for instance, in the final issue of IHRLA's *Young India* (1920), along with a number of quotations from U.S. nationalists and poets, including Patrick Henry, Walt Whitman, and Ralph Waldo Emerson.[83] As Dohra Ahmad argues, this mode of analogy meant that India would be represented by "America's past," and more broadly, would become a more nebulous, abstract category characterized by a "highly familiar (to American readers) yearning for freedom." The dangers of such analogies, Ahmad suggests, were that they "eras[ed] historical specificity."[84] The fact that the poem appeared in both a Gadar Party publication and an IHRLA publication, for instance, illustrate just how ideologically flexible and abstract such analogies could become. Lowell's conception of "freedom" was capacious enough to accommodate both organizations. How to achieve that freedom, of course, was still up for debate.

Members of the FFI regularly used such analogies in their speeches, reframing the cause of Indian independence into the symbols and narratives of American nationalism. On April 10, 1919, the FFI organized a mass meeting at the Central Opera House in New York City, which drew close to eight hundred people, a good faction of whom were supporters of the Irish cause. The vice president of FFI, Dudley Field Malone, gave a rousing speech, which one intelligence agent confessed was a "magnificent oratorical performance."[85] Malone insisted that the cause for Indian freedom was more than a "nationalistic aspiration," it was "part of a movement of mankind."[86] This vision transcended race, Malone told the audience, "it does not make any difference whether men are black or white, whether they are Chinamen or

Japanese, they are demanding justice and liberty for mankind."[87] Like Smedley, Malone focused on the arrest and eventual deportation of the Indian men, drawing an analogy to colonial America's historical past.

> What would have happened to Benjamin Franklin who spent six years in France, engaged in propaganda for the freedom of the colonies where he charmed men by the brilliance of his intellect and women by his gallantry, if he had been thrown into jail and was sent over to England because the French thought he belonged to the English and put to trial? If it was proper for Franklin to come to France to urge freedom for the colonies it is eminently proper in this republic that every representative of freedom everywhere should urge the people to assist the freedom of his nation.[88]

A month later, on May 17, 1919, the FFI organized another large dinner at the Yorkville Casino on 86th Street in Manhattan. According to an agent in attendance, the crowd was an eclectic mix of progressives and radicals from every walk of life, including "a good many Sinn Feiners, anarchists, Bolsheviks, IWWs [Industrial Workers of the World], radical Socialists, school teachers, ministers, doctors, other professional persons with radical inclinations, and society women who donate funds for propaganda about India as well as about Ireland."[89] Basanta Kumar Roy, who served as the editor for the organization's news service, described a series of mass strikes in India that April, at which point he asked the attendees, "Are you Americans going to stand for this? Have you the feeling of George Washington, Franklin, and Abe Lincoln?"[90]

How do we read such forms of address? Each speaker relied on an ahistorical reading of the American past, centered on a series of nationalist patriarchs who had become so abstracted that they resembled only the vaguest symbols of national freedom. Any critical pressure on these analogies would surely make them fall apart. How much can the putative "freedom" of the settler colonial subject, for instance, be thought of in the same terms as the anticolonial movement for an independent India, let alone the demand for the freedom of political prisoners? Yet these forms of strategic ahistoricism were integral to the rhetorical design of FFI propaganda. Consider a pamphlet titled "America on British Rule in India," which was circulated by the FFI in 1920 (Figure 2.2). The cover indicates that the pamphlet was originally a work of Irish nationalist propaganda published by the Wolfe Tone Co. in New York, but was redistributed by the FFI: an FFI stamp on the cover renders its Irish American origins into a kind of palimpsestic trace.[91] The pamphlet promised writings by an eclectic cast of American figures, including Andrew Carnegie, Mark Twain, Bishop Henry Potter, and Theodore Roosevelt, but by the time the FFI distributed them, they were already

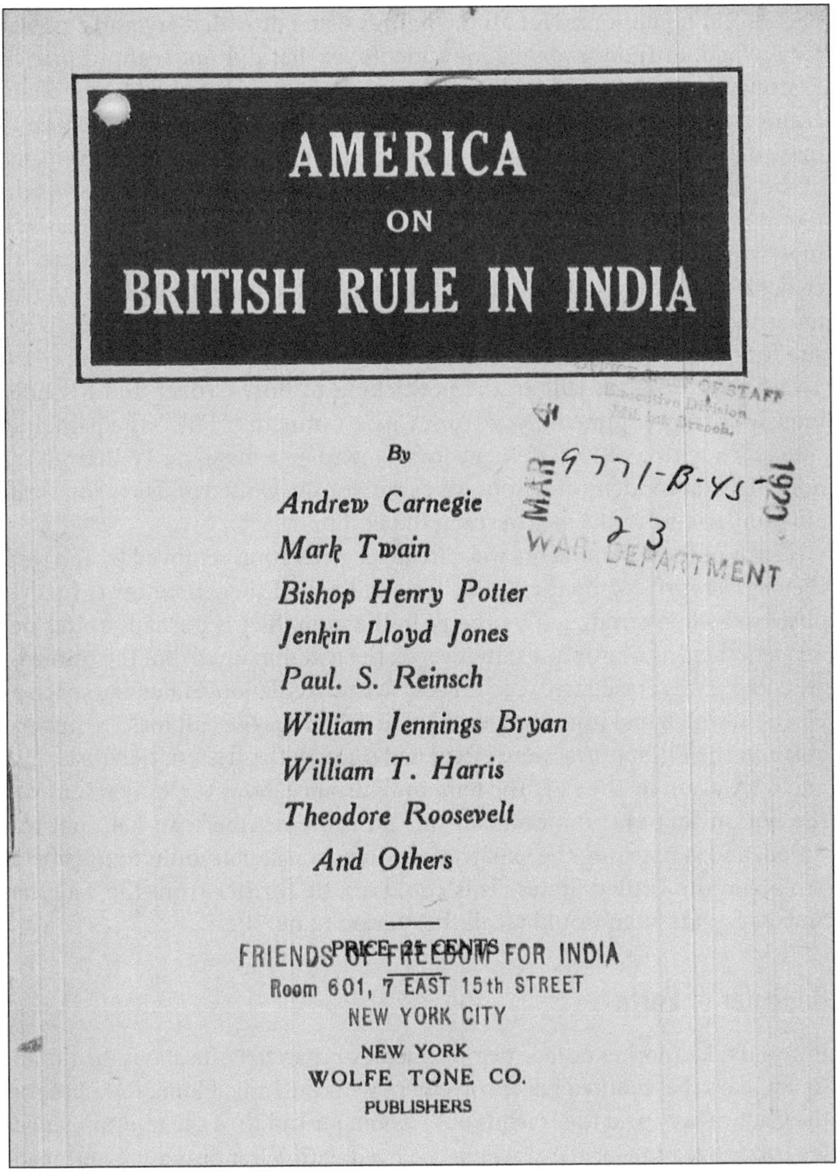

FIGURE 2.2 "America on British Rule in India" (Wolfe Tone Co.). (National Archives at College Park, Maryland)

decade-old quotations. Not all the figures listed provided favorable quotes for the Indian Independence movement, yet that did not seem to matter. Roosevelt's statement, culled from a speech delivered at the Metropolitan Memorial Methodist Episcopal Church, expressed predictable magnanimity toward British rule, describing it as "one of the most admirable achievements of the European race during the last two centuries."[92] The quote appears directly before responses by a number of prominent American progressives, mostly members of the turn-of-the-century Anti-Imperialist League, all critics of U.S. imperialism in the Philippines. One page draws from the famous industrialist Andrew Carnegie, who sympathizes with the Indian desire for national independence, while a particularly pithy quote from Mark Twain likens British rule to the politicking of Boss Croker and his infamously corrupt regime in New York City's Tammany Hall.[93] The pamphlet concludes with a 1910 statement from newspaper magnate William Randolph Hearst condemning Roosevelt's call for the United States to join Britain's imperialist ranks in governing the Philippines.[94]

Each of these statements was already a generation removed by the time they were reprinted by the Wolfe Tone press, and their intent was further obscured when circulated by the FFI. The pamphlet is perhaps better described, then, as a palimpsest in reverse; the text remained, but the immediate context was erased with each successive recirculation. Statements such as Hearst's, which had initially been used to denounce the call for U.S. imperialism in the Philippines, were circulated once by the Irish nationalist cause and once again by the FFI. The temporal distance, however, only reinforced the notion that anti-imperialism was an age-old American national tradition, and supporting the expatriate Indians was tantamount to the liberal project of the United States. This could not be further from the way that Smedley, years later, would recall that period in her life.

Daughter of Earth

It would take another decade before Smedley began to write about the tumultuous years that marked her involvement with the India Home Rule League, the Gadar Party, and the Friends of Freedom for India. In the interim, Smedley had moved to Germany, where she lived with Virendranath Chattopadhyay, or "Chatto," as he was known, a leading figure of the Berlin Indian Committee (BIC). With Chattopadhyay, Smedley again found herself at another important node in the clandestine network of expatriate Indian radicalism. She penned articles and provided lectures about India—occasionally under the name "Frau Violet Ali Khan Hussain"—at German universities.[95] She described their home in Berlin as a kind of halfway house for itinerant Indian radicals, dignitaries, and downtrodden students who had never before left India. Their house was "a small edition of that of a great joint family of India" with "Moslems and Hindus of every caste," regularly streaming in and out.[96] This included friends such as future Pakistani prime minister Muhammad Ali Jinnah and his wife Maryam, as well as members of Chattopadhyay's family like his younger sister Suhasini, who would become an important member of the Indian Communist Party, and his older sister Sarojini Naidu's son and daughter.[97] Inside the home, Smedley also took on a role as a caretaker, nursing ailing Indian students back to health, entertaining guests, and constantly being "harassed by domestic difficulties."[98]

Chattopadhyay was a complicated figure in the radical Indian movement abroad. The eldest son of a distinguished Bengali family, Chatto had helped establish the BIC, working as a liaison between the German Foreign Office and the Gadar Party. He was also partially responsible for the Gadar Party's turn toward Communism in 1919.[99] In 1921, Chattopadhyay, Smedley, and a delegation of Indian revolutionaries in Berlin traveled to Moscow to attend the Third Congress of the Comintern, where they attempted to garner Soviet support for the Indian nationalist movement.[100] Such an appeal came into conflict with M. N. Roy's thesis posed at the Second Congress of the Comintern a year earlier, which had opposed the Communist support of anticolonial nationalism on the grounds of its bourgeois class politics.[101] While Lenin did meet with Chattopadhyay, he concluded that the Soviet government would not support such an effort. Many decades later, Roy described how Smedley, with the support of Chattopadhyay, had wanted to be one of the representatives to see Lenin and make the case before a small commission set up to hear the Indian delegation, but was opposed on the grounds of her status as a non-Indian. While Roy did not mention it directly, Smedley's status as the sole woman among the delegation may very well have influenced his opposition.

Smedley described her relationship with Chattopadhyay as the unlikely union of "two eras" and "two cultures," which were drawn together by a shared antagonism for British empire and American capitalism:

> I was an American working woman, the product of a distorted commercial civilization, he a high-caste Indian with a cultivated, labyrinthine Brahmin mind and a British classical education. Though he hated everything British, he had an even deeper contempt for an American capitalism which judged all things by their money value.[102]

Biographer Ruth Price notes that by the early 1920s, their on-off relationship had turned toxic, with Smedley confessing to her close friend Florence Lennon that she had endured years of emotional and physical abuse from Chattopadhyay.[103] By 1925, she ended the relationship in an acrimonious split.[104] After several bouts of physical and mental illness, no doubt exacerbated by their relationship, Smedley left Germany. At first, she attempted to move to India, but because of her earlier record with Indian radicals in the U.S., colonial officials prevented her from securing a visa, thereby dashing plans to visit the country that had become so pivotal to her political life. She moved instead to Denmark, then Czechoslovakia, where she completed her novel *Daughter of Earth*, a book she described as "a desperate attempt to reorient [her] life."[105]

The novel traces the life of Marie Brown, from her childhood in Trinidad, Colorado, her work as a teacher in California, her failed marriage, and eventual move to New York, where she becomes involved with a group of Indian activists. While Smedley compressed the timeline and changed names, most events from the novel closely follow events from her life, so much so that many reviewers categorized the book as autobiography. Even the protagonist's name, "Marie Brown," stemmed from Smedley's life; the name was the alias that Smedley had used during her time with the Indian expatriates in FFI, a fact noted regularly in Military Information Division files.[106]

Daughter of Earth was finally published in 1929.[107] Walter Carmon of *New Masses* compared the book to heavyweights such as Upton Sinclair and Jack London, adding (somewhat patronizingly) that "no woman has written like this before."[108] Even Carmon's tentative grasp of the feminist politics of the novel—he writes, for instance, that "the social system that makes life a misery for man has added additional burdens to women"—gives way to his praise for its sheer scope: "Here is pioneering farm life in Missouri; mining camps ablaze with class conflict; free speech fights of the I.W.W. on the coast; Hindu revolutionaries; war hysteria which sends her to the Tombs for six months." He concludes by deeming the book a proletarian masterpiece, a novel about a "woman, a proletarian to her marrow [. . .] a fellow-worker [. . .] one of us."[109] Carmon's statement of solidarity across gender lines flattens the complex political landscape of the novel to a single figure: fellow-worker. The "Hindu revolutionaries," wedged between the Wobblies and the Tombs, are little more than an afterthought.

More recently, Smedley's novel has been described by scholars as one of the first American proletarian novels and the "Ur-text of women's proletarian fiction."[110] In categorizing the novel as a central work of proletarian fiction, literary historians place Smedley at the very beginnings of the Left's Cultural Front, treating the novel as a kind of feminist counterweight and corrective to the male-dominated canon of the American literary Left. In doing so, however, all the messiness of the novel's racial, class, and gender politics becomes subsumed under the proletarian subject.

This same tendency to emphasize the proletarian and feminist politics of the novel at the expense of its important intersections with race and empire are reflected in the publication history. While the chapter on "Hindu revolutionaries" makes up the longest part of the book (amounting to two-thirds of the entire novel and serving as the key event in its conclusion), critics,

Use Restriction

This device is restricted to indoor use when operating in the 5150 to 5350 MHz frequency range. This restriction applies in: AT, BE, BG, CH, CY, CZ, DE, DK, EE, EL, ES, FI, FR, HR, HU, IE, IS, IT, LI, LT, LU, LV, MT, NL, NO, PL, PT, RO, SE, SI, SK, TR, UK.

European Union—Disposal Information

The symbol above means that according to local laws and regulations your product and/or its battery shall be disposed of separately from household waste. When this product reaches its end of life, take it to a collection point designated by local authorities. The separate collection and recycling of your product and/or its battery at the time of disposal will help conserve natural resources and ensure that it is recycled in a manner that protects human health and the environment.

Class 1 Laser Information

This device is classified as a Class 1 Laser product per IEC60825-1:2007 and IEC60825-1:2014. This device complies with 21 CFR 1040.10 and 1040.11 except for deviations pursuant to Laser Notice 50, dated June 24, 2007. This device contains one or more lasers that could be damaged during repair or disassembly, which could result in hazardous exposure to infrared laser emissions that are not visible. This equipment should be serviced by Apple or an authorized service provider.

CLASS 1 LASER PRODUCT

iPhone

Before using iPhone, review the *iPhone User Guide* at support.apple.com/guide/iphone. You can also use Apple Books to download the guide (where available). Retain documentation for future reference.

Safety and Handling
See "Safety, handling, and support" in the *iPhone User Guide*.

Exposure to Radio Frequency
On iPhone, go to Settings > General > Legal & Regulatory > RF Exposure. Or go to www.apple.com/legal/rfexposure.

Battery
Don't attempt to replace the iPhone battery yourself—you may damage the battery, which could cause overheating, fire, and injury. The lithium-ion battery in your iPhone should be serviced or recycled by Apple or an authorized service provider, and must be recycled or disposed of separately from household waste. Dispose of batteries according to your local environmental laws and guidelines. For information about Apple lithium-ion batteries and battery service and recycling, go to www.apple.com/batteries/service-and-recycling.

Hearing Aid Compatibility (HAC)
Go to www.apple.com/support/hac, or see "Hearing devices" in the *iPhone User Guide*.

Avoiding Hearing Damage
To prevent possible hearing damage, do not listen at high volume levels for long periods. More information about sound and hearing is available online at www.apple.com/sound and in "Important safety information" in the *iPhone User Guide*.

Medical Device Interference
iPhone contains magnets that may interfere with medical devices. See "Important safety information" in the *iPhone User Guide*.

Apple One-Year Limited Warranty Summary
Apple warrants the included hardware product and accessories against defects in materials and workmanship for one year from the date of original retail purchase. Apple does not warrant against normal wear and tear, nor damage caused by accident or abuse. To obtain service, call Apple or visit an Apple Store or an Apple Authorized Service Provider—available service options are dependent on the country in which service is requested and may be restricted to the original country of sale. Call charges and international shipping charges may apply, depending on the location. Subject to the full terms and detailed information on obtaining service available at www.apple.com/legal/warranty and support.apple.com, if you submit a valid claim under this warranty, Apple will either repair, replace, or refund your iPhone at its own discretion. Warranty benefits are in addition to rights provided under local consumer laws. You may be required to furnish proof of purchase details when making a claim under this warranty.

For Australian Consumers: Our goods come with guarantees that cannot be excluded under the Australian Consumer Law. You are entitled to a replacement or refund for a major failure and for compensation for any other reasonably foreseeable loss or damage. You are also entitled to have the goods repaired or replaced if the goods fail to be of acceptable quality and the failure does not amount to a major failure. Apple Pty Ltd, PO Box A2629, Sydney South, NSW 1235. Tel: 133-622.

Regulatory
Regulatory certification information is available on this device. Go to Settings > General > Legal & Regulatory. Additional regulatory information is in "Safety, handling, and support" in the *iPhone User Guide*.

FCC and ISED Canada Compliance
This device complies with part 15 of the FCC Rules and ISED Canada licence-exempt RSS standard(s). Operation is subject to the following two conditions: (1) this device may not cause harmful interference, and (2) this device must accept any interference received, including interference that may cause undesired operation.

EU Compliance
Apple Inc. hereby declares that this wireless device is in compliance with Directive 2014/53/EU.

A copy of the EU Declaration of Conformity, including device frequency bands and maximum radio-frequency power, is available at www.apple.com/euro/compliance. Apple's EU representative is Apple Distribution International, Hollyhill Industrial Estate, Cork, Ireland.

publishers, reviewers, even Smedley herself seemed unsure about what to do with it.[111] Smedley explained to her close friend Florence Lennon that at least one early reader of the novel found the last chapter too sensational for the rest of the book and recommended getting rid of it. Smedley, however, was undeterred: "I worked like hell to get that last part done, and corrected it and worked on it . . . I am finished with it and tired of it and sick of it and hope never to see its dirty face again."[112] Her publisher, Malcolm Crowley, also wanted to axe the final chapter and in the second edition, published in 1934, the chapter fell swiftly under the editorial chopping block, excised of all but one reference to her encounter with Indian revolutionaries. The entire "Indian plot," so central to the narrative, goes missing.

As one might expect, literary scholars have paid careful attention to that section. The most compelling reading comes from Paula Rabinowitz, who argues that Marie's engagement with the Indian revolutionaries provides a "nurturing, feminine, collective space," offering a momentary resolution of the "narrative conditions" wrought by gendered difference.[113] But even this reading tends to subsume one social category under another. Racial minoritization and colonization becomes a space for the recuperation of working-class white womanhood; the Indian cause winds up becoming little more for Marie Brown than a site to work through the contradictions of her subject-position as a white woman, realizing she is neither at home in the American socialist circles nor in the Indian movement to which she had become so attached. It is partly through such readings that critics like Sondra Guttman, Barbara Foley, Paula Rabinowitz, and others have suggested in their own nuanced ways that *Daughter of Earth* "fails in its quest to inspire revolutionary consciousness."[114]

Convincing as such analyses are, they tend to overlook the way in which *Daughter of Earth* attempted to conceptualize the relationship between the hierarchies of gender, class, and race and the entanglements of patriarchy, capitalism, and colonialism. For Smedley, this conceptualizing occurred at the level of experience. While she had become active in the socialist circles and the study groups of New York, she explained in a 1927 essay for *New Masses* that it was ultimately the experience of "poverty and subjection" that forced her to think about the way that the relations of class, gender, and race were yoked together:

From the depths of poverty and subjection myself, I always instinctively identified myself with the poor and enslaved. The fact that I was a woman, and hated it, also intensified this tendency. I championed the cause of my own class, the workers; also of women as a sex; the Negro as a race; and I eventually ended in the revolutionary movement for the freedom of India. This was not only because it was a movement for freedom, but also because it was a movement just about as distant from American life and thought as any movement

can be. To forget my own unhappy life, I fled into this movement of
a distant, foreign people. [. . .] I have identified myself so completely
with it that I have almost ceased to be American.[115]

While this passage opens with Smedley's personal experience with poverty,
and her proxy identifications with workers, women, and African Americans,
it ends with a moment of disidentification. "I have almost ceased to be American," Smedley writes, fleeing into a movement of "distant, foreign people." In
a sense, Smedley's own self-narrative is at odds with the rhetorical strategies
that marked her journalistic and propaganda work. The Friends of Freedom
for India attempted to domesticate anticolonialism, I have argued. Smedley
and the group refracted the cause of "Indian freedom" through American
liberalism, making a distant struggle feel proximal to her audience in the
United States. Here, however, Smedley describes how she sought the movement for Indian revolution precisely because it was "distant" and "foreign."

There is a note of escapism here, which echoes Smedley's own life trajec-
tory; in the 1920s, she fled the United States for Europe and eventually Asia,
where a decade later she became a reporter following Communist China
and, according to biographer Price, served as a Soviet spy. But another way
to perceive her comment is to think through the ways of seeing afforded by
those in positions of exile and estrangement. The working title for *Daughter
of Earth* was fittingly *Outcast*. Where the title "Daughter of Earth" imagines
a sense of global belonging and the transcendence of political borders, "Outcast" offers its opposite: no belonging, only alienation and estrangement. Yet
the two titles are also connected in that they seek to unsettle categories of
belonging and attachment. Georg Lukács's description of "the novel form"
as "transcendental homelessness" seems particularly appropriate for the narrative Smedley spins.[116]

These themes—outcast, homelessness, estrangement—bring to mind the
figure of the exile, who Edward Said defines as a figure who exists "outside
habitual order [. . .] nomadic, decentred, contrapuntal."[117] I want to suggest
that Smedley's (and by proxy, Marie Brown's) identification with the Indian
revolutionaries—exiles in their own right—signals something similar. Her
connection with the Indians offers her more than just the immediate identification with the racial other, or an entry point into a politics of anticolonialism,
but forces her to adopt the perspective of the exile, who constantly decenters
social forms and undoes "habitual order." To give an example from this chapter's epigraph, Marie describes how working with the group of Indian revolutionaries forced her to reimagine the meanings of the World War. She explains,
"The War was always before our eyes in that house, and I came to see it
through the eyes of men from Asia—eyes that watched and were cynical about
the phrases of democracy. Sad eyes, eyes filled with despair at times."[118] Far
from the triumphalism of FFI propaganda, which posed tidy analogies be-

tween U.S. history and the Indian cause, *Daughter of Earth* describes the unsettling perspective that Marie's encounter with the exiled and expatriate Indians offers her. It is "through the eyes" of the Indian radicals that she begins to grasp the stakes of the war beyond the national concerns of the United States, the sloganeering "phrases of democracy," and the socialist concerns of her American comrades; the war transforms Marie into a different kind of internationalist, routed through Asia and not exclusively the Soviet Union. The novel thus adopts a transnational refraction, through which it unsettles entrenched understandings of the world and helps the reader imagine new social relations outside of those forged through capitalism and colonialism. This occurs most dramatically in the final chapter of *Daughter of Earth*, where Smedley challenges the form of the proletarian novel by rearranging and reimagining the relationship between anticolonialism and socialism.

Smedley's attempt to connect the struggle of the American proletariat with the struggle for Indian freedom was not without peer or precedent. In an issue of *New Masses* from 1930, editor Mike Gold explained his own ambivalent position about the Indian swadeshi movement. "Gandhi is a striking figure [who] [. . .] in his own way [has been] putting up a valiant fight for Indian freedom," Gold admitted, before arguing that Gandhi's "mind is shallow and reactionary" and that he opposes workers and "all forms of trade unionism."[119] Such an argument was fairly common, parroted by Marie's white comrades in *Daughter of Earth*, who argued that any national revolution would only benefit the colonial bourgeoisie. Lenin himself described something similar in the First Congress of the Comintern in 1919, maintaining that the Communist project served as a precondition for the freedom of the colonized world. "The liberation of the colonies is only thinkable along with the liberation of workers in the metropolis," Lenin argued, adding that "just as capitalist Europe has drawn the backward parts of the earth into the capitalist maelstrom, so too will socialist Europe come to the assistance of the colonies with its technology, its organization and its intellectual influence."[120] Lenin's statement was a retort to Woodrow Wilson's "Fourteen Points," which called for an "impartial adjustment of all colonial claims."[121] For Lenin, the preconditions for anticolonial revolution could only ever be European Communism and could not be achieved through Wilsonian bourgeois democracy. As Kris Manjapra explains, "Lenin insisted on the need for a relationship of tutelage between European communists and Asian anticolonial movements."[122]

In *Daughter of Earth*, Smedley intimated that the struggle for the Western worker and for Indian decolonization were indeed linked, but she emphasized a dialectical relationship that challenged the immediate Eurocentrism in Lenin's statement. The liberation of the colony was not predicated on the liberation of the Euro-American worker, but rather, the liberation of the worker could not occur without the liberation of the colony.

Smedley had argued as much to her friend Florence Lennon as early as 1921: "More and more do I see that only a successful revolution in India can break England's back forever and free Europe itself. It is not a national question concerning India any longer; it is purely international."[123] While Smedley's argument was more a provocation than Lenin's thesis, which would form Soviet state policy, her comments were not baseless. As a work of proletarian fiction, *Daughter of Earth* was invested in the project of arousing different forms of radical class consciousness in its reader. Rather than laying out the contradictions of capitalism, Smedley's novel attempted to "reorient" its reader by mapping a web of connections between imperialism, capitalist exploitation, and racial and gendered exploitation both at home and abroad. To return to her 1927 *New Masses* statement, Smedley did not solely fight for "the cause of my own class; the workers" or "women as a sex" or "the Negro as a race" or "the revolutionary movement for the freedom of India."[124] Rather she saw these as deeply interconnected struggles. The work of her novel was to illustrate that thesis, by staging a series of dialogues between her protagonist Marie and the secondary characters she encounters.

Before delving further into this argument, a gloss of U.S. proletarian fiction and its development may be useful, especially to underscore the uniqueness of *Daughter of Earth*. As Barbara Foley explains, U.S. proletarian novels emerged from the crucible of the Great Depression and the Communist-led Cultural Front and varied aesthetically, drawing from a number of forms and genres, from social realism to modernist experimentation, fictional autobiography to "collective novels." Aside from these formal differences, the center of the American proletarian novel was the idea that literature could raise a radical working-class consciousness in its reader.[125] As Jon-Christian Suggs argues, "Left novelists in general wanted to produce fictions that, when read by the working class and middle classes, enhanced that audience's understanding of and probability of its enlistment in the contradictions of the American working class experience."[126] What exactly constituted the American proletariat and who the subject of proletarian fiction was, however, continued to be the source of several debates. One such dispute between prominent figures in the U.S. literary Left illustrates the tenor of such squabbles: Writer Martin Russak had believed that the proletarian novel could only have as its subject the working class, and not the "emotions and reactions and values of the upper or middle classes or the [. . .] hoboes and tramps [of the lumpen proletariat]."[127] Mike Gold, on the other hand, had thought that the genre could accommodate the strivings of both the proletariat and revolutionary middle class.[128] The journal *New Masses* defined proletariat in an expansive way that not only included industrialized labor, but also "poorer farmers, the unemployed, and even the lower fringes of the petty bourgeoisie as well as its industrial workers."[129] This debate was further compounded by questions about whether proletarian literature was by, for, or about workers.[130] Trotsky described "proletarian culture" as an oxymoron, given that the Communist project would eventually lead to the dissolution of class society itself. "The proletariat acquires power for the purpose of doing away forever with class culture and to make way for human culture," Trotsky explained: "We frequently seem to forget this."[131]

The relationship between the genre of the proletarian novel and the Communist Party USA spurred its own set of debates, with one set of critics arguing that "proletarian literature was the literature of a party disguised as the literature of a class."[132] However, the relationship between the genre and the Soviet Union was far more complicated, Foley explains: "The key formal innovations associated with American literary proletarianism [. . .] had precedents in the revolutionary literary experiments being carried on in the USSR as well as in Germany and other countries with developed proletarian cultural movements."[133] By the 1930s, the journal *International Literature*, sponsored by the Comintern, had become a major source for Americans to keep up with leftist literature in the Soviet Union as well as Germany, Italy, Hungary, England, France, Japan, and China.[134] Nevertheless, suggesting that American proletarian literature aped Soviet directives is misleading, not accounting for the complex and idiosyncratic developments in American proletarian literature; influence rather than coercive prescription more accurately described the relationship.

Even before the journal *International Literature* was published, Smedley had closely followed and written about various forms of radical fiction and art from across the globe, including India, Germany, China, and Denmark. In a short essay published for the *New York Call*, Smedley described the "spirit of revolt" in contemporary Indian poetry, citing poets such as Benoy Kumar Sarkar—Lajpat Rai's fellow traveler on the S.S. *Philadelphia*—whose work captured the defiant voice of "Young Asia" as opposed to the "mystical, nebulous, [and] [. . .] spiritual" Indian literature with which most Americans were familiar. More than a record of colonial despair, poetry such as Sarkar's, Smedley argued, painted "a picture of wretchedness almost inconceivable" but also contained glimmers of hope through "the seething and ever-accumulating thoughts of revolts."[135] In her writings for the *Modern Review*, she frequently remarked on the relationship between revolutionary art and modern society, publishing essays on Chinese and Indian literature, as well as on German literature, film, and visual art. In a review for Sarkar's *The Bliss of a Moment*, Smedley wrote how most Americans did not care about the formal and aesthetic qualities such as "diction or melody" of poetry, but instead cared "for the message contained in it."[136] Thus, Sarkar's direct poetry was "more closely allied to [American] [. . .] mental habits than all the works of Kipling."[137] The call for more protest art, which captured the suffering and resistance of subjected people across the world, was a consistent theme in Smedley's critical writing.

In a *Modern Review* essay titled "The Negro Renaissance" (for which Smedley received photographs and references from W.E.B. Du Bois), she described the development of African American literature, referencing the work of Du Bois, Jessie Fauset, Jean Toomer, James Weldon Johnson, and Elise Johnson McDougal.[138] Tracing the earliest representations of Black characters in white American literature ("as comic relief, as sentiment, [. . .] as the faithful subordinate dog of the white man"), Smedley noted the dawn of a Black cultural renaissance, which had produced arguably the only distinctive form of American art.[139] She was still interested in literature's role as a pedagogical device to understand and articulate larger forces of oppression, but she centered that role around subjective experience. She wrote, "[Black writers] have taught us that Negro literature can never be written by white writers, but only by the Negro, for it requires a study, both objective and subjective, of those subtle forces that sustain a folk in its hopes and joys, that stiffens them in sorrow and pain."[140] These themes carried over in Smedley's assessment of other literary scenes. In a piece on Chinese literature from the 1920s, she characterized a growing conflict between what she described as reactionary bourgeois writers, social revolutionaries, and a "confused" and "chaotic" class in the middle who leans toward social revolution. The role of the poet, according to Smedley, was to be an aid to social revolution. In a line that evokes her novel's title, she explained:

> if it be said that poets should be absolved from the necessity of thinking or writing on social themes, one may ask in the words of a Chinese revolutionary poet: "*What* is a poet?" Is he a man who has dropped from the sky? Or is he not a product of the earth, of society, and does he not support, tolerate, or oppose society as it exists to-day?[141]

These lofty questions informed Smedley's examination of writers and artists across the globe, including Norwegian writer Henrik Ibsen, Danish actor Betty Nansen, and the German painter Käthe Köllwitz, the latter two of whom had become close acquaintances during Smedley's stay in Europe. One of her finest essays in the *Modern Review*, in fact, reviewed the career of Köllwitz and allowed her to further develop her ideas about the value of art to the working classes. For Smedley, Köllwitz's paintings did more than provide dignity to the toiling peasant and industrial laborer; they provided a "synthesis of social problems of the western world."[142] Moreover, Smedley described how often Köllwitz's paintings depicted laboring women, and the specific forms of gendered labor that working-class and peasant women engaged in—gleaning on farms, working as charwomen in the homes of the rich, and being mothers. Accompanied by a number of images, Smedley's essay described these paintings as producing a "new kind of art" in which the viewer can "see a simplification of forces driving the masses."[143]

In reading Smedley's essays on world literature, one notices a number of recurring themes. First, Smedley rehearsed a familiar leftist position on art, citing favorably the art of social realism and expressing distaste for what she perceived as the staid petit bourgeois interest in beauty and art for art's sake. Second, she rarely wrote about literature by white Americans, instead drawing inspiration from Indian, Chinese, German, and African American writing. And though her ambitions were international, she eschewed the proclivities of American leftists who spent the bulk of their attention on Soviet literature. Third, Smedley saw the purpose of literature and art as not just evoking pity or simply reaching the masses, but providing a "synthesis of social problems," to explain rather than to describe.

The seventh and final chapter of *Daughter of Earth* thus begins with an important series of episodes that map out the interconnections between class, race, and gender as social categories tied to a larger system of exploitation. Up until that point, the novel remains fairly autobiographical and rooted in the political and geographical landscapes of the United States. It traces Marie's life from her upbringing in Colorado to her eventual entry into political activism with socialists, the I.W.W., and other Marxists in California and New York. Her encounters with socialists often highlight the discrepancy between her experiences of a proletarianized life and their high-minded theories about exploitation. While the socialists provide dreary lectures on "technical Marxist subject[s]," Smedley emphasizes the irony that Marie's class position prevents her from connecting with them. "I sat in beaten wonderment and confusion amongst them," Marie explains, scathingly describing a socialist crowd that discussed "the Russian revolution as it were their private property."[144] Literature, too, provided her with very few points of entry. When she begins to move among the bohemian circles of New York, Marie describes her discomfort with conversations on literature and the arts. She explains:

> As with music, so with literature: I read for the story, knowing nothing of style, of form, or of authors. Poetry had always been foreign to me, for I could not understand why people did not write as they spoke, naturally, and not in verse. [. . .] I simply could not appreciate them. Only if they told a story of endeavor, of struggle, could I understand their purpose.[145]

At the start of the seventh chapter Marie finally mentions a work of fiction that has impacted her. "For weeks," she explains, "I had abandoned other European and English writers, for [Maxim] Gorki held my entire attention [. . .] It was not only what he wrote [. . .] it was his spirit; he treasured women and the intimate tenderness between man and woman; and he expressed the yearnings for beauty in the hearts of the masses."[146] There is a double-move here, from the presumably bourgeois writing of "European and English writers" to the revolutionary proletarian literature of Gorki's *The Mother* (1906), a move that is both ideological (bourgeois to revolutionary), as well as geographical (West to East). Like her socialist friends, Marie too is drawn to the Soviet Union as a source of inspiration, but unlike her American comrades, she looks even further east to Asia.

The India Plot

While *Daughter of Earth* drew extensively from Smedley's engagement with the expatriate Indian nationalist scene, she also scrambled many details, reordering events and creating a number of composite characters. The real-life Smedley first engaged with Indian radical networks as a reporter covering the Gadar Party, but Marie first comes in contact with an Indian lecturer named Sardar Ranjit Singh at her college on the West Coast. In the novel, Singh's speech is censored by the University Board of Trustees and faculty, a fact that alarms Marie, who later overhears a few pro-British faculty members describing him as a "traitor" and a "seditionist."[147] If we compare this scene from the novel with Smedley's biography, we might note how she compressed three life events: First, the rally in Fresno, in which *Gadar* editor Ram Chandra had warned of the British censoring the news in the United States; second, Smedley's initial encounter with Lajpat Rai, who delivered a lecture at the New York Civic Club that led to her work with the IHRLA; and third, a lecture on campus from K. D. Shastri (later secretary of the IHRLA) at San Diego Normal School in 1913, which drew faculty censorship.[148] In the process of narrative compression, the wide ideological differences between the Gadar Party and IHRLA are collapsed. Even the character Sardar Ranjit Singh appears to be a composite between Lajpat Rai and Gadar Party leader Bhagwan Singh.[149]

Purnima Bose persuasively argues that Smedley's choice to present Marie's initial interest in Indian nationalism through her encounter with the Indian lecturer and "University of California's censorship of a lecture on the topic" was deliberate.[150] This was a calculated "narrative absence," Bose argues, which served several functions. It hid the Gadar Party's "transnational links to Germany," which would have discredited the movement to an American readership suspicious if not downright antagonistic to Germany in the years after the war. It also helped to obscure certain names and facts that may have jeopardized the safety of Gadar Party members and their American collaborators, and revealed too much about her personal relationship with Virendranath Chattopadhyay.[151] *Daughter of Earth*, in other words, obscures its own radical tracks, preventing it from serving as a playbook for American and British intelligence.

I would add to Bose's argument that another important takeaway is that Smedley was less interested in conveying the intricacies and political rifts within the anticolonial Indian nationalist movement than she was in narrating the protagonist's developing relationship with the movement more broadly, a relationship that marked the possibility of cross-racial solidarity. In the initial meeting between Marie and Singh, for instance, Smedley underscored the subjective gap between Marie's American identity and the Indians' status as racialized and colonized others. When Marie first meets Singh, she comments that "something about him made me feel very sad."[152] In considering the reasons for her immediate identification with him, she considers that it was their shared experience of being "the subjected," "being humiliated." This soon gives way to her recognition of the difference that marks their experience: perhaps, Marie thinks aloud, "it was that he was a man of color in a land that judges men by color."[153] From the perspective of Singh, or at least as Marie imagines it, she is interpellated as "only one of my [American] countrymen."[154]

The distance between the perspectives of Marie and Singh, the American woman and the "man of color," soon narrows. When they meet again in New York, Marie becomes a disciple, volunteering to work for Singh as a secretary for his cause, studying with him in an effort to understand the world from the perspective of the colonized. Their relationship is described initially through the terms of courtship. Marie explains, "a man came into my life. A lover—no."[155] The language of romantic intimacy quickly gives way to the language of father and daughter, as Marie describes his paternal affections for her: "Perhaps he was lonely in exile; or perhaps my need for affection, for someone to love, for someone to take the place of a father."[156] Her work with him leads to her entry into the scene of Indian expatriates, where she is treated with equal parts suspicion and affection, as rival, comrade, and eventually sister. On that latter point, Purnima Bose suggests that "the transformation of [. . .] political relationships into familial ones" is a significant way in which Smedley imagined terms of solidarity. Marie, who has felt rejected from her family, from her husband, and from the political circles she has moved in, finally discovers a home through the intimate bonds she forges with the Indian radicals. She sees how her comrades "took the place of my father, of my brother who was dead."[157] Through this new network of kin, Marie's sense of belonging changes; she begins to see world events "through the eyes of men from Asia" and, exposed to their discussions, comes to understand the "basis of racial consciousness."[158] Singh himself suggests that they share more than what divides them, telling her one day, "I often hope that women, also, will work for freedom for all people. They should know, like the working class, and like all Asia, what subjection means."[159]

Richard Jean So has cautioned against reading *Daughter of Earth* as a novel that primarily marks the American Left's engagement with the non-West through "terms of solidarity or sympathy," suggesting that such attempts tend to "assimilate 'the foreign' as mere examples of an internally coherent U.S. cultural pluralism."[160] We see a version of this in Singh's statement, which compares the categories of womanhood, the working class, and racialized Asia as discrete and separate, never considering how these categories might be multiply embodied. The conspicuous absence or even consideration of women of color in *Daughter of Earth*, for instance, bears critical scrutiny. Smedley had written essays on women in India—publishing an interview in the *Independent Hindustan* with Lila Singh, an Indian "suffragist" who had traveled to the United States; a sprawling historical survey of women in India in the *Hindusthanee Student*, that spans 1000 B.C. to the present; and an essay on women of India in the *New York Call*, which ties the suppression of women to colonial rule.[161] In that latter essay, Smedley wrote, "A free India would have difficulties to solve, but the struggle would be against one foe, instead of two."[162] While *Daughter of Earth* rarely considers the embodied experience of women of color, it does challenge easy expressions of solidarity across social hierarchies, albeit from the perspective of working-class white womanhood.

Comparisons of social conditions weave throughout *Daughter of Earth*, as Marie continues to grapple with the various ways that the social forms of race, class, and gender are interconnected. In one scene, she describes an argument she has with a white professor, who had served as an adviser to a rubber baron in South America. In describing the labor conditions of the rubber plantation workers, all of whom were Black, the professor explains that they "did not object to a working day."[163] Marie describes being unable to argue—"I felt deeply . . . and thought little"—but nevertheless sensing race as a social relation that structured a global capitalist system. She challenges the professor: "How do you know what they feel or think—what do you know of their suffering—what could you know? And do you believe that Negroes are less sensitive than we are just because they are black?"[164] Soon, she imagines a scene of the Black laborers, connecting them to her brothers and father.

> The picture of those black men, working in the deadening heat for unearthly hours, just for enough to keep life in their bodies [. . .] My emotions were deeply touched when I thought of those black men— big men perhaps with stooped shoulders, laboring blindly, watching the earth as they worked [. . .] could it be that I saw my father, and perhaps my brothers, in all that was dumb and helpless before existence, all that was denied humanity, all that was defeated? . . . It was but chance that I was born white and not black; free and not slave; I believed a truth is a truth only when it covers the generality, and not just me.[165]

Smedley's aestheticizing of Black male bodies is discomfiting to be sure, a tendency throughout her writing that appears again in Marie's gratuitous physical descriptions of her Indian comrades. Nevertheless, Marie attempts to draw a connection between her family and the men in the rubber plantation, linking the class exploitation of proletarianized labor in the United States to the exploitation of Black workers in South America. Yet, she is also attentive to the ways that the exploitation of Black workers was predicated on racial difference. "It was but chance that I was born white and not black, free and not slave" Marie explains, casting a qualification on the comparison. Hers is an attempt to reach a theory of exploitation—a truth that "covers the generality," as she puts it. Such a description suggests that the novel was always meant to be more than autobiography; it was an attempt to form a synthesis—an ambitious, international, and intersectional "synthesis of social problems" of the entire globe.

While her apprenticeship with Singh draws her deeper into the expatriate Indian movement, Marie continues to be challenged by white socialists, who question her commitments for a "distant," "nationalist revolution" that they imagined would only serve "Indian capitalists and feudal landlords."[166] Guided by the Indians who encourage her to undo her Eurocentricity, Marie continues to map another kind of global imaginary, which saw Asia not as peripheral but central to an internationalist project of freedom. For Marie, the struggles of the American proletariat and colonized Indians were far more linked than had been previously imagined. She explains:

> I talked much with my Indian friends those days, and each day tried to convince my [socialist] comrades that without the freedom of Asiatic peoples, the European or American workers could not gain their emancipation; that one of the chief pillars of world capitalism was to be found in the subjection of Asiatic peoples. Above my desk I hung a map showing India as the strategic base from which China, the Near and Middle East, and a part of Africa, were dominated. I also explained to them that Russia was almost as distant as India, and yet their eyes were always following the Russian Revolution. There would one day be a revolution in India, I said, and they would then be ignorant of the conditions there.[167]

In this passage, Marie re-maps the global imaginary of the American Left, effectively placing India, instead of Moscow, at the center of the international struggle against capitalist exploitation. India was "the strategic base" that connected China, the Middle East, and Africa through the relations of colonialism. Echoing this geographical reorientation, *Daughter of Earth* attempts to connect the working-class and underclass affinity to a broader imaginary of anticolonialism. Marie draws a series of connections between her brother, killed in a war "fought by capitalists," and the Indian radicals during World War I, caught in a war between empires that was not of their making. She thus begins to see herself as the subject of a vast global system of capitalism, a network of exploitative relations that culminates in colonialism.

Ultimately, Marie challenges her mentor Singh as well. When Singh confesses that when thinking about the plight of colonized India he never "think[s] of classes," Marie snaps back at what she perceives as his facile nationalism absent of any class analysis: "If you were a peasant, you would think also of the landlord; and if you were a worker, you would think also of your boss."[168] Later in the novel, Singh suggests that the struggle against imperialism "is not just a struggle against the Capitalist system, but of all Asia against the western world."[169] Upon hearing this, Marie once again protests Singh's evasion of class analysis in favor of a civilizational discourse. If the revolutionary vanguard was Asia against the West, Marie asks, then what about Russia? Singh responds, "It is at least half Asiatic." Marie fires back again, "race has nothing to do with it. It is a new world order being born. That order is neither eastern or western."[170] Interestingly, Smedley stages these debates in a series of dialectical relationships, voiced through each character. Nationalism collides with class hierarchies, and anti-imperialism comes up against internationalism, symbolized in Marie's description of a new world marked by neither East nor West.

What ultimately draws Marie to the Indian movement is less a theoretical entrée into the world of anticolonialism, and more the emotional attachments she forms with the men in the movement. She confesses:

> I read and talked and argued. Yet I worked with and clung to the Indians. Why? Forced to find answers, I was driven more and more to study Indian history and conditions, and more to analyze my own motives. But I could not tell my American friends one bond that held me to the Indians—the bond of love. They would have smiled, for they would have seen only sex love. And yet it was not sex love. Throughout my life I had needed and longed for the warmth of human affection.[171]

No one embodies this "bond of love" as much as Singh does for Marie, a connection that "endured the strain of class, of political, and intellectual differences."[172] Even her initial descriptions of Singh are marked by an uneasy categorization, first as an unrequited lover, and later as a paternal figure. *Daughter of Earth* draws on the language of intimacy to describe both the symbolic and real political connections that are built between Marie and her Indian comrades. When she marries fellow comrade Anand Manvekar the couple serves as a metonym for the forging of a new political relationship; the "marriage" between Anand and Marie represent a putative marriage between East and West, anticolonialism and socialism. Nevertheless, Marie's agreement to marry Anand is also characterized as ambivalent at best, symbolized through a series of images that evoke lightness and darkness, vitality and decay, borders and crossings: "A lightness prevailed, and under the touch of his hands I felt the walls of protection that I had built to guard my soul for so many years begin to crumble into dust."[173] On one hand, the passage describes a "wall of protection" that breaks down, an image that at once suggests the sexual union of two physical bodies and the metaphorical union between two geopolitical bodies. On the other hand, Smedley's language evokes a profoundly uneasy image, one which resonates with an earlier scene of rape.

In arguing that *Daughter of Earth* crafts solidarities between white working-class interests and global anticolonialism through the language of intimacy and intersectionality, we nevertheless have to contend with the novel's traumatic conclusion. While the novel portrays Marie's deepening involvement and identification with the political cause of her Indian comrades, a scene of sexual assault changes the course of the plot, forever altering Marie's relationship to the Indian anticolonialist movement. In a pivotal scene, Juan Diaz—an Indian comrade who Marie describes as "cynical" and "irritating," and who "believed in the sincerity of few men and of no women"—visits her in her room one night in order to ask for the whereabouts of another comrade.[174] In the ensuing scene, Diaz sexually assaults her. As he leaves, Diaz begs Marie to never speak a word of this, for risk of it ruining his political work. That night, Marie turns on the gas oven in her room and attempts suicide. She is saved by a window left open, and during her recovery never mentions her encounter with Diaz to anyone. In the scenes that follow, Marie also partially blames herself, considering how she enabled Diaz: "I see that this thing could never have happened without either my conscious or unconscious consent."[175]

This pivotal scene has generated much discussion among scholars of Smedley's work. Paula Rabinowitz argues that this scene "break[s] forever Marie's illusion of the nurturing, feminine, collective space of the Indian movement, much as her mother's abusiveness and her abused body destroyed Marie's desire to mother."[176] Through a structural reading, Rabinowitz suggests that if the feminized Indian movement offered a momentary resolution of the "narrative conditions" wrought by gendered difference, then the rape scene undoes it. Indeed, Diaz continues to haunt Marie. Even as she recovers and finds a resolution of political and emotional desire through her relationship with Anand, who she eventually marries, the rumors of the rape ultimately undo her marriage and that resolution.

Biographers have speculated on identifying the real-life counterpart of Juan Diaz, reaching different conclusions. Janice and Stephen MacKinnon make the case that Diaz was based on Herambalal Gupta, who served as the liaison between the Berlin India Committee and the Gadar Party, and whose alias while organizing in Mexico was Juan Lopez.[177] Gupta would later become a British agent, much like Diaz is revealed to be in the novel. In her more recent biography of Smedley, Ruth Price concluded that the character was a composite of M. N. Roy and Gupta, but it was Roy with whom Smedley had a "disastrous sexual encounter."[178]

The emphasis placed on revealing the historical identity of Juan Diaz is troubling, in part because it overlooks Smedley's own strategic narration of the scene, in which she took deliberate efforts to mark Diaz through specific racial, religious, and political signs. Unlike any of the other Indian characters in the novel, Diaz is described as "Eurasian—half Hindu, half Portuguese, a Christian by religion."[179] He is "fairer than the others," and by the novel's end, eventually revealed to be a British spy. In more than one way, Diaz is a figure marked by a series of conflicted loyalties between East and West: a man of color who is "fair," a Hindu who has European blood, and an Indian radical who deep down is a British stooge. If the real-life Juan Diaz was Gupta, Roy, or a composite of both, then Smedley went to some pains to disassociate them from Diaz. As far as the record shows, neither Roy nor Gupta were Christian, nor were they of mixed race descent.

Thus, Smedley positioned Diaz as a figure who remains outside of the Indian movement, and outside in ways that conferred him power and privilege at every level. Diaz's political betrayal of the Indian movement is echoed in his sexual violation of Marie. His social positioning as partially white, partially European, and a closeted imperialist allows the novel to hold onto the possibility that the patriarchal violence that leads to Marie's estrangement from the Indian movement was only enabled by an outsider. In other words, there is a calculated attempt by Smedley to resolve Diaz's rape as a violation of the Indian movement itself. To characterize Diaz more closely to Gupta or Roy—as Indians central to the movement—would render such a resolution impossible.

Exile

It would be an overstatement to read the novel's conclusion as a forecast of revolutionary failure. Marie's marriage to Anand ends, yet it is precisely that failure that allows Marie to recognize that the institution of marriage and patriarchy have betrayed her. The novel concludes abruptly, with Marie leaving Anand, packing her things and exiting their home. The last sentence of the novel reads, "Out of this house—out of this country. . . ."[180] It is a curious, but also fitting conclusion for the novel. The subject is missing, and instead we have a phrase nearly repeated and joined with a dash, as if drawing an equivalence between "house" and "country." In the last moments of the novel, Marie moves outside the sphere of the domestic in two senses—the domestic sphere of the home and the domestic borders of the nation. She has finally achieved what she once told the socialist friends who had reminded her of her American national identity: "I have no country . . . my country-men are the men and women who work against oppression."[181] In the novel's conclusion, Marie takes concrete steps toward that new internationalist sub-jectivity—once exiled in her own country, she has now become an exile abroad.

In the decades that followed, Smedley's career would move further east-ward to China, where she published her most notable works. To a certain extent, one might read Smedley's engagement with India as the preface to her much longer and more politically important career in China. But her writing and organizing in the 1910s and 1920s were more than a prologue; they al-lowed her to think through an important set of ideas about the relations of kin and comrade, the sense of belonging felt by "countrymen" and exiles. Both her propaganda work with the Friends of Freedom for India and her more literary work in *Daughter of Earth* hinged on reimagining the relation-ship between the United States and India. If the FFI organization evoked "friend" as a noncommittal term for solidarity and support, then in *Daugh-ter of Earth* she deepened her investments into that term, considering the relationship between intimacy and political community.

Such friendships were tested as Smedley gravitated further to the Com-munist Left. Just a year before Lajpat Rai's death in 1928, she and Rai were engaged in a public political spat that played out in the Lahore-based newspa-per the *People*, edited by Rai. Smedley had written a series of articles titled "England's War Preparations in Asia," which raised critical objections to the Indian nationalist movement largely from a Marxist perspective.[182] Rai re-sponded by calling Smedley "a partisan," "not only anti-British, but pro-Bol-shevik," and was suspicious of her claims that Soviet Russia did not have imperialist designs on India.[183] But it was his mentee's condescending tone that seemed to irk him the most. "Miss Smedley is mistaken if she thinks we are all babies and do not understand even elementary politics," Rai wrote, adding that "sitting in Berlin, [. . .] she calls us traitors, cowards, and fools."[184] As Bill Mul-len has noted, Rai also revealed his "deep Hindutva roots" when he argued that "religionism is the curse of India, and no Muslim can to-day be anything but a Communalist."[185] Smedley responded once again in the *People*, objecting to Rai's personal attacks, his argument that Communism was somehow "a form of communalism," and most critically his "sweeping statements about Muslims."[186] From Smedley's vantage, the policy of Indian leaders was akin to "cattle trade": In return for reforms, you "strengthen the British Empire, rivet the chains more tightly about India."[187] Driving that latter point home, she echoed the words of Marie Rogers debating Sardar Ranjit Singh:

The class to which you belong, to which most of the Indian leaders belong, the owning class, the master class, makes war on the working class, on the dispossessed. It has done it for ages. Every time the workers, or the peasants, or the slaves have raised their heads in an attempt to throw off the yoke of subjection, it has been the master class, the "respectable" class, that has beaten them down, imprisoned them, and made new laws to hold them more securely in slavery.[188]

They would not speak again. In the 1929 special issue of the *People* memorializing Rai, Smedley expressed grief over her former mentor's death, which had come after sustaining injuries from an attack by the colonial police. She recalled her time with Rai as transformative, describing how after she had met him "my life entered new channels."[189]

By the time of Rai's passing, Smedley had outgrown Rai and, to a certain degree, the Indian movement altogether. If she had expressed her personal indebtedness to Rai for his mentorship, by the end of their relationship, Smedley had also spotted the limits of Rai's anticolonialism—the Hindu communalism that underpinned many of his arguments, the ways in which his nationalism outweighed his class analysis. But if we return to *Daughter of Earth*, published the same year as their public debate, we see how her novel conceptualized her encounter with Rai and the others within the Indian movement differently. If in her row with Rai in the pages of the *People* she expressed the stiff assurances of the Soviet line, then the novel captured something more intimate—the dialogue between the working-class American and Indian nationalist, through whom she began to channel a nascent internationalism and feel her sense of self, refracted: a daughter of earth and no longer a subject of America.

3

Killing Kipling

Dhan Gopal Mukerji and America's India

[P]eople believed that the British administration had not
lost all sense of frankness and sincerity, until the new
doctrine of the white man's burden was propounded by the
banjo-bards, and the jingo poets.

—LAJPAT RAI, 1907

"A Brilliant Painter of Indian Life"

In November 1920, the *Bulletin for the Brooklyn Institute of Arts and Sciences* advertised a lecture that promised to compare two giants of Indian literature: On one end was Rudyard Kipling, who "embodies the highest possible ideal of imperialism," and the other was Rabindranath Tagore, whose "eloquent plea" called for the "release of the soul of India from foreign control."[1] As if enacting Kipling's "Ballad of the East and West" in the form of a bookish debate, the Brooklyn Institute pitted the two writers as the literary equivalents of the Colonel and Kamal—"two great men," "two great poets," and "humanitarians" whose differences only appeared in their "deductions."[2]

Tucked away in the notice's text was the name of the lecturer—not Rudyard or Rabindranath—but the young and then largely unknown Indian American writer Dhan Gopal Mukerji.[3] A migrant from Bengal who had been residing in the United States for the previous decade, Mukerji had started to lecture around the country, presenting himself as a cultural interlocutor, an authentic "Brahmin philosopher" and "Hindu poet" from India who also knew the customs of his adopted home in America. If someone could explain the difference between "The India of Kipling and Tagore" to "Homo Americanus" (as he once referred to his American readers), it might as well have been him.[4]

Mukerji was something of an adjacent figure in the network of Indian activists in the United States discussed thus far. While his name appeared in military intelligence reports as a person of interest, he was not directly involved in either the India Home Rule League, the Gadar Party, or the Friends of Freedom for India. As Daniel Elam has argued, Mukerji was a "middlebrow" anticolonialist, publishing in venues accessible to an American audience whose interest in the region was formed by mild curiosity rather than any lasting political or ideological investments.[5] Whereas figures like Rai and Smedley had published in progressive and radical newspapers, Mukerji's writing found a home in the lite Orientalist fare of *Asia* magazine and youth magazines such as *Boys' Life* and *American Boy*, where he often placed his juvenile fiction.

By the end of his brief but prolific career, Mukerji would publish just short of thirty books, an eclectic catalog that included works of poetry, drama, fiction, travel books, children's literature, religious commentary, and at least one guide to meditation. But it was as a children's writer that Mukerji found his audience and acclaim. In 1927, he was awarded the prestigious Newbery medal for his children's novel *Gay-Neck, the Story of a Pigeon*, a work that remains in print today.[6] As Elizabeth Seeger wrote in a eulogy after his untimely death in 1936, "American children [. . .] found in Dhan Gopal Mukerji an interpreter after their own hearts. [. . .] Though he spoke to hundreds of adult audiences . . . he gave his best to children."[7] While his career was cut tragically short when he took his own life at the age of forty-six, by the late 1920s Mukerji had become arguably one of the most well-known Anglophone Indian writers in the world, certainly the most famous in the United States.

That distinction came in part from the relatively little that Americans knew about Indian writing in the first decades of the twentieth century. While they may have come across Tagore's poetry or some works of Orientalist scholarship, American readers were more likely to know the stories of Kipling. "Kipling's India," Harold Isaacs once explained, was "part of the mental baggage carried about by a great many Americans of youthful maturity or older."[8] In his 1918 travelogue *America through Hindu Eyes*, Indu Bhushan De Majumdar recalled the regularity with which he was asked about Kipling. Even Lajpat Rai himself noted in *USAHIS* that "Americans in general know very little [of India]; perhaps not more than what they read in Kipling's books."[9] When he first entered the American literary scene, Mukerji was well aware of this, and attempted to loosen the powerful grip that Kipling had on American imaginaries of India. In the opening pages of his 1923 memoir *Caste and Outcast*, in fact, Mukerji begins with a note on Kipling, drawing a distinction between "the point of view of the most humble Hindu" and Kipling, "a brilliant painter of Indian life."[10] He writes:

> I use the word painter advisedly, for everything that the eye alone can take in, that Mr. Kipling not only sees but completely conveys. No one, however, except a Hindu, to whom the religion of his coun-

try is more real than all its material aspects put together, can understand Indian life from within. But here is the dilemma—to convey this in a manner consistent with the western idea of what a book ought to be. I fear it is impossible.[11]

To see India as Kipling posed one kind of a problem. Like a painting, Kipling's India was crafted with exacting detail, drawing in everything the "eye alone [could] take in." But also like a painting, it could only ever capture surfaces. This was arguably a bit of salesmanship; for Mukerji to call Kipling's India a "brilliant" yet superficial representation conveniently placed himself in the position of the authentic, native interlocutor. He often referred to Kipling in books and lectures as shorthand for a set of stereotypical representations of India that had become familiar to American readers. From the outset of his career, Mukerji presented lectures on "The Truth about Kipling's India," contrasting Kipling with figures like Gandhi and Tagore (as he did in Brooklyn), pitting the colonial writer against the native subject.[12] Critics such as Rimi Chatterjee have gone further, arguing that revising Kipling's fiction was a key facet of the critical work that Mukerji undertook throughout his career.[13] The goal, it seemed, was to show American audiences another India than the one which they had become accustomed to reading about. As he once told a crowd in Nashville in his characteristically circuitous style, "What you do see in Kipling's India is nothing compared to what you do not see in India."[14] There were elements of India, in other words, that were imperceptible to the foreign eye—even for an Anglo-Indian like Kipling.

Indeed, Mukerji's literary project attempted not only to present American readers with a different India than Kipling's, but to demonstrate how their access to India was always mediated by their Orientalist ways of seeing, which were encoded in Western literary genres. In his rebuke of Kipling in *Caste and Outcast*, for instance, Mukerji openly admits the limitations of literary form. To convey Indian life "from within" was made difficult, if not impossible, when relegated to the "western idea of what a book ought to be."[15] As a result, Mukerji was especially promiscuous with genres, constantly experimenting with aesthetic forms and conventions. Some of this was due to the marketing constraints imposed by his publisher E. P. Dutton, which stipulated that he write two "juvenile books" for each "adult book." But even beyond the categories of "adult" and "juvenile" writing, Mukerji often transgressed generic boundaries: memoirs read like travelogues,[16] travelogues contained fictitious characters, and his children's books, filled with fables gleaned from his childhood in Bengal, included state-of-the-world pronouncements about postwar society.

Instead of presenting India as a site that American readers could access unencumbered, Mukerji developed strategies of disruption—a key facet in the practice of transnational refraction—that made it clear that theirs was a translated and mediated experience. In other words, Mukerji did not simply replace one representation with another, but he demonstrated that his readers' ways of seeing were, in fact, distortions wrought from a colonial gaze. In this chapter, I consider this idea through three different types of writing from Mukerji's oeuvre: first, Mukerji's autobiographical text, *Caste and Outcast* (1923), in which he intervened in a discourse that was accreting around the "Hindu" in America; second, his travelogue *Visit India with Me* (1929), which was less a travel book geared for American audiences that his publisher insisted it was, and more a text that critiqued American Orientalist ways of seeing India; third, Mukerji's children's writing, in which he directly countered Kipling's tales of "imperial boyhood" to imagine a child whose relationship to India—and to the rest of the colonized world—stood outside of the colonial relationship implicit in Kipling's work. As the chapter unfolds and examines these three sites in Mukerji's extensive body of writing, we pay attention to the constraints on his literary and political project, constraints that were the product of Mukerji's own upper-caste Hindu background as well as those placed on him as he sought a readership in the United States.

"The Militarism of Nirvana"

In 1910, a twenty-year-old Mukerji arrived on the West Coast of the United States. As Gordon Chang notes, Mukerji shared two very different stories about his motivations to come to America. One, recounted in his memoir *Caste and Outcast*, described a familiar route by which young upper-class Indians migrated to the United States for higher education.[17] Mukerji had traveled to Japan to study textile engineering in an effort to "learn Western scientific methods of production," but disenchanted by the rigors of industrial life, he quit.[18] Before embarking on his return voyage to India, however, Mukerji met a fellow Indian expatriate, who spent time in the United States and painted "an Arabian Nights' picture" of America.[19] Drawn by the promise of opportunities abroad, Mukerji paid for the low-cost steerage passage on a transpacific steamship, and after a seventeen-day journey arrived in San Francisco in 1910.

The other, far more dramatic story involved his elder brother Jadu Gopal Mukherjee, a prominent Indian revolutionary who had been under the watch of the colonial government for organizing violent actions against the British in Bengal. In this version, Jadu was promised amnesty by the British in exchange for surrender. In an about-face, however, British authorities ordered his arrest and jailed him. Before being sent to prison, Jadu tipped off Dhan Gopal (then acting as a courier for his brother) about the betrayal and urged him to rally support abroad for the independence movement. "Mukerji escaped by diving into the Ganges River in Calcutta," Chang writes, and found "refuge aboard a Dutch ship, which happened to be bound for Japan."[20]

In Japan, Mukerji worked a series of odd jobs and inadvertently accrued a debt with a Japanese ship. To pay it off, he served as a contract laborer on board, eventually jumping ship in the United States and making his way to California.

Which rendition of this origin story is true is not entirely clear, although the former—shaped by the everyday realities of study and labor—was repeated more often, turning up in *Caste and Outcast* as well as in E. P. Dutton's publicity materials.[21] Read together, both tales of arrival combine elements that were common to South Asian pathways to North America at the time: as steerage passenger, contract laborer, student, and anticolonial revolutionary. As a document of early South Asian America, *Caste and Outcast* depicts the lives that were forged along these routes to the United States. When Mukerji navigates California as a young Indian immigrant in the country, he finds himself traversing a number of social worlds that were already being formed by Indian settlers, students, and radicals who had arrived in the decade prior to his arrival.

Mukerji describes his first days in the United States through a series of fish-out-of-water anecdotes, each illustrating the bemused reaction of Americans upon hearing his stilted Victorian English. When the luggage handler tosses his trunk down from the heights of the ship deck, Mukerji whimsically quotes Milton: "Him the Almighty Power hurled headlong flaming from the ethereal sky." The handler responds, "Cut it out! You're too fresh!"[22] The next morning, during breakfast at his boarding house, Mukerji asks for sugar, which the landlady reluctantly hands to him after "some fuss." He tells her, "This reduces the entire discussion to a *reductio ad absurdum*," to which the landlady responds, "My God, what's that?"[23] Soon after his arrival, Mukerji attends classes at Berkeley. Despite some initial enthusiasm, he is left "disgruntled" by the apathy of his fellow students who, he complains, are only "there to pass examinations and learn a vocation."[24] His "true" education comes outside of the classroom, when he falls in with a group of socialists, anarchists, and Wobblies with whom he discusses loftier questions about work and capitalism, the abolition of the state, the institution of marriage, and the nature of freedom. Alongside the American leftists, Mukerji finds himself in debates with Indian students and revolutionaries in San Francisco, Berkeley, Oakland, and Palo Alto.

Much like the debates that Marie Brown has with socialists and Indian revolutionaries in *Daughter of Earth*, the argument around anticolonialism in *Caste and Outcast* is presented as an open question rather than a rigid political doctrine. If anything, Mukerji expresses far more skepticism about the project of anticolonial nationalism than do the socialists in *Daughter of Earth*, who chasten Marie for subsuming the workers' revolution under the anticolonial struggle. At first, Mukerji describes the Indian students as zealous nationalists whose desire for a politically free India overshadows any question about what such freedom would putatively look like. His discussions with "the typical Indian revolutionist" are equally dismissive. "He wanted to cut the throat of every English official," Mukerji comments, challenging his comrade to consider how revolutionary violence may simply "supersede British massacres by our own."[25] If Indian revolutionaries found British conquest as violent and industrial development as a "soulless," "destructive" project, then Mukerji surmised that the revolutionary's critique was perhaps misplaced.[26] Was the issue imperialism or capitalism? How would "overcom[ing] imperialism by a nationalism just as crude and greedy" be the answer?[27] The Indian revolutionary scoffs at Mukerji, claiming that he talked like a "soulless Socialist" who was "tainted with a pro-Western bias."[28]

The only position that Mukerji considers seriously is voiced by a "recent arrival from India," whom he refers to as "Nanda." Nanda speaks of a master–slave dialectic, in which anticolonial nationalism provides a crucial step toward the West saving itself. He explains, "In order to give the spirituality of India to the modern barbarism of Europe [. . .] we [must] have a victorious India free from all foreign control."[29] Mukerji repeats this argument to his American socialist and anarchist friends, one of whom is receptive, at least on principle. The "most humiliated in this India–British transaction are the British," his comrade Frank explains. "They are damning their souls by exploiting a race in the name of British liberty."[30]

It was not as though Mukerji was unsympathetic to all forms of Indian anticolonialism. In an essay published in the *Modern Review*, Mukerji was quoted defending the revolutionaries from an Indian expatriate who warned would-be Indian students in the United States to steer clear and not be seduced by their cause.[31] Mukerji, then a first-year student at Berkeley, criticized the expatriate for his "charlatanry," punctuating his critique with yet another pithy quote from Milton: "To what pit thou seest, from what height fallen."[32]

In *Caste and Outcast*, Mukerji underplays his own intimate acquaintance with Indian revolutionaries residing and traveling through the Bay Area at the time. In California, Mukerji was immersed in a milieu that included several high-profile Indian expatriate nationalists, many of whom he had been acquainted with through his brother, Jadu Gopal. One friend, known then as Naren Bhattacharya, described how Dhan Gopal had welcomed him to California, and encouraged him to "wipe out the past and begin as a new man."[33] Bhattacharya was reborn as M. N. Roy at Stanford University that same evening. Dhan Gopal helped Roy make several introductions in the Bay Area, including with the Berkeley professor Arthur Upham Pope, who had been a longstanding sympathizer for the Indian cause. Years later, during a deposition at the Hindu–German conspiracy trial, Pope admitted to meeting Roy through Mukerji, who he described as "a very brilliant Hindu, and [. . .] clear of all this political mixup."[34] Even if not directly involved with the Gadar Party, Dhan Gopal continued to serve as a liaison, relaying messages between radicals. When Sailendranath Ghose (Smedley's collaborator with the FFI) arrived in the United States in 1917, he first stayed with Mukerji in California in order to be put in touch with Roy.[35] British intelligence officers kept Mukerji under their watch; in one memo, they named him as a possible subject to interrogate for more information on the Hindu radicals.[36]

While his brother Jadu Gopal and late cousin "Bagha" Jatin Mukerjee were both advocates for armed insurrection against the British, Dhan Gopal was sympathetic, while also skeptical about the aims of nationalist revolution, at least in writing. In letters to his close friend Jawaharlal Nehru, particularly those written in the late 1920s, Mukerji wrote favorably of the older guard of the Indian nationalist movement—he described Gandhi as a saint, subscribing to his strategies of "non-violent non-cooperation" and joked that if he had to choose between Jawaharlal or Motilal Nehru, he would "choose the old rooster" every time.[37] Mukerji also confessed that he bore none of Nehru's "love of Communism," doubting that socialism could succeed in India given its different conditions than "war-worn" Russia.[38]

The political debates in *Caste and Outcast*, however, published just over a decade after his arrival in the United States, focused on a more radical brand of anticolonial politics. Maia Ramnath has read the book as a "picaresque autobiography" that both allegorizes "debates within anarchist discourse" and "presents a microcosm of the Indian movement in that context."[39] Daniel Elam, on the other hand, has described the book's blurring of genres as a form of autobiography that "flirt[s] with the boundaries of the travelogue." This hybrid genre suggests a larger poetics of anticolonialism, in which Mukerji not only presents "the Indian movement" but also the movement of Indians through "errant" routes carved out by empire. *Caste and Outcast* offers a different type of cosmopolitanism for Elam, who writes that Mukerji's is "a cosmopolitanism rooted in the shared injustices of racism and colonialism, and it remains determinedly rooted to those injustices and histories even as it proposes a new civilization to U.S. audiences."[40] Elam's emphasis on form provides a critical way of articulating the subdued anticolonial politics of *Caste and Outcast*, reading against what, at times, appear as Mukerji's explicit disavowal of the expatriate nationalists and their agenda.

A different type of reading opens up entirely when considering the stakes of representation for Indians in postwar America. Either by coincidence or by design, *Caste and Outcast* proved to be an extremely timely book. Its publication in 1923 came the same year as the catastrophic *US v. Bhagat Singh Thind* Supreme Court decision, which effectively prohibited Indians from the right to naturalization. This decision, along with the Immigration Act of 1924 one year later, cemented a nearly quarter-century period of exclusion during which legal immigration from India came to a standstill and

Indian immigrants lost their rights to citizenship. These immigration laws also acutely impacted Mukerji and his wife, Ethel Ray Dugan, whom he had met at Stanford.[41]

The *Thind* case rested on the racial classification of Bhagat Singh Thind, a Sikh Punjabi migrant who had enlisted in the U.S. Army during the First World War and was granted, then subsequently stripped of, citizenship. Using simultaneously racist and casteist logic, Thind had argued his case on the basis that as a "high caste Hindu," he was by definition Caucasian and thereby eligible for naturalization based on the racial prerequisites for American citizenship.[42] The Supreme Court ruled against him. By "white persons," the court argued, the original framers of the law had never intended that citizenship be extended to "people of primarily Asiatic stock." In the decision, Justice George Sutherland argued that "the words 'free white persons' are words of common speech, to be interpreted in accordance with the understanding of the common man." Thind was invariably not white and invariably, not American. "Hindus [are] Too Brunette to Vote," one headline read— and that, according to the court, was a matter of common sense.[43]

Even before the *Thind* decision, dominant images of Indians in the United States had clustered around two prevalent narratives about the "Hindu" as a threat to American society, producing its own form of racial common sense. First was the fomenting discourse that positioned migrant Indian workers as a scourge of cheap labor, much in the same way that the "Yellow Peril" image stoked paranoid fears among white workers in the late nineteenth century. Headlines warning of a "Dusky Peril," a "Tide of Turbans," and "Hindu Invasion" contributed to the widespread fear of Indian labor as a racial threat that would undermine white settler livelihoods along the Pacific Coast. Second was the characterization of "Hindus" as part of a "Heathen Invasion," as one journal put it, which centered on popular images from films and newspaper scandals about mystics, yogis, fakirs, Vedantists, and the occasional con artist.[44] Both the "Dusky Peril" and "Heathen Invasion" narratives indexed different types of fears, to be sure. But together they spoke to a broader social fear around the Indian presence in the United States, which dovetailed into gendered and sexualized anxieties of cross-racial mixture and miscegenation. *Caste and Outcast* intervened in these discourses insofar as they presented Mukerji's own entanglement in them. Yet Mukerji's focus was not so much about presenting a respectable counter-image as it was about underscoring the way in which American perspectives were clouded by a gaze that prevented them from actually knowing the Indian.

In a chapter titled "California Fields," for example, Mukerji described summers spent working on asparagus and celery farms alongside teams of "Hindu" and Muslim agricultural laborers.[45] While Mukerji at times paints a sympathetic picture of the workers, he also reinforces the attitude that Asians posed an economic threat to white labor. The result was an ambivalent and at times negative portrait. On the one hand, Mukerji describes his initial "disgust" for their seemingly excessive "love of work": "They worked longer hours than any other laborer would dream of working, and it was no wonder the American union laborer wanted to exclude them."[46] On the other hand, Mukerji also explains how working conditions were responsible for the laborers' state of abjection: "Soon I came to see that my countrymen, who had few vices at home, with six months of this kind of work had been reduced to such a condition that they were drinking up their wages in order to forget they were alive."[47] His description of Muslim laborers, in particular, were even more unfavorable. As Rimi Chatterjee points out, Mukerji presented several disparaging illustrations of Muslims, which mobilized colonial and Hindu communal fears of Muslims as especially oppressive to women and habitually prone to violence.[48]

That these kind of sentiments came from a member of the Indian student community is not entirely surprising. Mukerji hailed from neither the same class nor region of the Punjabi migrants who had taken up such forms of labor. In contrast to Mukerji's fluent English, the agricultural workers spoke very little English, and unlike his political pedigree and years of colonial education, many had served as rank-and-file soldiers of the colonial army. In essays published by Bengali American students such as Girindra Mukerji and Sarangadhar Das, agricultural workers were often depicted as the students' pitiable and uneducated others, whose lives were spent in deplorable working conditions wrought by U.S. and Canadian capitalist interests. Girindra Mukerji described the negative perception of the Indian laboring element for whom "the better class of the Hindus blushed for shame."[49] Sarangadhar Das, on the other hand, suggested that the xenophobia and racism that the workers faced was partially due to their own steadfast refusal to assimilate. If they would just rid themselves of their turbans, Das opined, then "no one could distinguish them from Southern Americans or Southern Europeans."[50] As Balbir Singh has argued, Das's commentary betrayed a common assimilationist narrative, which urged the erasure of all possible markers of racial and religious difference as a means to fully integrate into society.[51] These writers often cited the "racial" bond between the Hindu and the American Caucasian, based off their perceived shared ancestry as "Aryan." The "blind religious fanaticism" of the laboring class was perceived as a particular obstacle preventing the acceptance of Indian migrants in American society as racial kin. In contrast, Indian students (Chapter 1) were described as having rid themselves of the caste prejudice and religious distinctions that had been so salient back home, marking them as model subjects for citizenship.

Dhan Gopal Mukerji was not immune from describing the laboring class of Indian émigrés in such condescending ways. Yet, read from another perspective, the episodes with the laborers also serve to foreground the divide that occurs across language. This divide reverses the power dynamic between the English-speaking, white, American reader and the Indian migrant, placing the former in the position of ignorance and vulnerability. In an episode with Salvation Army missionaries, for instance, Mukerji gives the laborers the upper hand in a comic exchange of translations. When Mukerji tries to explain who the Salvation Army men were, he translates, "They represent the Militarism of Nirvana."[52] The workers burst into laughter. When he tries to explain that the men promise that "Bibi Miriam's Son" will wipe away their sins, one laborer replies, "Why does he look for other people's sins like a rat looking for holes?"[53] In another episode with the Muslim laborers, mistranslation is characterized as a tactic of worker resistance. When the Muslim bookkeeper, who kept track of the number of laborers, speaks to the overseer, he makes sure his words are deliberately misinterpreted in order to grant the workers a higher wage. "Whenever the bookkeeper said thirty," Mukerji writes, "the overseer translated thirty into forty. The bookkeeper would then make a profound bow as if the overseer's word were law."[54] One might argue that Mukerji uses this scene to criticize the bookkeeper's hypocrisy, who is forbidden by religion from lying but nevertheless refuses to correct the overseer. But these episodes also reinforce a broader theme in Mukerji's writing, which emphasized the linguistic and cultural gap that prevented white Americans from fully knowing the Indian migrant.

Whereas the Indian migrant laborer posed one kind of threat to American society, the Hindu "holy man" presented another. A 1912 Washington Post article put it succinctly: "The Hindu as a factor in the labor problem has so far not troubled the eastern United States. . . . The Hindu problem of the East lies in the presence of the swamis, or teachers, educated and able men, who with their swarthy faces and dreamy-looking eyes stand in themselves symbolic of the mystery of the Orient."[55] As Kirin Narayan explains, the "Hindu holy man," from the late nineteenth century onward, had become a well-traveled stereotype in American media, appearing in magazines such as National Geographic, in colonial-era postcards, and silent films such as Thomas Edison's 1902 short titled Hindoo Fakir. Through such representations, the Hindu male body, Narayan argues, "became a site in which cultural difference was first derisively emphasized and then commodified for entertainment."[56] Mass-culture American Orientalism had helped promulgate the image of the Hindu as a mystic and magician, a fraud and fakir, appearing in popular songs such as "Hindu Man" (1921) and "Hindu Moon" (1922).[57] Coinciding with the commoditization of the "Hindu body" was an increased interest, among middle class Americans especially, in the occult and spiritualism, which was either advertised as or confused with Hindu practices such as hatha yoga. Such interests gave way to a series of sensationalized stories, describing white American women falling prey to Indian spiritualists. Pierre Bernard, who dubbed himself "The Omnipotent Oom," was an

FIGURE 3.1 "American Women Victims of Hindu Mysticism," *Vancouver World*, Second Section (February 24, 1912), 6.

Iowa-born hatha yoga practitioner in the United States who made headlines after he was accused of attempting to kidnap and sexually molest two teenage women who had joined his institute. Rustom Rustomjee, the colonial apologist introduced in Chapter 1, warned a crowd of Congregational ministers at Boston's Pilgrim Hall in 1913 that "American women who become interested in the so-called Hindu religions that handsome young Swami fakirs bring to the country are in danger of the lunatic asylum." He added that he had once assisted the police in raiding one of these fakir's "sacred rites" gathering, where members "drank wine from skulls in an orgy that shocked even the [NYPD]."[58] A less salacious but more prominent case involved Sarah Bull, a student of Swami Vivekananda who, in her will, had left her entire estate to the Vivekananda's Vedanta Society. News of this case led to a series of panicked headlines across the country. *The Washington Post* reported "American Women Victims of Hindu Mysticism,"[59] and the *Hampton Columbian Magazine* took out a twelve-page cover story warning of American women losing "their fortunes and reason" to heathen Hindu priests (Figure 3.1).[60] By the 1910s, the trope of the Asian man preying upon "vulnerable" white women had become commonplace in Hollywood productions such as Cecil B. DeMille's *The Cheat* (1915) and Robert Leonard's *The Love Girl* (1916). These stories exacerbated the public's anxiety over the interracial mixture of Asian men and white women. As Philip Deslippe has shown, even the mere association with yoga was enough cause to impeach an Oklahoma governor in the late 1920s.[61]

Caste and Outcast tends to such anxieties in a chapter titled "Spiritualism," which captured the middle-class fascination with India as a space of occult "Eastern wisdom."[62] In the chapter, Mukerji describes his encounters with a Bay Area socialite who offers him free lodging in exchange for one strange request. Every day, Mukerji would be summoned to the parlor room to wear a turban and "Hindu robe" and sit quietly for an hour.[63] Unbeknownst to him, the woman and a coterie of Berkeley socialites had been conducting evening séances, and Mukerji's "Oriental" presence was intended to lend authenticity to the spectacle. Mukerji soon realizes this, after his landlord lets slip that she assumed he was a "spiritualist."

> In amazement, I exclaimed, "What the devil are they doing in this house?" [. . .]
> The woman said, "Why, we materialize the spirits here and ask for messages."
> I said, "You don't mean to tell me you are a spiritualist?"
> "Of course," she said. "Aren't you one?"
> "I don't think I am," I answered.
> "Every Hindu is one," she insisted. "Spiritualism comes from India."
> "How do you know it comes from India? I have never seen it there," I declared, "except among very questionable people."
> She said, "But in America they are very respectable people, people like myself."
> "Are you sure you are respectable?" I asked her.[64]

For the cost of a month's lodging, Mukerji inhabits the body of the commoditized Hindu "holy man" and is reduced to a prop on an Orientalist set piece. The woman's instructions, to stand quietly or to play along if someone asks him a question, further objectifies him. Only when Mukerji begins to respond does he disrupt that discourse, challenging the woman's assertions with matter-of-fact responses about India. While the woman "insist[s]" that Spiritualism comes from India, Mukerji responds by drawing on experience ("I have never seen it there.") In doing so, he pokes fun at the naïveté of the spiritualist crowd while undermining the common trope of the Indian spiritualist predator preying upon vulnerable white women. If anyone was being taken advantage of, it was Mukerji, whose poverty forces him to succumb to the racist visions of the Berkeley middle class.

Mukerji unsettles the discourses that defined the "Hindu" in America, either by subverting the paranoia that surrounded the spiritualist craze or by exposing the actual conditions of Indian labor. The spiritualists and the Salvation Army missionaries both project a series of meanings onto the Indian body. For the spiritualist, Mukerji's body is the object of Orientalist desires that imagine an alternative to rational modernity, regardless of whether it was a real or fabricated "Indian" religious practice. For the Salvation Army missionaries, Mukerji and his laboring compatriots are the object of paternal compassion and religious condescension. In these two examples, *Caste and Outcast* undermines such narratives, by illustrating how little American readers—including those reading the book—actually knew about the Indians around them.

This motif continued to appear in Mukerji's nonfiction, which like *Caste and Outcast* often combined elements of autobiography with travelogue.[65] In Chapter 1, I discussed how Indian expatriates, such as Lajpat Rai, had adapted the travel narrative to describe the lives of Indian migrants and students in the United States. Such narratives altered the common directionality of the Euro-American travelogue, making visible the encumbered imperial routes of the colonized subject. Mukerji's travelogues did the opposite, taking his American readers on journeys into contemporary India. *Visit India with Me* (1929), a book that was marketed by publisher E. P. Dutton as a guidebook, was the most obvious example of this genre. But even a book such as *My Brother's Face* (1924), which partially narrates the life of Mukerji's revolutionary brother Jadu Gopal, contained elements of travelogue, presenting to his American readership a contemporary India that was agitating for freedom.

My Brother's Face (1924) begins by explaining the reason for Mukerji's homecoming trip to India after spending nearly twelve years in America. During a lecture at the New York Town Hall, Mukerji experiences something between an epiphany and a nervous breakdown; he "looked into the faces of [his] audience" and discovered himself "a man without a message."[66] This crisis of confidence may have been an element of fiction to frame the book, or very well may have been based in Mukerji's experiences as a struggling writer. Mukerji was a frequent and often unhappy lecturer, who regularly traveled across middle America to supplement his book sales. The grueling schedule took a personal toll on his physical and psychological health. In one letter addressed to his publisher John Macrae, Mukerji complained about the work: "This lecture tour is a damnable business. I wish my body could stand it. When will you sell books enough in order to keep me from lecturing for a living? Do work it out if you want to keep a decent author alive."[67]

My Brother's Face soon turns its attention away from Mukerji's psychological ailments, and looks toward his voyage to India alongside a group of sojourners from Europe and the United States:

The ship I took was a small vessel filled with tradesman and pleasure-seekers going to India, whose conversation revolved around what to see in the shortest time, what to buy, and how to uphold the dignity of the Nordic race. Fortunately, among them were one scholar and some missionaries who spoke of other things.[68]

In the first few pages, Mukerji patiently eavesdrops, biting his tongue as he relays the strange argument that unfolds between "the Tradesman," "the Missionary," "the Pleasure-Seeker," and "The Scholar," each name indexing a different type that travels to India and cumulatively representing a "miniature" of the Occident.[69] The archetypal names recall the opening passage in Joseph Conrad's *Heart of Darkness*, as the protagonist Marlow sits with the Lawyer, the Accountant, and the Director on a ship on the Thames, reflecting on England's precolonial past and his voyage through the Congo. In *My Brother's Face,* however, the band of travelers reflects on British India instead of the Belgian Congo, and Mukerji illustrates how their understanding of India is, in effect, a projection of their own desires. The belligerent Tradesman, "the dominating figure of the West," describes the Orient as a "country of slaves" and further complains about how the "Orientals" will soon be demanding equality with the "white man."[70] "Where will the white man be then?" the Tradesman quips.[71] The Scholar is presented as a man with a broader sense of history; he objects to the Tradesman's racist comments with patient responses, pointing out that "there were other races who [. . .] ruled the world in their time."[72] Nevertheless, he also condescends to Mukerji, displaying his own form of Western arrogance. After hearing Mukerji quote from the *Rig Veda*, for instance, the Scholar responds, "I don't like your translation."[73] In spite of his protests, the Scholar still finds Mukerji an able conversationalist, and asks him, "Can you tell me whether all India has accepted the theory that an Italian adventurer built the Taj Mahal?"[74] Mukerji responds firmly to the Scholar's Eurocentric conjecture, advising him "to read what Indian art critics and archaeologists think about their own works of art!" From Scholar to Tradesman, Missionary to Pleasure-Seeker, each of these figures represent one facet of what Mukerji describes as the "Occidental's write-up of the Orient."[75]

This is a curious opening for a book that is ostensibly about Mukerji's attempt to "find a message" after his breakdown, and one that purports to tell the story of his revolutionary brother. Yet it is also consistent with the goals of Mukerji's literary project, which pointed to the mediations and gaze that structured American perceptions of India. That same strategy appears in his travel book *Visit India with Me* (1929), which traces his journey through an itinerary of sites in India alongside an American colleague with an almost absurdly American last name. His travel partner, John Edgar Eagles, we come to learn, had trained as a Sanskritist but abandoned a future in academics to pursue a thirty-year career in "making money."[76] Recently retired, Eagles enlists Mukerji as his translator and guide, as he finally pursues his dream of traveling to India or the "wisdom land," as Eagles calls it. Mukerji promises to show Eagles—and metonymically, his American audience—another India from the one Eagles had read about in books by Max Müller, John Freeman Clarke, and Rudyard Kipling.[77] *Visit India* would be Eagles's guide (and by extension, his readers' guide) into a contemporary India from the authentic perspective of a "Hindu."[78] As indicated in his book contract, *Visit India with Me* was meant to be a "guide-book to India," replete with half-tone photographs chosen by Mukerji himself.[79] It was to include Mukerji's commentary about Indian history and art, as well as first-person accounts of famous sites and cities of the subcontinent. The primary audience was not "sociological students," publisher John Macrae reminded Mukerji, but rather "people from the English speaking countries who were planning to travel in India and see the glories of the country."[80] Macrae had also suggested that Mukerji cut the statistical footnotes in the initial drafts, for fear of "antagoniz[ing]" his readers.[81] In a private letter, Mukerji confessed to Nehru that his hopes for the book were modest, to simply "do some good to Homo Americanus by giving him accurate information about India."[82]

When *Visit India with Me* turns to the political climate in the colony, with agitations from the Indian nationalist movement exploding across cities across the subcontinent, Mukerji steps aside and allows Eagles to become the narrator. In one chapter, we learn that the two arrive in Calcutta—Mukerji's self-described "detestable home town"—at the very same time that an Indian National Congress meeting was taking place. Instead of commenting directly, Mukerji defers to the voice of Eagles, telling his readers, "I think it would be well to see this tremendous gathering through his eyes."[83] A long quotation follows, from a letter Eagles has sent to his brother. Eagles describes the scene dramatically, with the independent faction of the Congress rallying behind the cause of "complete separation from the British Empire."[84] Just as the crowd erupts into a mob, with Eagles commenting that "he expected they were all going out in a few minutes to blow up the British Empire," Gandhi appears, "harmless as a dove," "wily as a serpent," and more "foxy" than Henry VIII.[85] Elsewhere, Eagles insists on meeting Mukerji's brother Jadu Gopal. Mukerji advises against it, warning Eagles that his brother had turned bitter after his "unwarranted arrest and complete incarceration for four years."[86] When Eagles eventually does meet Jadu Gopal the narrative perspective once again shifts to Eagles, who describes his encounter in a letter to his wife. Jadu Gopal tells Eagles of the effects of British rule, from uneven development to the brutal repression of activists, and repeats the need to free India from colonization. The British, Jadu Gopal tells Eagles, "desire to protect their Indian Empire. We, like the Ganges in flood, seek to wash the Empire clean."[87]

We will return to *Visit India with Me*, in a later chapter, to consider the way that the book also served as an important response to Katherine Mayo's wildly popular exposé *Mother India* in 1927. But for now, it is useful to note how Mukerji consistently deferred an anticolonial voice, avoiding a direct polemical tone and allowing his American partner to experience and convey arguments for him. Mukerji claims that he has "never capitalized England's unjust treatment of [his] people," instead attempting to protect his readers from the harsh realities of colonial rule.[88] The reader comes across the Indian present, with the various factions of nationalism—from the claims of Sreenivasa Iyengar, Jadu Gopal Mukherjee, and Gandhi—as though eavesdropping on a private conversation between Eagles and his family.

When it came to pointing out the Eurocentricity that structured American ways of seeing India, Mukerji was quick to call out his travel partner. Early on, as the two make their way east, Mukerji encourages his friend to "divest your mind of all the American preconceptions" and urges him to "see the East without Western sentimentality."[89] Eagles, however, disregards his friends' warnings, often to comic effect. In Egypt, Eagles is confronted by a beggar, and before Mukerji can "intercept," his partner gives a "dollar bill to the rascal."[90] In Ellora, when the two are invited to visit the Nizam of Hyderabad, Eagles's mind quickly turns to a series of clichés of Oriental splendor, at which point Mukerji tempers his friends' enthusiasm. "My dear sir," Mukerji tells him, "there will be no amber and amethyst walls, no peacocks decorating the housetops, nor elephants on plots of gold [. . .] You may be entertained with the comforts of a second-class American hotel there. That is all that the Nizam can do for you."[91] Eagles embodies a liberal American gaze, expecting Oriental splendor, cautiously receptive to the anticolonial argument, and disenchanted by the materialism of American society. He is the "Pleasure-Seeker" of *My Brother's Face*, quick to contest the more brutish perspective of the capitalist Tradesman, but still guided by Orientalist fantasies of an East that is fixed in time and readily available for personal spiritual renewal. In Eagles, Mukerji finds a voice for the archetypal American, through which he could affect American perspectives and assumptions about India. Eagles was also, if it was not always obvious to its readers, a totally fictitious character. As Mukerji writes, in an easily passed-over "note of warning" that precedes the title page: "In order to give the guidebook a human interest I have invented an American gentleman through whose eyes we see everything."[92]

The reviews for *Visit India with Me* were ambivalent about Mukerji's fictional device. John Clair Minot of the *San Francisco Chronicle* noted that "there is genius in the indirection of it all. [. . .] [Mukerji] takes us on a leisurely tour of India, a journey that not only leads us to all the places of importance and interest, but also allows us to go intimately behind the scenes. He does it by serving as guide for an imaginary American, Mr. Eagles."[93] Another critic described the purpose of the book as serving as a guide to "contemporary life" in India and to major works of Indian art, which would "enable [American readers] to perceive in them the same symbolism as the

Hindu does." This was done through the "manufactured Mr. Eagles . . . through whose eyes the reader sees the point of interest."[94] Mary Gould Ogilvie of the *Tulsa Daily World,* called the book a "soft answer" to Katherine Mayo that challenged the "American belief in the beneficence of British civilization and 'white race egotism.'"[95] Not all reviewers were so enamored with the fabricated Eagles character. The *Los Angeles Times* reviewer described Eagles as an "admirable 'yes man.'"[96] The *Argonaut* deemed Eagles "interesting but impossible" and that "Mukerji could have made a better book had he allowed his readers to see his India through his own eyes."[97]

As the reviewers all note, the Eagles persona provided Mukerji's American readers with a cultural touchstone, a point of reference through which they could connect with the otherwise foreign and indecipherable world of Indian art, culture, and life. For Mukerji, this had a few different consequences: It was a way to represent the Indian nationalist movement while also maintaining a position of political disinterestedness and objectiveness. It is significant, for instance, that most of the arguments against British rule in *Visit* were voiced through a fictitious epistolary dialogue between Eagles, his American wife, and his brother. But more crucially, Mukerji's construction of Eagles allowed him to clearly lay out his conception of the liberal American gaze. Even book reviewers seemed to pick up on this, by the sheer number of times they emphasize vision, ways of seeing, and points of view. Mukerji's strategy brings to mind the intervention of Mary Louise Pratt's foundational study on travel writing, *Imperial Eyes* (1992), which underscores the ideological power embedded in the travelogue and its historic role in empire-building. Pratt writes that the travel book, from its inception in the eighteenth century onward, has been "a key instrument . . . in creating the 'domestic subject' of empire," in effect producing "the rest of the world" at key junctures of European expansion.[98] In her centuries-spanning study, Pratt also describes the generic protagonist of these books, who she dubs the "seeing-man," as the "white male subject of European landscape discourse— he whose imperial eyes passively look out and possess."[99]

John Edgar Eagles serves as a version of the disembodied "white male subject" of the travel book, although Mukerji thoroughly embeds him within in a social context. By including Eagles as a character in constant dialogue with Mukerji's narrative voice, he gestures toward the familiar figure of the "seeing-man" but also presents his American way of seeing as short-sighted and frequently comical. That gaze was, as one reviewer remarked, the product of "white race egotism." It was also, even for the liberal Eagles, the product of old and obsolete sources of knowledge. In the opening pages of *Visit India with Me,* recall that Mukerji describes how Eagles's ideas about India were derived from only a few scant sources, including Max Müller's *India— What Can It Teach Us* (1883) and Rudyard Kipling's *Kim* (1901).[100] When Mukerji warns Eagles that he need not go to India, because "Max Müller's

India is the eternal reality which you don't need to go anywhere to find," he intimates that Müller's was an abstracted India, fixed in time, captured in "sacred texts" but also not reflected in modern India.[101] Mukerji himself shared certain traits with Müller, who also reinforced the India as a symbolic antithesis to Western modernity. But Kipling's India, for Mukerji, would prove to be a far greater problem with which he continued to engage and challenge throughout his career.

Kipling's India

What exactly was "Kipling's India"? To answer that, we return to the striking passage that begins Mukerji's memoir *Caste and Outcast*. In the book's opening pages, Mukerji refers to the difficulty of the task that lies ahead of him, while invoking Kipling as a point of comparison.

> Indian life cannot be understood with even moderate justice if its constant background of religious thought remain unrealized. That is the difference between the point of view of the most humble Hindu and such a brilliant painter of Indian life as Mr. Kipling. I use the word painter advisedly, for everything that the eye alone can take in, that Mr. Kipling not only sees but completely conveys. No one, however, except a Hindu, to whom the religion of his country is more real than all its material aspects put together, can understand Indian life from within. But here is the dilemma—to convey this in a manner consistent with the western idea of what a book ought to be. I fear it is impossible.[102]

There is something at once exceedingly humble and boastful about this statement. Mukerji apologizes to his American readers in advance, explaining the difficulty in conveying the "real meaning" of the events in his childhood without a "continual" series of editorial interruptions. At the same time, he makes a claim about authority, reminding his audience that only a Hindu such as himself (or, for that matter, even "the most humble Hindu") could express the realities of India, a privilege that does not, and by definition could not, extend to Kipling. (Presumably, it is also a privilege that could not extend to Sikhs or Muslims, revealing Mukerji's investments in Hindu majoritarian ideology). The problem was not that Kipling's India was an ersatz one; it was that Kipling's India could only ever be a painting: magnificently detailed, brilliant, and ornate, but nevertheless, static and superficial—the work of a European "eye." Years later, a similarly worded critique was lodged even more forcefully against right-wing journalist Katherine Mayo, whose book *Mother India* presented a damning critique of the social evils of India to undermine the demands of the anticolonial movement.

Mukerji claimed he was reluctant to read *Mother India* because it was the work of the typical tourist, who "never touch[es] the depths and enjoy[s] exploiting the surfaces."[103] While Mayo had access to "facts," she was unable to make sense of "the truth about India." Mukerji explains, "There are realities there which Miss Mayo's racial myopia makes it impossible for her to see."[104] As dissimilar as Mayo was to Kipling, Mukerji insisted that both writers were unable to see beyond surfaces; their "racial myopia" prevented them from reformulating these close-up details into a picture that tells the whole story. Mukerji's critique directly countered Kipling's own imperial hubris, which, as Kris Manjapra argues, was built on a Victorian worldview that claimed "universal knowledge of the world."[105] Hence, Kipling could write, with complete confidence, that "one of the few advantages that India has over England is a great Knowability."[106]

Kipling figured frequently in Mukerji's writing, even from his earliest publications. When he lectured across the country in the late 1910s and early 1920s, Mukerji used "Kipling's India" as shorthand for a preconceived idea of India, one that had increasingly grown out-of-date. In Joliet, Illinois, he lectured on "The Truth about Kipling's India," yet in much of the lecture he described the sweep of modernization across India that rendered books such as *Kim* as quaint reminders of a long-lost era. "You must read Kipling's India. He paints wonderful pictures of the earlier India," he told his audience, adding an ever so slight critique of Kipling's datedness: "There is nothing like that now."[107] Years later, in Bronxville, New York, Mukerji updated the lecture, presenting on "The India of Kipling [and] the India of Gandhi." "At the outset," *The Bronxville Review* reported, "the lecturer referred to the fact that the impression which the Occident for the past quarter of a century has had of India was that which Rudyard Kipling portrayed in his many writings on India, and especially in his widely known work 'Kim.'" This "India of Kipling belonged to a bygone generation," Mukerji argued; it was entirely different from the India of today, which had shaken Britain through the upheavals of the nationalist movement.[108]

The India of Kipling was the India of a bygone era. Mukerji reminded his American audience of this, time and again in his lecture and his books. Over time, that argument became more incisive. Kipling came to stand in for not only the Western gaze that could never fully "understand Indian life from within" or the quaint India before industrialization, but an arrogant view that fixed India into its past and still believed in the beneficence of imperial rule.[109] In *My Brother's Face* (1924), Mukerji cautioned "all Americans who read Kipling that if they goto (*sic*) India now they will find no longer the country that he wrote about thirty years ago. [. . .] Gandhism has taken away from us our last bit of faith in the virtue of the European, as well as our cherished belief in the permanence of our social institutions."[110] The datedness of Kipling now referred to a dated politics, which history had turned obsolete. Six years later, in *Disillusioned India* (1930), Mukerji was even more forthright: "Young India believes that [Britain] remains there because of her financial interests. Rudyard Kipling, on the other hand, places England in India to carry on the White Man's burden."[111]

As much as Mukerji disavowed Kipling's imperialist politics in his lectures and nonfiction, he could not fully escape Kipling's literary influence. In the field of juvenile literature, especially, Kipling cast a long shadow that often eclipsed Mukerji's work. For instance, there is no way around the fact that the titles in Mukerji's bibliography bear more than a passing resemblance to Kipling's books and stories. For Mukerji's *Kari the Elephant* (1922), his first children's book, there's Kipling's "Toomai of the Elephants" (1893). Mukerji's *Jungle Beasts and Men* (1923) obviously recalls *The Jungle Book* (1894) while *Hari, the Jungle Lad* (1924) makes nods to Mowgli, Kipling's famous feral Indian boy. Even Mukerji's lone adult novel *The Secret Listeners of the East* (1926) shares the same geography and Anglo-Russian intrigue of *Kim*. As Rimi Chatterjee puts it, Kipling served as an "intimate enemy" of Mukerji, a "pernicious model [he tried] to displace by means of his own fiction."[112] But what exactly was Mukerji trying to displace? Was this simply his attempt to claim a native authenticity that the Anglo-Indian Kipling could never fully embody? Was there an anticolonial politics behind the claim? Before delving into those questions, it is worth considering what exactly Mukerji was revising. What was the "truth about Kipling's India," which he promised to expose to American audiences? And for that matter, what did Kipling mean to American audiences?

Most discussions about Kipling's reception in the United States revolve around two small but significant details: The first is biographical, the second ideological. At the turn of the century, a twenty-something Kipling moved to the United States after marrying Caroline Balestier, an American woman from Brattleboro, Vermont. The two settled in a bungalow overlooking the Connecticut River that they named Naulakha (after its construction costs of "nine lakh" rupees). Between 1892 and 1896, they lived in their home in Vermont, and during this period Kipling began to pen many of the stories that were later compiled in *The Jungle Book* and also started work on *Kim*.[113] Kipling had initially taken kindly to the United States, once remarking that there were only two places he wanted to live: Bombay or Brattleboro. But he also wrote, with predictable British bemusement, about the crude manner of life in the United States. Some of these impressions were collected in *American Notes* (1899), which is filled with pages of observations, ranging from the American predilection for gun violence ("fifty per cent of the men in the public saloons carry pistols"), to the life of politics, to more baldly racist statements about "Negroes" and "Chinamen" in urban spaces such as San Francisco.[114] But behind those anecdotes, and in spite of his disdain, Kipling also wrote about American national identity, and not without some gentle digs: "A Hindoo is a Hindoo and a brother to the man who knows his vernacular. And a Frenchman is French because he speaks his own language. But the American has no language. He is dialect, slang, provincialism, accent, and so forth."[115] Such commentary presented a gibe about the derivative national and linguistic identity of America, but it nevertheless implied and reestablished the sense of kinship that connected the United States and Britain. America may very well have been "dialect," "slang," and "accent," but it decidedly shared a language with England. The United States, in other words, was a vernacular form of Britain.

Kipling mentioned the ties between Britain and the United States even more dramatically and memorably in his 1899 poem "The White Man's Burden." Originally published in *McClure's Magazine* with the subtitle "The United States and the Philippines," the poem was Kipling's call for America to finally accept its imperial destiny and carry the heavy burden of colonization alongside its ally Britain. The poem signaled not only the imperial mission shared by Britain and the United States, but that their commonality was forged through the racial kinship of Anglo-Saxon whiteness. As Gretchen Murphy notes, the poem had become extremely popular in the United States, and was followed by a sudden popularity in all things Kipling—a "Kipling boom," as one publication put it.[116] "The White Man's Burden" not only introduced a new generation of American writers to Kipling, but, as Judith Plotz observes, it became a timely example of Kipling's commitment to "an Anglo-American 'special relationship.'"[117]

Perhaps this was what Mukerji objected to—the interimperial Anglo-Saxon relationship promoted, as well as embodied, by Kipling. What drew the United States and Britain together, according to Kipling, was the shared inheritance of imperial destiny, the shared racial identity of whiteness, and, of course, the shared language of English. In drawing such strong ties between the United States and Britain, Kipling fostered an Anglo-American alliance. In contrast, Mukerji sought in his project the possibility of imagining a different kind of relationship between the United States and India, one not predicated on a colonial relationship or on shared racial lineage. Following Kipling's racial analogies, though, India's relationship with the United States could only ever be one of subordination, the Indian colony to the Anglo-American metropolitan center.

While useful, this simple calculus of racial and ideological partnerships and parallels also feels a little too tidy. What's more, criticizing Kipling's imperialist values was not particularly unique, even during his lifetime. Though a popular writer, Kipling had a fair share of detractors who lambasted him for everything, from his purple prose to his outright arrogance. One British critic dismissed Kipling as a "second-rate journalist," who trafficked in "superficiality, jingoism, and aggressive cocksureness," while another devoted an entire book-length study to Kipling's "hooliganism."[118] In the United States, several anti-imperialist writers parodied Kipling's "White Man's Burden," reversing the terms of the poem. One particularly poignant American critic wrote, "The trouble with the kind of White Man's Burden that Kipling talks about is that it really means the Brown Man's Burden."[119] The Indian journalist Saint Nihal Singh (Chapter 1), who resided in the United States in the first few decades of the twentieth century, followed suit, placing the "brown man's burden" onto Indians in the United States after the Bellingham riots of 1907.[120] As Seema Sohi explains, Singh "called on Indian migrants to take up the 'brown man's burden,' an expression of self-determination directed at both liberating India from British rule and challenging racial exclusion in North America."[121] Kipling's "Burden," then, served as a useful target, typifying the racial Anglo-American alliance based off of an idea of racial supremacy.

By the early part of the century, Kipling and his writing had produced some of the most dominant and ubiquitous representations of India that American readers had encountered. One Indian traveler who learned this firsthand was Indu Bhushan De Majumdar, a student who first came to the United States in 1906 to pursue a master's degree in agriculture. In his travel book *America through Hindu Eyes,* Majumdar described the popular misconceptions that Americans had of India. The average American, he explained, knows little about India other than images of "palmists, jugglers, and snake-charmers" and those produced by Kipling.[122] In one amusing episode from his account, Majumdar recalled a visit to New Haven, where he was repeatedly asked questions about Rudyard Kipling and his version of India. One graduate student approached him, asking, "Mr. De, in this country we know India mostly through Kipling. Have you read his *Kim*? [. . .] Tell me, Mr. De, is the story true to life?"[123] After describing Kipling's poem "The Naulakha," that same student inquired, "Do the people of India smoke opium much?"[124] Another student, upon seeing Majumdar, chimed in, reciting portions of Kipling's "Mandalay," before assaulting him with a barrage of questions: "Do the women of India smoke, Mr. De?" "Are the elephants used in India for piling timber?" "Do they use much garlic . . . ?" After another series of questions, all drawn from Kipling's shelf, the student seemed to suddenly become aware of the increasingly fantastical nature of his own inquiries. He asked Majumdar, "Tell me, Mr. De, are Kipling's pictures over-coloured?" The next day, reporters from the *New Haven Register,* who were following Majumdar during his visit, published a column on him with the byline: "Don't mention Kipling to him." "The mere mention of Kipling now," the article warned, "is sufficient to put Mr. De to full flight."[125]

Kipling's status as an authentic Indian writer was an issue that had already cropped up in American literary circles by the time Mukerji began to publish. In an essay titled "Rudyard Kipling Seen through Hindu Eyes" published in the influential Boston-based *North American Review* in 1914, the Indian critic A. R. Sarath-Roy took Kipling to task, arguing that he was no authority on India, only "a writer of the life of foreigners in India."[126] Kipling may very well have known the "machinery of the Indian Government" and the characters of the Indian Service, but as a whole, he had "misrepresented, ridiculed, and maligned the people of India." As Mukerji would do a decade later, Sarath-Roy paused to praise Kipling's descriptions of India, noting that his "pictures" were "full of realistic and interesting details." Nevertheless, he also stated that Kipling "saw through other peoples (*sic*) eyes," "extol[ling] his people at the expense of India."[127] That sentiment was apparently a common one felt by Kipling's Indian readers. Sarath-Roy recalled a conversation at the Calcutta Club, in which a group of Bengali intellectuals questioned whether Kipling's children's stories were not in fact plagiarized from his Indian *ayah*. The Calcutta Club group summarily concluded, "Rudyard Kipling is an ingrate. [. . .] The man as a man is an ingrate."[128]

Hucheshwar Gurusidha Mudgal, the Indian-born editor of Pan-Africanist Marcus Garvey's *Negro World*, devoted an entire "Foreign Affairs" column in 1922 about Kipling. Describing Kipling as an imperialist and nationalist, Mudgal accused Kipling of "slander[ing] and misrepresent[ing]" India in such a way that always emphasized the very worst sides of "human nature." Through his column, Mudgal threw some choice insults at Kipling, at one point describing him as committing so many writerly sins that Lucifer would "hang his head down in shame," and at another calling him a "stinking carcass with gaudy clothing and fragrant flowers on." Mudgal ended his column with a quote from the *New York World*, which cemented the Anglo-Indian writer's racist reputation: "If Kipling were an American he would be a King Kleagle of the Ku Klux Klan."[129]

Mukerji was never so direct in attacking or parodying Kipling. As critics such as Harish Trivedi have suggested, he was often marketed as the native counterpart to Kipling; magazines regularly advertised Mukerji's fiction with a reference to Kipling, describing them as "an account of the wild life that gave Rudyard Kipling the opportunity to write the great jungle books."[130] Few American literary critics could resist the opportunity to use Kipling as a yardstick for assessing the success or failures of Mukerji's fiction. From Mukerji's end, what was at stake in Kipling's India was the Orientalist gaze that structured it, one that reduced India to a site for generating imperial subjects. This came in conflict with Mukerji's insistence that India could be a site for a different kind of knowledge for Americans, not for the mastery of another place, but rather to illustrate how ideologies of racial supremacy and imperialist arrogance—"racial myopia," as he put it—clouded their ways of seeing. This idea, that India was the space for the rearing of imperial subjects, can be traced throughout much of Kipling's oeuvre, not only in his nationalistic poetry but in his children's books.

There are few better examples of Kipling's service to the discourse of imperial boyhood, perhaps, than the role his juvenile fiction played in the development of the scouting movement in Britain and the United States. A close acquaintance of Kipling, Robert Baden-Powell—or "B.-P." as he was known—had developed the scout movement in Britain in the first decade of the twentieth century. A decorated officer in the British Army, Baden-Powell's military career was spent across the empire: he had served in India as a sub-lieutenant, in the Crimean War with the 13th Hussars, and eventually as a captain in campaigns in Africa, against the Kingdom of Zulu, the Ashanti Empire, and the Ndebele.[131] His most famous stint as an officer came in the Siege of Mafeking during the Second Boer War, which made him a national hero. While British accounts of the siege foregrounded Baden-Powell's heroics, it obscured the racist way that he had ensured the survival of the white garrison.[132] Joseph Bristow notes, "In order to conserve rations for the whites, [Baden-Powell] executed a 'leave-here-or-starve-here' policy," which had left the native population resembling, according to one account, "black spectres and living skeletons."[133]

Baden-Powell had long held an interest in the education of Britain's young men, or what was known then as "boy's work." In 1899, he published a pamphlet titled *Aids to Scouting for N.C.O.s and Men*, filled with games and exercises to develop young scouts and imbibe them with a character of "grit," "pluck," and "ability." While Baden-Powell insisted that scouting work was not the same as "soldiering," the examples were often drawn from British imperial warfare. In *Aids to Scouting*, he described how the British scout must "be good beyond all nationalities [. . .] because he is called upon to act not only against civilized enemies in civilized countries, like France and Germany, but he has to take on the crafty Afghan in his mountains, or the Zulu in the open South African downs, the Burmese in his forests, the Soudanese on the Egyptian desert—all requiring different methods of working."[134] Baden-Powell's clear division between "civilized" European and the uncivilized Afghan, Zulu, Burmese, and "Soudanese" betrayed not only a deeply embedded racism, but also made clear who was counted as the unruly subjects of the British Empire.

After the Siege of Mafeking, Baden-Powell used his fame to further develop the Boy Scouts. In 1907, he recruited twenty boys for a trial camp on Brownsea Island off the southern coast of England, where he developed several of the ideas that would later be popularized in the Boy Scouts. The culmination of the camp was the 1908 publication of *Scouting for Boys*, a handbook organized into a series of chapters called "Camp Fire Yarns." Each "yarn" conveyed a skill or a lesson, ranging from the weighty task of defining a scout's role and purpose, to the skills of camping, spooring, and tying useful knots.[135] The book's very first "Camp Fire Yarn" used the example of Kimball O'Hara, the protagonist of Kipling's *Kim*, to define the scouts' mission. In the chapter, Baden-Powell describes how Kim had learned the ways of India through close observation: he had "learned to talk their language," to "know their ways," to "dress himself in Indian clothes." All of this "special knowledge of native habits and customs" allowed Kim to become a useful intelligence agent for the British.[136] Between illustrating a few of Kim's exploits—when he helps an adult agent successfully pass as an Indian beggar, and when he identifies an agent in disguise—Baden-Powell chimes in with a series of important lessons. "Noticing and remembering small details," he explains, are important in the training of a scout.[137] Encouraging his readers to further explore Kipling's work, he writes, "These and other adventures of Kim are well worth reading because they illustrate the kind of valuable work a Boy Scout can do for his country in times of emergency if he is sufficiently trained and sufficiently intelligent."[138]

The example of *Kim* points to the umbilical ties between Kipling's creations and the emergence of the scouts. It also points to a theme that goes unstated in *Scouting for Boys*. Kim's skills are developed in part because he is both a part of India, but also apart from India; he is able to pass as an Indian, even while his Britishness remains intact. This has been a key critical approach to *Kim*, which scholars have long studied under the postcolonial themes of racial passing, hybridity, and colonial subjectivity. But this component of *Kim* was also a central part of the scout system itself. Hence, Baden-Powell's very first example of what constitutes a scout is the ability for the white child to extract knowledge from native spaces, to master colonial societies, while remaining firmly in the employ of the empire.

Throughout *Scouting for Boys*, Baden-Powell provides scouting lessons by using examples drawn from his military experience and from the racial subjects he encountered across the British Empire. The scouts' uniform, he explains, was inspired by the khaki uniforms worn by the South African Constabulary.[139] The scout's dance was drawn from "the young men of the Kikuyu tribe."[140] The aborigines of Australia could teach young boys the use of smoke signals, while in India, one could learn camouflage by observing the method by which "gipsies" hunt jackals. These motifs were carried over during the American development of the Boy Scouts by figures such as Ernest Thompson Seton, whose "Woodcraft Indians" group regularly drew on his own fanciful ideas of Native American practices.[141] While the particular examples changed, the broader form of the scouts' relationship to the racial other remained intact; Boy Scouts performed a cursory "respect" for other cultures, but ultimately instrumentalized their others from the outposts of empire in service of developing the perfect scout.

Kipling's *Kim*, after all, follows the very same logic. In *Kim*, India and the Grand Trunk Road are the playground for Kimball O'Hara's picaresque adventures. As Javed Majeed explains, in the novel "India is spread out for the reader as a surface to explore."[142] The setting allows O'Hara to explore Indian spaces and even adopt Indian practices as a means to safely express his uninhibited masculine energy. But in the end, all of that cultural slumming must be repackaged into a series of skills that can aid the broader project of

British empire. Hence, while Baden-Powell ends *Scouting for Boys* with the lesson that a scout joins a "world brotherhood," one nevertheless had to abide by the rules, wear the khaki uniform, and, in short, enlist in a "pretend" British imperial army.[143]

Kim was not the only book by Kipling that Baden-Powell used to develop his scouting philosophy. In response to the popularity of the scouting movement, Baden-Powell created the Cub Scouts for younger boys, using *The Jungle Book* as the central text upon which the Cub Scout structure was based.[144] After receiving Kipling's blessings, Baden-Powell acknowledged his friend in his dedication: "To Rudyard Kipling, who has done so much to put the right spirit into our rising manhood."[145] The *Wolf Cub's Handbook* replaced the "Camp Fire Yarns" with "Bites," the first few of which summarize stories in *The Jungle Book* and develop a series of games and dances based off of the characters' names. The lessons themselves point to how Kipling's India was so abstracted that it had effectively become an empty signifier. Whatever content about India the stories contained was vacated, and instead what remained was an India that served as a vehicle for the identity play of white boys. Thus, when the Boy Scouts of America adapted the Cub Scouts program in the mid-century, the group transposed the Indian geography of *The Jungle Book* to the American plains—the wolf Akela became the Indian "chief" of the Webelos tribe, "bright in his warrior's headdress and in ceremonial paint" and Mowgli was translated as a "little Indian boy in [a] tee-pee."[146] Kipling's India was not simply adaptable to the discourse of Anglo-American boyhood; it was a constitutive element of it.

The history and controversies that surrounded the scouting movement in India, which first landed in the subcontinent in 1911, illustrate its close ideological attachments to the broader British imperial project. A headline for an April 1926 edition of the Gadar Party publication the *United States of India* described the Boy and Girl Scout movement in India as "one of the storm centers in the national movement of freedom."[147] The essay explains that for the first six years of its existence in India, the Boy Scouts organization was open exclusively to British children, and prohibited Indian boys and girls from joining. When Indians were finally allowed to participate in the Scouts organization, they were prohibited from equal access:

> The right of Indian boys and girls to join Scout organizations was denied by the British-Indian Government until as late as 1916, and then they were permitted to join only under the most careful tutorship of English, or pro-English guidance, and only under restrictions such as no European or American Scout organization would think of imposing upon Youth. No Indian boy or girl Scout for example, can learn riding or shooting, although these are requirements of English and other Scout organizations.[148]

After permission was granted to allow Indians to join the Scouts, three Indian Boy and Girl Scout associations were formed under the leadership of Home Rule leader Annie Besant and Congress leader Pandit Malaviya in Madras, Allahabad, and one of the "Native States." The Indian scouts were a kind of vernacular outfit, the khaki uniform replaced with hand-woven *khaddar*, the fleur-de-lis replaced with a Crescent and Swastika ("the symbol of unity between Mohammedans and Hindus"), and instead of the imperialist lessons of Baden-Powell, the scouts were instilled with patriotic lessons about Indian freedom. According to the essay, the British government quickly became so alarmed by the Indian scouts' rapidly growing membership that Baden-Powell personally traveled to India to "amalgamate all these Indian scouts into the English Association, otherwise they would become dangerous to the British Government."[149]

Killing Kipling

If Kipling represented India as a readily accessible psychic and physical playground for the development of Anglo-American imperial subjects, then Mukerji's India represented a space that was far more difficult to access. The India that his readership viewed, Mukerji constantly reminded them, was always a mediated experience. That mediation occurred first and foremost because it was the product of a literary translation. Purnima Mankekar and Akhil Gupta explain that while Mukerji, like all autobiographers, attempted to "strike a chord of identification in its readers," he insisted on reminding his readers of the "differences between his experiences" and theirs.[150] Gupta and Mankekar argue that *Caste and Outcast* more resembles "the genre of canonical ethnographic writing that seeks to render the unfamiliar and, in some instances, the exotic, intelligible and familiar."[151] They add that part of Mukerji's project in *Caste and Outcast* was to underscore the limits of "cultural translation" itself:

> Mukerji seems to be conscious of the limits to cultural translation: there are certain things, he seems to imply, that are, quite simply, untranslatable. Although he believes that, as someone who has crossed cultural borders, he is uniquely qualified to describe both cultures, he posits an immutable difference between "the oriental and the occidental mind."[152]

This theme of cultural translation occurs in several of Mukerji's books. In *Visit India with Me*, Mukerji's fictitious American travel partner, Eagles, constantly asks him to translate for him. When surprised by the meaning behind an Indian concierge's formal salutation, Eagles asks Mukerji, "Do they talk like this all the time in India?" The hotel agent overhears, responding in English, "Only amongst ourselves, sir." Eagles then turns to Mukerji and tells him, "I wish you would count me as one of your own and talk to me like that." Mukerji promises that he will, that he would "fill his ears with golden speech wherever we went," a promise not to only his travel partner but to his American audience.[153]

In his children's fiction, Mukerji also provided reminders of the mediated and translated nature of his work. In the introduction of his 1931 *Bunny, Hound and Clown*, Mukerji describes the pains he underwent to translate the stories of his childhood in Bengal for an English-speaking audience in the United States. He explains, "It has been the ambition of my life to put into the hands of American boys and girls a document that will portray the living soul of a Hindu boy."[154] Such a translational practice necessitated developing new idioms for expression. Mukerji describes the difficulty, for instance, in "transcribing Hindu cradle-tales from Indian folk-speech into Modern English," given that the latter no longer had a "picturesque" idiom that could convey the "grace and directness" of Bengali.[155] Mukerji was quick to note that the loss of such texture in English could be attributed to the broader forces of industrialization, a move that cleverly challenges the fitness of the English language itself and slyly undermines the notion of Anglophone supremacy. The role of cultural translator—of having a foot in English and a foot in Bengali, one in the United States and the other in India—meant that Mukerji alone was positioned to evaluate both "cultures." Thus, he could defend the literary culture of India against Lord Thomas Babington Macaulay's infamous statement about the "intrinsic superiority of Western literature."[156] Not only was Indian literature beautiful and captivating, according to Mukerji, but it had proven to be popular among American youth. "In the presence of such glaring evidence to the contrary," Mukerji writes, "to exclaim that we have no adequate juvenile literature in India is blasphemy."[157]

Mukerji, of course, took juvenile literature seriously, not only because his own children's books were far more successful than his adult books, but because such literature was inherently political, especially in the context of British India. Much like Kipling's tales of imperial boyhood, an ideological and pedagogical impulse drove Indian children's fiction during the colonial era. In the example of children's literature in Bengal, scholars Supriya Goswami and Satadru Sen have described the considerable efforts made by authors and editors to construct the native child as a counterweight to colonial discourse, a figure imagined to undermine "forms of colonial and official authority."[158] Sen explains how literary childhood, in the works of prominent Bengali authors such as Abanindranath Tagore and Jogendra Nath Gupta, was imbued with "modern-masculine agency," a direct contest to a colonial regime that had derided and doubted native capacity.[159] Goswami goes even further, arguing that the literary Bengali child was imagined as "far more capable of subverting empire and challenging the laws of the land than Bengali adults, who are often enfeebled or emasculated by colonization."[160]

However, unlike the Indian children's literature that Sen and Goswami describe, in which nationalist aspirations were projected onto the Bengali child, Mukerji's children's stories were directed toward an altogether different type of child—a cosmopolitan, and presumably, American one.[161] In an essay titled "Why I Write in English about Hindu Life," Mukerji describes the convergence of two themes that were prevalent in his writing: the need to translate, and the importance of conveying India to American children: "I was surprised to find that there was not much understanding of the soul and character of India here. [. . .] Since I believe that children best understand foreign civilizations and foreign ways, I set out to write for *them*."[162] In several of the introductions to his children's books, he outlined what he saw as the role of children in the larger project for global peace. In the lengthy introduction to his 1931 book *Bunny, Hound and Clown*, Mukerji explains:

> I hold that until a nation appreciates the common culture of another nation it will not be able to understand the value of international peace. We need peace between nations, because peace alone can augment the forces of true culture. If we know early in life how good our neighbor's culture can be, we shall think twice before we decide to destroy it by warfare. Of the many agencies working for international amity, appreciation of the cultures of other races is a very potent one. And this appreciation should be made into an art and a habit of the young of every land.[163]

This is lofty language for a children's book that included stories titled "How the Sea Was Turned Salty" and "A Conceited Fly." The lingering effects of World War I haunt Mukerji's juvenile fiction, as he describes the devastation wrought by the war and the omnipresent threat of more violence ("think twice before we decide to destroy [our neighbor's culture]"). Mukerji also evokes the discourse of the League of Nations, as he describes how the hope of "peace between nations," "international amity," and "international peace" could come out of the habits of "the young of every land." It is useful to pause and consider Jacqueline Rose's powerful argument about children's fiction, that it is never about "what the child wants, but of what the adult desires."[164] Comparing the ideal child that Kipling "desired" to the one that Mukerji imagined presents both stark contrasts and broad convergences. In both cases, the Anglo-American child is the beneficiary of tales from the "East," and in both cases, the child learns through those tales his (rarely, her) position within the globe. But this comes with vastly different intentions. Kipling's juvenile fiction imagined the boy as an untamed being, who needed to be molded into the service of empire. For Mukerji, the American child was to be a global neighbor, one for whom understanding India was a means of inculcating values of "international amity" rather than national pride.

We see this distinction when comparing Kipling's famous *The Jungle Book* (1894) to Mukerji's children's novels. Many scholars have argued that the jungle setting of Kipling's book represents a deeper allegory for forms of social order, whether that be the order of "natural law" or colonial hierarchy. In his influential study, Shamsul Islam points to the way that the Mowgli stories present the "law of the jungle" as an outgrowth of an earlier period of "primitive" lawlessness, which had been generated over time by values of common good and continuously enforced by those in power. More recently, Supriya Goswami describes *The Jungle Book* as a thinly veiled colonial allegory, with the "bandar-log" or monkey-people as stand-ins for the Indian natives who "mimic" the law of the jungle without fully internalizing its logic.[165] In contrast to Kipling, Mukerji's children's fiction presents the jungle as a space absent of authority and hierarchy. Rimli Bhattacharya argues that in Mukerji's children's books, the jungle serves as a "utopic" even liberating space that enables a "re-imagining of caste, ethnicity, and gender."[166] In books such as *Gay-Neck* and *Ghond the Hunter* (1928), Mukerji imagines friendships across caste lines and forms of kinship outside of the parent–child dyad; in *Gay-Neck*, for instance, a Brahmin boy finds a paternal figure in an elder hunter. Bhattacharya explains, "The jungle, as the non-domestic, non-urban (not settled), non-institutional space, affords a site for experimenting with interpenetrative discourses of kinship, hierarchy and social relations."[167] In this regard, Mukerji's children's fiction is less about the fixity of a static culture, in which social structure could not be upended, and more about a space "where social relations could be reconfigured [. . .] outside the normative paradigm of the quasi-emergent 'colonial bourgeoisie.'"[168]

Even while Mukerji's "jungle" represents a liberating space that could act as a temporary reprieve from colonial authority, empire continues to exert its influence on his book's native subjects. In *Gay-Neck*, the protagonist's pigeon has been selected to serve as a carrier for the British Army, while his elder friend, the hunter Ghond, is also recruited by the British to serve on a reconnaissance mission. Ghond is "equipped with rope ladders, a lasso and knives" but not firearms. The narrator explains, "The British Government forbids the use of firearms to the common people of India, and so we carried no rifles."[169] A similar line appears in *Hari, the Jungle Lad* during a scene in which the protagonist and his father attempt to capture or kill a tiger that has attacked villagers. The father tells his son: "Since we are not allowed firearms (this, as you may know, is a law of the British government), we have only one thing to do."[170] In both lines, an authorial voice intrudes on the narrative, as either an aside or a parenthetical, reminding the reader of the ways that colonial authority has penetrated even the most remote areas of India and indeed, the most remote Indian lives. In both cases, the "ban of firearms" presents an added danger to the protagonists—for Ghond as he is enlisted as a scout for the British Army, and for Hari and his father, who are left defenseless in their village. Mukerji's children's novels may very well present the jungle as a space of utopian possibility, but those spaces are consistently constrained by the colonial government and its wartime machinations. This was a subtle but significant critique of the colonial administration, one carefully woven into the plot of children's stories.

Whatever anticolonial critique Mukerji may have mustered was immediately tempered by the realities and limitations of the publishing industry in which he worked. Mukerji struggled to earn his keep as an American writer, a fact he registered in letter after letter to his publisher John Macrae. Even while he received awards for his fiction, Mukerji also faced scrutiny over his status as an American writer. When *Gay-Neck* won the John Newbery medal for the most distinguished contribution to American literature for children in 1928, several critics praised the novel and claimed that Mukerji had inherited the "mantle of Kipling." Others registered concern over his eligibility to receive such an award. The *Des Moines Register*, for instance, praised *Gay-Neck* for promoting "international understanding," but questioned whether Mukerji should have been awarded an American award: "How does Mukerji happen to be receiving a medal that is always given [. . .] 'for the most distinguished contribution to children's literature from an American pen'? Is Mukerji's an 'American pen'?"[171]

I have argued that central to Mukerji's oeuvre was a project of reader reorientation; he attempted to rescue "India" from representations such as those of Baden-Powell and Kipling, for whom India was just one site among many imperial outposts that could help mold the Anglo-American "imperial boy." But even that argument must contend with the realities of the American publishing industry. Ironically, many of Mukerji's stories were published in *Boys' Life*, the official publication of the Boy Scouts of America.[172] *Hari, The Jungle Lad*, for instance, was first serialized in the magazine in 1924. While the text in both the E. P. Dutton and the *Boys' Life* versions are identical, the context of the stories shift dramatically when they appear in these magazines, surrounded on either side by safari tales told by retired British officers and primitive cave-man fantasies such as "Og, Son of Fire." In these magazines, Mukerji's tales of childhood in India were recirculated as Kipling-inflected fantasies for American boys, in spite of his desire for American children to view India without a colonial gaze. Thus, despite his attempt to disrupt Kipling, Mukerji's juvenile fiction continued to circulate in a field that made it indistinguishable from the discourse of American "boy work," a discourse that readily imagined the shaping of imperial subjects for the new century.

If the formal limits and publishing constraints of children's fiction kept Mukerji from launching a more robust anticolonial critique, then it only makes sense to turn to *The Secret Listeners of the East* (1926), Mukerji's sole adult novel, to see what he was capable of when his hands were less tethered.

Set in India and Afghanistan in 1919, immediately after the end of World War I, *Secret Listeners* begins with an arresting and grotesque image. General Gastry, the leader of the Scout Movement in British India, is found dead on a train, his "face battered beyond recognition" and his left ear mysteriously sliced off.[173] It is perhaps tempting to read in this gruesome spectacle a case of literary fratricide, but Gastry's death serves a much larger purpose in the novel than the murderous fantasies of the author. The Bengali protagonist and narrator, Nirmal Chatterjee, himself a scoutmaster and friend of Gastry's, launches an investigation that takes him from Bengal to the Northwest frontier into a world of clandestine societies and revolutionary intrigue. Over the course of the novel, Chatterjee discovers that Gastry was the victim of a "secret order of Jehadis." No hapless bystander, Gastry had been killed for his work with the British consular service, where he served as a "surveywalker," mapping "all the Mohammedan lands, intending [. . .] to give it over to the British."[174] His murder, in effect, was an act of political violence. At stake was Gastry's map, which produced an image of India whose sole purpose was to assist in the domination of the last unincorporated region of British territory.

Secret Listeners illustrates Mukerji's own conflicted political commitments. On one hand, the novel demonstrates Mukerji's recurring theme about the power of colonial visualities: like Baden-Powell and Kipling's India, Gastry's map was an image of India shaped entirely by a colonial gaze and whose only function was to further extend the British imperial project. On the other hand, the novel also betrays Mukerji's own deeply held prejudices. The novel's anticolonial fantasy of violence is projected onto the figure of the Muslim, whose violent actions are suspected to be motivated as much by religious reasons as political ones. Early on, Chatterjee suggests that "the Mohammedans [had been] forming a secret society on the frontiers of India, and, under the guise of a religious sect, carrying on a war through assassination upon their European enemies."[175]

When Chatterjee finally uncovers the murderer Abdul Rahim, however, his motives are revealed sympathetically. Rahim describes serving for the British in the World War, yet growing increasingly conflicted by his role as a soldier on the frontlines of empire. Rahim describes witnessing the death of a Turkish soldier who cries "Allah" at precisely the same time that one of his fellow soldiers does the same, a moment that forced him to question his own allegiances. He confesses that the atrocities of colonial rule have impacted him personally. The Jallianwala Bagh massacre, in which the British Indian Army opened fire on a crowd of unarmed protesters, occurred at the same time as his sister-in-law and nephew were "blown up by bombs dropped by the Englishman."[176] Rahim continues to explain to Chatterjee just how much the contradictions of being an Indian in the British Army had clarified his own marginal position:

On our return to India in 1908 we were enrolled in the Indian army. We were trained and became officers, rising to the rank of Rasseldars. After that our promotions were slow. Beyond and above us were Englishmen whose positions no coffee-colored men could take. No Indian in the army was allowed to poach on the rich preserves of British officials and officers. Our faces were branded, as it were, with the mark of inferiority. Though we were men, we were forced to toil like ants in the anthill of the lower ranks, while our white overseers strutted above us. Every Asiatic is a dog in the eyes of the white man.[177]

Here, Rahim's biography is marked constantly by the barriers produced by the rule of colonial difference, a rule predicated on the idea of racial inferiority. No "coffee-colored men" could possibly surpass their "white overseers," Rahim notes. What begins, then, as a detective novel transforms into something of a polemic, with Mukerji using the figure of the Muslim to do his anticolonial bidding.

The Secret Listeners of the East received mixed reviews after its publication in 1926. Part of the blame for its lukewarm reception could be attributed to its occasional miscategorization as a children's novel. The *New York Herald* had assumed as much before publishing a correction, calling *Secret Listeners* as much a "juvenile" as *Kim*.[178] Another notice described it as a tale teeming with as much incident and plotting as *Kim* "but also, alas! without the genius of that great story!"[179] Other reviewers commented on the political content of the novel, describing it as a "tale of oriental political intrigue" that demonstrated the "hatred for an encroaching white race" by an organization hell-bent on overthrowing "Caucasian domination in India"; or a novel that proved to be "not only a thrilling tale" but "an enlightening document on Oriental affairs."[180] At least one review, however, was far more critical, invoking Kipling as the yardstick against which *Secret Listeners* was to be measured:

> Naturally, Mr. Mukerji knows his India, being a Brahman of the Brahmans, but in this instance he has failed to make it real and vivid to Occidental senses. We do not see it or smell it or hear it—as we do in "Kim," for example. The story is told in the most matter-of-fact way; stupendous adventures are casually encountered and recorded. Whether or not the book is written for boys, so good a story should have been treated less cavalierly and more color put into Mr. Mukerji's careful English.[181]

In its insistence that narratives about India ought to cater to the sights, sounds, even "smells" desired by "Occidental" taste, the reviewer in *The Independent* made it clear that, in spite of Mukerji's project to provide an alternative, the American audience still would rather experience Kipling's India and judged any representation of India according to its proximity to Kipling. Even if Mukerji had convinced Americans that Kipling's India was not the real thing, that it was just an image refracted through an imperialist's eye, it was by and large, the picture that Americans preferred.

4

The Dark Alliance

Refracting India in W.E.B. Du Bois's Dark Princess

W.E.B. Du Bois was fretting over details. In the fall of 1927, he was completing *Dark Princess*, a novel that, he explained to friends, "touch[ed] slightly upon India."[1] Never having visited the British colony, Du Bois questioned if, for instance, the name of the novel's invented "Indian country" Bwodpur sounded "sufficiently Indian" or whether it was appropriate to use the word "priest" for Hindu pujaris and Muslim imams.[2] He wrote to Lajpat Rai, who he had befriended a decade earlier, explaining that the novel "touches India incidentally in the person of an Indian princess" and that he looked forward to any criticism Rai could offer.[3] He also reached out to Dhan Gopal Mukerji, asking if he might offer some feedback. In a letter posted on October 29, he wrote to Mukerji:

> I want very much to have someone who knows India and its customs to read three or four pages of the manuscript and criticize any errors or inconsistencies in which I may have failed. I never had the pleasure of visiting India and my knowledge is solely from reading and my acquaintanceship with Indians. Would you be willing to do me this service?[4]

Mukerji responded at once, suggesting only "slight changes in your narration."[5] As far as Mukerji could tell or was willing to admit to Du Bois, the book had told "at least the facts that I know accurately." "Beyond that," he explained, "I can't criticize your mss., nor alter them."[6] For a writer who had spent much of his career trying to challenge the Orientalist gaze of his American readership, Mukerji's reticence to critique Du Bois's novel may come off as surprising. The India that Du Bois imagined in *Dark Princess*, after all, conjured an image of the subcontinent filled with bejeweled princesses and wealthy princes, Hindu gods and ancient Indian kingdoms. The novel was stuffed with allusions to Western art's fantasies of the East, from Scheherazade to "March of the Sardar," Purcell's *The Fairy Queen* to *A Midsummer Night's Dream.*[7] Even Mukerji's literary rival Rudyard Kipling managed to make an appearance by way of a reference to *The Jungle Book*. As Madhumita Lahiri succinctly puts it, "the Orientalism of the novel is difficult to contest."[8]

For all its representational faux pas, Du Bois's *Dark Princess* was a work that attempted to look beyond the gaze that rendered the East as a site for Western consumption and imperial fantasy. Instead, Du Bois rendered India into a space of *anti-imperial* fantasy, breathing life into the histories and struggles that he had long believed linked the subcontinent to Black America. The novel tells the story of Matthew Towns, an African American medical student who leaves the United States in a self-imposed exile in Europe, where he comes in contact with a clandestine circle of Asian and Middle Eastern anticolonialists led by the Indian princess Kautilya. While Matthew and Kautilya's destinies appear intertwined after their first encounter, the novel strings him along a circuitous sequence of events, including a failed plot to destroy a train boarded with Klansmen, a short period of imprisonment in which he becomes a political cause célèbre, and a cold marriage to a skillful woman who helps him become elected to state legislature from a Black district of Chicago. Alienated by the corruption in urban politics, Towns flees just before taking office and eventually consummates his relationship with the princess. By the end, the two marry and have a child, whose birth in the last pages symbolically augurs a Black–Asian future.

Provisionally titled "Dark Alliance"[9] and "The Princess and the Porter,"[10] *Dark Princess* was the culmination of Du Bois's long-standing interest in India, which by the 1920s had led him into the network of Indian expatriate nationalists and their allies in New York. As a charter member of the Civic Club of Manhattan, he had come to know several figures from the club's "India group." He befriended Lajpat Rai in the late 1910s, once sharing a stage when the two were invited to speak at an event sponsored by the Intercollegiate Socialist Society in New York. Some years later, when Agnes Smedley organized the Friends of Freedom for India, Du Bois accepted a role on the organization's national council. Such relationships reflected Du Bois's ongoing solidarity with anticolonial movements, which he announced in columns of the *Crisis* in the decades to follow. His engagement with Indian anticolonialism also inflected the kind of questions raised by *Dark Princess*. The novel shared with Rai's *The United States of America* an attempt to rethink political identity by comparing the struggles of race in the United States and in India, and much like Smedley's *Daughter of Earth*, Du Bois's

American protagonist is alienated by repeated instances of marginalization, rediscovering a sense of community and self in Indian anticolonialism. For both Smedley and Rai, I have argued, these forms of Indian–American exchange exemplified the practices of transnational refraction, a means of seeing through the eyes of the other that disrupted their entrenched understandings of race, class, and caste and invested those social identities with new meaning.

The "gaze of others," of course, had already been a formative idea in Du Bois's concepts about race. In his monumental work *The Souls of Black Folk* (1903), he had developed a series of visual metaphors to describe the Black experience in a post-Civil War America. In *Souls*, Du Bois detailed how Black subjectivity was structured through "double consciousness," the "negotiation of disparate gazes"[11] by which African Americans were forced to "always [look] at one's self through the eyes of others" who looked on in "amused contempt and pity."[12] He discussed the racial veil that prevented white Americans, reared in the ideologies of racism, from seeing African Americans as equals or as part of the nation.[13] That same veil mediated the Black American experience, gifting them with a "second-sight" into the United States but yielding no "true self-consciousness."[14] Written a quarter century after *Souls*, *Dark Princess* built upon these ideas, transposing double consciousness onto a global scale and a political milieu that witnessed the rise of anticolonial movements in Asia, Africa, and Latin America. It speculated on how the political and civic struggle of African Americans fit into the nascent anticolonial world following World War I, and pondered how the racial veil that shaped Black life in the United States compared to the imperialist veil through which much of the world's populations appeared as objects of conquest, rule, and extraction. It also considered the veil that stood between the lives of the colonial Indian and African American, preventing them from seeing and recognizing one another.

In its bold experiment with aesthetic form and transnational fantasy, *Dark Princess* attempted to think through these issues. In the process, the novel offered the possibility of imagining a reordered future for Black America, or as he put it in his 1926 essay "Criteria of Negro Art," "a vision of what the world could be if it were really a beautiful world [. . .] [the] sort of a world we want to create for ourselves and for all America."[15] In stretching the canvas of the novel from the nation to the globe, *Dark Princess* attempted to imagine a postwar future in which Euro-American cultural and political hegemony had been replaced by a world led by what he often referred to as "the darker nations." Yet that still raised the question: Why was India's nationalist struggle, as opposed to any other anticolonial movement, so important to Du Bois for conceiving that world? And why did Du Bois use the tropes of Orientalism as a means of imagining the future he had envisioned for "ourselves and for all America"?

Deus Ex India

In spite of Du Bois calling it his favorite work, *Dark Princess* was published in 1928 to largely mixed reviews. At least one of his contemporaries, the writer George Schuyler, praised the novel's bold aesthetic experiments. Schuyler had apparently stopped reading midway to write Du Bois a letter, praising the novel as a "masterful" work and "great [. . .] portrayal of the soul of our people" that reduced him to tears.[16] According to scholar Claudia Tate, however, many privately held misgivings about the work even while outwardly praising it. Alain Locke, for instance, lauded the novel for breaking new ground, while also deeming it "not wholly successful." For Locke, the novel suffered from "strained melodramatic [plot] convergences" and "an epic theme [. . .] befogged by false romanticizing." Such sequences, he thought, overshadowed the "sound realism that throws a new light on many a contemporary Negro situation."[17] Several reviewers, in fact, echoed the opinion that the novel's foray into romance and melodrama masked the real (and realist) political content. The *New York Age* wrote that the novel was a "rattling good story," but claimed that its realist Chicago section was far more convincing than the other chapters, which had the "flamboyancy of an [E. Phillips] Oppenheim thriller."[18] The *New York Times* shared that sentiment, calling the plot "flamboyant and unconvincing," while also condescendingly suggesting that Du Bois's talents would have been better used to "show the natural ability [or nobility] of the colored man" as white-authored works such as DuBose Heyward's *Porgy* (1925) had.[19] What reviewers took exception to was the plot's departure from grounded realism and its melodramatic flights into international romance. All of this may have appeared to critics as an eccentric exercise for a figure who had otherwise been so committed to African American history and politics. As with Smedley's reviewers, no one seemed to know exactly what to do with the entire Indian subplot.

As one might expect, contemporary critics have been far more generous in their appraisal of the novel, noting its unique and almost prescient engagement with anticolonialism and internationalism. Madhumita Lahiri has argued that while the novel eschewed the cultural accuracy that Du Bois called for in "Criteria of Negro Art," it laid "claim to a life of fantasy and desire" that reflected not the world as it is but as it might be.[20] Along those same lines, Dohra Ahmad has noted that the novel deliberately toggled between realism and romance to capture the tension between a politics of limitation and possibility, a contrast that is marked in the different spaces in which the novel travels—the domestic world of the United States, and the "utopian" international world heralded by the Indian princess.[21]

For the first three-quarters of the novel, Matthew Towns tries on a variety of guises that represent distinct avenues of Black political and social advancement in the early twentieth century. Like the coterie of writers of the Harlem Renaissance in Paris or Du Bois, himself, who studied in Germany, Matthew attempts to escape the United States during his short-lived period of exile in Berlin. In the second chapter, he works as a Pullman porter, attempting to unionize his fellow workers for better conditions. When a fellow porter is lynched, Matthew plots a conspiracy alongside a character named Miguel Perigua—a thinly veiled caricature of Du Bois's rival Marcus Garvey—to derail a train filled with Klansmen, abandoning the plan only when he happens to see the Indian princess on board. In the lengthy third chapter, set in Chicago, Matthew marries the "self-made and independent" Sara Andrews, who helps release him from prison and thrusts him into the machinery of city politics, where he slowly becomes disaffected as his values are compromised by the corruption of the system.[22] Each of these sections marked the road of realist politics for Du Bois—the fight for labor, the world of Black nationalism, and the incremental wins of electoral politics—and each of these avenues distinctively fail him. It is only in the fourth chapter, the fantastical "Maharajah of Bwodpur," where the novel fully embraces a politics outside of these "realist" possibilities, which it teases in the beginning.

Indeed, from the outset, Du Bois indicates that the promise of the novel lay elsewhere, in a politics that transcends the boundaries of the nation-state and turns to the globe for a larger theater of struggle. We learn that Matthew has dropped out of Manhattan medical school after the dean notifies him that due to his racial identity he will be unable to register for obstetrics and, in a sort of racist catch-22, will therefore not meet the requirements for graduation. With the pathways of social mobility blocked, Matthew begins his journey on the S.S. *Orizaba*, where he is effectively caught in geographical and historical limbo, somewhere between the West and the East, along a route that marks a reversal of the historic Middle Passage voyage. Unaware of his final destination, he remains certain that it will at least not entail a return to the United States. In these opening notes, Du Bois depicts Matthew as an allegorical stand-in for Black America in the postwar period, for whom the promise of racial justice in the United States has seemingly stalled in a social and political dead-end. When Matthew looks at the horizon, he notes that "America had disappeared."[23] In a letter to his mother, he states that he "cannot and will not stand America longer."[24] A few pages later in Berlin, he confesses that "America was impossible—unthinkable."[25] With the United States fading in the distance, Matthew instead gazes at the "edge of the world" where he sees a set of indeterminate forms: "the curled grace of billows," "changing blues and greens," and "shining shapes," descriptions of water that evoke an image of the globe itself.[26] The novel thus begins with an alternative orientation—Matthew, unmoored by national attachments, begins to open up to a global consciousness, however inchoate it first appears to him. In other words, the domestic space of America had become impossible for the Black subject, leaving only two options: fleeing the United States or transforming it.

By the end of *Dark Princess*, Du Bois will propose an imaginary for national transformation, but in the novel's opening scene, Matthew simply opts for escape. He lists a set of possible destinations, each one offering reprieve from the nightmare of the America:

> Where *was* he going? The ship was going to Antwerp. But that, to Matthew, was sheer accident. He was going *away* first of all. After that? Well, he had thought of France. There they were at least civilized in their prejudices. But his French was poor. He had studied German because his teachers regarded German medicine as superior to all other. He would then go to Germany. From there? Well, there was Moscow. Perhaps they could use a man in Russia whose heart was hate. Perhaps he would move on to the Near or Far East and find hard work and peace. At any rate, he was going somewhere.[27]

While France and Germany represent the ideals of the Western Enlightenment and Russia exemplifies the radical promise of Communism, none offer an escape from Matthew's racial interpellation. With the exception of the nebulously described "Near or Far East," each of these possible destinations were coordinates on a Western map, and in each case, the specter of race would follow him: either in a more bearable form of racism ("civilized in their prejudice") or in a form of tokenization, in which Matthew's Blackness would be instrumentalized for the Soviet cause ("they could use a man [. . .] whose heart was hate"). The "Near or Far East" still occupies an unknown state, formless and undefined; Matthew at this stage can only imagine it as a sort of ascetic respite, erasing identity in exchange for labor and nothing more. As it happens, Matthew never follows through on that itinerary and instead his exile facilitates the bitter realization that there is seemingly no escape from the racist gaze that follows him, nor is there a way to shake the "double consciousness" through which he interprets such glances. As Du Bois would continue to write in his essays, "the problem of the twentieth century is the problem of the color line" and that line cut not only through the United States but it belted the world as a whole.

What *Dark Princess* illustrated perhaps better than his nonfiction were the ways that the global color line—often depicted in large-scale barriers (colonial rule, apartheid, segregation) raised by whites against nonwhites—extended into subtler facets and lived experiences of the veil.[28] Indeed, throughout his journey, from the ship deck to Europe, Matthew is constantly dogged by this sense of always "seeing oneself through the eyes of others." On the *Orizaba*, he senses that the passengers "spoke about him . . . each word heard and unheard pierced him."[29] In Berlin, he notices a white woman catching his eye, but quickly realizes she's a sex worker who "thought him a South American, an Egyptian, or a rajah with money."[30] While sitting at the Viktoria café on the Unter den Linden in Berlin, Matthew is overwhelmed by the panoptic presence of the "white leviathan"—a reference to the buildings of Humboldt University of Berlin rendered into an abstraction of racial power—which he describes as "that mighty organization of white folk which he felt himself so bitterly in revolt."[31] In that image, Matthew comes to realize that the "white leviathan" spreads its tentacles across the Atlantic, representing the "same, vast, remorseless machine in Berlin as in New York."[32] Just as America is impossible, so too is Europe.

It is precisely at this moment, in a plot device that will repeat throughout Matthew's trials, that Princess Kautilya enters the scene. Appearing as a splash of color in the otherwise "yellowish and pinkish parchment" world of Berlin, Kautilya embodies the "glow of golden brown" set against the white world that transfixes and seemingly transforms Matthew.[33] "Never after that first glance," Matthew thinks to himself, "was he or *the world* quite the same."[34] In a bout of chivalry that even seems to surprise himself, Matthew rescues the princess from a drunk and lecherous white American. The gesture is rewarded with an invitation to join her and her proverbial royal court—members of a "great committee of darker peoples" constituted by all "those who suffer under the arrogance and tyranny of the white world" and were willing to fight against it.[35] Matthew, it appears, has arrived.

And yet, as the following scene makes abundantly clear, he hasn't. In the scene that unfolds, Matthew comes to witness a form of anticolonial alliance—an aristocratic form of "colored cosmopolitanism," to use Nico Slate's term—that ultimately proves to be politically flawed, and almost comically so. Matthew awkwardly enters the space of the committee, in which representatives of the darker nations—including Japanese, Chinese, Egyptian, Arab, and Indian delegates, elite and aristocratic in manner—converse confidently on subjects of Western art such as Picasso and Kandinsky, Proust and Croce's *Aesthetics*.[36] These are characters who resemble Homi Bhabha's "mimic men"—figures who are an "effect of a flawed colonial mimesis," or, to paraphrase Macaulay, a class of persons non-European in color, but European in tastes.[37] Matthew perceives in this strange and alternative space an anticolonial world that transgresses the "color line." At dinner, white servants wait on people of color, while discussions characterized white workers and ruling classes alike as "inferior races." Matthew eavesdrops on the other guests:

> It started on lines so familiar to Matthew that he had to shut his eyes and stare again at their swarthy faces: Superior races—the right to rule—born to command—inferior breeds—the lower classes—the rabble. [. . .] How contemptuous was the young Indian of inferior

races! But how humorous it was to Matthew to see all tables turned; the rabble now was the white workers of Europe; the inferior races were the ruling whites of Europe and America. The superior races were yellow and brown.[38]

While these words initially appear to delight Matthew, the pleasures of the racial uncanny soon wear off as he comes to realize that the committee members' mimicry entails not just parroting European tastes but adopting their logic of racial hierarchy. When it comes time to discuss the "Negro," for instance, Matthew senses the "shadow of a color line within a color line, a prejudice within prejudice" as members of the committee question whether African Americans had a rightful place in their anticolonial assemblage.[39] While Matthew suggests that "Negroes belong in the foremost ranks" of their coalition, a Japanese member responds that while he maintains "every human sympathy," the question of "ability, qualifications, and real possibilities of the black race" are still uncertain.[40] Again, the condition of double consciousness rears its heads even in the space of this anticolonial committee, viewing Matthew with pity and disdain, if not outright contempt.

Kautilya is the sole exception. She challenges the committee's view, citing a Moscow report that spoke of the revolutionary potential of African Americans who constitute a "nation today, a modern nation worthy to stand beside any nation."[41] While the rest of the committee balk at this suggestion, Kautilya entrusts Matthew with a mission to report notes back on a "carefully planned uprising of the American blacks" currently under way, a mission that will set in motion the line of occupations—Pullman porter, Chicago politician, etc.—that he takes up upon his return to the United States.[42] Kautilya herself decides to embark on a trip to the United States herself, telling Matthew, "I have started to fight for the dark and oppressed peoples of the world; now suddenly I have seen a light."[43] Kautilya's words almost appear as a negative image of Matthew's first encounter with her. Where Matthew initially felt "a sense of color" against the whiteness of his environment, only able to sense but not articulate the importance of their encounter, Kautilya has developed that feeling of recognition into a vision of politics— a "light" in the struggle for dark peoples of the world, hope amidst the glaring ideological failures of the colored committee.[44]

Sanda Mayzaw Lwin has noted how the encounter between Kautilya and Matthew revises an autobiographical scene from The Souls of Black Folk, which was central in Du Bois's development of the double consciousness concept. In a childhood tableau set in school, a white girl refuses to exchange cards with a young Du Bois, and he would later recall the incident as a formative moment in his racial, social, and political development. At the time, he noted that "it dawned upon me with a certain suddenness that I was different from the others."[45] Contrasting that scene with Kautilya and Matthew's first meeting in *Dark Princess*, Lwin argues that "both of these formative encounters involve being looked at by an other who is racialized and gendered differently—the white girl who sees the young Du Bois's blackness and rejects his token of friendship, and the Asian princess who sees Matthew Towns and calls on him to live up to his potential as a world leader."[46] Both cases mark racial interpellation. In the schoolyard, the white girl makes Du Bois conscious of his otherness and—much like Frantz Fanon's evocative scene of interpellation in *Black Skin, White Masks*—he is "sealed into [a] crushing objecthood."[47] But Du Bois presents Kautilya's racial interpellation of Matthew not as an objectification of his Blackness, as much as a feeling of mutual recognition. In that moment, Matthew ponders not how he was "different from the [white] others," but rather, how he was similar to the colonized and colored masses. Over the course of the novel, he attempts to make sense of this alternative gaze that comes from an other who sees him, not with the objection and pity he has come to expect through the color line, but as the vanguard of twentieth century anticolonialism.

In what follows, we look at why India, of all places, was so central to this revision of double consciousness and what compelled Du Bois to posit it as the lens through which Black America could reimagine itself within a global, anticolonial framework.

Friends of Freedom

Du Bois's interest in India developed in earnest when he resided in New York City during World War I. He had been one of the charter members of Manhattan's Civic Club, an interracial collective of liberals, radicals, and bohemians often remembered in the annals of literary history for hosting what James Weldon Johnson would call the "coming out" party for the Harlem Renaissance.[48] In the late 1910s, the Civic Club had hosted the "India Group" (Chapter 2), which was composed of a committed but ideologically diverse cast of Indian supporters including Agnes Smedley, Lajpat Rai, and Sailendranath Ghose. Whether Du Bois directly participated in the group is not entirely clear, but during that decade, he had become an acquaintance of Rai, Ghose, Smedley, and other New York-based Indian activists such as K. D. Shastri, the chairman of the Hindustanee Students' Convention who later became secretary of the IHRLA. In the years that followed, letters to Du Bois from figures such as Smedley and Ghose invariably began with a reminder that Du Bois had first crossed paths with them at the Civic Club.[49]

Among all these figures from the expatriate Indian network, Rai had the most lasting relationship with Du Bois. When he arrived in the United States in 1914, Rai had drawn on Du Bois's contacts as he made his tour across the American South, details of which found their way into his study *The United States of America*. In one of their earliest recorded meetings on September

21, 1917, the pair were invited to speak on a panel sponsored by the Intercollegiate Socialist Society. Rai and Du Bois took turns discussing, and to a large degree casting suspicion on, the Wilsonian promise that the war would make the world "safe for democracy."[50] Du Bois began his comments by turning toward America's checkered historical record, pointing out that neither the American Revolution nor the Civil War had actually been fought for the inclusion of African Americans into the fold of citizenship. Even Abraham Lincoln, "the man called the Emancipator," had repeatedly stated that his primary concern was maintaining the union between North and South and "would maintain slavery to preserve the Union."[51] When it was Lajpat Rai's turn to speak, he began with a nod to Du Bois, offering that "Problems of the Hindu and of the negro and cognate problems are not local, but world problems."[52] In a freewheeling talk, Rai railed against the war effort by criticizing the hypocrisy of the Allies claiming that their cause was to defend democracy while evading their role as imperialist powers colonizing the globe. He eluded to former U.S. Secretary of State Elihu Root's famous quote supporting America's entry into the war: "To be safe, democracy must kill its enemy [. . .] The world can not be half democratic and half autocratic."[53] Rai pointed out the incongruities between empire and democracy, noting how empire by definition is autocratic:

> The question is not whether the world can be half democratic and half autocratic [as in the Allies and Central Powers], but one-tenth democratic and nine-tenths autocratic. The vast bulk of the peoples of the world live in Africa and Asia. Do you see any proposals as to how the populations of Asia and Africa are to be included in the new democracy after the war?[54]

Both Rai and Du Bois challenged the Allied Powers' rhetoric of democracy, reminding the audience that Euro-American empire was at the roots of the Great War. In his 1915 essay "The African Roots of War" published in *The Atlantic*, Du Bois went so far as describing the cause of the war emerging from the European scramble for the African continent, a contest that entailed "lying treaties, [. . .] murder, assassination, mutilation, rape, and torture" by the Allies and Central Powers alike.[55] Throughout his essay, Du Bois pointed to the way that modern democratic regimes went "hand in hand" with the inequalities wrought by racial difference, that the wealth and accumulation that fueled modernity came from the exploitation of "the darker nations of the world."[56] If it was peace that American liberals were after, then, Du Bois contended, "we must extend the democratic ideal to the yellow, brown, and black peoples."[57] Both Rai and Du Bois reframed the war as an imperial contest among Americans and Europeans rather than as a battle between the autocrats of the Central Powers and democratic Allies. To paraphrase a line from Agnes Smedley's *Daughter of Earth*, Rai and Du Bois constantly had their eyes on the war, and their eyes were "cynical about the phrases of democracy."[58]

By the 1910s, Du Bois had continued to express support for anti-imperialist movements, finding in their challenge to the color line a link to the cause of freedom for African Americans. During the war, he continued his efforts to support the Indian cause, lending his name to the national council of the Friends of Freedom for India (Chapter 2). Sifting through Du Bois's personal papers, one notices a number of materials related to the organization: "A Manifesto of the Indian National Party" (the same "party" that led to the arrests of Ghose and Smedley), rubber-stamped with "Compliments of Friends of Freedom for India"; a pamphlet titled "Women and New India" authored by Agnes Smedley; and a note on "How to Form a Regular Branch of the Friends of Freedom for India" with the modest recruitment requirement of "ten or more individuals."[59] The Gadar Party publication *Independent Hindustan* had reported that Du Bois had attended the National Convention of the Friends of Freedom for India on December 5, 1920, held in New York, but does not reveal much besides his attendance.[60] These papers suggest that Du Bois was more an ally and friend, willing to lend his name and share contacts, but not an on-the-ground activist for the movement.

While Du Bois may have only been peripherally involved in the expatriate Indian anticolonial movement, the colonial situation in India continued to interest him intellectually throughout the decade. As editor of the NAACP's the *Crisis*, he often struck up correspondences with figures directly involved in India. In 1924, he had exchanged letters with the Hindi writer Banarsidas Chaturvedi, who had been residing at the Gandhi ashram in Ahmedabad when he first contacted Du Bois to request copies of the *Crisis*. The two floated the idea of a possible visit to India and the rest of Asia, and Chaturvedi ensured Du Bois that he was well known among the Indian educated classes who "feel as strongly on colour problems as the people of your race."[61] Chaturvedi suggested that Du Bois also make a stop in nearby East Africa, an outpost of the Indian diaspora, so that he witness the "important part India can play in the regeneration of the African races."[62] While Du Bois cited costs as preventing him from making the voyage, he did agree to Chaturvedi's request for a contribution to a special issue of the Hindi magazine *Chand* "devoted to the cause of Indians abroad."[63] Du Bois crafted a statement that framed the shared struggle of African Americans and Indians against the "color bar":

> Twelve million Americans of Negro descent, grandchildren and great grandchildren of Africans, forcibly stolen and brought to America, are fighting here in the midst of the United States a spiritual battle for freedom, citizenship and the right to be themselves

both in color of skin and manner of thought. This is the same terrible battle of the color bar which our brothers in India are fighting. We stretch out, therefore, hands of fellowship and understanding across the world and ask for sympathy in our difficulties just as you in your strife for a new country and a new freedom have the good wishes of every Negro in America.[64]

Du Bois's statement of solidarity, which drew connections between the "spiritual battle for freedom" fought by African Americans and "terrible battle of the color bar" faced by Indians, was predicated on the idea that their movements were interrelated. Du Bois had long argued that the struggle against racial inequality was the connective tissue between Asia and Black America, between anticolonial struggles for self-determination and the fight for equal rights in the United States. His "color line" concept had been developed to frame the problem of American racism as a "local phase" of an international problem, placing the struggle of African Americans into a global field that included colonized Africa, the Americas, and the West Indies, as well as "the brown and yellow myriads" in Asia.[65] Du Bois was convinced that the same color line that ran through Mississippi, Harlem, and Chicago ran through places like Bombay and Johannesburg, each coordinate marking a site of colonial rule. Racism was the mechanism that allowed the machinery of colonialism—in Asia, Africa, the Caribbean, Pacific Islands, and the United States—to operate.

It was this fact that undermined interracial working-class solidarities in the United States, Du Bois would argue in *Black Reconstruction* (1935), and rendered the white proletariat class as pawns in an imperialist game. Du Bois contended that white laborers in the South had "by persistent propaganda and police force" sided with their white exploiters, that their allegiance to whiteness would overrule any form of cross-racial class consciousness. "The South," he wrote, "is not interested in freedom for dark India."[66] This theme appeared in Du Bois's writing as early as the 1920s. In a column from the *Crisis* themed around "Socialism and the Negro," Du Bois had answered a query from a young radical who had challenged him to consider how the global white proletariat was not to blame for imperialism and the plight of "Negroes and other dark peoples" worldwide. Du Bois responded, "I maintain that the English working classes *are* exploiting India [. . .] that the working classes of America *are* subjugating Santo Domingo and Haiti. [. . .] He is a co-worker in the miserable modern subjugation of over half the world."[67] As Du Bois continued to develop the concept of the color line, he used it to signal not only the relationships of Jim Crow, colonialism, and the legacies of slavery, but to mark the ideological barrier—the veil—that prevented interracial solidarities from forming with the white working class. Race complicated the relations of class, and India was shorthand for the colonial example that made this abundantly clear.

Du Bois's correspondence and affiliation with Indian intellectuals was at least partially why India remained so persistently on his radar. A steady stream of letters from editors of Indian newspapers such as the *Guardian* in Calcutta and the *People* in Lahore turn up in Du Bois's archive, often requesting a free exchange with the *Crisis*. Other Indians would contact Du Bois as an authority on the "Negro Question," such as K. Paramu Pillai, a headmaster at a high school in Travancore and Malayali translator of Booker T. Washington. Pillai had written a letter to Du Bois in 1908 requesting his publications and adding that he was "keen on the American negro question, and that negro war for life and liberty."[68] Du Bois's status as a prominent intellectual also meant that he crossed paths with Indian anticolonialists during his travels. In 1911, Du Bois attended the Universal Race Congress in London, which organized leaders from around the globe to discuss the "general relations subsisting between the peoples of the West and those of the East, between so-called white and so-called coloured peoples, with a view to encouraging in between them a fuller understanding."[69] There, Du Bois would have seen Brahmo Samaj leader Brajendra Nath Seal, who delivered a speech on the meaning of "race, tribe, and nation" during the first session of the conference.[70] Incidentally, the NAACP's Mary White Ovington, also in attendance, would later claim that it was at the Race Congress that Du Bois met the real-life inspiration for *Dark Princess*: "I think I saw the dark princess in 1911 as she came down the steps of the ballroom at the last meeting [. . .] By the Princess's side was one of the most distinguished men at the Conference, Burghardt Du Bois."[71] The two were discussing the race problem, Ovington added.

The mystery surrounding who was the source of the inspiration for Princess Kautilya has left scholars taking on the role of literary detective, retracing steps that have led to a coterie of characters from Indian nationalist history. Homi Bhabha has suggested the real princess may have been Madame Bhikaji Cama, a Parsi revolutionary who attended the International Socialist Congress in Stuttgart when Du Bois was studying in Berlin.[72] Other scholars have suggested that the inspiration for the princess was Lajpat Rai, given their documented friendship during the war. Madhumita Lahiri, for instance, convincingly demonstrates how Kautilya's background resembles an amalgam of Indian nationalists, including Rai, Annie Besant, and Gandhi. Like Besant, who had worked with a matchworker's union, Kautilya works for a time in the "box-makers' union," and like Gandhi, Kautilya works with the ambulance corps during the war. Lahiri also explains that Kautilya's "domestic program" resembles Rai's Arya Samaj, both in its position on religion ("go back to the ancient simplicity of Brahma") as well as its political efforts on challenging caste, investing in public welfare, and establishing public schools.[73] Nico Slate suggests that the inspiration may have been Sarojini Naidu, who lectured in the United States just before the publication of *Dark*

Princess, while Bill Mullen goes so far as proposing that the romance in *Dark Princess* was partially inspired by the cross-racial relationship between Agnes Smedley and Virendranath Chattopadhyay, with several allusions also made to Rai and the Berlin Committee, as a whole.[74]

Read separately, each of these arguments are reasonable conjectures, strung together from a myriad of historical clues. When taken together, they illustrate how interconnected the expatriate nationalist movement was, how it spanned continents, including North America, Asia, and Europe. While the exact inspiration may be impossible to determine, critics such as Vermonja Alston have also cautioned against the temptation to "turn fantasy into fact," pointing to the long history of critics reading African American literature through a narrow realist lens.[75] Alston instead proposes that the only way to understand Kautilya is as a composite, stitched together from Du Bois's readings and his relationships.[76] Kautilya could only ever be a character cobbled together from different sources, an assemblage of lives and texts. To go back to the letter that Du Bois sent to Dhan Gopal Mukerji, he admitted that all he knew of India was from reading and his "acquaintances from India."[77]

But the scholarly impulse to search for the real-life correlative of Du Bois's "princess" may stem less from a bad faith effort to read African American literature as sociology, or fiction as fact, and instead come from the desire to excavate a history of collaboration, in which Indian and African American activists had together sought to challenge the color line. Historical scholarship by Gerald Horne, Bill Mullen, Vijay Prashad, Nico Slate, and many others have pointed out how the lives of African Americans and South Asian immigrants had been intertwined since the late nineteenth century.[78] Though the story of how the U.S. civil rights movement had adopted principles of noncooperation and civil disobedience from Gandhi is well known, scholars have more recently pointed to other histories of exchange that tell a more variegated story about the contours of international solidarity. Richard Wright's visit to the Bandung Conference of 1955, which resulted in his volume *The Color Curtain* (1956) had conceived of emergent "Third World" solidarities between the recently decolonized nations in Asia and Africa and oppressed peoples in the West.[79] On the other hand, when Dalit leader B. R. Ambedkar briefly corresponded with Du Bois about the National Negro Congress petition to the United States, which attempted to secure minority rights through the U.N. council, he implicitly challenged the analogy between colonized Indians and African Americans, pointing to the caste hierarchies that stratified the "color line."[80] Historian Vivek Bald's archival recovery of two waves of Bengali migrants—peddlers who arrived to the United States in the late nineteenth century, and Muslim lascar sailors who jumped ship during the height of the Asian exclusion era—highlight the role that Black and Puerto Rican communities, and women in particular, played in providing refuge and forming new, syncretic communities.[81] These histories challenge the late twentieth-century discourse that characterized South Asians as a "model minority," the image of a politically acquiescent, financially ascendant, and often aspirationally white figure who plays into a racial discourse that discredits the prevalence and persistence of racism in America. It is in that spirit that we might take a different tack and ask what purpose did the character Kautilya, or for that matter the India imagined in *Dark Princess*, serve? What do they enable for Matthew Towns and for the broader politics of the novel? And how does the novel contribute to what community historian Anirvan Chatterjee describe as "the secret history of South Asian and African American solidarity"?[82]

The intersections between African American and Indian figures during the interwar period when Du Bois wrote *Dark Princess* provide scant but significant evidence of the ways that both communities had either sought or seen in one another's struggle an echo of their own. Future Congress Party leader Jayaprakash Narayan spent much of the 1920s as a graduate student in the Midwest, where he worked in the Black quarters of Chicago as a peddler. Pranav Jani has suggested that Narayan's experiences of racism impacted his political development as he adopted more radical positions after returning to India in 1929 to join the noncooperation movement.[83] H. G. Mudgal (Chapter 3), another Indian student who came to the United States for higher education, worked for the *Daily Negro Times* and its successor *Negro World*, both mouthpieces for Pan-Africanist Marcus Garvey and his organization the Universal Negro Improvement Association (UNIA).[84] By 1930, Mudgal was hired as the acting managing editor for *Negro World*, becoming a familiar name in Harlem political circles, where he regularly gave speeches, organized panels, and turned up for debates defending the movement's vision for racial uplift through economic empowerment. In his columns, Mudgal often stressed the interconnected nature of the African American struggle with worldwide anti-imperialist movements. Issues of *Negro World* often published articles about the Indian nationalist movement, including a steady output of news reports, announcements for lectures, and occasional editorials. For Mudgal, it was clear that anticolonial and national struggles in India, Egypt, China, and Africa would "have an effect on the destiny of the Negro, not only in Africa but even in the United States."[85]

The support for Indian freedom that appeared in the African American press was substantial enough to become a concern for British and American intelligence. Just a few days after Rai and Du Bois's joint speech for the Intercollegiate Socialist Society, Du Bois received a letter from a major in the Department of War with a veiled threat. "Mr. Lajpat Rai seems anxious for trouble," the letter read. "Did anything of his address bear upon the negro question in this country?"[86] A memo from the U.S. Military Intelligence Division during the same period singled out the "revolutionary Negro newspaper" the *Messenger,* among other radical papers, for publishing "one-sided and virulent articles" from Indian expatriate nationalists.[87] As it happens, several other Black newspapers had taken an interest in the Indian independence movement. In his "Views and Reviews" column for the *New York Age,* James Weldon Johnson compared the strategies of Irish and Indian anticolonialism to African American resistance. "The Irish, the East Indian, and the Negro in America are at present engaged in a battle for rights, but each is employing distinctly different methods."[88] Johnson commented that African Americans ought to observe and study these movements with care, given their potential value for struggles at home. In another editorial, Johnson added that while the violent methods of the Irish were neither practical nor available to African Americans, the Gandhian methods of noncooperation very well might be: "Suppose, for example, that a colored man was arrested and placed in jail, and there were threats of lynching him, what would be the effect if all of the colored people in that community, town or city, put into practice [. . .] principles of non-cooperation?" Johnson hedged on the effectiveness, but added that a strike by "colored women" might produce immediate impact, since "the prospect of having to do their own work would strike greater terror to the hearts of the white ladies of the South than if the Negroes were threatening with guns."[89]

Under the editorship of Du Bois, the *Crisis* reported news from India, printing a slew of stories on the noncooperation movement, including a piece by Indian American Syud Hossain and notices from the Friends of Freedom for India.[90] In the early 1920s, Du Bois had included several pieces on Gandhi, among them a five-page profile, a hagiographic poem, and a shorter piece titled "India's Saint," featuring approving quotes by NAACP leader John Haynes Holmes, India Home Rule League secretary J. T. Sunderland, and FFI member Basanta Kumar Roy.[91] Stories about Gandhi and the noncooperation movement also turned up in *The Brownies' Book,* a children's magazine edited by Du Bois and Jessie Fauset.[92] In his monthly column "As the Crow Flies," Du Bois took his young readers on an itinerary across the British Empire, documenting the unrest in Egypt, Ireland, and India. "Hundred millions of brown people are much incensed at the injustice of English rule," he explained, adding that a "large part of them are trying to secure their freedom."[93]

Du Bois's engagement with the Indian movement certainly influenced and shaped the narrative of *Dark Princess.* From his direct interactions with figures such as Lajpat Rai and organizations like the FFI to his study of the Indian political situation, we can trace how his thinking influenced the invention of Kautilya. This is a thought echoed by many, including Vijay Prashad who argues that the community of Indian radicals and progressives that Du Bois had come across provided the "social and historical basis" for the princess.[94] But Prashad points out that Du Bois had also critically misread them, rendering them as aristocratic and, for inexplicable reasons, "felt the need to exoticize them and to gender Asia female."[95] Vermonja Alston adds that Kautilya is a feminized "synecdoche" of a particularly Hegelian construction of India, "an exotic jewel, a marvel to which all nations must journey."[96] We might add that Princess Kautilya represents "Mother India" herself, much like the illustration that adorned covers of the *United States of India* (Figure 0.3) bridging East and West.

If the Indian movement had become a "site of struggle against imperialism and racism" for Black America, then, Kautilya, as an embodiment of India, functioned as the regenerative other through which Matthew Towns could begin to see himself anew.[97] There is admittedly something troubling about this. Indian women become a means to an end, a sort of fictitious surrogate that birth an "Afro-Asian" future. Tamara Bhalla points out that in the novel and its scholarly response, femininity and women altogether are disavowed within Black–Asian political imaginaries, compounding a heteronormative and patriarchal Orientalism that are "overlooked as the collateral damage of the novel's visionary perspective on transnational and cross-racial alliance."[98] The novel's gendered fault lines might be attributed to shortcomings in ideology. Several scholars have noted that the gender and sexual politics that run through the novel are in keeping with certain strains in Du Bois's thought: the "essentialist representations of reproductive heterosexuality,"[99] the prescriptive ideas around Black masculinity and femininity, even the flirtation with oligarchic politics signal certain shortcomings in the novel's radical potential.[100] But some of this could also be attributable to literary form itself; the romance as a genre was predicated on a narrative resolution that entailed heterosexual pairings. Matthew and Kautilya—like Hermia and Lysander or Elizabeth and Mr. Darcy—are, by the very structure of "romance," bound for, and bound to, one another.

In spite of these incisive criticisms, it is worth ruminating on the possibilities that *Dark Princess* offered in its time, and how they compared to the forms of transnational politics and writing that this book has thus far discussed. To return to our key term, we might consider how, more than an embodiment of India, Kautilya is a character who facilitates a form of transnational refraction, a means to rethink the position of African Americans within the global anticolonial struggle. Taking refraction as a point of focus, we especially notice how much *Dark Princess* resembles *Daughter of Earth*, each novel staging a generative back-and-forth exchange between an American and Indian radical. In Chapter 2, I argued how the dialogue and debate between Marie Brown and Sardar Ranjit Singh illustrate the dialectics of transnational refraction, the way that antipodean worlds collide, each rendering the other transformed. Singh reorients Marie's perspective, challenging her Eurocentricity while pushing her to draw the connections between the struggles against capitalism and colonialism; Marie, in response, tells

Singh of a "new order being born [. . .] neither eastern or western."[101] In the case of *Dark Princess*, a similar reorientation occurs for both Matthew and Kautilya, not only through the obvious consummation of their romance as most critics have suggested, but through an epistolary exchange that takes place in its final chapter.

Much like in *Daughter of Earth*, in Du Bois's novel, it is the figure of the Indian anticolonalist rather than the Bolshevik, as one might have expected, that provides the catalyst for this new global synthesis. And while Bill Mullen reminds us that the political positions alluded to in *Dark Princess* had real-life corollaries in the Comintern politics of the 1920s, it is ultimately the Indian figure that so powerfully provides Matthew with the lens to envision a new global imaginary. What marked *Dark Princess* as so distinctive from Smedley's contemporary novel, however, was that Du Bois eschewed proletarian realism, instead utilizing the genre of fantasy—a racially recoded and deeply Orientalist fantasy, at that—to imagine this newly ordered world.

Vijay Prashad is correct in arguing that within the long, historical tradition of Black–Indian political solidarity, India was imagined by African American activists as a "site of struggle against imperialism and racism" rather than a world as imagined by the Orientalists.[102] But, as we will see, Orientalist thought was melded with political struggle in the fantastical imaginaries of Du Bois's novel.

Bwodpur and the Black South

Du Bois's engagement with the history and mythology of India appears most prominently in the novel's final section, titled "The Maharajah of Bwodpur." After the long third chapter, Matthew has finally broken off his marriage to Sara, and both he and Kautilya dream of their future work in battling the color line. Rather than discussing the nuts and bolts of anticolonial revolution, however, their language delves curiously into the mythic, evoking Hindu gods and goddesses and an ancient history of India far removed from the present. In one scene, Matthew and Kautilya walk along the shoreline of Chicago and (in an echo of the opening on the S.S. *Orizaba*) stare into Lake Michigan's "waving waters."[103] Matthew playfully teases her, calling her Scheherazade and asking her "from what fairyland you came?"[104] In a long passage, Kautilya describes her India through a mixture of cosmology, fable, and myth, a reflection of Du Bois's erudite but eclectic reading list. "India! India! Out of black India the world was born," Kautilya begins, describing the subcontinent as the big bang of humanity. In her eyes, India is the place where the world was conceived and "the world shall creep to die."[105] It is a place of superlatives, where the mountains are "the loftiest," the rivers are "the mightiest," the plains are "widest," and oceans "broadest."[106] "All that the world has done, India did," Kautilya continues, and without any misgivings boasts, "and that more marvelously, more magnificently."[107] Her India is a microcosm of world religions "from divine Gotama to the sons of Mahmoud and the stepsons of the Christ," where human beings appear in "every shape and [. . .] hue," and, in a quick reference to Kipling's *The Jungle Book*, she mentions "the Bandar-log" or monkey-men, who are also part of the "drama of life" that unfolds daily in the subcontinent.[108]

Such descriptions of India as a site of fantasy have lead critics such as Dohra Ahmad to rightly charge that "India and Kautilya function not as a geographical reality and a human reality [. . .] but rather as conceptual categories powered by the vocabulary and imagery of Orientalism."[109] Even in the passage above, Du Bois seems to wear his Orientalist references openly, from the nod to *Arabian Nights* ("tell me beautiful things, Scheherazade"), Kipling ("the laugh of the Bandar-log"), and Shakespeare ("fairyland"). The novel's dedication to "Titania XXVII" (as in the year '27) was an obvious nod to *A Midsummer Night's Dream*, a tale that also involved an Indian boy kept offstage for the length of the story.[110] The princess's namesake itself comes from the fourth-century B.C. minister of the Mauryan emperor Chandragupta and author of *Arthashastra*, a treatise on Indian statecraft and political power, which had been translated into English just a decade earlier in 1915. The Vedas make a brief cameo as well. Just before her monologue on India, Kautilya is described laying "aside [her] books" and reading "the sacred words of the Rig-veda" as if she emerges wholly out of the texts themselves.[111]

More than fairytale and fantasy, however, Du Bois's greatest influences in *Dark Princess's* India seemed to have come from Orientalist scholarship. Through his own racial interpretation, Du Bois transforms Orientalist histories of India into ones that resonate with the history of Black America. *Dark Princess* renders India as a mythological—almost primordial—site of "blackness," the missing link in an ancient African–Asian civilization. This was of a piece with Du Bois's later writings on India, particularly in his work of history *The World and Africa*, published two decades later in 1947. In the chapter "Asia in Africa," Du Bois frames the history of ancient India into a Manichean narrative of whites and Blacks, which implicitly offered analogies to African American history.[112] This begins with Du Bois's reference to a prehistoric land bridge that had connected the two continents, placing Black people as central figures in the development of South Asian civilization:

The ethnic history of India would seem to be first a prehistoric substratum of Negrillos or black dwarfs; then the pre-Dravidians, a taller, larger type of Negro; then the Dravidians, Negroes with some mixture of Mongoloid and later of Caucasoid stocks. The Dravidian Negroes laid the bases of Indian culture thousands of years before the Christian era. On these descended through Afghanistan an Asiatic or Eastern European element, usually called Aryan.

> The *Rig Veda*, ancient sacred hymns of India, tells of the fierce
> struggles between these whites and blacks for the mastery of India.
> It sings of Aryan deities who rushed furiously into battle against the
> black foe. The hymns praise Indra, the white deity, for having killed
> fifty thousand blacks, "piercing the citadel of the enemy" and forcing
> the blacks to run out in distress [. . .] The blacks under their renowned
> leader Krishna, that is, "The Black," fought back with valor. The
> whites long held the conquered blacks in caste servitude, but eventu-
> ally the color line disappeared before commerce and industry, inter-
> marriage, and defense against enemies from without.[113]

In this lengthy passage, Du Bois draws on what Thomas Trautmann has
described as the "racial theory of Indian civilization," a master narrative of
India that posited that the culture and peoples of the subcontinent were the
outcome of the conquest and eventual mixture of "light-skinned civilizing
invaders (the Aryans) and dark-skinned barbarian aborigines (often identified as Dravidians)."[114] German philologists such as Max Müller had drawn
on theories of language to postulate that Indo-Aryan languages (Hindi, Bengali, Punjabi, Marathi, etc.) and European languages shared a common an-
cestor, which led to his belief that modern Indian and Englishman shared
the same "blood."[115] By the late nineteenth century, a consensus had formed
around this theory and it was widely accepted by various disciplines.

British Orientalists such as Herbert Hope Risley, Arthur Anthony Macdonell, and Arthur Berriedale Keith, who were less interested in theories of
language than they were of the racial science of anthropometry, took Müller's readings of the *Rig Veda* and ran with them. They quoted selectively,
drawing huge conclusions from a scant few passages and relying on iffy
translations to render the theory of Aryan invasion of India into a racial
contest. In one story, which described the Vedic god Indra stripping the
"black skin" (*krisna tvach*) of a demon (*asura*) named "The Black" (*krisna*),
they saw evidence of differences in complexion.[116] They drew on Müller's
translation of "*vrsasipra*" as "without a nose" to mean "flat-nosed," fueling
their theories of nose width as another telltale sign of racial difference.[117]
Such forms of interpretation attempted to extract "objective facts" from mythology, rather than considering the specific meanings of the terms within
their mythological framing. As a result, Trautmann explains, British Orientalists like Macdonell and Keith were especially prone to "back-projection of
systems of racial segregation in the American South and South Africa onto
early Indian history."[118] Victorian ideas of racial division were mapped onto
the social geography of ancient India. Such projections also helped reinforce
the present hierarchies of the British Empire: "the relations of the British
'new invader from Europe' with the peoples of India is prefigured thousands
of years before by the invading Aryans."[119] For British Orientalists, race, and

especially the division between white and black races, was a "permanent, transhistorical" fact, which had been shaping the ancient Indian world and continued into the present nineteenth century.[120] The proof was in the Vedas, or so it appeared to the Orientalists.

Trautmann explains that these were misreadings of a history that scholars could not know, a reflection of their modern biases and beliefs rather than an objective understanding of the ancient past. As it turns out, Du Bois drew heavily from the overall claims in the Orientalists' racial interpretation of Aryan invasion, never questioning them. And like them, he took the meaning of Aryan invasion in India to be an example of the racial conquest of whites against blacks, guilty too of "back-projecting" the institutions of imperialism and segregation onto this unknowable past. But importantly, unlike British Orientalists, his interpretation undermined the notion that ancient India justified racial domination or that the Aryans were in anyway superior to the people they conquered. Instead, he plumbed this Orientalist "history" for a narrative of racial resistance and resilience. Indigenous, Dravidian India was indisputably "Negro," Du Bois argued, and it remained so in spite of racial mixture. Du Bois then turned to Hindu mythology to place characters into this racial matrix. Indra, the Vedic god of heaven is described as "the white deity," a powerful murderer and dispossessor of "fifty thousand blacks." Krishna "The Black" is reimagined as a historical leader of the persecuted. If the British Orientalists had used stories in the *Rig Veda* as a means of reinforcing ideas of racial difference and white supremacy, then Du Bois used those same stories to center ideas of transhistorical Black suffering and resistance.

I am less interested in pointing out the problems in Du Bois's claims, which, for all intents and purposes, are only as problematic as the sources he cited. What is more compelling to think through are the effects that his re-coding of the then-prominent racial theory of Indian civilization had at the time. For one, Du Bois's narrative of India challenged the racial identification of Indians as exclusively "Aryan," "Caucasian," and, hence, "white." As discussed in Chapter 1, Indian migrants and nationalists had drawn on this category of "Aryan" to make claims for citizenship as well as to contest the justification of colonial rule on racial grounds. Du Bois had repeatedly challenged what he perceived as the imagined "white" alliance among Indians, who were "tempt[ed] to stand apart from the darker peoples and seek her affinities among whites [. . .] wish[ing] to regard herself as 'Aryan' rather than 'colored.'"[121] In addition, we might consider how Du Bois scripted a narrative of ancient Indian history that provided evidence for India as an ancient "Black" civilization, replete with epic tales of Black resistance against white thralldom. This ancient Black India effectively undermined the Eurocentrism of history, which had foregrounded "white" contributions to world culture and diminished contributions from the darker world. As Alys Weinbaum argues, Du Bois's India undermines the notion that "Europe and specifically Greece were the origin of civilization."[122] Vermonja Alston too has suggested that Du Bois had revised Hegel's *Philosophy of History,* replacing the birth of civilization from ancient Greece to ancient India.[123] If ancient India was rooted in the West—as the "racial theory of Indian civilization" claims it was—then it too could be understood as an outgrowth of the Occident, a branch off the trunk of European culture. In categorizing ancient India as indisputably Black, Du Bois untied the genealogical threads that connected Asia to Europe and drew attention to the ones connecting it to Africa.

We can describe this doubled interpretation—that is, the revisionist interpretation of an Orientalist interpretation—as a kind of refraction of a refraction. Du Bois disrupted the white Eurocentric gaze through which British Orientalists had interpreted the origins of ancient Indian civilization, and instead, interpreted it through an Afrocentric lens. While he did not dispute their evidence nor attempt to undermine their claims, he chose instead to provide a different interpretation of the story the evidence told. He recast the genre, so to speak: the Aryan invasion of India was not a triumphant tale of white conquest, but instead, a story of resistance in which the oppressed "Blacks" were the protagonist. The society they constructed, according to Du Bois, also challenged the racial order in ways that were bewildering for the twentieth-century reader.

In his chapter "Asia in Africa" from *The World and Africa,* Du Bois describes ancient India as a topsy-turvy world of power relations that disrupted modern understandings of racial hierarchy, a dense forest of myth, knowledge, and imagination into which one could escape the color line. In one passage, in fact, Du Bois argues that in ancient India the "color line" was undone. In an echo of the dinner scene in *Dark Princess,* Du Bois explains how in India "whites enlisted in the service of blacks," and even the caste-privileged "Brahmans are as black and as flat-nosed as the early Negro chiefs."[124] Power, in other words, did not depend on color and complexion. Just as he rendered Krishna into a Black leader of *racial* resistance, Du Bois argued that Buddha was also Black and of "negroid type," drawing on a theory floated by Egyptologist Gerald Massey.[125] For Du Bois, ancient India's histories and mythologies contained enough signs and symbols for him to rework into a narrative of a great Black civilization that flourished outside of the West. This imagined past could be put in service for an imaginary future for the darker world.

Twenty years before the publication of *The World and Africa* (1947), Du Bois introduced several of these themes in Bwodpur, the fictitious Indian kingdom of *Dark Princess.* Kautilya's description of her kingdom bears more than a passing resemblance to Du Bois's take on the racial theory of Indian civilization. She explains, "We came out of the black South in ancient days [. . .] then, scorning the yoke of the Aryan invaders, moved to Bwodpur, and there we gave birth to Buddha, black Buddha of the curly hair."[126] That Kauti-lya's people flee the "black South" to escape the "Aryan invaders" clearly echoes the Aryan invasion theory, but it also resembles another place in the novel's transnational imaginary. The ancient "white Aryans" who oppress the black Dravidians in the subcontinent's south provide an analogy to the white Americans under whose "yoke" African Americans suffer in the U.S. South. The racial theory of Indian civilization, posited by nineteenth-century British Orientalism and reimagined by Du Bois, serves as one of the mythic intertexts of the novel, lurking just beneath the novel's realist veneer. The color line that belts the United States also shaped Bwodpur.

Projecting Black India onto the Black Belt and Hindu signifiers onto African American characters is a running theme that cuts through *Dark Princess*. Through Kautilya, Black characters are described as Hindu gods and goddesses, Vedic traditions are connected to African spirituality in quick asides and discussions. Shortly after Matthew and Kautilya consum-mate their relationship, for instance, they call one another "Krishna" and "Radha."[127] What might have simply marked an innocuous (if somewhat cloying) exchange of affection transforms when considering Du Bois's inter-pretation of Krishna as a mythic Black leader of resistance. As Madhumita Lahiri has argued, Kautilya's nickname both elevates Matthew into the pro-phetic "enlightened race leader" who, through a form of "aesthetic trans-figuration," rescues "black sexuality from pathologization."[128] In another scene, the princess tells Matthew about her shock of recognition when she first meets his mother in the South and saw "Kali, the Black One; wife of Siva, Mother of the World!"[129] Matthew's mother is reimagined as a goddess from the Hindu mythos, a figure of feminine strength, who, Rebecka Rut-ledge Fisher suggests, is transformed into a "Pan-Africanist, maternal ideal, and a symbol of Indian nationalism."[130] Kautilya goes on to describe how upon seeing his mother she "knew that [she] was looking upon one of the ancient prophets of India." When she describes the old woman's religious rituals, she identifies them as West African ones originating and passed down from India.[131] Through Matthew's mother, Kautilya deciphers the civ-ilizational links that connect African America to India, "the intimacy of continents" (to use Lisa Lowe's phrase) whose links have been obscured through history.[132] Those visions appear to her as refracted glimpses that come in and out of focus, each driven by Du Bois's larger project in the novel to link Blackness to India.

Kautilya effectively serves, then, as a transnational prism to enable these visions across history, a means by which Du Bois recodes and reinterprets the mythologies of ancient India and projects them onto the landscape of Black America. The result is an uncanny rendering of the Black South, as glimpsed through the eyes of India, an India that itself was an invention of Du Bois. It is not only that Kautilya sees her Hindu mythos come alive in the Black characters she surrounds herself with, she also begins to reimagine how the Black South can serve as the key site in extending the struggles of anticolonialism and anti-racism into the heart of twentieth-century U.S. empire. By the end of the novel, Du Bois pushes the transnational connections that linked the myth and ancient history of Indian and Black people into the present, transforming them into a synthesis of internationalism that delivers on the promise stated at the outset of the novel: that "Pan-Africa belongs logically with Pan-Asia."[133] In a series of letters that the two exchange, Kautilya tries to share her way of seeing Black America—and specifically, Virginia—with Matthew.

The Virginia that Kautilya sees, however, is far removed from the place Matthew first describes in the beginning of the novel. While Matthew affectionately describes his mother and her farm, Virginia comes to represent a dead-end of progress. Early on, Matthew tells Kautilya how his life in Virginia would have culminated in a life of vocational training that "insisted on making [him] a farmer," a reference to the Hampton Institute and the political compromise of Booker T. Washington.[134] Kautilya, however, attempts to convince him that the seeds of the anticolonial world are planted in the Black Belt of the U.S. South. In one of her missives to Matthew, she describes a walk she takes with his mother, and the heady connection she felt between the social landscape of Virginia and her "world":

> This world is really much nearer to our world than I had thought [. . .] the river winds in stately curve down Jamestown-of-the-Slaves. We went down the other day, walking part of the way through the woods and dells, toward the great highway of the Atlantic. Think, Matthew, take your geography and trace it: from Hampton Roads to Guiana is a world of colored folk, and a world, men tell me, physically beautiful beyond conception; socially enslaved, industrially ruined, spiritually dead; but ready for the breath of Life and Resurrection. South is Latin America, east is Africa, and east of east lies my own Asia.[135]

The geography that Kautilya encourages Matthew to trace is, at first glance, a puzzling one. What exactly connects Hampton Roads, Virginia to Guiana, a British colony in South America? One answer comes from their shared history of conquest, slavery, and colonization and another, related to the first, comes from an Englishman who links the two places. Sir Walter Raleigh, the explorer who in the sixteenth century established the Virginia colony in North America, had, some years later, sailed to the west coast of South America in search of El Dorado, publishing an account of his voyage in *The Discoverie of Guiana*. The exploits of Walter Raleigh are not a particularly important detail in Matthew's "geography," but the chain of events that his encounter with the New World set off certainly are. The Guianas, divided and conquered by Dutch, Spanish, French, and British powers, were an example of the colonial machinery that cleaved Africa, Asia, and the Americas and created the global color line. Like Virginia, Guiana witnessed the decimation of indigenous people and the import of enslaved Africans—in Jamestown to work in tobacco and cotton fields, and in British Guiana to work in the sugar plantations. With the 1833 abolition of slavery in the British Empire, Guiana turned to indentured laborers from India, who continued to work in sugar plantations under horrific conditions. For Du Bois, Guiana may have represented the forces that brought the peoples of Africa and India together in the New World, a microcosm of the interconnected "world of colored folk" he imagined. Kautilya's insistence that Matthew "trace this geography" is an attempt to make him imagine the interconnections between the colonial world and the Black communities of Hampton Roads.

Matthew is unable to see or even accept the reconfigured geography that Kautilya proposes. He challenges her, stating that Virginia does not represent a site of anticolonial regeneration but a world of social death, home of "mob and rape and rope and faggot."[136] Instead, he is resigned to the fact that his political work remains in Chicago, a space of electoral politics and a Northern escape from Southern racism, which he believes to be "the epitome of America" and the "crossroads of the world—midway between Atlantic and Pacific, North and South Poles."[137] It is only in Chicago where Matthew believes he can work toward restoring the "balance and cooperation of the white and black worlds."[138] But Kautilya insists that the answer lies in the South, citing his mother's prophesies of a "new age" being born in Virginia. In Black America, Kautilya "see[s] a mighty synthesis":

> Here in Virginia you are at the edge of a black world. The black belt of the Congo, the Nile, and the Ganges reaches by way of Guiana, Haiti, and Jamaica, like a red arrow, up into the heart of white America. Thus I see a mighty synthesis: you can work in Africa and Asia right here in America if you work in the Black Belt. [. . .] I have been sore bewildered by this mighty America, this ruthless, terrible, intriguing Thing. My home and heart is India. Your heart of hearts is Africa. You may stand here, Matthew—here, halfway between Maine and Florida, between the Atlantic and the Pacific, with Europe in your face and China at your back; [. . .] and yet be in the Land of the Blacks.[139]

The contrast between Kautilya and Matthew's mappings—between claiming either Chicago or Virginia as "halfway between the Atlantic and Pacific"—is significant, and critics have interpreted how Du Bois sets the two places as foils against one another. The cold and gritty "realism" of Chicago is countered by the lush verdant fantasy of Virginia, mirroring what Dohra Ahmad has argued as the contest between a politics of limitation and a utopian politics of possibility. Daniel Elam has also commented on this passage, explaining how it "reroutes our imagination and renders peripheries into centers, ultimately undoing both."[140] Indeed, in the passage "white America" seems surrounded, a speck within a larger geographical canvas that includes Egypt, India, the Congo, the West Indies, China, and even Europe. Kautilya's map blows down the domestic borders of the nation-state, and the politics of Black America are reconceived as part of an international landscape that can challenge the color line. If the only itinerary that Matthew could have imagined in the opening scene of the novel to escape the racism of the United States were France, Germany, Russia, and the nebulous "Far East," Kautilya has reconstituted the terrain for politics, not as a place of escape but of confrontation.

Describing *Dark Princess* as a work of utopian imagination, scholar Amor Kohli argues that Du Bois presented a prescient model for the global South, "the land of the southern United States, Latin America, Africa and Asia are consolidated by a merging of the fertile, long-suffering black US South and a romanticized India."[141] For Kohli, Virginia is transformed into a "gestational" utopia; quite literally, by the novel's close the virgin land becomes the birthplace of Kautilya and Matthew's messianic son.[142] In the final pages, the two are married in a syncretic ceremony that entails his mother whispering "the first words of the old slave song of world revolution" and Brahmin priests and Muslim imams anointing the baby Madhu Chandragupta Singh as "Messenger and Messiah to all the Darker Worlds."[143] A common and convincing reading of the novel focuses on the allegory of Madhu's birth, interpreting the arrival of the mixed race child as a portent for an Afro-Asian future. As Paul Gilroy puts it, the messianic son represents a "dream of global co-operation among people of color" that would see different iterations across the history of the twentieth century—at the League Against Imperialism in Brussels in 1927, the Bandung Conference of 1955, and the multiple imaginaries of the "Third World" that persisted into the 1960s.[144]

But what interests me more about the conclusion is the epistolary back-and-forth that Du Bois stages between Kautilya and Matthew, which comes just before the arrival of their child. I want to suggest that this exchange represents the transnational refraction that Du Bois's engagement with the Indian cause had allowed him, what seeing Black America through his colleagues from the East had once provided. Matthew initially perceives Virginia as solely a site of Black trauma, while Kautilya insists on its potential, the traumatic epicenter of modernity that has now produced the conditions for an anticolonial vanguard. Like two optic lenses which, at just the right angles come into focus, Kautilya and Matthew's exchange together produce a new vision of the world, transformed.

It is for this reason that we might read the union of Kautilya and Matthew as the embodiment of an anticolonial, transracial, and transnational way of seeing. Just as the Indian anticolonialists that Marie Brown encounters in *Daughter of Earth* disrupted the ways by which she apprehended World War I, Kautilya persuades Matthew to reimagine Black America as the seat of global revolution. Whether Kautilya's real-life counterpart was Lajpat Rai, Bhikaiji Cama, or Banarsidas Chaturvedi is beside the point; what Du Bois borrowed from each of them was the tendency to compare, to see in Black America the "cognate problems" of India. In the end, perhaps, that comparative gaze is what allowed Du Bois to imagine in *Dark Princess* the rightful place of both Black America and India in the global struggle against racism.

Colored India

Decades after *Dark Princess*, Du Bois continued to urge the Indian and African American community to learn from one another's struggles. In an essay from 1935, he pressed for more literature that could lead to "sympathetic understanding" between African Americans and Indians, citing Rai's *The United States of America* as the "best effort in this line."[145] In Du Bois's mind, Rai had avoided writing a "conventional history of white America for the information of colored India," instead noting that he devoted a "quarter of his space" to a thoughtful and intelligent interpretation of the issues facing African Americans.[146] What had enabled this was friendship, Du Bois thought. While exiled, Rai had "gained wide acquaintance with American Negroes" as he travelled across the country.[147] It was unfortunate that African Americans had not written similar studies of India—works that could "orientate the thought of the people concerning the problems of that land"—but Du Bois also knew that impediments raised by the British and Americans that had made such connections nearly impossible. "If the *visé* (*sic*) is obtained," Du Bois added, "usually it is under the pledge to limit his words and activities."[148] Even if one were to circumvent those barriers, for both Blacks and Indians a voyage on a steamship "often involve[d] racial discrimination"—a harsh reality experienced by Rai on the S.S. *Philadelphia*, and illustrated in the opening scene of *Dark Princess*.[149]

In his commentary, Du Bois framed white America and Britain as the middlemen, mediating the terms of the Black and Indian encounter either by direct censorship or by making connections difficult to sustain. If we extend that thought, we might consider the various ways by which the images of Indians and African Americans were always mediated by Euro-American discourses on race. In his speech "Criteria for Negro Art," delivered just a year earlier, Du Bois had railed against the distorted and degrading representations of "colored people" that had become de facto in the white publishing industry. "They want Uncle Toms, Topsies, good 'darkies,' and clowns," Du Bois had told the crowd at the 1926 NAACP conference.[150] When his publishers sent a preliminary illustration of the Indian princess for the dust-jacket of *Dark Princess*, Du Bois saw even more evidence of this. The artist had "succeeded in making [the princess] ugly," he noted, adding that "no white American artist can paint a colored person without making it a caricature."[151]

In asking what might have been lost had Rai written a history of "white America" for "colored India," if he had only imbibed what white Americans had provided him, Du Bois seemed to imply another question: What might Black America be missing if they only hear the British and British-sympathizing version of the Indian story? As it turned out, the publication of Katherine Mayo's *Mother India* in 1927, which would spur a heated debate about the status of Indian colony that extended for years, would provide an opportunity to answer that question.

5

Uncle Sham

Katherine Mayo's Mother India *and Parodic Anti-imperialism*

Let us look over Uncle Sam, the giant; Uncle Sam, the father
of democracy; Uncle Sam, the would-be President of the
world; Uncle Sam whose morals are measured in great
dimensions, who is the patron of Christian Missions and
the outlawry of war.

—K. L. GAUBA, *Uncle Sham* (1929)

W hen the American writer Katherine Mayo was guided through the
streets of British Calcutta, she claimed to have discovered not one but
two cities: The first was "big, western, modern" and full of the sort of
buildings that "might belong to a prosperous American city"; the second, an
"Indian town of temples, mosques, bazaars" organized by labyrinthine alleys
that transgressed the "rectangular lines" of the city map.[1] Moving deeper into
that second city, Mayo jotted down sights that would later horrify, titillate,
and enrage the hundreds of thousands of readers that her book would attract
in the years to come. She wrote of a crowd surrounding two priests who
hacked the head off a goat, and a woman who sprang forward, dropping on
all fours to lap up its blood. Further along, Mayo wrote of scores of men and
mendicants, "fat," "hairy," and "begging," and a burning-ghat, in which the
corpse of a young woman—"blessed among women, in that she is saved from
widowhood"—was lit aflame over a funeral pyre.[2] These characters were the
opening players in Mayo's wildly popular 1927 exposé *Mother India*, the culmination of three months she spent in the country. Over the course of the
book, Mayo introduced such figures as the child bride and impotent Indian
male, the lower-caste "Untouchable" and the upper-caste Brahmin to provide
an indelible set of images of the subcontinent that would circulate as the
book became a worldwide best seller. Emphasizing the social ills of India's
population, Mayo's book was a sensationalist account of the native bodies
that made up colonial India, but its purpose was broader than providing the
Western reader a voyeuristic lens on India. Published during nationalist

agitations against the controversial Government of India Act of 1919, which had denied Indians dominion status within the Empire, and during domestic political challenges to the U.S. 1924 Immigration Act, which barred Indian immigrants from naturalization, Mayo's book seemed to pose two implicit questions for its American readers: Were these the same people clamoring for independence? And would you want them as neighbors?

Two years later, a Parsi man in New Jersey named Dinshah Ghadiali gave testimony to a host of sordid sights in Mayo's own country, where he had resided since 1911. All the barbarism of *Mother India* detailed by Mayo—who Ghadiali nicknamed "Baronness Munchausen, Fabricatress of Libels on India"—was present in the United States, he explained, only amplified.[3] On a tour of the infamous Union Stockyards of Chicago, he wrote of a steel wheel studded with chains and hooks, where one butcher hooked a pig's leg, and another slit its throat, before the hog was dismembered piecemeal by workers that resembled "medical students gloating over a dissected carcass."[4] In response to the cremation scene in Calcutta, Ghadiali wrote that the Americans preferred their dead embalmed and casketed, "slowly eaten off by myriads of worms [. . .] as long as they do not *see with their eyes* what is happening."[5] In a chapter-for-chapter rebuttal, Ghadiali populated his version of America with figures analogous to Mayo's Indians: Klansmen, "long-suppressed Negroes," "sex wolves" in Atlantic City, and "oversexed" women. India at least had colonial governance to blame for any perceived social backwardness, but what, Ghadiali implied, was America's excuse?

A clever reversal of barbs, Ghadiali's book—somewhat misleadingly titled *American Sex Problems* (1929)—was just one of many responses to *Mother India* that deflected Mayo's criticism of India and mimicked her "muckraking" rhetoric to criticize the United States. As trivial as some of his examples might seem, Ghadiali's book was emblematic of the blistering narratives about the United States that gained notoriety during the controversy that followed *Mother India*'s publication. These narratives, which engaged in what I call "parodic anti-imperialism," ranged from earnest rebuttals to vitriolic diatribes, refracting Katherine Mayo's racial gaze by adopting her rhetorical form. Quite literally, Indian responses to *Mother India* parodied Mayo's culturalist arguments against India's self-governance by redirecting their critiques toward social life in the United States. In particular, Mayo outlined an uneven list of social ills—ranging from alleged sexual dysfunction, the prevalence of disease, and the very real oppression of Dalits and women—to prove that India was unprepared for any degree of national sovereignty. By emphasizing the "grotesqueries" of American social life—rampant venereal diseases of Americans and their "oversexed" bodies, news of lynchings against African Americans and the disenfranchisement of the country's minority communities—Indian writers returned the favor, rupturing the discourse of the United States as a moral giant on the postwar world stage.[6]

A critical part of this transnational episode of "books and battles," as one publication described it, was how the controversy surrounding *Mother India* opened up new ways for Indian writers to articulate the relations of caste and race at both global and national scales.[7] Mayo's text forced the Indian nationalist Lajpat Rai to reconsider the United States as the anticolonial and historically anti-British emblem he had imagined it to be during his visits to the United States in the first two decades of the twentieth century. Instead, he began to articulate a global division between the "white" West and the colored nations. Others such as Ghadiali and K. L. Gauba cited instances of racial discrimination to disparage the United States for its hypocritical discourse of democracy. Yet in engaging and adopting rather than challenging and discrediting Mayo's racial arguments they betrayed a deeply casteist view of the Indian nation. In his study of the long history of African American and Indian collaboration, Nico Slate argues that responses to Katherine Mayo led to forms of "transnational justification," whereby Indians and Americans claimed that the relations of caste were worse than race, or vice versa. This chapter goes further, arguing that responses to Mayo accepted her basic racial framework, a prevalent feature of imperialist rhetoric that posited a triangulation between colonial master, native elite, and native subaltern. The effects were at times generative and at other times reactionary, but nevertheless forced these writers to explicitly articulate the racial and caste character of the Indian nation.

In what follows, I examine the framework of "racial triangulation" that marked Mayo's writing, which spanned colonial states, including Dutch Guiana, the Philippines, and India.[8] Second, I trace the way in which Mayo's own pro-imperialist and racial ideology was reworked in five immediate responses to the book: Lajpat Rai's *Unhappy India* (1928), K. L. Gauba's *Uncle Sham* (1929), Dinshah Ghadiali's *American Sex Problems* (1929), Dhan Gopal Mukerji's *A Son of Mother India Answers* (1928), and Sudhindra Bose's *Mother America* (1934). These responses were unique, among the fifty book-length rejoinders to *Mother India*, in that they focused heavily on the history and social practices of the United States, rather than refuting the factual claims of Mayo's study. In recent years, several scholars have examined how the debates unleashed by *Mother India* in the United States raised questions about American identity, memory, and immigration policy.[9] Anupama Arora and Asha Nadkarni have both examined how *Mother India* conflated a pro-imperialist discourse with an agenda to prevent Indian immigration to the United States. In her exhaustive history of the controversy, Mrinalini Sinha discusses how Mayo's emphasis on the social problems of colonial India, with particular regard to the condition of Indian women, enabled Indian nationalists to critique British rule as an impediment to social reform.[10] However divergent the specific politics and circumstances of each of these Indian rebuttals, they all undermined the way that Mayo placed the Indian national question onto a social platform—or as K. L. Gauba put it, "from the Constitutional plane to a pathological base."[11] But the participation by Indians and Indian expatriates in the United States, and how the controversy reformulated Indian nationalist imaginings of caste and race has been only marginally examined. As writers rendered the United States into a "civilization" ridden with archaic and irrational cultural practices, they interrogated the meaning of race and caste in India, the United States, and the world at large.

Racial Triangulation

A century before the slogans "Build the Wall" and "Blue Lives Matter" had become the rallying cry for the American Right, Katherine Mayo had churned out a number of short stories and hard-bound books stating much the same. As Christina Joseph and Anandam Kavoori have argued, Mayo's writings, from her earliest fiction and nonfiction to her popular muckraking books later on, expressed a continuous articulation of "specific racial tropes and culturally essentializing contrasts between an Anglo-Saxon 'self' and cultural 'others.'"[12] Her early books, such as *Justice to All* (1917), *The Standard-Bearers* (1918), *Mounted Justice* (1922), rendered tales of the Pennsylvania State Police that pit the heroic white policeman against a variety of social threats, including the dangers of labor radicalism, the criminality of Blacks, and the persistent "horde of foreigners" imagined to be flooding the country. In these books, Mayo portrayed immigrants as a frightening rogues' gallery of immigrant types from "mercurial" Italian and Poles to "savage Hun[s]" and "Cossack horde[s]."[13] Mayo's dramatic tales of police heroics reflected the typical xenophobic and racist views of her American middle-class readers in the early twentieth century.[14]

Even earlier, Mayo had sharpened her racial views in short stories about Dutch Guiana, published between 1911 and 1913 in the pages of the *Atlantic Monthly* and *Scribner's Magazine*. Having resided in the Dutch colony for eight years with her father, a mining engineer, Mayo observed firsthand the operations of a colonial state managing and disciplining a set of subjugated populations. In the case of Dutch Guiana, this included the population of formerly enslaved Africans and indentured laborers from colonial India. In Mayo's stories of Dutch Guiana, Mrinalini Sinha explains, Mayo constructed a tripartite colonial order between "strong and paternalistic whites, loyal and well-tamed blacks, and sly and mysterious Hindus."[15] The Indian indentured laborers, in particular, Sinha argues, "threaten the proper ordering of colonial society."[16] Indeed, throughout Mayo's fiction about Dutch Guiana, we first observe a racial triangulation framework between different types of colonial subjects that she continued to project onto other colonial contexts.

Mayo cast her white characters as indulgent but occasionally flappable colonial masters and the "Negro" characters as docile, if somewhat irksome, colonial subjects. In an early *Atlantic Monthly* story titled "Big Mary," for instance, Mayo likens one Black character, in terms of "strength," "patience," and "intelligence" to an ox that could be "led by whoever pulled on his nose ring."[17] With overwrought detail, she describes the difference between white and Black physiognomies. In contrast to the "flat-nosed, ape-eared, slant-chinned, broad-jawed" features of the colony's Black population, the white colonial master is "ruddy, hearty, fine-featured [. . .] with silver hair [. . .] clear and kind blue eyes."[18] These physiognomies were mapped onto a social and biological evolutionary scale, in which the Black characters lagged centuries behind. Later in the story, for instance, Mayo characterized the difference between the "slight little figure" of the "colonial mistress" Nora and the "rough-hewn form of the great Negress" Mary as the "contrast of the Twentieth Century with the Age of Stone." Despite their alleged primitive qualities, however, Mayo described how the "limitless good-will and sympathy" and willingness to defer to their masters made figures like Mary the ideal colonial subjects.[19]

The Indian indentured laborers in these stories, however, were not so easily categorized. In "My Law and Thine," Sirpal, a man hailing from Calcutta, is described as possessing a face that seemed "benign enough" but still appeared as an "inscrutable mask—legacy of centuries of a mode of thought, locked and sealed from the occidental mind."[20] Later in the story, the otherwise deferential Sirpal gruesomely murders his adulterous wife, defending himself on the grounds of his cultural beliefs. During his arrest, he requests of the police "that the law of their land may be obeyed on me even as I have obeyed the law that is mine."[21] In contrast to the Black characters, Sirpal retains his "immutable [. . .] cultural difference" behind his benign appearance, as Joseph and Kavoori argue.[22] While Mayo often wrote with a guarded paternalism toward the formerly enslaved Black population of Dutch Guiana, allowing them to be easily tucked into the colonial fold, the Indian, whose culture was allegedly centuries old and quarantined from Western influence, was "inscrutable" and, moreover, dangerous. Associating Indians with an unpredictable and violently misogynist ancient culture would prove to be an important trope in *Mother India*, symptomatic of Mayo's imperial feminism, which posited the Indian woman as a figure to be rescued by Western empire.[23] Central to Mayo's racial triangulation was the uneven relationship between colonial master, docile subject, and a threatening third figure that stood somewhere in between. This triangulation would provide the critical framework for Mayo to interpret all colonial relations and interpellate all colonial subjects. It would also prove influential in her arguments against Indian immigration to the United States.

After a decade of writing books that took up mainly domestic concerns, Mayo returned to her earlier interest in colonialism when she published *The Isles of Fear: An Examination of America's Task in the Philippines* in 1925. In

The Isles of Fear, Mayo asserted that U.S. colonial presence was all that kept the Philippines from descending into its earlier "history of destruction, decay, and loot."[24] Responding to the anti-imperialist petitions for the "Filipinization" of the colonial government, Mayo argued that thus far such policies had had disastrous consequences in the Philippines, specifically discrediting the Jones Law of 1917, which contained a declaration to grant independence to the U.S. colony. The power of *The Isles of Fear* came not only from its polemics against the perceived liberal acquiescence of U.S. colonial legislation, but, as Paul Teed has argued, from the way Mayo reclaimed and reordered American symbols, which had been used by both Filipino nationalists and American anti-imperialists to underscore the contradiction between America's anticolonial iconography and its imperial designs. One such American was William Jennings Bryan, who had declared that if Americans pursued a colonial policy in the Philippines, they would defile the legacy of 1776 and would have to "muffle the tones of the old Liberty Bell."[25] Aware of these rhetorical strategies, Mayo attempted to delegitimize comparisons between Filipino nationalists and America's Founding Fathers.[26] "To picture to yourself the figure of the little cacique," Mayo explained to her American readers, "you must first deliver from your mind from the treacherously recurring subconscious idea that he is a brown-skinned New England squire living in a tropical Lexington or Concord."[27] Filipinos, already divided among their many rival populations, Mayo argued, could only understand patriotism as a means for gaining personal profit. While colonial education had afforded them access to books on American history, they did not have the capacity to fully assimilate the meanings of that history. The Filipino "interprets our national history, by his own race experience and sets up parallels where none exist."[28] While allusions to Abraham Lincoln, Daniel Webster, and Patrick Henry circulated in Filipino nationalist speeches (much as they did in expatriate Indian nationalist appeals), Mayo claimed that Filipinos lacked the "preliminary training" that went into creating the "President, the orator, the public favourite," and eventually, the American nation-state.[29] Not surprisingly, training the native population for eventual independence was the common rhetoric by which U.S. imperialists justified their imperial mission in the Philippines.

After undermining the American analogy, Mayo complicated the picture of the Philippines by effectively denying the subjects of the colonial state any claims to national unity. "What do you mean when you speak of the people of the Philippine Islands? Do you think of them as a political body? A social body? A distinct race? Do you think of them as a minor nation, represented by delegates to Washington?" Mayo asked, to which she herself replied, "If you do, you start wrong."[30] Throughout *The Isles of Fear*, in fact, Mayo set up a familiar triangle of colonial relations reminiscent of her Dutch Guiana tales: on one vertex was the American ruler, on another, the docile peasantry (*tao*), and on the third, the sly and manipulative urban class (*caciques*). Beyond the class distinctions between peasantry and urban classes, Mayo insisted that ethnic divisions in the Philippines—between the southern Moro, the Christian Filipino, and the Igorot—were as vast as the distinction between nations: "The line of demarcation is to them at least as definite and as sensitive as is, to a Frenchman, the line that protects France from the terror across the Rhine."[31] The overall effect was to undermine the relationship between the United States and the Philippines as metropole and colony; the "isles of fear" were rendered too complicated and too ridden with intranational conflict for simple anticolonial platitudes.

The Isles of Fear received largely positive reviews on both sides of the Atlantic. Nicholas Roosevelt of the *New York Times* recommended that the book be read by "every Congressman and by all politicians and editors who have occasion to discuss the Philippine Islands."[32] A similar endorsement turned up in the pages of the London *Times Literary Supplement* by a commenter who immediately saw its pertinence to British colonialism: "We venture to believe that [*The Isles of Fear*] will leave its mark on America's thinking about the Philippine problem and in due time of England's thinking about India and Egypt too ... It is a book which no serious student of British Imperial problems can afford to ignore."[33] One such student of empire was the English official Lionel Curtis, a member of the Round Table group that authored the Government of India Act of 1919. Curtis contributed a preface for the British edition of *The Isles of Fear*, in which he described Mayo's clarity: "In Miss Mayo's view of nature there are two colours, black and white. The medium in which she draws scarcely permits her to indicate shades between these extremes."[34] Indeed, Mayo's Manichaean view of the U.S.-administered Philippines was transplanted almost directly to India where she traveled two years later.

Irrespective of the differences between the centuries-old British dominion of India and the decades-old American administrative control of the Philippines, Mayo modeled *Mother India* largely on *The Isles of Fear*. Like the Philippines, India could not constitute a nation, given its volatile array of populations prone to "periodic destructive outbursts of sulphur and flame."[35] In a chapter from *Mother India* titled "We Both Meant Well," Mayo further drew comparisons between British rule of India with American rule of the Philippines, arguing that the former was an even greater challenge to govern. "In the Philippines," she explained, "no social bars exist—no caste distinctions except the distinction between *cacique* and *tao*—rich man and poor man—exploiter and exploited. In India something like three thousand castes split into mutually repellent groups [constitute] the Hindu three-quarters of the population."[36] Still, these thousands of castes were simplistically interpellated into Mayo's schematic colonial triangulation. British colonial governance, she argued, was all that prevented the full-scale domination of the upper castes over the lower castes. In *Mother India,* Mayo cobbled together several historical

narratives—including the "racial theory of Indian civilization" (Chapter 4)—
to present a pro-imperialist history of caste in India:

> Madras, the citadel of Brahmanic Hinduism. Citadel also of the rem-
> nant of the ancient folk, the dark-skinned Dravidians. Brahmanic
> Hinduism broke them, cast them down and tramped upon them,
> commanded them in their multi-millions to be pariahs, outcasts,
> ignorant and poor. Then came the Briton, for whatever reason, estab-
> lishing peace, order, and such measure of democracy as could sur-
> vive in the soil.[37]

In this passage, Mayo produced an absurdly terse historical narrative detail-
ing the history of India as a history of successive conquests. Brahmins conquer "dark-skinned Dravidians," and turn them into "pariahs and outcasts."
The British magnanimously arrive on the scene, without motive or imperial
design, appearing "for whatever reason." While there, they bring the workings of "peace," "order," and "democracy" to a continent that is endemically
unsuitable to all three. Here, the triangulation between "Briton," Brahmins,
and Dravidian-pariahs takes the place of Mayo's familiar racial triangulation between white savior, native oppressor, and racially marked underclass.
Compare that passage to one from *The Isles of Fear*, in which she formulated
a triangulation between the *cacique, tao,* and American:

> Malays as they are, no caste system exists among them. And they
> show but two classes—the *cacique*, or moneyed class, which bosses
> and from which all politicians come; and the *tao*, or peasant class,
> which is bossed, and which has, in practice, no voice whatever in
> governmental or political affairs.[38]

While conceding the differences in social organization between India and
the Philippines (namely, the absence of the caste system), Mayo implied that
the native hierarchy prevents the possibilities of democratic self-governance.
In the Philippines, were it not for the "intervention of the Anglo-Saxon spirit," she wrote, "the voice of the victim would scarcely have been raised."[39]
Like the Briton in India, the Anglo-Saxon American was all that could retain
order and promote democracy, rescuing the subaltern from the elite, be that
pariah from Brahmin, *tao* from *cacique*, exploited from exploiter.

For Mayo, however, writing *Mother India* was as much about defining a
racialized American national identity as it was about undermining Indian
national identity. Paul Teed explains how Mayo's emphasis on the shared
colonial projects of Britain and the United States underplayed earlier iterations of America's anti-British history, thereby ameliorating the antagonistic
history that served as the birth of the United States. A key facet that Mayo

used to emphasize these imperial connections was the shared "Anglo-Saxon" racial identity that connected these two countries.[40] In *Mother India*, for instance, Mayo contrasts the Indian, who she described as a "broken-nerved, low-spirited, [and] petulant" from an "ancient" civilization, with the "Anglo-Saxon [who was] just coming into full glory."[41] Much like Kipling's "white-man's burden" had imagined, for Mayo the twentieth century belonged to the British and the American, who embodied the spirit of a new age.

Mayo's vision of the United States as racially Anglo-American had important implications for questions of immigration. While Mayo was writing *Mother India*, a group of Indian immigrants began to challenge the restrictive racial requirements for American citizenship that had emerged earlier with the passing of the Immigration Act of 1924. These recent challenges to the Immigration Act had partly motivated Mayo to write *Mother India*. According to a letter from Mayo's acquaintance Emily Lutyens, on May 1928, Mayo lectured at a meeting at the house of Lady Sarah Lyttleton in London, where she allegedly explained her three reasons for writing *Mother India*: one, to counteract anti-British propaganda carried on by Indians residing in the United States; two, to investigate the menace to the health of America that India presented; and three, to petition the enactment of the Hindu Citizenship Bill pending in Congress.[42] Mayo later denied making such claims.

The Hindu Citizenship Bill of 1926 (S. 4505), proposed by New York senator Royal Copeland, aimed to reverse the effects of two legislative acts that had targeted Indian migrants in the United States. The 1923 Supreme Court decision in *US v. Thind* (Chapter 3), had prevented Indians from naturalization rights and effectively stripped citizenship from those Indians who had already gained it. One year after the *Thind* decision, two Republicans—Washington congressman Albert Johnson and Pennsylvania senator David Reed—went further, developing the Johnson–Reed Act on 1924, which restricted immigration by closing the door to migrants who were ineligible for naturalization. Together, the 1917 "Asiatic Barred Zone" Act, the *Thind* case, and 1924 Immigration Act effectively ended all legal immigration of Indians. Public opposition to the United States ruling against the *Thind* decision and the subsequent restriction of Indian naturalization came from several corners of the country. Vaishno Das Bagai—an import business and general store owner based in the Bay Area, who had ties to the Gadar Party—decided to end his life rather than live under the restrictive purgatory of noncitizenship.[43] In his suicide note, published in the *San Francisco Examiner* on March 17, 1928, Bagai described the anguish caused by the new legislation: "In year 1921 the Federal court at San Francisco accepted me as a naturalized citizen of the United States and issued to my name the final certificate, giving therein the name and of my wife and three sons. [. . .] But now they come to me and say, I am no longer an American citizen. They will not permit me to buy my home, and lo, they even shall not issue me a passport to go back to India. [. . .] Is life worth living in a gilded cage?"[44]

When Senator Royal Copeland proposed a bill in 1926 to "restore by legislation the Hindus to the place they were original assigned by Congress among peoples eligible to citizenship in the United States," Indian immigrants quickly rallied to support his efforts. Former FFI organizer and radical Sailendranath Ghose, who in the 1920s had become the secretary for the India Freedom Foundation (IFF), helped organize a "Hindu Night" fundraiser to support "the fight to maintain for the people of India the right to become American citizens," mailing invitations to luminaries such as W.E.B. Du Bois (Figure 5.1). In an address delivered at the testimonial dinner organized by the IFF, Copeland argued for the inclusion of "Hindus" as citizens, "who possess all that original Americans have except color alone." "Color," however, did not assume race, Copeland insisted: "The Hindu has the skull, the features, the hands, the figure, and above all else the intelligence of what we call American [. . .] he possesses every physical trait of the Northern Europeans races except his possession of a tinted skin."[45] Copeland's biological argument ultimately suggested that his problem with the *Thind* case was not the use of race as a prerequisite for citizenship, but that the court's reliance on "color" as a marker of race was misguided. Beyond the immediate effects that the *Thind* decision and the 1924 Act imposed on the thousands of Indians whose future status as U.S. citizens was now jeopardized, the Act, and the debates that preceded and succeeded it, marked a broader shift in the meanings that the United States carried internationally. The effect was a reworking of whiteness in American racial discourse that avoided the ambiguities that previous racial typologies produced, replacing it with a definition that created stronger ties between Americans and Western Europeans. Mayo's writings were inflected with such an ideology, invoking an Anglo-Saxon racial identity for the United States and its allies. When *Mother India* was published in 1927, it fed into these various political discourses motivated by race—namely, the international politics of empire in India and the Philippines, and the domestic politics of exclusion within the borders of the United States.

Mother India quickly became an international best seller, going into nine reprints and selling 140,000 copies in its first year of publication alone, before its eventual translation into seven European and six Indian languages. By 1930, the response to the book included fifty book-length endorsements and rebuttals, a short-lived Broadway play, and plans to adapt the book into a Hollywood film. As a defense of the British Raj, *Mother India* was famously celebrated by the British monarch, colonial officials, the British public, and the press.[46] The leftward-leaning British *New Statesman* published a review that stated that the common reader "will feel that these religious baby-violators," by which he meant Indians, "ought to be wiped off the face of the earth [. . .] There appears to be no rational possibility of democracy in India."[47]

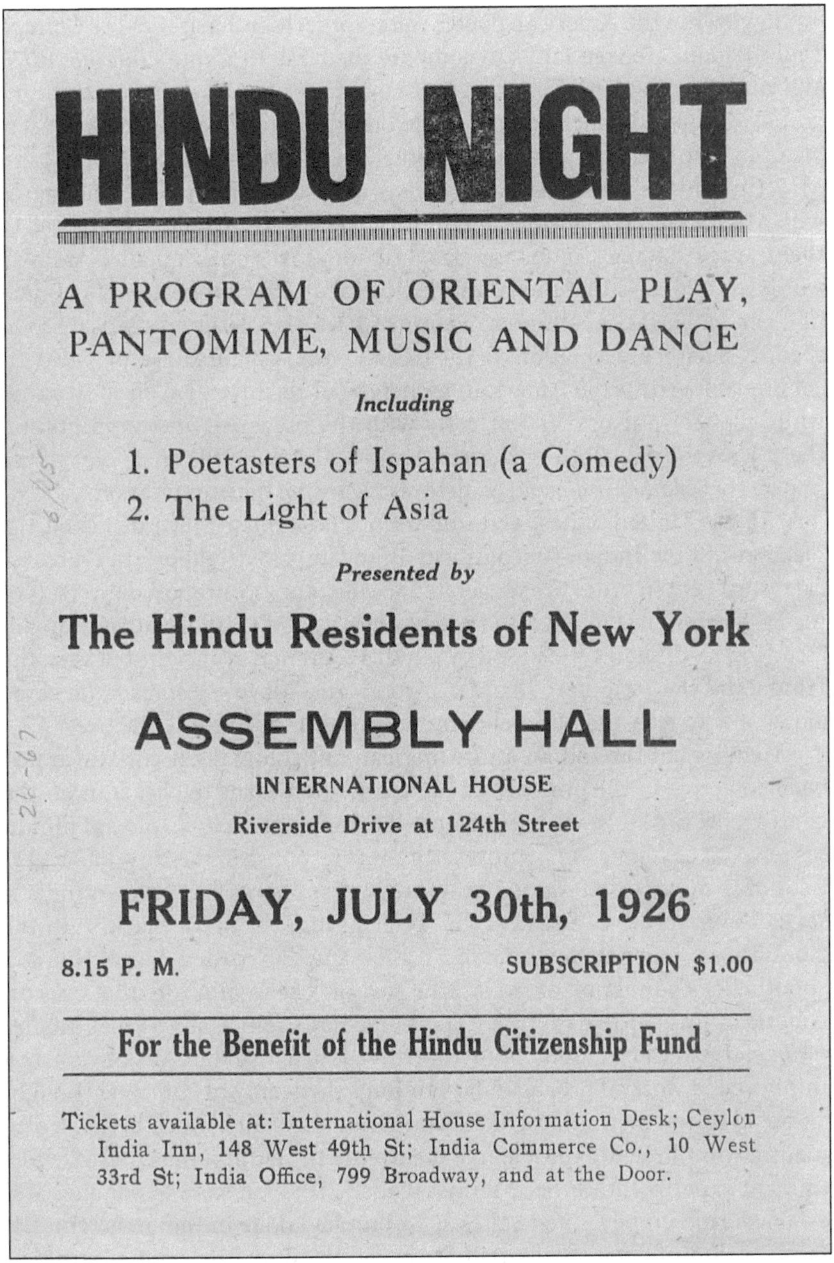

HINDU NIGHT

A PROGRAM OF ORIENTAL PLAY,
PANTOMIME, MUSIC AND DANCE

Including

1. Poetasters of Ispahan (a Comedy)
2. The Light of Asia

Presented by

The Hindu Residents of New York

ASSEMBLY HALL

INTERNATIONAL HOUSE

Riverside Drive at 124th Street

FRIDAY, JULY 30th, 1926

8.15 P. M.   SUBSCRIPTION $1.00

For the Benefit of the Hindu Citizenship Fund

Tickets available at: International House Information Desk; Ceylon
India Inn, 148 West 49th St; India Commerce Co., 10 West
33rd St; India Office, 799 Broadway, and at the Door.

FIGURE 5.1 Notice for "Hindu Night" fundraiser in support of Royal Copeland's
S. 4505 Bill, as sent to W.E.B. Du Bois from Sailendranath Ghose of the India
Freedom Foundation. (Used by permission of Department of Special Collections and
University Archives, W.E.B. Du Bois Library, University of Massachusetts Amherst)

Reviews in the American papers were similarly enthusiastic. The *Chicago Daily Tribune* went so far as to compare the book to Dante's *Inferno*; P. W. Wilson, in a *New York Times* review, saw Mayo's book as a "contemporary gospel of empire," which rethought the view of empire from tyranny to "service and sacrifice, of hygiene and healing, of education and [. . .] liberty"; and M. F. Cummings of the *Los Angeles Times* argued that both those who "agree with Miss Mayo's conclusions and those who [. . .] are unalterably opposed to them, agree that the Hindus as a class lack initiative and originality" (Mayo's words exactly) and that their "self-dedication to the moot cause of national unity and their racial enthusiasm in general, which is easily aroused, are soon spent."[48] Such representations of the Indian—whose figure bore an antithetical imprint against the American archetype of the inventive, hard-working white pioneer—also fit in perfectly with the prevalent anti-immigration rhetoric of the day. Both Anupama Arora and Asha Nadkarni point to the impact that *Mother India* had on debates regarding the immigration of "Hindus" to the United States, and underscore how often Mayo deployed the metaphor of the Indian subcontinent as an "unruly neighbor" and disease-carrying agent in order to exaggerate the effects of any proposed reversals of the 1924 Immigration Act.[49] In the face of Copeland's Hindu Citizenship Bill asserting no difference—"moral or physical," cranial or racial—between the Hindu and the "original" "Nordic" Americans, Mayo's *Mother India* came along only to reify that difference on the grounds of cultural practice.[50]

Members of the Indian and American anticolonial network, who had been so active in the previous decade, also took turns to chime in on the controversy. Du Bois, who sent Lajpat Rai copies of the *Crisis* to aid him in his rebuttal *Unhappy India*, provided a short response in the November 1927 issue of the *Crisis*, describing Katherine Mayo's charge that "brown India is sexually immoral" as a case of the "pot call[ing] the kettle black."[51] In the Communist journal *New Masses*, Agnes Smedley called Mayo's book a "bootlicker's handbook of India," the sort of "cheap film rot" that only an American was capable of.[52] Central to Smedley's criticism was that *Mother India* claimed to be a book of investigative journalism but was obviously a thinly veiled work of propaganda—an English viceroy or someone "bought and paid for by the Indian Office" could not have done much better. Colonialism was the central problem of the twentieth century; thus, she offered a thought experiment for her Marxist readers: If Japan were to conquer and establish rule in the United States as Britain had done in India, then in that same period of time the United States would surely become a "stinking swamp of social evils and disease just as India is today."[53]

Mother India gained even more notoriety from reports of the controversy it produced in India and the United States, and the backlash among Indians in America and at home were a consistent source of headlines. Gandhi had famously called the book "the report of a drain inspector sent out with the one purpose of opening and examining the drains of the country [. . .] or [giving] a graphic description of the stench exuded."⁵⁴ The nationalist poet and artist Sarojini Naidu (whose brother was Virendranath Chattopadhyay) had been hand-selected by Gandhi to tour the United States, in part to contest Mayo's comments directly.⁵⁵ In an interview in the *Brownville Herald*, Naidu objected to *Mother India* as "all wrong, very much exaggerated, and altogether unjust."⁵⁶ In San Francisco, the *United States of India*, the official publication of the Pacific Coast Hindustani Association, had declared that the book was a "cowardly stab," before dedicating the issue entirely to Mayo, reprinting responses from Gandhi, Tagore, and Lajpat Rai. Chief among its complaints was that "an American writer had been used to give [the] book a semblance of impartiality and [. . .] to make it carry more weight with [the] American public."⁵⁷

Several newspaper accounts highlighted a deeply gendered narrative that presented Indian men as excoriating American women for their moral and sexual transgressions. The *Chicago Daily Tribune* cited a Calcutta newspaper article protesting *Mother India*, in which a "Hindu leader [called] the American woman" with "her flashy black eyes, slim, sinuous figure, her knack of talking seductive English, and her air of wicked abandon, [. . .] the ideal of villainous," and warned that "the only safe thing to do is to shut American girls between 15 and 25 in cages."⁵⁸ Bipin Chandra Pal, the Bengali Indian nationalist, was quoted responding to Mayo in the Indian weekly *Forward*, citing a trip to Chicago where he witnessed one hundred and fifty women "sitting at a number of marble tables spreading over the hall with intent to let themselves on hire."⁵⁹ Elsewhere, the press reported on Indian protests in the United States. On January 21, 1928, outside the New York Town Hall building where Mayo was giving a lecture on "The Women and Children of India," the *New York Times* reported that a few Indian men burned copies of her book amid a crowd of spectators. Inside the hall, an Indian professor from Lucknow University protested the distorted picture Mayo painted, to which she coolly responded, "I don't care to debate the facts."⁶⁰ Indeed, a theme common in *Mother India* reviews was the stark contrast between the excitable Indian and the dispassionate Mayo. When asked for a book she most wished she had written, for instance, Mayo replied, "the Indian census."⁶¹

As the opinion that the Indians were overreacting circulated, so too did the opinion that Mayo's facts could deceive; that facts, themselves, could provide a false image of Europe, or Mayo's homeland, if one were to redirect Mayo's gaze westward. One commentator, Reverend Dr. Arthur Field Waken, wrote to the *New York Times*, praising *Mother India*, but nevertheless calling for a book of equal force for the United States (even suggesting the title, "Uncle Sam"), which would describe "the slums, coal mining districts, graft, neglect of national parks, and similar evils."⁶² Satirist Corey Ford, under the pen name John Riddelhi (a play on his usual penname, John Riddell), published an editorial titled "A Step-Son of Mother India's Aunt Answers" in

Vanity Fair. "Although I have been to America, a fact which obviously qualifies me to write it without any prejudice whatsoever," Ford quipped, "I am nevertheless informed on good authority of the following terrible fact: *A number of people die in America every year.*"[63] In 1927, modernist painter and writer Wyndham Lewis, in a review of Mayo's book that appeared in his journal the *Enemy*, skewered *Mother India*, deeming it a book that deserved a spot in the "Pantheon of Hate" for the "insidious manner it [put] the British Government in the position of Machiavellian power."[64] Lewis painted a scenario in reverse (dispensing with the rules of capitalization):

> Miss Mayo knows that if an indian lady journalist, for instance, hurried to America on such a mission as Miss Mayo's she could very easily draw an equally untruthful picture. [. . .] [she] could quote Mencken for bits about the monstrosities of Prohibition [. . .] and she could wind up by saying that America is "a physical menace." [S]he might remark [. . .] these [American] mothers put on flesh-coloured tights and went and danced all night, while their husbands stole out, gun in hand, and went lynching Negroes in the next block. [. . .] And then, of course, she could quote Prescott's *Conquest of Mexico* to give an idea of the sort of blood sacrifices currently perpetuated by the Americans. This she could easily mix up with the Ku Klux Klan and say they disemboweled fifty Negroes a day in any fair-sized american city.[65]

Lewis's description was prophetic. While it is unlikely that many Indian writers got hold of Lewis's modernist journal the *Enemy*, in the years that followed *Mother India*'s publication, they began to adopt Mayo's muckraking style, a few even using the sources that Lewis mentioned. In *Uncle Sham*, for instance, K. L. Gauba quoted verbatim from H. L. Mencken's compiled volumes of *Americana*, prompting one *New York Times* reviewer to blame Mencken directly for Gauba's book.[66] Even more prescient was Lewis's identification of one of the major areas of American life that Indian writers highlighted in their responses to *Mother India*: the rampant racial inequalities of the United States. Such responses were more than simplistic, frivolous, or even retributive constructions of the United States, but posed deconstructions of Mayo's unique brand of American imperialist discourse. For many writers, the co-opting of Mayo's rhetoric served as both send-up and immanent critique, parodying Mayo in order to expose the logic that held together her construction of India, a logic that directly linked racial essences to the capacity for political self-rule. Out of the fifty-odd book-length responses that emerged in the wake of *Mother India*, we look at rejoinders bracketed under the category of *tu quoque* logic, the "you too" argument. To be sure, the effects of such arguments are more interesting than the effectiveness of their strategies; with the possible exception of K. L. Gauba's *Uncle Sham*, after all, none of these books had a serious impact in countering the enormous sway Mayo's book had on global imaginings of India. But while all responses to *Mother India* foregrounded the role of colonial discourse in maintaining the common sense of empire, texts such as Rai's or Gauba's attempted to expose the logic of colonial discourse by creating "muckraked" narratives of American life, with varying impact. American narratives of social fissure became the sites to interrogate and perforate the imperialist discourse of Mayo specifically, and challenge the politics of race, nation, empire, and transnationalism in the postwar world, more generally. Adopting Mayo's muckraking style also meant that their books produced forms of anticolonial parody.

Parody, as Linda Hutcheon has famously argued, is a form both notoriously complex and ubiquitous in the twentieth century, which can refer to a whole host of practices, including satire, quotation, pastiche, appropriation, and plagiarism. Irrespective of the specific form it takes, at the center of all of parody is "repetition with critical distance."[67] That critical distance, according to Hutcheon, implies a sense of irony that can be "playful as well as belittling," "critically constructive as well as destructive."[68] Because parody involves the repetition of the form it attempts to critique, it also invites a slippage in meaning that can serve to reinforce its object of criticism. As Hutcheon puts it, "parody is doubly coded in political terms: it both legitimizes and subverts that which it parodies."[69] Hutcheon's discussion naturally brings to mind Homi Bhabha's concept of colonial mimicry, "the desire for a reformed, recognizable Other, *as a subject of a difference that is almost the same, but not quite.*"[70] Bhabha discusses the way in which the colonized subject, whose mimicry brings him or her ever closer to the colonizer, threatens to disrupt the authority of colonial difference altogether.

Something else is at stake in the Mayo rejoinders, however. In the case of the Mayo responses, Hutcheon's insistence that parody legitimizes the object of its critique through repetition is particularly important. The "parodies" that Gauba and Ghadiali produced in their books not only repeated the muckraking form of writing that Mayo engaged in, but also repeated the forms of argument—namely, the pathologizing of culture—that Mayo used so effectively to delegitimize the cause for anticolonial nationalism. In doing so, as we will see, they legitimized Mayo's cultural logic.

Caste and the Limits of Parodic Anti-Imperialism

The earliest book-length responses to *Mother India* followed more or less the same strategy: first, they contested Mayo's observations, refuting her facts when possible and giving mention to the Indian-led caste and women's reform movements that Mayo had failed to note; second, they pulled a number from Mayo's book and highlighted social fissures or "deviancy" in the United States, whether that be the country's long history of racism or its supposedly depraved sexual practices. One of the first to strike back was C. S. Ranga Iyer, a member of the Indian Legislative Assembly, whose rebuttal *Father India: A Reply to Mother India* (1927) hit the shelves within months of *Mother India*'s publication. In addition to outlining the reform efforts of eighteenth- and nineteenth-century Indian leaders, Iyer, who was mired in the social mores of the early twentieth century, used American judge Ben Lindsey's *Revolt of Modern Youth* (1924) to counter Mayo's discussion of child betrothal in India with lurid details of the immoral "sex atmosphere in which the girls of America live."[71] All the "outrageously improper" behaviors of Americans still did not prove, according to Iyer, that "the United States are not fit for Swaraj and should be placed under the tutelage of the more moral if dark-coloured inhabitants of the Philippine Islands."[72] Through a rhetorical reversal, Iyer made explicit the imperial relations of the United States and the Philippines, while effectively disconnecting the link between presumed cultural superiority and the right to colonial governance, or self-governance, for that matter.

Among the responses to *Mother India*, only Gauba's work rivaled Mayo's exposé in terms of sales and notoriety. By 1929, Gauba, the son of Punjabi industrialist and millionaire Lala Harkishen Lal, claimed to have amassed his own fortune on the basis of profits from *Uncle Sham*, his response to Mayo. A year earlier, observing the relative commercial failures of most responses to Mayo, including Lajpat Rai's *Unhappy India* (discussed in the next section), Gauba pitched his idea to Rai in his *Sunday Times* column, "Musings of a Punjabi":

> I give Lala Lajpat Rai a tip. If he wants to make money, *Unhappy India* is much too stale a theme. India has been unhappy a long time and it is not likely to be happy soon. In these days people are more interested in masturbation, prostitutes, and the married pastimes of unmarried young ladies. [. . .] I am afraid the answer to the book like *Mother India* is not: "Your picture is very exaggerated, we have good men and women; our social reform movement is vigorous; look at the statistics [. . .]." To my mind the effective reply is: "My American friend offered me whisky. I asked him how he got it. He said in America, money can buy everything, every department, every state official, every policeman . . ."[73]

Gauba had not spent any time in the United States, his only American contact being a "blue-blooded Bostonian" he had met in London, who supplied him with references. He reasoned that "if Miss Mayo could write of India after spending three months in the country," he would do one better and write about America without ever having gone there. Gauba soon took to books and magazines of both "pornographic and surrealistic" quality, printed in the United States and sold at Lahore book stalls.[74] Compiling a list of texts like Judge Ben Lindsey's *Revolt of Modern Youth* (1928), Stephen Graham's *New York Nights* (1927), and Mencken's compiled *Americana* volumes, Gauba traveled to the opulent Cecil hotel in the mountains of Simla, where he wrote for three months of the monsoon season.[75] By the end, he had completed *Uncle Sham: The Strange Tale of a Civilisation Gone Amok*, publishing the book under the "Times Publishing Company." As an early order of business, he allegedly sent a copy to Katherine Mayo with the personal inscription: "To one drain inspector from another."[76]

Uncle Sham was more popular among the public than it was in the press. The book went through twenty printings in ten months, with more than 100,000 books sold in a year—enough that one American traveler noticed the book was a "best seller on news-stands all over India."[77] *Uncle Sham* appeared in the American press as well when a minor controversy arose after customs officials seized the book and banned it from entering the United States.[78] Eventually, an American edition was published by Claude Kendall, and soon American readers weighed in.[79] A *Los Angeles Times* reviewer took *Uncle Sham* as an indication of the newfound hostility India felt toward the United States as a result of *Mother India*: "World fellowship may be a fine thing, but today is not the time to talk to Indians of spiritual unity with America. They hate us over there. On every news stand in Bombay, Calcutta and other Indian cities are cheap reprints of 'Uncle Sham' containing a collection of clippings from our own journals [. . .] all to show us up as a nation of hypocrites."[80] In a syndicated review, Ronald Kenyon described the book through an allegorical scene: "On the sunny plains at Lahore, India, an Old gentleman with a goaty (*sic*) beard and wearing striped trousers has been pegged out. Under the glare of the Indian sky, he is tied hands and feet while a polished young gentleman proceeds to dissect him. His scalpel is dipped in vitriol and he murmurs apologies as he proceeds to take the hide off our old friend Uncle Sam of the United States."[81] Gauba's quick-witted insults and vitriol drew applause from supporters and disapproval from detractors, but either way, *Uncle Sham* was far less a radical reinterpretation of Mayo's racial framework than it was a full-on imitation.

Uncle Sham begins at a dinner table, a postwar banquet where a presidential hopeful (flanked on both sides by a "bootleg king" and a "flirt") pronounces that America is both "the world's most powerful nation" and "the moral giant of history."[82] Over the course of the book, Gauba undermines that claim by adopting terms that indexed transgressive sexualities, much like Mayo had in *Mother India*. If India was "oversexed" and sexually depraved, then the United States had its own share of excessive and degenerate sexual practices captured in chapters titled "The Virgin," "Fairies," "The Sowing," and "The Grease Spot." Mayo had drawn on the language of sexual perversion, linking transgressive and excessive sexual desire to other areas of social life, which only further underscored her argument that the Hindu was especially unfit for self-governance. "Little in the popular Hindu code suggests self-restraint in any direction, least of all in sex relations," Mayo wrote, drawing causal links between that lack of "self-restraint" and a series of practices, including pedophilia, child marriage, homosexuality, masturbation, and the worship of phallic avatars, each either tacitly accepted by or symptomatic of Hindu society.[83] By the age of twenty-five to thirty, nearly 80 percent of Indian men were impotent, Mayo added, who used the large number of "Indian-owned newspapers" advertising euphemistic "magical drugs," "mechanical contrivances," and "pillars of strength to prop up your decaying body" as evidence of her claims.[84] In providing such sensational and titillating details of the depraved sexuality of the Hindu male, Mayo developed a simultaneously racialized and sexualized argument against the Hindu's ability to govern. But she also went further to suggest that the Hindu male's excessive libidinal energy was intimately linked to the native's *desire* to revolt, in the first place. In one key passage, Mayo drew a link between "political unrest" and "sexual exaggeration," implicitly pathologizing anticolonial thought and revolt as a byproduct of a perverted mind:

> Bengal is the seat of bitterest political unrest—the producer of India's main crop of anarchists, bomb-throwers and assassins. Bengal is also among the most sexually exaggerated regions of India; and medical and police authorities in any country observe the link between that quality and 'queer' criminal minds—the exhaustion of normal avenues of excitement creating a thirst and a search in the abnormal for gratification.[85]

Mayo's use of the term "queer" to mark the Bengali is astounding, to say the least. As Victor Mendoza has argued about the context of early twentieth-century U.S. imperialism in the Philippines, "queer" as a racial signifier was placed on native populations to describe not only same-sex intimacies, as it was beginning to be used in the United States, but a whole host of nonnormative configurations, including "fashion styles," "polygamy," "gender inversion," and the transgression of "Victorian bourgeois gender norms."[86] "Queer," as Mendoza explains, was both a "'racializing' signifier" as well as "an imperialist one."[87] In the case of Mayo's incredible formulation, the queerness of the Bengali was linked to a kind of revolutionary bloodlust. Exhausted in his insatiable desire for "normal avenues" of sexual arousal, he turns to the "abnormal for gratification." This abnormality was, of all things, political anarchism. In such a formulation, anticolonial violence could also be read as a queer or abnormal outgrowth against the normative form of colonial governance. It was this argument that prompted Agnes Smedley to quip, in her scathing review of Mayo, "The bomb-throwing of Bengal is to her a sign of perversion; perhaps the revolutionaries of Russia were also perverts!"[88]

With *Uncle Sham*, Gauba drew on the licentiousness of his subject matter when marketing the book to an Indian audience. The cover for the U.S. edition (Figure 5.2a) featured an image of Uncle Sam, crouched over and removing a mask that revealed an ugly, pock-marked face (in-step with a muckraking narrative, exposing the ugly truths about the nation). The Indian version (Figure 5.2b), on the other hand, featured a drawing of a burlesque dancer, legs raised as she tumbles in a martini glass. At least half of *Uncle Sham* is focused primarily on the sex lives of Americans, drawn from a wide array of muckraking journalism, social reform literature, and sex education. Gauba emphasized sexual promiscuity among youth and adults, chronic masturbation among young American men, the high divorce rates among Americans, and the prominence of prostitution in the country, each detail feeding into his larger argument that "the same ugly features of life" that Mayo highlighted in *Mother India* were just as commonly identifiable in the United States.[89] But more than just instances of "sexual excess," Gauba also emphasized the "inversion" of gendered and sexual norms in the United States, drawing on examples of masculine women, "Nancy boys," "fairies," and what "science calls [. . .] homosexuality."[90] Quoting Edith Houghton Hooker's *The Laws of Sex* (1921) and Graham's *New York Nights* (1927), Gauba added:

> Such [homosexual] unions are not rare in the United States. Uni-sexual intimacies are the delight of certain perverted localities. "Women dance together unashamed to the murmuring chorus of 'Fairies, fairies.'" As a poet explains: "Fairy land's not far from Washington Square." Says Stephen Graham: "This is something not imitated in London, where it may still be a charming compliment to call a girl a fairy."[91]

Gauba drew on the modern category of the "homosexual" as a means to undermine the notion of the United States as the normative metropolitan nation. His heavy use of quotations bounced between two registers—the sensationalist language of muckraking and the emergent field of sexology, the latter adding "scientific" weight to his claims.

American sexuality was not the only target of Gauba's parody. Gauba devoted a good deal of *Uncle Sham* to racism in the United States to indicate the hypocrisy at the heart of American democracy:

> The relation of the White and Negro populations in the United States—generally spoken of as the Negro problem—is the most grave and perplexing of domestic issues. It is also, perhaps, the largest blot on the institutions of the American democracy. The racial distinction, discrimination and antipathy constitute eloquent testimony upon the vaunted liberty of United States citizenship.[92]

Figure 5.2 (a) The American and facing page (b) Indian covers of *Uncle Sham*. (New York: Claude Kendall, 1929/Lahore: Times Publishing Company, 1929)

In two chapters titled "K.K.K." and "The Negro," Gauba contrasted the image of the United States as the self-proclaimed "world's greatest democracy" with statistics of poverty, unequal incarceration rates, and crimes against African Americans culled from the Chicago Commission of Race Relations' report *The Negro in Chicago* (1922). For instance, Gauba invented a scene at the signing of the Treaty of Versailles, where "President Wilson was sitting in judgment upon German atrocities, [while] a Negro was publicly roasted."[93] Elsewhere, Gauba contrasted the "War of Democracy, the War to save Civilization," which united "Black men, tan men, Negroes, Japs, Chinese, Lithuanians, Poles, French, English and Americans" with a scene months later when Chicago was engaged in "one of the wildest Negro hunts in history."[94] The power in his juxtapositions was the product of different framing devices—the international United States was set against the domestic United States—paralleling, in ways, Mayo's own strategy of presenting the Indian nation as a set of contrasts between Indian modernity and its archaic, oppressive culture; imagined political unity versus real cultural dissolution. Anti-Black racism was not the only realm of social life that Gauba presented, however. The Ku Klux Klan's "triumvirate of 'hates,'" targeting the Catholic, Jew, as well as "the alien and Negro," was cited as yet another example of "*perverted* Americanism."[95]

The African American press seemed to be of two opinions regarding *Uncle Sham*. On the positive end was the sharp social critic George Schuyler. In his column for *The Pittsburgh Courier*, he recommended *Uncle Sham*, calling it a "devastating book" and for its cover price of three dollars, a "good Christmas present."[96] "[Gauba] tells the truth about our liberty, the treatment of the Negro, our boss-ruled politics, [. . .] and American Imperialism," Schuyler added.[97] In an anonymous editorial about the 1934 film *Imitation of Life* published in Baltimore-based *Afro-American*, Gauba's name turned up again: "If you think our white folks haven't their weak points pick up Kanhaya Gamba's (*sic*) 'Uncle Sham,' which deals with American dope dens, vice rings, graft in cities, its sex dives and sin dens, its venereal diseases, its working of children, its lynchings, its fairies, its outlaws, racketeers, bootleggers and a thousand and one sins our country has."[98] Over the years, *Uncle Sham* had gained enough notoriety to become shorthand for a muckraked image of America.

But it appears that *Uncle Sham* as an idea was more appreciated by the African American press than was the book itself, which Schuyler likely never read in its entirety. In a more detailed review published in both the *Afro-American* and *Pittsburgh Courier*, Ralph Brewing took Gauba to task for his inconsistent assessment of racial inequality in the United States. While embracing the book's "ribald" take on the "so-called Negro Problem" in which Gauba asserted that "the southern lynching jamboree is an expression of the Ku Kluxers' sexual inferiority complex," Brewing also pointed out that

Gauba's positions on race were not all that progressive.[99] Gauba had written that miscegenation was "one of the greatest menaces with which our white civilization is faced," a statement that prompted Brewing to ask, "What does the author mean by 'our' white civilization? Does he mean that by choice he has adopted the white civilization as his own? [. . .] Since when did England invite her Hindu subjects as equals in the Anglo-American supremacy of the world?" Furthermore, when Gauba wrote that the craving for "swarthy flesh is one of the new diseases of the modern age," Brewing reminded Gauba that "his own flesh is swarthy." He concluded, with good reason, that Gauba's attitude toward "the Negro is identical with that of American white men," that his disapproval of miscegenation was worded in the same "prejudiced language of the notorious K.K.K.," and that, on further reading, Gauba's attack on America on the account of the Negro Problem was little more than a rhetorical point and not a gesture of solidarity.[100] Gauba's moral ambivalence toward racism extended to his comments on American exclusion, as well: "Every country has a right to control imports and aliens. There can be no grouse therefore if Scotch Whiskey is bootleg and the Chinese cannot acquire United States citizenship."[101]

Dinshah Ghadiali, in his self-published book *American Sex Problems*, wrote of race in a similarly ambivalent fashion. Just as Gauba had done before him, Ghadiali responded to Mayo's chapters on untouchability with a chapter of his own on American race relations, inexplicably titled "The Negro President in the White House." Ghadiali wrote, "One does not have to retreat into the caves and jungles of 'mysterious India' to find the counterpart of this story [of Untouchables] enacted in the United States."[102] At first, Ghadiali showed compassion, mentioning the history of slavery—citing Harriet Beecher Stowe's *Uncle Tom's Cabin* as required reading—and listing the daily inequities of Jim Crow laws and the threat of lynching regularly faced by African Americans in the South. But far from promoting a racial solidarity between the Indian and African American, or even a sympathetic parallel between the violence against African American and Dalits, Ghadiali forwarded the view that the "fatal error" in emancipation was not the extension of human liberty, "which by birthright was theirs," but the extension of equal voting to the freed Blacks. With language almost identical to Mayo's assessment of the essential character of the Indian and his unfitness for self-rule, Ghadiali wrote that "the Negro, nearly a quarter of a million years behind in point of evolution as a race, could not digest liberty" and (borrowing Gauba's language) "ran amuck."[103] Even while Ghadiali's imitation of Mayo attempted to tarnish the sterling image of the United States, his writing also expressed horrific opinions about Dalits, justifying the stigmatized status of their labor through a combination of biological and social explanation: "The high class vegetarian Hindu [. . .] must have had cogent reasons for the debarring from social intercourse the 'Untouchable' who constantly wallowed in filth and lived on dead animal carcasses. [. . .] They are human 'buzzards.'"[104] Ghadiali's reactionary views on African Americans were not unlike his views on Dalits: they both represented nationally inassimilable subjects far behind on the racial, evolutionary scale. In *American Sex Problems*, Ghadiali's parodic response used the basic discursive framework of *Mother India* to represent the United States, but left that basic framework intact. If, as Linda Hutcheon has argued, parody both "legitimizes and subverts that which it parodies," then all that had been subverted in both *Uncle Sham* and *American Sex Problems* was the notion that the United States was somehow immune from critique. On the other hand, the books adopted and then doubled-down on the racist and casteist argument that supported and justified a social hierarchy between Blacks and whites, Dalits and Brahmins.

Dhan Gopal Mukerji seemed to be aware of the perils in responding to Mayo through parody. In his preface to *A Son of Mother India Answers* (1928), Mukerji pointed to the disadvantage that critics faced in attempting to undermine a book that presented "a positive thesis to advance." "Denials and doubts" leave readers "cold," Mukerji argued, suggesting instead that effective rebuttals required the same kind of "pictorial" and "picturesque" qualities that made Mayo's book so effective. This left only a few available options for the critic:[105]

> In order to give added life and vim, two obvious courses are open. One is to say *Tu quoque!* There are horrible products of Western civilization which might be thrown in the teeth of the traducer of the East—the abject slums of this industrial nation, the appalling white slavery of that. And so on. The other course would be to lighten up one's reply with invective—and invective, shrewdly used, can be very telling."[106]

Mukerji hints at, but never fully articulates, a parodic response, highlighting two instances of social abjection in the United States—urban slums and "white slaves," a term that referred to the trafficking of white women for the "purpose of prostitution or debauchery"—which would be easy for any writer to mobilize.[107] Yet he largely avoided such an approach, claiming to take the high road and arguing for a temperate response that was in character with, in his words, "the way of India."[108] A slim one hundred pages, *A Son of Mother India Answers* largely comes off as a kind of cross-examination; page after page checks Mayo's claims against his own facts culled from census reports.

To a great extent, Mukerji's *Visit India with Me*, published one year later, was a far more nuanced response to Mayo, although he never named it as a response as such. As discussed in Chapter 2, *Visit India* was marketed by E. P. Dutton as a guidebook, meant for "people from the English speaking countries" planning to travel to India. But through his fictitious American character John Edgar Eagles, Mukerji used the book to expose and critique what he perceived as the Orientalist gaze that structured American perceptions and representations of India. Eagles is representative of an American "liberal" voice, certainly more liberal in thought than the imperial apologia of Katherine Mayo; he is susceptible to believing Orientalist myths about India as a space of spiritual renewal, and cautious but sympathetic to arguments for Indian decolonization. Mukerji stages a number of "conversations" between Eagles and political actors, including his brother, the revolutionary Jadu Gopal Mukherjee, and Gandhi. During the dialogue between Eagles and Gandhi, *Visit India* raises the comparison between the mistreatment of Blacks in America and Dalits in India, much like Ghadiali and Gauba had done before. Eagles explains:

> Gandhi began by pointing out the parallel problem of the Negro race in America. "Yet," he said, "there can be no true comparison between the two. They are dissimilars. Depressed and oppressed as the untouchable is in his own land, there is no legal discrimination in force against him as it is in the case of the Negro in America. Then, though our orthodoxy sometimes betrays a hardness of heart that cannot but cause deep anguish to a humanitarian, the superstitious prejudice against the untouchable never breaks out into such savage fury as it does sometimes in America against the Negro. But in India such things are impossible because of our tradition of nonviolence. [. . .] The prejudice against untouchability is fast wearing out. I wish somebody could assure me that the tide of color prejudice had spent itself in America."[109]

The notion that there was no equivalence to lynching against Dalits because of an Indian "tradition of nonviolence" was as egregiously false then as it continues to be now.[110] The point, however, is to note how the repudiation of Mayo's argument about the violence meted out against the "untouchable" meant, in the case of Mukerji, a total disavowal of the problems that afflicted the lower castes in India. As if directly responding to Mayo's triangulation of colonial patriarch, native bourgeoisie, and underclass, Mukerji's "Gandhi" voices his desire to obliterate that lattermost category. Doing so would reshape that colonizer–colonized–underclass triangle to a Manichaean struggle between colonizer and colonized, Britain and a unified India. Mukerji's Gandhi explains, "I realize that even your Negroes have a love of country that our unlynched Pariahs lack. That is why I want to abolish the Pariah's class. I want unity at any cost among our people."[111] Ironically, these words predict the devastating outcome of the 1932 Poona Pact, in which Gandhi effectively led a hunger strike against a ruling that would provide "depressed classes" with separate electorates, forcing B. R. Ambedkar to eventually concede. In "abolish[ing] the Pariah's class," Mukerji's Gandhi effectively undermines Dalit self-determination—"unity at any cost," indeed.

Recasting the "World Menace"

Perhaps the most powerful response to *Mother India* came in 1928, when Lajpat Rai published *Unhappy India*. Rai's text emphasized the role that imperialist discourse played in perpetuating myths about native culture and the belief in the necessity of colonial rule. "It is a part of the imperial game to paint the subject people in the blackest colours, and to slander and libel them most shamelessly," Rai explained, adding that the "object is to produce and perpetuate the slave mentality of the subject people, and to obtain moral sanction of the rest of the world for usurping the rights, properties, and liberties of other peoples."[112] Rai's choice of words (producing the "slave mentality of the subject people") cleverly reworked Mayo's own terminology. In the second chapter of *Mother India* titled "Slave Mentality," Mayo went into great detail to describe the psychology of the Indian—melancholic, ineffective, and inert—linking those traits to Hindu cultural practices. The cause, Mayo wrote, was "simply, his manner of getting into the world and his sex-life thenceforward," after which she began her lurid discussion of the sex lives of Indians.[113] In using Mayo's own term, and describing it as the byproduct of imperialist discourse rather than any kind of essence of the Indian psyche (i.e., "enslavement" rather than "slave mentality"), Rai demystified the language of Mayo. "Her object was to whitewash British imperialism," Rai wrote, and "to her all that there is in India is wrong and is so because the Hindu is either a savage sensual beast, or a pervert, or both."[114] Informing his readers about Mayo's contacts, including the aforementioned Lionel Curtis, Rai insisted that the motive of *Mother India* was "political and racial," despite the author's claims of neutrality inherent by being an American.

Surpassing *Mother India* in length, *Unhappy India* collated Rai's previous writings on the United States from his 1916 volume *The United States of America: A Hindu's Impressions and a Study* with line-by-line assessments of Mayo's arguments. But far different than his earlier writings on the United States, *Unhappy India* signaled a reevaluation of his earlier praise of the United States. In *Unhappy India*, Rai forwarded a transnational concept of "whiteness" that did not distinguish the United States from Britain. This was a significant shift from Rai's writings from his 1905 visit to the East Coast of the United States, or even his 1916 volume, in which he emphasized America's anticolonial and anti-British history and argued that "the Hindus come from the same racial stock as the Europeans" (Chapter 1).[115] Part of this was the specifics of the controversy: Rai and others were responding to an American and not an English writer, and hence, the United States figured largely into any kind of rebuttal. But it seems fair to suggest that Rai was also responding to Mayo's own racial discourse, which had pit a homogenous white West (Dutch, American, and English) against the rest of the colonized world. This racial bifurcation even inflected the preface, when Rai explained that he quoted extensively from American sources because "white peoples of the West are not prepared to accept and believe any testimony but that of persons of their own race and colour."[116]

Nevertheless, armed with issues of the NAACP organ the *Crisis*, sent to him by his acquaintance W.E.B. Du Bois, Rai devoted two chapters titled "Less Than the Pariah" to cite examples of American racism. These chapters were direct rebuttals to Mayo's chapters on untouchability—titled "Less Than Men" and "Behold, A Light!"—in which she had narrated the cruelties inflicted upon Dalits by upper-caste Hindus. The "light" referred to in the latter chapter was none other than the Prince of Wales, whose visit to New Delhi was boycotted by Gandhi and the Indian National Congress, but attended by what Mayo offensively described as a "swarm of Untouchables" who literally sang praises of the prince, king, and government. Mayo was again setting up her familiar triangulation of colonial power, wherein the colonial ruler rescues the native downtrodden from native elite.[117] In reality, any meaningful political alliance between Mayo and Dalit leaders such as B. R. Ambedkar never existed, due to the latter's own critique of British rule. As Mrinalini Sinha documents, during his visit to the United States in 1931, Ambedkar was heavily recruited by Mayo. Mayo, however, was rebuffed by Ambedkar, who had issues with Mayo's misquoting of him in *Mother India's* 1931 sequel, *Volume II*.[118]

In *Unhappy India*, Rai's basic argument was that if the practices of untouchability were enough to disqualify Indians from self-rule, then how could one justify the legitimacy of the Declaration of Independence, signed when the country's economy was run on the backs of slave labor: "One would have thought that the Americans would be the last people to declare Hindus to be unfit for *Swaraj* and democracy because of the existence of a class of untouchables among them," Rai wrote.[119] The two chapters on racism in *Unhappy India* were filled with statistics of lynching from 1911 compiled in Rai's earlier monograph *The United States of America*, and further abetted with short excerpts from 1927 issues of the *Crisis*. Among the many incidents of lynching that Rai catalogued, the East St. Louis riots of 1917, as documented in the *Crisis*, captured Rai's attention the most.

Before devoting ten pages to the incident that left somewhere between one hundred to one hundred and fifty African Americans killed, Rai issued the following statement: "A brief account of the Massacre of East St. Louis in 1917 will serve to disillusion those who believe in the moral superiority of the white man."[120] In fact, what was unique about *Unhappy India* was the way that Rai introduced the "white man" as the other, a foil to "the black or brown or yellow peoples," among whom he counted himself in 1928.[121] Moreover, throughout the two chapters, there was a deliberate pairing of the United States and the British Empire, caught together in the larger folds of the "white man," "white world," and "white civilization." In one sentence Rai wrote about East St. Louis, the next he wrote of Indians around the outposts of the empire unable to enter "the white people's hotels, restaurants, cafés, and other places," and in the next he explained that "all this becomes a tame affair when one considers the treatment meted out to the African natives whose trustees the white people pretend to be."[122] Rai moved swiftly from the Black subjects in the United States to Indian subjects in the British Empire to the Black African subject in unmarked European colonies. Rhetorically, he was mapping his own figurations of colonial power to replace Mayo's.

The East St. Louis riots figured largely into the work of Du Bois, in particular in his work *Darkwater: Voices from within the Veil* (1920). Du Bois wrote in "epic language" (as Amy Kaplan describes it) about the East St. Louis riots, viewing the violence not only as the "legacy of southern history and slavery, but as a part of the world history of a global economic system."[123] Indeed, in a passage reminiscent of *Dark Princess*, Du Bois mapped the riots onto a global geography, spanning New World and Old:

> It was the old world horror come to life again: all that Jews suffered in Spain and Poland; all that peasants suffered in France, and Indians in Calcutta; all that aroused human deviltry had accomplished in ages past they did in East St. Louis, while the rags of six thousand half-naked black men and women fluttered across the bridges of the calm Mississippi."[124]

In many ways, Rai's slippery analogies are reminiscent of Du Bois's, who also constructed race as an organizing force in the world. Two decades after seeing himself as a revolutionary in the pedigree of Washington and part of the same "racial stock," Rai connected a line between anti-Black racism in America, anti-Indian racism in the British Raj, and a more broadly defined, global white racism that targeted the colonized worldwide. Rai had said as much in the opening pages of *Unhappy India*, describing the mentality of the "white races of the world—Europe and America," who had kept subject peoples under their domination through the guise of the "white man's burden."[125]

Even more remarkable was just how far Rai drew that line of equivalence. "Yet another class of America's mercilessly persecuted untouchables is that of the Red Indians," he wrote in one passage. "They have come up to the level of the African natives. Just as for the Masai in East Africa, [. . .] the richest lands are under the white men, so the Red Indian gets the 'worst lands in which life could be sustained at all.'"[126] Whereas in earlier writings Rai had expressed an ambivalence about the pathos of the "Indians (Red)," the effect of *Mother India* was to force Rai to imagine the division of power in the world as a bifurcation between whites and "non-whites":

> White imperialism is the greatest world menace known to history, and its racial arrogance rests on the assumption that those who are not 'white' are 'less than men.' It has deprived vast populations of political and civic liberties, and is ruthlessly exploiting them for economic ends. [. . .] Unless it is promptly and effectively brought under check it promises not merely to bomb out non-white civilization, but even to end *all* civilization in a death dance—a dress rehearsal of which we have had in the World War of 1914—inspired by greed and jealousy.[127]

Rai's use of "world menace," a phrase that was repeated throughout several other responses to Mayo, was another term lifted directly from the language of *Mother India*. In a chapter titled "World Menace," Mayo discussed the cases of malaria, bubonic plague, and cholera in India, and the pandemic threat that disease posed on the United States. Her discussion of disease, and the bodies that transmit them, however, was a thinly veiled euphemism for the movement of people to the shores of the United States. "In estimating the safety of the United States from infection, the elements of 'carriers' must be considered," wrote Mayo, by which she meant, of course, that small trickle of Indian migrants who constituted the "Hindu menace" in the newspapers of the day. Mayo's *Mother India* connected the politics of imperialism with the politics of immigration, and as Asha Nadkarni argues, both these concerns were "materialize[d] through the discourse of public health."[128] Rai responded to Mayo's fixation on disease by reminding his readers that the historical "carriers" of disease have always been colonizers from Europe, adding that the term Indians use for syphilis is "*frangi rog*," the foreigner's disease.[129] In describing white imperialism as the world menace of the ages, Rai effectively reversed and replaced Mayo's metaphor, from disease to a "death dance," from the imagined threat of pandemics to the historical threat of world war, which had ravaged the globe a decade earlier.

Several scholars have rightly suggested that Rai's *Unhappy India* ultimately attempted to downplay the atrocities of the caste system by emphasizing American racism. In observing Rai's commentary that racial discrimination against African Americans was worse than the practice of untouchability, for instance, Nico Slate argues that Rai "transformed a transnational [race/caste] analogy with which he attacked injustice in the United States and India into a reactionary shield."[130] Similarly, Kamala Visweswaran points out that while Lajpat Rai asserted that untouchability was "an absolute indefensible, inhuman and barbarous institution," he also described it as no worse than "what the white man has done to non-white people."[131] Ambedkar responded sharply to Rai's duplicitous *tu quoque* rhetoric, arguing that "the Hindus try to defend [untouchability]" by using a "line of defense that [they] have never upheld slavery as other nations have done."[132] What I am suggesting here is the powerful impact of Mayo's racial triangulation between whites, native elites, and native subalterns. By being drawn into her terms of debate, Rai collapsed the distinctions between elite and subaltern, upholding a binarial logic between colonizer and colonized, whites and natives, which ultimately undermined subaltern challenges to a unified Indian nation. In parroting Mayo's formulations, Rai, like Gauba, Mukerji, and Ghadiali, replicated a structure that absorbed the Dalit subject into the nation as an object of rescue, rather than as a subject with agency.

Despite the stature of Lajpat Rai in India and abroad, *Unhappy India* failed to make much of a mark and was overshadowed by his death that same year. Rai died from injuries sustained from police attacks against protestors of the Simon Commission—a legislative body made up completely of British ministers of parliament, who were to decide on the type of constitutional reform for the Indian colonial state. The Mayo controversy pushed Rai toward a worldview that in many ways used Mayo's racial framework against itself. Mayo's "trans-imperial" category of the white master, who carried the "white man's burden" of colonization, was adopted by Rai, who used it to extend his critique of British imperialism to the United States.

A late response to the *Mother India* controversy came from the pen of Sudhindra Bose. Bose had arrived in the United States decades earlier, in 1903, when he worked as an assistant steward for Standard Oil. Later, he became a student at the University of Iowa, where he eventually became a lecturer on Asian politics. While Bose's *Mother America* (1934) was explicitly prefaced as "not a rejoinder to the production of Miss Mayo," its suggestive title and long passages refuting Mayo's claims prove otherwise.[133] Like his peers, Bose made the familiar argument that America's democracy was deeply compromised on the basis that politically "the Negro is not the equal of the white American."[134] Bose, who had written earlier about his experiences in the United States in the *Modern Review* and a book titled *Fifteen Years in America* (1920) outlined the segregation faced by African Americans in a chapter titled "American Negroes." "The Negro must travel in a Jim Crow car, eat in a Jim Crow hotel, worship in a Jim Crow church, and be buried in a Jim Crow cemetery," Bose wrote, and echoing Rai's conclusions nearly two decades earlier, he added that "he is the American pariah."[135] But while Bose sometimes drew analogies between the lower caste "pariah" and African Americans, he also tended to see the equivalence between the Indian nationalist struggle and the Black struggle for rights in the United States: "I surely believe that the Afro-American has made more progress along certain lines during the past sixty years that we in India, under the English rule, for a hundred."[136] In using race as a category to describe both caste-oppression of the Dalit subject within Indian society and the colonial oppression of the Indian subject, Bose undermined the triangulation between English overseer, Indian nationalist, and the oppressed Dalit upon which Mayo's imperialist discourse depended.

But *Mother America* was unique among rejoinders in that it also interrogated the hagiographies of national leaders and the mythos of the nationalist history of the United States. Others had touched on the hypocrisy of the Declaration of Independence, but Bose destabilized the entire history of the American nation, by rendering the narrative of national revolution into a muddy, multivocal, and less-than-heroic movement. The American Revolution was far from the "unanimous affair" that history books had portrayed it as, Bose asserted, and instead represented history's first "movement of the 'discontented,' 'disloyal,' minority." Basing his position off of Walter Wey's study *New Democracy* (1912), Bose explained that the "'better classes' of the colonists did not believe at all in the doctrines of the Declaration, especially in its immediate democracy."[137] In presenting the colonial American population as ruptured between the loyalists and revolutionaries, Bose deliberately drew parallels between the loyalists and nationalists in colonial India:

> While the country was in the midst of a terrible life and death struggle, the American Tories—"the vile trash," as the patriots called them—not only had no sympathy for the Revolution, but they went straight against their country, and actually fought on the side of the English. In other words, the Tories of the colonies looked to England, much as the Loyalists of India do today. [. . .] Independence was considered barbarism, and the American revolutionists were painted as savages.[138]

Bose questioned the heroism of the American Revolution by underscoring the importance of foreign aid in the death of the British: "How did the little scattered Thirteen Colonies with three million heterogeneous inhabitants win the war against eight million Britishers with ships on every sea? The truth of the matter is that had Americans depended entirely on their own meager resources and received no outside aid, they would in all probability have been beaten and the Revolution lost."[139] Yet, the irony is, despite the nation's existence was dependent of foreign aid, "Americans today detest a foreigner."[140]

In Bose's narratives, the American Revolution was full of folly. He described the story of General Charles Lee, who, at the moment when he was supposed to advance his army, "retreated almost before the English had fired a shot." That particular story ends with George Washington dashing in front of Lee, calling Lee a "damned poltroon," before rescuing the army from an annihilation that would have "ended the Revolution right there."[141] *Mother America* spent a good deal of its discussion of American history on the figures of Washington and Lincoln, pulling both leaders off the pedestals of national hagiography. Washington, in Bose's *Mother America*, did not exactly resemble the lionized, "apotheosized" father of the nation. Instead, Washington appeared as a "great card player, an inveterate dance, a distiller of good whiskey, [. . .] a champion curser," and a "ladies' man."[142] Further undermining notions of an exceptionalist American identity, Bose described Washington as "an Englishman with English background and English viewpoints" who also "imported his ideas as well as his wardrobe from England."[143] The Father of the Nation "in spite of his democratic leanings, was an aristocrat at heart" who "kept, bought and sold slaves."[144]

As for the other towering figure of American history, Abraham Lincoln was also not spared Bose's treatment:

> That Lincoln's primary concern was not the emancipation of the slaves, but the saving of the nation as a whole and united can be demonstrated by his own words. "My paramount object in this struggle," wrote Lincoln to the editor of the New York *Tribune*, "is to save the Union, and is not either to save or to destroy slavery. If I could save the Union without freeing any slave, I would do it."[145]

On one hand, we may read Bose's reworking of the symbols of American national identity as a petty response to Mayo's discrediting of the legitimacy of the Indian nationalist movement and its leaders. On the other hand, his narratives of American history emphasized the way in which American nationhood itself was full of contradictions from its inception, and even through the crisis of the Civil War, leaders held desperately onto the notion of national unity in spite of its fragments. Extending that idea to Mayo's *Mother India*, which ultimately argued that the fragments of the Indian nation were irreconcilable without a colonial presence, Bose's reconstruction of America's national narratives contested her framework by underscoring American nationhood as equally tenuous as that of the imagined Indian nation.

Reading Gauba, Rai, Mukerji, Ghadiali, and Bose as key Indian responses to *Mother India* offers a way to think about how Mayo's muckraking book unwittingly constructed a "cosmopolitan thought zone," to use Kris Manjapra and Sugata Bose's term. Bose and Manjapra explain, "Cosmopolitan thought zones [are] heterotopias that call forth conversation [. . .] generated by the pragmatic need to get things done in communities with highly different others."[146] The "thought zone" inaugurated by the circulation of *Mother India* produced not only the hegemonic image of India that circulated in the American imaginary in the post-World War I era, nor did it just reinforce a white racial identity of America, as scholars Teed and Nadkarni have argued. The book's many *tu quoque* responses from Indians contributed to a drastic overhaul of the image of the United States in Indian nationalist discourse:

the dominant narratives of America went from anti-British revolution to a socially fragmented civilization, fissured on the lines of race. But while engaging with Mayo's racial framework produced new articulations of the global and national meanings of race and caste, these writers left with deeply problematic conclusions. In the case of Ghadiali and Gauba, the "Negro Problem" produced no analogies to the colonial condition of India, but rather provided a platform to reinforce deeply casteist views of the Indian nation and racist views of Black America. In the case of Lajpat Rai, the history of African Americans expanded their analogous range and supported a broad bifurcation of the world into categories of race—the "white races of the world" and their "colored" subjects—at the expense of seriously engaging caste. The controversy around *Mother India*, and the parodies that it produced, marked a historically important if also cautionary example in the history of transnational refractions. To peer through the lens of Mayo's racial imperialism, to accept its terms of debate rather than redefine them, was to risk replicating the injustices it produced.

The view of America from India, and India from America, had changed and would never quite seem the same.

Afterword

Refracting the Past

I n spite of the powerful grip that Katherine Mayo's book held on the American public, at least some were hopeful that her influence was on the wane at the end of the decade. In April 1929, Dhan Gopal Mukerji had written to his friend Jawaharlal Nehru to let him know that the rebuttals that were published in response to *Mother India* had, to his mind, succeeded, and that the lectures that Sarojini Naidu delivered across the country had been especially effective.[1] "Outside of a few lickspittles," Mukerji wrote, "the people of the U.S.A. are convinced that Mayo is a liar."[2] He only complained that Naidu had left the lecture market dry for those among them still residing in the country: "No one wants to hear us after her oratory of last season."[3]

By the end of the 1920s, the economy of the United States shuddered under the weight of the Great Depression and the mood in the country, as a whole, had changed. Mukerji described to Nehru how the political atmosphere in the United States had also shifted, the Anglo-American alliance that people like he, Smedley, and Rai had so fervently fought against had, by and large, come to an end. "Since the interests of America and the British Empire do not converge[,] America will not interpret Indian events in a British spirit," he wrote, adding that America would be neither "pro-British" nor "pro-Hindu," but "pro-American." For Mukerji, this geopolitical shift was cause to celebrate: "That ghastly pro-European spirit that Wilsonism created here is dead. *Requiescat in pace!*"[4]

In hindsight, of course, Mukerji was far too confident in predicting the demise of the Anglo-American alliance, which would continue unabated, growing stronger in each decade that led up to World War II. But his comments about America no longer being "pro-Hindu" were not off the mark. With the 1917 "Asiatic Barred Zone" Act, the *Thind* decision, and the 1924 Johnson–Reed Act, the United States had all but ensured that the legal immigration of Indians was next to impossible, thereby making America no longer a hospitable ground for expatriate Indian nationalism.[5] By 1930, the community of American and Indian writers that this book traces had long since been disbanded. Before the decade was up, Lajpat Rai had died from injuries sustained during a protest against the Simon Commission, and was memorialized as a martyr for Indian freedom. After stints in Germany, Denmark, and Czechoslovakia, Agnes Smedley moved even further east to China, where she became a wartime correspondent. During that same period, Du Bois also made his way to Asia in a visit to China and Japan, and while India did not make it onto his itinerary, he continued to support the broad struggle against British empire in the pages of the *Crisis*. In 1936, Mukerji took his own life after a long struggle with depression. The same year, he confessed to Nehru in a letter that amid the economic downturn, the American people had become largely indifferent to the Indian struggle.[6]

The decade and a half between the late 1910s and 1920s in the United States marked a unique and intensive period of activity surrounding the question of Indian independence. American liberals and radicals had viewed India not as a distant cause, but a refraction of political struggles at home. Through India, they saw, larger issues that afflicted the twentieth century—about race and the color line, immigration and national borders, caste, class, and gender inequalities. They asked themselves what possible implications a "free India" would have on the United States. While the Indian radicals and progressives who settled in America in the early twentieth century may have once perceived the country as a refuge from the oppression of colonialism, what they found in the United States was a new site of struggle, as they faced forms of racism, surveillance, exclusion, and imprisonment. At stake in these legislative measures and acts of political suppression were key questions about American democracy: In what ways did the Indian struggle against British rule relate to the battles against capitalism, racism, and colonialism in the United States? What global role would the United States play in the new century? These were bold questions, painted in the broadest strokes, but during this brief moment in history, writers such as Du Bois, Smedley, Mukerji, Rai, and even to a certain degree Katherine Mayo, had wrestled with them publicly, asking their readers and one another to consider them as well. As the decade came to a close, that project—brimming with energy during World War I—had begun to fade.

What they left behind was an astonishing archive of writing: the novels and travelogues they composed, the pamphlets, journals, and broadsheets they printed and circulated. Newspapers recorded their speeches, published their editorials, and reported on their cleverly orchestrated protests. Private letters revealed their feelings of doubt, their rivalries and wit, and the occasional moment of political heartbreak, as their efforts appeared to them to fall on unsympathetic ears. By examining this compendium of writing, *The United States of India* reveals a complicated history that tells us about their hard-won solidarities, their contradictions and shared struggles, and above all else, their effort to think through the differences they encountered. As Indian migrants and expatriates made sense of the racial stratification of the United States, their North American allies tried to connect to the broad struggle of Indian freedom. This entailed a practice of seeing across difference—a process I have called transnational refraction—which often meant identifying with others whose lives were remarkably different than their own, drawing comparisons between their own conditions and those of their allies. In that process, refractions had the potential of disrupting their fixed ways of looking at the world.

If, as the saying goes, the past is another country, then this book itself constitutes its own version of a transnational refraction. *The United States of India* was written a century after the events in this study took place. While the historical characters in this book occupied a social world that feels radically different than our current political landscape, at times, aspects of their world reflect our own. The exclusionary United States of a century ago has reappeared in full force, emboldened by an administration that has openly admitted to policies of racial profiling and immigrant deportation which previous regimes had enacted discreetly. Take, for instance, the Immigration Act of 1917, known also as the "Asiatic Barred Zone" Act. Motivated by fears and anxieties surrounding Asian labor and Indian political radicalism, Congress passed the Act, adding a provision that excluded the migration of all people from a geographical region that included all of what we now refer to as South Asia. Exactly one hundred years later in January 2017, the president of the United States passed Executive Order 13769, banning migrants and travelers from seven predominantly Muslim countries, each considered a national security risk. As Seema Sohi has pointed out, the executive order, colloquially known as the "Muslim ban," adopted the logic of the 1917 Act by not explicitly excluding people by identity, but by region, geography serving as a euphemism for racial and religious identity.[7] While liberal protests against the Trump administration have resorted to slogans (much like those of the FFI), claiming that "this is not our country," *The United States of India* reminds us that, in fact, such ideologies of racism, xenophobia, and exclusion have been pervasive and, in fact, constitutive to the development of the United States.

On the other end of the globe, India, a century ago, was a colony in the throes of anticolonial movements, a symbol of hope among the "darker nations" for a future unfettered by the relations of empire. Today, however, the postcolonial republic has increasingly taken its cues from the most regressive aspects of the United States, subscribing to a majoritarian nationalism that has targeted vulnerable populations within the state and exhibited its own forms of colonial occupation through its coercive militarized rule in Kashmir and the Northeast. Most recently, under the Bharatiya Janata Party-led government, India has peddled a nationalist ideology that marries Hindu fundamentalism with the "shining" advances of neoliberal capitalism.[8] If India once signaled the promise of an anticolonial future for radicals such as Du Bois and Smedley, then today it resembles the vanguard of right-wing authoritarianism, brutally suppressing movements of political resistance and self-determination, and fanning the flames of violence that continues to afflict Dalit, Muslim, and other minority communities. In his grim assessment of the nation on the occasion of the seventieth anniversary of Indian Independence, Pankaj Mishra writes, "It turns out that the racist imperialism Du Bois despised can resurrect itself even among its former victims: There can be English rule without the Englishman."[9] Refraction, perhaps, provides a meaningful way to continue the vital task of examining how these histories form the foundation of our contemporary moment, how the oppressive structures of the past find new life in the present.

But there is also a more personal scale by which the histories in this book can refract our present. To give a very recent example, in a chapter of Amitava Kumar's novel *Immigrant, Montana* (published as *The Lovers* in India, 2018), the protagonist Kailash, an Indian graduate student in the United States, is encouraged by his advisor to research the life of Agnes Smedley and the activities of her Indian expatriate associates. Kailash is quickly drawn to the drama of Smedley's biography, tracing her steps from her earliest days in Missouri to her life in New York, where she is mentored by Lajpat Rai, and eventually arrested in a conspiracy hatched with her husband Virendranath Chattopadhyay (Kumar recasts Sailendranath Ghose as Chatto, and sets their volatile relationship in the United States instead of Berlin). As Kailash works on his thesis, he begins to identify with the characters of his research: "For a few pages, I would see the world with Smedley's eyes, and then, with a feeling of uneasy identification, with her husband's."[10] While it may seem more fitting for Kailash to identify with the Indian-born Chatto, he is instead drawn to Smedley, sensing how her experience of class displacement begins to reflect his own experiences as a Bihari in an American graduate school. At one point, he pauses over Smedley's stories about her working-class brother and father, and considers how "her words took me back to my own relatives in Bihar. Their small worlds, their plain poverty, and the ordinary complications of their difficult lives."[11] In Amitava Kumar's novel, Smedley's description of seeing through "eyes from men of Asia" comes full circle. Her deep identification with Indian radicals, captured in *Daughter of Earth*, becomes the prism through which Kumar's Indian migrant remembers home. Like the assembly of lenses inside a camera, Kailash sees through the eyes of Smedley, who at the turn of the century adopted the perspectives of her Indian radical friends. These layered reflections capture something about both the kinds of unlikely identifications experienced in diaspora as well as the ways of seeing that history enables. Refractions can allow for unexpected moments of connection, across space and across time.

One of the goals in this book is to take seriously the strange and sometimes surprising direction that such refractions take. What political possibilities open up when we consider the ways that Lajpat Rai and W.E.B. Du Bois found friendship through their shared struggle against the global color line? What limitations do we recognize in early Indian immigrants who both railed against British Empire, but evaded the history of, and their own participation in, the ongoing process of American settler colonialism? In uncovering these stories, I hope to highlight the ways that refractions often led to contradictions, imagining one form of freedom at the expense of another. These contradictions are particularly important when considering the relevance of early histories of South Asian America to our contemporary moment. To name just a few: Throughout the book, we see how, in navigating discriminatory laws, Indian immigrants formally made claims to whiteness, but in doing so they espoused a "racist response to racism," as Sucheta Mazumdar describes it, that reinforced a system of white supremacy.[12] We see how upper-caste Indian writers would acknowledge the violence of the caste system (from which they benefited), but just as quickly disavow it by foregrounding their experiences of racism in the United States and India. Consider, too, how Lajpat Rai, who could be so sharp and cutting in his critiques of colonialism, also upheld Islamophobic ideologies and forms of Hindu nationalism that we see horrific repercussions of today. As important as it is to engage the stories of solidarity and resistance from the South Asian American past, it may be an even more critical task to engage its contradictions, because they continue to persist and shape our present.

If we were to extend that metaphor, this book—as a historical refraction in and of itself—also works through its own set of contradictions. To give just one example, throughout the community of Indian and American anticolonialists in this study, there was a startling lack of women, and particularly, women of color. While lecturers like Sarojini Naidu and, later Kamaladevi Chattopadhyay, had toured the United States to counter the power of Mayo's *Mother India*, the network I focus on for the most part consisted of Indian men. In their critique of recent historical scholarship on solidarities between Black and Asian American groups, Vanita Reddy and Anantha Sudhakar have argued that there are certain epistemological limitations in such projects of historical recuperation, which, by focusing on public records and institutional archives, almost always focus on "men as political and historical actors in the construction of cross-racial solidarities."[13] Such methodological and ideological limitations "marginalize, render illegible, or simply elide" queer and women's experiences within this field of cross-racial solidarity.[14] This criticism can certainly be made about this book, which, in its attention to the lives and the written work of a transnational network of actors, largely misses out on the lives of women of color, or on queer socialities. Scholars such as Nayan Shah and Karen Leonard have shown that such socialities were constitutive to the lives of immigrants from South Asia who settled in North America during the early twentieth century.[15]

The point is not to disavow these histories but to scrutinize them further, to take seriously the ideological limits that bound them because those same limits often structure our contemporary ways of seeing. Part of the objective in this book is to consider how these limitations were constituted by form— rhetorical, literary, and social—which opened certain political possibilities, while foreclosing others. As we discussed in the last chapter, while the parodic response to Katherine Mayo's powerful muckraker provided a platform for Indian writers to discuss the injustice of African Americans, it also meant that these writers would downplay upper-caste violence against members of lower-caste and Dalit communities. In Chapter 2, we discussed how the Friends of Freedom for India had used the example of British interference and meddling as a means to rally support for Indian prisoners, but such calls also uncritically adopted a language of American nationalism and sovereignty, which ignored the legacies of colonialism and racial violence that the country was built upon. Indeed, the term "The United States of India" itself, as a model of transnational refraction, centered the language of the nation-state while pushing other forms of affiliation and political imagining to the periphery.

In the end, however, if there is something to take away from this network of Indian and American writers, perhaps it is that their stories remind us that solidarities and affinities are a hard-earned gesture, fraught with contradictions but guided nonetheless by the promise of a better future. Solidarity emerges only out of a willful act of seeing through the eyes of another, whose life we can only understand in glimpses. As we look back on this history a century later, what traces of their lives do we see in ourselves?

Notes

INTRODUCTION

1. Lala Lajpat Rai, *The Collected Works of Lala Lajpat Rai*, vol. 2, ed. Bal Ram Nanda (New Delhi: Manohar, 2003), 180.

2. Ibid.

3. Ibid.

4. Ibid., 182.

5. Ibid., 182–183.

6. Paul Giles's concept of "virtualization" shares certain elements of what I describe as transnational refraction. In his study on transatlantic Anglophone literary culture between Britain and the United States, Giles discusses how writers on each side of the Atlantic influenced and even wrote against one another, leading to forms of estrangement and defamiliarization that revealed nationalist and exceptionalist myths as flat, "hollowed out" virtual constructions. In his reading of Giles's work, John Muthyala summarizes, "America becomes a site not of reflection but of refraction, digression, oblique reassessment of societies and cultures that lie outside the formal boundaries of the U.S. nation-state." Paul Giles, *Virtual Americas: Transnational Fictions and the Transatlantic Imaginary* (Durham, NC: Duke University Press, 2002), 2; John Muthyala, *Dwelling in American: Dissent, Empire, and Globalization* (Hanover, NH: Dartmouth College Press, 2012), 38.

7. Rai, *Collected Works*, vol. 2, 179–180.

8. The term "Hindu" was used in the United States as a racial designation, referring to people from India, regardless of religion.

9. Agnes Smedley, *Daughter of Earth* (1929; reprint, New York: Feminist Press, 1987), 272.

10. W.E.B. Du Bois, "The Freeing of India" (1947); reprinted in W.E.B. Du Bois, *W.E.B. Du Bois in Asia: Crossing the World Color Line*, ed. Bill Mullen and Cathryn Watson (Jackson: University Press of Mississippi, 2005), 145.

11. Sucheta Mazumdar, "Colonial Impact and Punjabi Emigration to the United States," in *Labor Immigration under Capitalism: Asian Workers in the United States before World War II*, ed. Lucie Cheng and Edna Bonacich (Berkeley: University of California Press, 1984), 320–322.

12. Vivek Bald, *Bengali Harlem and the Lost Histories of South Asian America* (Cambridge, MA: Harvard University Press, 2013).

13. Priya Srinivasan, *Sweating Saris: Indian Dance as Transnational Labor* (Philadelphia, PA: Temple University Press, 2012), 47.

14. The two legislative restrictions, the Prevention of Seditious Meetings Act of 1907 and the Press Act of 1910, culminated in the Defense of India Act in 1915.

15. Unbeknownst to authorities, Sun Yat-sen used a doctored birth certificate to evade Chinese Exclusion laws.

16. Daniela Spenser, *The Impossible Triangle: Mexico, Soviet Russia, and the United States in the 1920s* (Durham, NC: Duke University Press, 1999), 39–40.

17. Michael Silvestri, *Ireland and India: Nationalism, Empire and Memory* (New York: Palgrave Macmillan, 2009), 38.

18. Bradford Perkins, *The Great Rapprochement: England and the United States, 1895–1914* (New York: Atheneum, 1968).

19. Srdjan Vucetic, *The Anglosphere: A Genealogy of a Racialized Identity in International Relations* (Stanford, CA: Stanford University Press, 2011), 24.

20. Lothrop Stoddard, *The Rising Tide of Color against White World-Supremacy* (New York: Charles Scribner's Sons, 1921); Darwin P. Kingsley, "Anglo-Saxon Solidarity," *English Speaking World* 4, no. 1 (January 1921): 9–11.

21. Seema Sohi, *Echoes of Mutiny: Race, Surveillance, and Indian Anticolonialism in North America* (New York: Oxford University Press, 2014), 4.

22. For example, as early as 1911, British authorities had followed the activities of Taraknath Das and attempted, but failed, to prevent his naturalization as an American citizen. See Don K. Dignan, "The Hindu Conspiracy in Anglo-American Relations during World War I," *Pacific Historical Review* 60, no. 1 (February 1971): 60; Joan M. Jensen, *Passage from India: Asian Indian Immigrants in North America* (New Haven, CT: Yale University Press, 1988), 173–174.

23. "Connection between Hindus and Radical Elements," Military Intelligence Division 9771/B-58, Record Group 165, National Archives, College Park, MD (hereafter cited as MID and RG).

24. Scholars have attributed various names to this organization including "Pacific Coast Hindustani Association," "Pacific Coast Hindi Association," and the "Hindi Association of the Pacific Coast." This may very well reflect the inconsistent use of the name by members, themselves; the Gadar Party, for instance, was sometimes spelled as Ghadar Party, and also known as the Hindustan Gadar Party.

25. Maia Ramnath, *Haj to Utopia: How the Ghadar Movement Charted Global Radicalism and Attempted to Overthrow the British Empire* (Berkeley: University of California Press, 2011), 37.

26. Ibid., 90.

27. Details of the case made for a steady stream of headlines, and the trial was featured in two tell-all police memoirs and a wartime silent film series about a German spy ring. In 1918, the Whartons Studio released *The Eagle's Eye*, a film serial that included an episode titled "The Great Hindu Conspiracy," based on a book by Courtney Ryley Cooper and former U.S. Secret Service Chief William James Flynn. Curiously, the story of the Hindu–German conspiracy was published in American newspapers but not the

book version. See "The Eagle's Eye," *Courier-Journal*, August 18, 1918, C4; Thomas J. Tunney and Paul Merrick Hollister, *Throttled! The Detection of the German and Anarchist Bomb Plotters* (Boston, MA: Small, Maynard, 1919); and, John Price Jones and Paul Merrick Hollister, *The German Secret Service in America* (Boston, MA: Small, Maynard, 1919).

28. Brent Hayes Edwards, *The Practice of Diaspora: Literature, Translation, and the Rise of Black Internationalism* (Cambridge, MA: Harvard University Press, 2003), 265.

29. Benedict Anderson, *The Spectre of Comparisons: Nationalisms, Southeast Asia, and the World* (London: Verso, 1998).

30. Saint Nihal Singh, "Colour Line in the United States of America and How the Negro Is Uplifting Himself despite Odds," *Modern Review* 4, nos. 5–6 (1908): 368, *South Asian American Digital Archive*, https://www.saada.org/item/20110621-216, accessed March 10, 2018.

31. M. K. Singh, *Encyclopaedia of Indian War of Independence (1857–1947): Revolutionary Phase*, vol. 11, *Lala Hardyal, Ajit Singh, Ramprasad Bismil and Ras Bihari Bose* (New Delhi: Anmol Publications, 2009), 12.

32. Partha Chatterjee, *The Nation and Its Fragments: Colonial and Postcolonial Histories* (Princeton, NJ: Princeton University Press, 1993), 16–26.

33. "Ourselves: The India Home Rule League of America," *Young India* 1, no. 1 (January 1918): 3, *South Asian American Digital Archive*, https://www.saada.org/item/20110912-359, accessed March 10, 2018.

34. Robert Morss Lovett and Agnes Smedley to David Starr Jordan, July 21, 1919, *South Asian American Digital Archive*, https://www.saada.org/item/20130513-2755, accessed March 10, 2018.

35. Chandra first arrived in the United States with his wife, Padmavati, after an eastbound itinerary that included stints in Peshawar and Delhi (where he edited nationalist newspapers), Hong Kong, Japan, and Seattle (where he briefly worked at a Parsi-owned export store), before eventually landing in the Bay Area. In 1914, Chandra was appointed by Har Dayal as the editor of *Gadar*, and would eventually become head of the Gadar Party. By January 1917, a rift had formed between leaders Chandra and Bhagwan Singh, which according to one report was due to "the failure of Ram Chandra to account for his disbursement of the German secret fund." Reports to Berlin indicated that the party was breaking up "because the Sikhs accused Ram Chandra of giving them nothing from all the money he got from the Germans." "Notes on the Accused, ca. 1918," *US v. Franz Bopp, Ram Chandra et al.*, Neutrality Violation Investigation Case Files, Record Group 118: Records of U.S. Attorneys, 1821–1994, *National Archives Catalog*, https://catalog.archives.gov/id/296681, accessed March 10, 2018.

36. Ram Chandra, *Exclusion of Hindus from America Due to British Influence* (San Francisco: Hindustan Gadar), 3, *South Asian American Digital Archive*, https://www.saada.org/item/20100916-121, accessed March 10, 2018.

37. Ibid., 8.

38. See William Jennings Bryan, *British Rule in India* (San Francisco: Yugantar Ashram, 1906), *South Asian American Digital Archive*, https://www.saada.org/item/20101015-123, accessed March 10, 2018. According to Dignan, Bryan had specifically sent a letter to the British ambassador Cecil Spring-Rice to convey that the pamphlet misrepresented his position. Dignan, "The Hindu Conspiracy in Anglo-American Relations during World War I," 65.

39. A dramatic example of this strategy came during deportation hearings for Gadar Party cofounder Har Dayal in 1914. Dayal was arrested on a warrant issued by the

Secretary of Labor in accordance with an immigration law that deemed any "anarchists or persons who believe in anarchy [. . .] or the assassination of public officials shall be deported." During the deportation hearing, Dayal quoted liberally from Bryan's statements against British Rule, and charged that the Wilson administration was "'licking the boots of England." "Relying on Bryan; Hindu Quotes Him in Defense," *Los Angeles Times*, March 27, 1914, I1; "A Servant, Says Dyal: Hindu Calls Wilson Britain's Tool," *Los Angeles Times*, March 29, 1914, I1.

40. Ram Chandra, *The Appeal of India to the President of the United States* (San Francisco: Hindustan Gadar), Box 1, Folder 30, South Asians in North America Collection, Bancroft Library Archives, University of California, Berkeley (hereafter cited as South Asians in North America Collection).

41. Ibid.

42. Erez Manela, *The Wilsonian Moment: Self-Determination and the International Origins of Anticolonial Nationalism* (New York: Oxford University Press, 2007), 40.

43. Chandra, *The Appeal of India*, 4.

44. "Britannia in India," *Los Angeles Times*, March 1, 1918, I2.

45. Ibid.

46. Padmavati Chandra. New York City. Interview May 1974, Box 4, Folder 1, South Asians in North America Collection.

47. Ramnath, *Haj to Utopia*, 137.

48. "Every Day in Every Way Is India Becoming More and More United and Democratic," *The United States of India* 1, no. 1 (July 1923), 3, *South Asian American Digital Archive*, https://www.saada.org/item/20110908-346, accessed March 10, 2018.

49. Ibid.

50. *The United States of India* 3, no. 8 (February 1926), 1, *South Asian American Digital Archive*, https://www.saada.org/item/20111129-505, accessed March 10, 2018.

51. Eamon De Valera, *India and Ireland* (New York: Friends of Freedom for India, 1920), 3.

52. See V. K. Gorey, *The United States of India: A Constructive Federal Solution* (Baroda: Padmaja Publications, 1946); J. S. Hodge, "The United States of India," *North American Review* 214, no. 791 (1921): 450–460.

53. Bhagat Singh Thind, "Political Prophecy Based on Truth of Life," December 13, 1939, *South Asian American Digital Archive*, https://www.saada.org/item/20110802-277, accessed March 10, 2018.

54. Taraknath Das, *India in World Politics* (New York: B. W. Huebsch, 1923), 78.

55. B. R. Ambedkar, *States and Minorities: What Are Their Rights and How to Secure Them in the Constitution of Free India* (1947; reprint, Delhi: Siddharth Books, 2008), 11.

56. Partha Chatterjee, *Nationalist Thought and the Colonial World: A Derivative Discourse?* (1986; reprint, Minneapolis: University of Minnesota Press, 2004).

57. Pandita Ramabai, *Pandita Ramabai's American Encounter: The Peoples of the United States* (1889), trans. and ed. Meera Kosambi (Bloomington: Indiana University Press, 2003), 136.

58. Meera Kosambi, "Introduction: Returning the American Gaze: Situating Pandita Ramabai's American Encounter," in Pandita Ramabai, *Pandita Ramabai's American Encounter*, 4.

59. Amitava Kumar, *Bombay-London-New York* (New York: Routledge, 2002), 8.

60. Yuko Kikuchi, "Introduction," in *Refracted Modernity: Visual Culture and Identity in Colonial Taiwan*, ed. Yuko Kikuchi (Honolulu: University of Hawai'i Press, 2007), 9.

61. Daniel Coleman, *Masculine Migrations: Reading the Postcolonial Male in "New Canadian" Narratives* (Toronto: University of Toronto Press, 1998), 3.

62. Christian Gutleben and Susana Onega, ed., *Refracting the Canon in Contemporary British Literature and Film* (New York: Rodopi, 2004), 9.

63. Ibid., 7.

64. Lajpat Rai, *The United States of America: A Hindu's Impressions and a Study* (Calcutta: R. Chatterji, 1916), 77.

65. Grace Kyungwon Hong and Roderick A. Ferguson, "Introduction," in *Strange Affinities: The Gender and Sexual Politics of Comparative Racialization*, ed. Grace Kyungwon Hong and Roderick A. Ferguson (Durham, NC: Duke University Press, 2011), 3.

66. Ibid., 11.

67. Lisa Lowe, *The Intimacies of Four Continents* (Durham, NC: Duke University Press, 2015), 2.

68. As Ann Stoler reminds us, "actors and agents" of colonialism alike constantly "reflected on analogous governing practices and [. . .] contexts from which lessons might be learned." Ann Laura Stoler, "Intimidations of Empire: Predicaments of the Tactile and Unseen," in *Haunted by Empire: Geographies of Intimacy in North American History*, ed. Ann Laura Stoler (Durham, NC: Duke University Press, 2006), 6.

69. Françoise Lionnet and Shu-mei Shih, "Introduction: Thinking through the Minor, Transnationally," in *Minor Transnationalism*, ed. Françoise Lionnet and Shu-mei Shih (Durham, NC: Duke University Press, 2005), 8.

70. Mary Louise Pratt, *Imperial Eyes: Travel Writing and Transculturation*, 2nd ed. (London: Routledge, 2008).

71. Nico Slate, *Colored Cosmopolitanism: The Shared Struggle for Freedom in the United States and India* (Cambridge, MA: Harvard University Press, 2012).

72. Yogita Goyal, *Romance, Diaspora, and Black Atlantic Literature* (Cambridge, UK: Cambridge University Press, 2013), 106–107.

73. Dohra Ahmad, "More than Romance: Genre and Geography in *Dark Princess*," *ELH* 69 (2002): 775–803.

74. Manela, *The Wilsonian Moment*, 5.

75. Pratt, *Imperial Eyes*, 167.

76. Paula Rabinowitz, *Labor & Desire: Women's Revolutionary Fiction in Depression America* (Chapel Hill: The University of North Carolina Press, 1991), 10.

77. Smedley, *Daughter of Earth*, 215.

78. W.E.B. Du Bois, *The Souls of Black Folk: Essays and Sketches* (Chicago: A.C. McClurg & Co., 1903), 3.

79. Lajpat Rai, *Unhappy India: Being a Reply to Miss Katherine Mayo's 'Mother India.'* (Calcutta: Banna Publishing Co., 1928), xv.

CHAPTER 1

1. Lala Lajpat Rai, *The Collected Works of Lala Lajpat Rai*, vol. 5, ed. Bal Ram Nanda (New Delhi: Manohar, 2006), 63.

2. As Nayan Shah argues, by the 1900s, trachoma not only had become the "signature disease of medical exclusion" but was disproportionately diagnosed to Asian immigrants, leading to higher rates of deportation. Nayan Shah, *Contagious Divides: Epidemics and Race in San Francisco's Chinatown* (Berkeley: University of California Press, 2001), 187; Lajpat Rai, *The Collected Works of Lala Lajpat Rai*, vol. 5, 64.

3. Partha Chatterjee, *The Nation and Its Fragments: Colonial and Postcolonial Histories* (Princeton, NJ: Princeton University Press, 1993), 16.

4. Inderpal Grewal, *Home and Harem: Nation, Gender, Empire and the Cultures of Travel* (Durham, NC: Duke University Press, 1996), 3.

5. Nico Slate, *Colored Cosmopolitanism: The Shared Struggle for Freedom in the United States and India* (Cambridge, MA: Harvard University Press, 2012), 37.

6. Lajpat Rai, *The United States of America: A Hindu's Impressions and a Study* (Calcutta: R. Chatterjee, 1916), 401.

7. W.E.B. Du Bois, "The Color Line Belts the World"; reprinted in W.E.B. Du Bois, *W.E.B. Du Bois in Asia: Crossing the World Color Line*, ed. Bill Mullen and Cathryn Watson (Jackson: University Press of Mississippi, 2005), 33.

8. Rai, *The Collected Works of Lala Lajpat Rai*, vol. 5, 187. The English were a common target in Rai's invective, and he occasionally pitted them against the French. In a February 1906 issue of the Urdu monthly *Zamana*, Rai contrasted the English to the French, pointing first to Voltaire as an emblem of political and cultural liberty against English conservatism. The article takes a quick turn for humor when Rai begins to draw distinctions between the socially liberated French and the painfully stuffy English, who "eat in silence," fear dressing in the wrong color combination, "believe in following the beaten track," and whose "teeth are uneven and mostly dirty" as opposed to the "clean, even and strong" teeth of the French. Lala Lajpat Rai, *The Collected Works of Lala Lajpat Rai*, vol. 2, ed. Bal Ram Nanda (New Delhi: Manohar, 2003), 209–216.

9. Rai, *The Collected Works of Lala Lajpat Rai*, vol. 5, 184–185.

10. Barkatullah would later teach Hindi at the Tokyo School of Foreign Languages, where he published the pan-Islamist journal *Islamic Fraternity*. Eventually, he returned to the United States in 1912 or 1914 (there are conflicting reports) to aid the San Francisco headquarters of the Gadar Party. Rai would meet Barkatullah again during that time, but being opposed to the Gadar Party's flirtation with the German government and their more radically conceived anticolonial revolution, Rai privately dismissed Barkatullah.

11. See Alan Raucher, "American Anti-Imperialists and the Pro-India Movement, 1900–1932," *Pacific Historical Review* 43, no. 1 (1974): 83–110; Christopher Lasch, "The Anti-Imperialists, the Philippines, and the Inequality of Man," *Journal of Southern History* 24, no. 3 (1958): 319–331.

12. Rai, *The Collected Works of Lala Lajpat Rai*, vol. 2, 187.

13. N. S. Hardikar, *Lala Lajpat Rai in America* (Delhi: Servants of the People Society, 1966), 5. Hardikar would eventually cofound the IHRLA with Rai.

14. For a detailed discussion of the intersections between eugenic feminism and Indian nationalism, see Asha Nadkarni, *Eugenic Feminism: Reproductive Nationalism in the United States and India* (Minneapolis: University of Minnesota Press, 2014).

15. Dohra Ahmad, *Landscapes of Hope: Anti-Colonial Utopianism in America* (New York: Oxford University Press, 2009), 69.

16. M. Churchill to A. Bruce Bielaski, November 22, 1918, MID 9771-72, RG 165; From Mil. Rep. on EPCC to Chief, Military Intelligence Section, Washington, DC, "Subject: Suspect card," MID 9771-72, RG 165.

17. J. A. Merton to H. T. Jones, October 30, 1918, MID 9771-72, RG 165; J. F. Williams, "Report Regarding Lajpat Rai, General Investigation," November 8, 1918, MID 9771-72, RG 165.

18. "Connection between Hindus and Radical Elements," MID 9771/B-58, RG 165.

19. Memorandum from Captain H. T. Jones to Captain Grosvenor, December 10, 1918, MID 9771-72, RG 165.

20. Bill Mullen, *Un-American: W.E.B. Du Bois and the Century of World Revolution* (Philadelphia, PA: Temple University Press, 2015), 101.

21. A central tenet to the Arya Samaj belief system was that Aryans composed the original inhabitants of India (or *aryavartan*), whose society and culture was believed to form the basis of an Indian nation from time immemorial.

22. Christophe Jaffrelot, *Dr. Ambedkar and Untouchability: Fighting the Indian Caste System* (New York: Columbia University Press, 2005), 71–72.

23. Chetan Bhatt, *Hindu Nationalism: Origins, Ideologies, and Modern Myths* (Oxford: Berg, 2001), 41, 50. Bhatt captures the contradictions of Rai's nationalism: on one hand, Rai "accepted the need for Hindu-Muslim unity, that Hindus and Muslims shared a [. . .] composite nationality" and also criticized the Arya Samaj, Swami Vivekananda, and Sister Nivedita for "fostering an intolerant Hindu communal consciousness," but on the other hand, he consistently denigrated Islam as an "intolerant, dogmatic religion" in comparison to Hinduism. Ibid., 71.

24. Lala Lajpat Rai, *The Collected Works of Lala Lajpat Rai*, vol. 12, ed. Bal Ram Nanda (New Delhi: Manohar, 2010), xvii.

25. Lajpat Rai, *Lala Lajpat Rai: The Man in His Word* (Madras: Ganesh & Co., 1907), 260–261.

26. Babli Sinha, "Dissensus, Education, and Lala Lajpat Rai's Encounter with W.E.B. Du Bois," *South Asian History and Culture* 6, no. 4 (2015): 465.

27. Several organizations shared a similar name to the India Home Rule League of America, and to make matters more confusing, several journals during this time were also titled *Young India*, so some clarification might be useful. There were at least three different organizations that were named after "India home rule." In 1905, Shyamji Krishnavarma established the India Home Rule Society in London, which would later be known as the India House, one of the most notable diasporic outposts in the Indian nationalist movement. In 1916, Bal Gangadhar Tilak established the India Home Rule League with branches across India. That same year, Annie Besant also established the All-India Home Rule League. *Young India* was the title of one of Gandhi's weekly newspapers. Rai also wrote a book titled *Young India: An Interpretation and a History of the Nationalist Movement from Within*, which was published in 1917 in New York by B. W. Huebsch.

28. "Ourselves: The India Home Rule League of America," *Young India* 1, no. 1 (January 1918): 3, *South Asian American Digital Archive*, https://www.saada.org/item/20110912-359, accessed March 10, 2018.

29. Ibid.

30. Ahmad, *Landscapes of Hope*, 80.

31. "Ourselves," *Young India*: 4.

32. Ahmad, *Landscapes of Hope*, 70.

33. "India and the World War," *Young India* 1, no. 2 (February 1918): 1, *South Asian American Digital Archive*, https://www.saada.org/item/20110912-360, accessed March 10, 2018.

34. My thanks to Varuni Bhatia for this Sanskrit translation.

35. Ahmad, *Landscapes of Hope*, 4.

36. Rai, *The United States of America*, iii.

37. W.E.B. Du Bois, "The Clash of Colour: Indians and American Negroes," *The Aryan Path* 7, no. 3 (March 1936): 113.

38. "A Hindu's Impressions of the United States," *New York Times*, January 21, 1917, BR2.

39. Javed Majeed, *Autobiography, Travel, and Post-National Identity: Gandhi, Nehru, and Iqbal* (New York: Palgrave Macmillan, 2007), 10.

40. Ibid., 19.

41. Ibid., 76.

42. Mary Louise Pratt, *Imperial Eyes: Travel Writing and Transculturation*, 2nd ed. (London: Routledge, 2008), 85.

43. For more on the *Komagata Maru* saga, see Ali Kazimi, *Continuous Journey* (Vancouver: Peripheral Visions, 2004); Hugh Johnston, *The Voyage of the Komagata Maru: The Sikh Challenge to Canada's Colour Bar* (Vancouver: University of British Columbia Press, 1989); Rajini Srikanth, "The *Komagata Maru*: Memory and Mobilization among the South Asian Diaspora in North America," in *Re/Collecting Early Asian America: Essays in Cultural History*, ed. Josephine D. Lee, Imogene L. Lim, Yuko Matsukawa (Philadelphia: Temple UP, 2002), 78–93.

44. Rabindra Kanungo, ed., *South Asians in the Canadian Mosaic* (Montreal: Kala Bharati, 1984), 17.

45. Rai, *The United States of America*, 400.

46. Rai, *The Collected Works of Lala Lajpat Rai*, vol. 5, 22.

47. Qtd. in Majeed, *Autobiography, Travel, and Post-National Identity*, 15.

48. Within the Indian context, Rai wrote of a past constituted by an "ancient Hindu race," described the British as a "fighting race," and described Muslims as believing they "belong to a race of rulers." Rai, *Lala Lajpat Rai: The Man in His Word*, 194, 197, 184, 260.

49. Ibid., 194.

50. Rai, *The United States of America*, 394.

51. Ibid., 395.

52. Ibid.

53. Ibid., 394.

54. Ibid., 396.

55. Qtd. in Anupama Rao, *The Caste Question: Dalits and the Politics of Modern India* (Berkeley: University of California Press, 2009), 128.

56. Rai, *The United States of America*, 77.

57. Ibid.

58. Ibid.

59. Ibid.

60. Ibid., 289.

61. Ibid., 388.

62. Ibid., 392.

63. Ibid., 389.

64. Ibid., 393.

65. In a remembrance written for Rai, published in 1929, Bose described how he was in frequent correspondence with Rai during his time in the United States. Bose had invited Rai to speak at Iowa, but circumstances prevented that meeting from occurring. Sudhindra Bose, "The Fighter Lajpat Rai," *People* (April 13, 1929): 20.

66. Sudhindra Bose, *Fifteen Years in America* (Calcutta: Kar Majumdar, 1920), 356.

67. Ibid., 356.

68. Ibid., 362.

69. Ibid., 353.

70. Ibid., 355.

71. Ibid., 356.

72. Ibid., 357.

73. Ibid., 365.

74. Ibid., 27.

75. Ibid., 358.

76. Sudhindra Bose, "Life in the Southern States," *Modern Review* 10, no. 2 (August 1911): 131.

77. To support this statement, Bose quotes Du Bois: "It must be frankly admitted that there is absolutely no logical method by which the treatment of black folks by white folks in this land can be squared with any reasonable statement or practice of Christian ideal." Bose, *Fifteen Years in America*, 361.

78. Saint Nihal Singh, "Colour Line in the United States of America and How the Negro Is Uplifting Himself Despite Odds," *Modern Review* 4, no. 5 (November 1908): 366.

79. Saint Nihal Singh, "A Negro Educator's Unique Ideals and Successful Methods," *Modern Review* 3, no. 1 (January 1908): 12.

80. Singh, "Colour Line," 367.

81. Ibid., 368.

82. Ibid.

83. Ibid.

84. Ibid., 372.

85. Vinay Lal, *The Other Indians: A Political and Cultural History of South Asians in America* (Los Angeles: Asian American Studies Press, 2008), 21–22.

86. Joan Jensen, *Passage from India: Asian Indian Immigrants in North America* (New Haven, CT: Yale University Press, 1988), 49–56.

87. "Proceedings of the Asian Exclusion League, San Francisco, February 1908," in *Proceedings of the Asiatic Exclusion League, 1907–1913* (New York: Arno Press, 1977), 8–9.

88. "Proceedings of the Asiatic Exclusion League, San Francisco, January 16, 1910," in Ibid., 9.

89. "Proceedings of the Asiatic Exclusion League, San Francisco, December 1907," in Ibid., 6.

90. "Proceedings of the Asiatic Exclusion League, San Francisco, September 1910," in Ibid., 46.

91. With the passing of the Fourteenth Amendment in 1868, African Americans gained the right to citizenship and naturalization as Congress included the right to naturalize for "persons of African nativity, or African descent," yet the restriction against Native American and Asian naturalization continued through the "'white person' prerequisite." Ian Haney López, *White by Law: The Legal Construction of Race*, 10th anniversary ed. (New York: New York University Press, 2006), 31.

92. Ibid., 172.

93. See Jensen, *Passage from India*, 246–269.

94. "Hindu Immigration Hearings Before the Committee on Immigration, Part 1" (Washington: Government Printing Office, 1914), 7, *South Asian American Digital Archive*, https://www.saada.org/item/20120113-581, accessed March 10, 2018.

95. Ibid., 13.

96. Doug Coulson has recently drawn attention to the role of caste in the momentous 1923 Supreme Court case *US v. Bhagat Singh Thind*, discussed in Chapter 3 of this book. Thind claimed "high caste" status as a means to prove that he was a descendant of "Aryans" and not the "dark races of India," further using the observance of caste endogamy to prove his "white" racial identity. The slippage between caste and race by congressmen during the 1914 hearing and the *Thind* case speak further to the instability of racial categories, and the racial classification of migrants from India more specifically. As Sucheta Mazumdar has

argued, Thind and other migrants' use of the categories of "Aryan" and "high-caste" constituted a "racist response to racism"; we might extend that thought to consider how such responses also entailed a casteist response to racism. Doug Coulson, *Race, Nation, and Refuge: The Rhetoric of Race in Asian American Citizenship Cases* (Albany: State University of New York Press, 2017), 61–62; Sucheta Mazumdar, "Racist Responses to Racism: The Aryan Myth and South Asians in the United States," *South Asia Bulletin* 9, no. 1 (1989): 47–55.

97. Haney López, *White by Law*, 5.

98. Mazumdar, "Racist Responses to Racism."

99. Rai, *The Collected Works of Lala Lajpat Rai*, vol. 5, 75.

100. Rai, *The Collected Works of Lala Lajpat Rai*, vol. 1, 371.

101. "Mr. Hardayal," *Young India* 2, no. 5 (May 1919): 104, *South Asian American Digital Archive*, https://www.saada.org/item/20130128-1270, accessed March 10, 2018.

102. Har Dayal, "India in America," *Modern Review* 10, no. 1 (July 1911): 4.

103. "A Servant, Says Dyal," *Los Angeles Times*, March 29, 1914, I1.

104. Har Dayal, "India in America," 11.

105. Rai, *The United States of America*, 401.

106. Ibid., 409.

107. Ibid., 411.

108. See Jasbir Puar, *Terrorist Assemblages: Homonationalism in Queer Times* (Durham, NC: Duke University Press, 2007), 177–78.

109. Rai, *The United States of America*, 412.

110. Ibid., 403.

111. Ibid., 405.

112. Girindra Mukerji, "The Hindu in America," *Overland Monthly* 51, no. 4 (April 1908): 305, *South Asian American Digital Archive*, https://www.saada.org/item/20111101-443, accessed March 10, 2018.

113. By emphasizing self-reliance, each of these narratives by Rai, Mukerji, and Dayal also countered the well-worn colonial discourse of Indian racial emasculation.

114. Sarangadhar Das, "Why Must We Emigrate to the United States of America," *Modern Review* 10, no. 1 (July 1911): 78–79.

115. Ibid., 78.

116. According to a Military Intelligence Report, Vaishya helped run the Baroda Laundry at 1490 Bonita Avenue, Berkeley, which allegedly was a meeting place for Gadar Party operatives. Vaishya was also thought to have attended the welcome dinner for *Gadar* editor Ram Chandra, when he came to San Francisco, organized by Har Dayal. "Premanend Valji Vaishya," MID 9771-64, RG 165.

117. Ibid.

118. Ibid.

119. Ibid.

120. B. R. Ambedkar, *The Essential Writings of B. R. Ambedkar*, ed. Valerian Rodrigues (New Delhi: Oxford University Press, 2002), 245.

121. "Letter from B. R. Ambedkar to W.E.B. Du Bois," *South Asian American Digital Archive*, https://www.saada.org/item/20140415-3544, accessed March 10, 2018.

122. This has not kept others from imagining what may have transpired. For the biopic *Dr. Babasaheb Ambedkar*, writers Sooni Taraporevala and Jabbar Patel had written a fictitious scene in which Ambedkar appears in a kitchen, working alongside a Black coworker, while the two discuss the differences between untouchability and racism. The scene occurs after a previous sequence in which Ambedkar is approached by Lajpat Rai

to participate in the India Home Rule League of America. *Dr. Babasaheb Ambedkar.* Dir. Jabbar Patel. Ultra Distributors Private Ltd., 2008. DVD.

123. Maud Ralston, "The India Society of Detroit," *Modern Review* 10, no. 3 (September 1911): 236, *South Asian American Digital Archive,* https://www.saada.org/item/201106 16-211, accessed March 10, 2018.

124. Ibid.

125. George Weller, "The Case of the Tan Stranger," *Saturday Evening Post* 12 (July 12, 1952): 103–104.

126. Ibid.

127. Sudhindra Bose, "Life in the Southern States of America," *Modern Review* 10, no. 2 (August 1911): 129–133.

128. Lala Lajpat Rai, *The Collected Works of Lala Lajpat Rai,* vol. 6, ed. Bal Ram Nanda (New Delhi: Manohar, 2006), 70.

129. Ibid.

130. Ibid.

131. Lajpat Rai, "Message," *Hindusthanee Student* 6, no. 2 (March 1916): 3.

132. Paul Kramer, *The Blood of Government: Race, Empire, the United States, and the Philippines* (Chapel Hill: The University of North Carolina Press, 2006), 365.

133. Ibid.

134. Lajpat Rai, "Making India Like Philippines," *Los Angeles Times,* May 11, 1915, III4.

135. Ibid.

136. Ibid.

137. Rai, *The United States of America,* 299.

138. E. Berkeley Tompkins, *Anti-Imperialism in the United States: The Great Debate* (Philadelphia: University of Pennsylvania Press, 1970), *1890–1920,* 152.

139. Lasch, "The Anti-Imperialists, the Philippines, and the Inequality of Man," 321.

140. Ibid., 326.

141. Rai, *The United States of America,* 297.

142. Erez Manela, *The Wilsonian Moment: Self-Determination and the International Origins of Anticolonial Nationalism* (New York: Oxford University Press, 2007), 88.

143. "Connection Between Hindus and Radical Elements," MID 9771-B-58, RG 165.

144. Milton Israel, *Communications and Power: Propaganda and the Press in the Indian Nationalist Struggle, 1920–1947* (Cambridge, MA: Cambridge University Press, 1994), 280.

145. Rustom Rustomjee, "Who Rules in India: A Reply to the Contention that Britain Holds All the Reins," *New York Times,* June 20, 1916, 10.

146. Rustom Rustomjee, "India's Loyalty Asserted: Unrest of a Few Home Rule Highbrows Is Not Representative," *New York Times,* June 24, 1915, 8.

147. Residing in the United States for more than a decade, Rustomjee disseminated propaganda not only on British rule in India, but on a variety of topics that dealt with immigration and racial governance. At the 1914 Sagamore Sociological conference, he spoke on the issue of Indian immigration in the United States, concluding "very reluctantly, that it will not be wise for America to receive immigrants from India." His argument distinguished "Aryan Indians"—described as "bright-faced, light-complexioned people"—from the working-class and presumably dark-skinned "coolies" currently entering the West Coast. In 1921, he served on the Advisory Board of the *English Speaking World,* a pro-imperialist monthly journal that regularly published articles supporting "Anglo-Saxon solidarity" and U.S.–British unity, while denouncing the Irish republican

and Indian nationalist movements. By 1922, the British had sent Rustomjee back to India after his decade-long stint in the United States. When he returned in 1924, according to historian Milton Israel, "he was regarded as an indiscreet ally who had allowed his official connections to become known." *Sagamore Sociological Conference Eighth Year,* Sagamore Beach, Massachusetts, June 30 to July 2, 1914; "In re: Indian Revolutionists, General Neutrality Matter," MID 9771-72, RG 165. For its part, the IHRLA journal *Young India* had called Rustomjee out on several occasions. See "Rustom Rustomji and Tagore," *Young India* 2, no. 9 (September 1919): 203–204.

148. Naeem Rathore, "Indian Nationalist Agitation in the United States: A Study of Lala Lajpat Rai and the India Home Rule League in America, 1914–1920," (PhD diss., Columbia University, 1965), 90.

149. Don K. Dignan, "The Hindu Conspiracy in Anglo-American Relations during World War I," *Pacific Historical Review* 40 no. 1 (February 1971): 60.

150. *United States v. Sailendra Nath Ghose, Agnes Smedley, and others*, Grand Jury Testimony, Henrietta Rodman, April 16, 1918, MID 9771-64, RG 165.

151. Ahmad, *Landscapes of Hope*, 120.

152. Rai, *The Collected Works of Lala Lajpat Rai*, vol. 6, 147.

153. Lala Lajpat Rai, "What India Wants: Liberty Like that of Canada or South Africa," *New York Times*, May 31, 1916, 12.

154. Rai, "Making India Like Philippines," III4.

155. David Brody, *Visualizing American Empire: Orientalism & Imperialism in the Philippines* (Chicago: University of Chicago Press, 2010).

156. Rai, "Making India Like Philippines," III4.

157. Ibid.

158. Rai, *The United States of America*, 389.

159. "Tributes to Mr. Rai," *Young India* 3, no. 2 (February 1920): 28–35.

160. Originally from Switzerland, Frieda Hauswirth was closely associated with Har Dayal, who gave her letters to pass along to Ram Chandra and Munshi Ram after he fled the United States. Hauswirth would later marry Sarangadhar Das, and in the 1930s published a number of books on India. Hauswirth wrote two chapters for *The United States of India*, including the "Outline of American History" and another chapter on the status of American women.

161. Rai, *The Collected Works of Lala Lajpat Rai*, vol. 6, 71.

162. Agnes Smedley, *Daughter of Earth* (1929; reprint, New York: Feminist Press, 1987), 272.

CHAPTER 2

1. The embassies that received the letter included Japan, Spain, Norway, Bolivia, Netherland, Costa Rica, Chile, Peru, Brazil, Denmark, Paraguay, Panama, and Honduras. Memorandum from R. H. Van Deman to Intelligence Officer, Western Department, March 23, 1918, MID 9771-72, RG 165.

2. Even more forceful than the letter written to Wilson, the letter to Trotsky describes the work of the INP as "throwing off the British autocracy" in an effort to destroy "the backbone of the most pernicious imperialism of the world—the Anglo-Saxon imperialism." Pulin Behari Bose to Woodrow Wilson, December 8, 1917, MID 9771-72, RG 65; Pulin Behari Bose to Leon Trotsky, December 12, 1917, MID 9771-72, RG 65.

3. The name Pulin Behari Bose appears to be a combination of Pulin Behari Das and Rash Behari Bose, both Bengali radicals. Rash Behari Bose was also listed on some

of the Indian National Party's stationery. Dohra Ahmad, *Landscapes of Hope: Anti-Colonial Utopianism in America* (New York: Oxford University Press, 2009), 221.

4. "The Hindu Activity in the United States," MID 9771-72, RG 65.

5. "Hold American Girl as an India Plotter," *New York Times*, March 19, 1918, 5.

6. Dada Amir Haider Khan, *Chains to Lose: Life and Struggles of a Revolutionary: Memoirs of Dada Amir Haider Khan,* ed. Hasan N. Gardezi (Karachi: Pakistan Study Centre, 2007), 238.

7. "Investigating War Expenses," *Ithaca Daily News*, July 1, 1919, 2.

8. Agnes Smedley, *Battle Hymn of China* (New York: A.A. Knopf, 1943), 8.

9. Walt Carmon, "Books," *New Masses* (August 1929): 17.

10. Paula Rabinowitz, *Labor & Desire: Women's Revolutionary Fiction in Depression America* (Chapel Hill: The University of North Carolina Press, 1991), 10.

11. Smedley, *Battle Hymn of China*, 5.

12. Ibid., 5.

13. Janice MacKinnon and Stephen MacKinnon, *Agnes Smedley: The Life and Times of an American Radical* (Berkeley: University of California Press, 1988), 22.

14. Ibid., 29.

15. Nayan Shah, *Stranger Intimacy: Contesting Race, Sexuality and the Law in the North American West* (Berkeley: University of California Press, 2012), 90.

16. Maia Ramnath, *Haj to Utopia: How the Ghadar Movement Charted Global Radicalism and Attempted to Overthrow the British Empire* (Berkeley: University of California Press, 2011), 32–33.

17. Shah, *Stranger Intimacy*, 90.

18. "All India Revolts Against Rule of Briton," *Fresno Morning Republican*, September 25, 1916, 12.

19. Ibid.

20. Ibid.

21. Allen Churchill, "The Female Reformed: Henrietta Rodman's Mädchen," in *On Bohemia: The Code of the Self-Exiled*, ed. César Graña and Marigay Graña (New Brunswick, NJ: Transaction Publishers, 1990), 277–279.

22. Qtd. in Kenneth E. Miller, *From Progressive to New Dealer: Frederic C. Howe and American Liberalism* (University Park: Pennsylvania State University Press, 2010), 233.

23. Naeem Rathore, "Indian Nationalist Agitation in the United States: A Study of Lala Lajpat Rai and the India Home Rule League in America, 1914–1920," (PhD diss., Columbia University, 1965), 85.

24. During a grand jury hearing for the case against Smedley and Ghose on April 16, 1918, the chief prosecutor, Robert P. Stephenson, asked Rodman how Smedley had become interested in India. Rodman replied, "I have an idea I knew. We all met Dr. Raw (*sic*) and he is a very interesting talker, and he had written several books, and I think probably she read them and talked with him and became interested in that way. We were all interested in India." Testimony by Truda Theresa Weil, a student at NYU who claimed to know Smedley six weeks before her arrest, states similarly. *United States v. Sailendra Nath Ghose, Agnes Smedley and others*, Grand Jury Testimony, Henrietta Rodman, April 17, 1918, MID 9771-72, RG 165; Memorandum by Inspector C.L. Converse on Truda Theresa Weil, September 6, 1917. MID 10541-722, RG 65.

25. *United States v. Sailendra Nath Ghose, Agnes Smedley and others*, Grand Jury Testimony, Lajpat Rai, April 16, 1918. MID 9771-72, RG 165.

26. Agnes Smedley, *Daughter of Earth* (1929; reprint, New York: Feminist Press, 1987), 269.

27. Rathore, "Indian Nationalist Agitation," 135.

28. *United States v. Sailendra Nath Ghose, Agnes Smedley and others*, Grand Jury Testimony, Henrietta Rodman, April 17, 1918, MID 9771-72, RG 165.

29. Darshan Singh Tatla, *The Sikh Diaspora: The Search for Statehood* (London: University College London Press, 1999), 92.

30. Vivek Bald, "'Lost' in the City: Spaces and Stories of South Asian New York, 1917–1965," *South Asian Popular Culture* 5, no. 1. (April 2007): 65.

31. Interrogation of J. B. Dev by Captain Lloyd, May 29, 1916, MID 9771-72, RG 165; also see Anita Mannur, "Indian Food in the U.S.: 1909–1921," *South Asian American Digital Archive*, https://www.saada.org/tides/article/20111018-417, accessed March 10, 2018.

32. Bald, "'Lost' in the City," 62–63.

33. Sailendra Nath Ghose, "An Indian Revolutionary: The Story of a Bengali Boy Developing in an Atmosphere of Student Radicalism," *Asia* (July 1927): 694.

34. Ibid., 674.

35. Sailendra Nath Ghose, "An Indian Revolutionary: The Story of a Bengali Boy in Flight from Physics Laboratory to Stoke Hole," *Asia* (September 1927): 772.

36. "The Hindu Conspiracy," April 10, 1918, Record Group 9771-72, RG 165.

37. Ghose, "An Indian Revolutionary: The Story of a Bengali Boy in Flight," 774.

38. A report filed in March 16, 1918 described Ghose's alias as "Miter," "Mitter," or "Mitra," and mentions his indictment by the Grand Jury in connection with the Hindu–German Conspiracy case. Intelligence Officer to Chief Military Intelligence Branch, March 16, 1918, MID 10497-514, RG 65; Telegram from Watkins to Major Nicholas Biddle, March 14, 1918, MID 10497-514, RG 165.

39. Smedley, *Battle Hymn of China*, 8.

40. Ruth Price, *The Lives of Agnes Smedley* (Oxford: Oxford University Press, 2005), 65–66.

41. Ramnath, *Haj to Utopia*, 130.

42. Office of Military Intelligence Report, March 22, 1918; U.S. Army Western Department Intelligence Office Report, March 19, 1918; U.S. Army Western Department Intelligence Office Report, March 22, 1918, MID 9771-72, RG 165.

43. Ramnath, *Haj to Utopia*, 130.

44. Price, *The Lives of Agnes Smedley*, 65; "The Hindu Conspiracy," April 10, 1918, MID 9771-72, RG 165.

45. Office of Military Intelligence Memorandum, March 19, 1918, MID 9771-72, RG 165.

46. MacKinnon and MacKinnon, *Agnes Smedley*, 46.

47. During this time, Smedley also ran the Hindu Defence Fund, which circulated letters to socialist, radical, and liberal groups, and newspapers such as the *Dial*. The National Civil Liberties Bureau had subscribed to the fund, and key figures in the Friends of Freedom for India, such as Dudley Field Malone, had spoken at a large gathering at Carnegie Hall on February 16, 1919, to support their case. On January 26, 1919, a concert and ball at Forward Hall was organized to raise funds for their defense. Memorandum from John B. Trevor to Director of Military Intelligence on "Society of Friends of Indian Freedom," March 11, 1919, MID 9771-B-45, RG 165.

48. Smedley, *Battle Hymn of China*, 8.

49. Taraknath Das to Agnes Smedley, May 12–13, 1919, MID 9771-72, RG 165.

50. Memorandum from J. P. to W. on Sakharam Ganesh Pandit, March 5, 1919, KV 2/2207—Soviet Intelligence Agents and Suspected Agents, The National Archives, Kew, Great Britain (hereafter cited as KV 2/2207).

51. Memorandum from J. P. to W. on Agnes Smedley and Sailendra Nath Ghose, February 27, 1919, KV 2/2207.

52. *United States v. Sailendra Nath Ghose, Agnes Smedley and others*, Grand Jury Testimony, Henrietta Rodman, April 16, 1918. MID 9771-72, RG 165.

53. Captain John B. Trevor explained that while Smedley was only listed as secretary of the organization, "it is obvious that Agnes Smedley and her Hindu associates are the moving spirits in this particular affair." John B. Trevor to Office of MID, April 15, 1919, MID 9771-B-45, RG 165.

54. An agent who attended the meeting also described how pledges were made out in honor of a variety of causes and people, including Soviet Russia, Eugene Debs, Mahatma Gandhi, Éamon de Valera, and "dead American soldiers recently brought here from France." Memorandum from Assistant Chief of Staff for Military Intelligence to Director, MID on "Anti-British Activities," March 21, 1921, MID 9771-B-70, RG 165.

55. Ibid.

56. There is some discrepancy about the actual start date of the FFI. One military intelligence report explains that "files do not show date of organization but it apparently started late in 1918 by Agnes Smedley." "Objects of the Organization," MID 9771-72, RG 165.

57. Ibid.

58. Agnes Smedley to Bhagwan Singh Gyanee, January 18, 1920, *South Asian American Digital Archive*, https://www.saada.org/item/20120321-680, accessed March 10, 2018.

59. Sergeant M. K. Bunde to Captain Wm. L Moffat Jr., February 29, 1920, MID 9771-72, RG 165.

60. Khan, *Chains to Lose*, 237.

61. Ibid., 239; see Vivek Bald, *Bengali Harlem and the Lost Histories of South Asian America* (Cambridge, MA: Harvard University Press, 2013), 144–148.

62. *India's Freedom in American Courts* (New York: Friends of Freedom for India, 1919), 7, *South Asian American Digital Archive*, https://www.saada.org/item/20111027-430, accessed March 10, 2018.

63. Ibid., 10.

64. Ibid., 4.

65. Ibid.

66. Ibid., 9.

67. "The Failure of British Rule in India" (New York: Friends of Freedom for India, 1919?), MID 9771-72, RG 165.

68. Sohi, *Echoes of Mutiny*, 174.

69. Ibid.

70. Ibid.

71. *India's Freedom in American Courts*, 10.

72. Kritika Agarwal, "Indian Laborers and Conspiracy on Ellis Island," *South Asian American Digital Archive*, https://www.saada.org/tides/article/20141020-3825, accessed March 10, 2018.

73. Basanta Koomar Roy, "Doing England's Dirty Work," *The Independent Hindustan* 1, no. 2 (October 1920): 29.

74. The IHRLA also covered news of the deportations; see N. S. Hardiker, "Deporting Indian Laborers," *Young India* 3, no. 2 (September 1920): 213–215.

75. American Federation of Labor to Santokh Singh, July 11, 1919. MID 9771-72, RG 165.

76. Agnes Smedley to Santokh Singh, July 11, 1919, MID 9771-72, RG 165.

77. Price, *The Lives of Agnes Smedley*, 79.

78. Smedley's contributions to the *New York Call* included several reports on the British Empire, world affairs, as well as domestic labor issues: "Britain Seeks to Expand Empire by Control of Air," *New York Call*, February 8, 1920, 6; "Britain Trembles for Fear of Losing East," *New York Call*, February 3, 1920, 6; "Nation Strives to Gain Liberty, Says Egyptian," *New York Call*, March 3, 1920, 5; "Passage of Measures Means Liberty's End, Declares Marshall, *New York Call*, May 15, 1920, 1.

79. Agnes Smedley, "Trinity of Starvation, Disease and Executions Bringing 'Peace' To India," *New York Call*, September 14, 1919, 5.

80. Ibid.

81. Kevin Grant, "The Limits of Exposure: Atrocity Photographs in the Congo Reform Campaign," in *Humanitarian Photography*, ed. Heide Fehrenbach and Davide Rodogno (Cambridge, MA: Cambridge University Press, 2015), 64.

82. Friends of Freedom for India to Dr. D. S. Jordan, July 21, 1919, *South Asian American Digital Archive*, https://www.saada.org/item/20130513-2755, accessed March 10, 2018.

83. Ahmad, *Landscapes of Hope*, 127–128.

84. Ibid., 128.

85. John G. Purdie to Lieutenant W.L. Moffat, Jr., April 11, 1919. MID 9771-B-45, RG 165.

86. Ibid.

87. Ibid.

88. Ibid.

89. "'Friends of Freedom for India' Dinner," May 23, 1919. MID 9771-72, RG 165.

90. Ibid.

91. Irish nationalist expressions of solidarity for India, and vice versa, were fairly common; the FFI, for example, hosted a dinner in honor of Éamon de Valera during his American tour in 1920. Ramnath, *Haj to Utopia*, 108–109. On September 5, 1920, Roy and members of the FFI had joined Irish Republicans in a reportedly five-mile parade in Philadelphia to support the cause of Indian and Irish independence; the ensuing report in the Gadar Party's *Independent Hindustan* again drew on the iconography of American Revolution, declaring that "Philadelphia Rings the Liberty Bell of India." "Philadelphia Rings the Liberty Bell," *Independent Hindustan* 1, no. 2 (October 1920): 44.

92. "America on British Rule in India" (New York: Wolfe Tone Co. Publishers), 12, MID 9771-72, RG 165.

93. Ibid., 15–17.

94. Ibid., 28–29.

95. Agnes Smedley to Florence Lennon, April 27, 1924, Florence Becker Lennon Papers, Special Collections and Archives, University of Colorado, Boulder (hereafter cited as Florence Becker Lennon Papers).

96. Smedley, *Battle Hymn of China*, 15.

97. Ibid., 15–19; Agnes Smedley to Florence Lennon, November 11, 1922, Florence Becker Lennon Papers.

98. Smedley, *Battle Hymn of China*, 15–19.

99. Ramnath, *Haj to Utopia*, 124.

100. This delegation included Bhupendranath Dutta, Virendranath Das Gupta, Nalini Gupta, Gulam Ambia Khan Luhani, and Pandurang Khankhoje. See Kris Manjapra, *M. N. Roy: Marxism and Colonial Cosmopolitanism* (New Delhi: Routledge 2010), 71;

Price, *The Lives of Agnes Smedley*, 86; M. N. Roy, *M. N. Roy's Memoirs* (Bombay: Allied Publishers Private Ltd, 1964), 479–483.

101. M. N. Roy had proposed this thesis as a member of the Communist Party of Mexico.

102. Smedley, *Battle Hymn of China*, 15.

103. Price, *The Lives of Agnes Smedley*, 111.

104. In a letter to Florence Lennon from Christmas Day 1923, Smedley described her separation from Chattopadhyay. At one point she writes, "He can't torture me any more as he used to do. But he has left me, nevertheless, destroyed nervously. Much of it, but not all, is on his bill, and much of the time I think I'll make him pay in more costly coin than dollars or pounds. But my feeling of protection arises and prevents." While they attempted to reconcile their relationship, by July 1925 Smedley had again left Chattopadhyay. Chatto was a consistent topic of discussion in many of the letters that Smedley sent to Lennon, which detail the emotional abuse and jealousy she endured on a constant basis from him. Agnes Smedley to Florence Lennon, December 25, 1923; Agnes Smedley to Florence Lennon, July 27, 1925, Florence Becker Lennon Papers.

105. Smedley, *Battle Hymn of China*, 23.

106. "The Hindu Conspiracy," April 10, 1918. MID 9771-72, RG 165.

107. Translations were soon published in Germany, France, Czechoslovakia, Holland, Spain, Sweden, Russia, Poland, Serbia, Italy, China, Japan, and Portugal. "Bitter Biography: Re-Issue of Book by Agnes Smedley," *South China Morning Post*, August 23, 1935, 15.

108. Carmon, "Books," 17.

109. Ibid.

110. See Rabinowitz, *Labor & Desire*, 10; Richard Jean So, *Transpacific Community: America, China, and the Rise and Fall of a Cultural Network* (New York: Columbia University Press, 2016), 9.

111. MacKinnon and MacKinnon, *Agnes Smedley*, 107.

112. Qtd. in Ibid., 115.

113. Rabinowitz, *Labor & Desire*, 12.

114. Sondra Guttman, "Working Toward 'Unity in Diversity': Rape and the Reconciliation of Color and Comrade in Agnes Smedley's *Daughter of Earth*," *Studies in the Novel* 32, no. 4 (Winter 2000): 489; Barbara Foley, *Radical Representations: Politics and Form in U.S. Proletarian Fiction, 1929–1941* (Durham, NC: Duke University Press, 1993).

115. "One Is Not Made of Wood: The True Story of a Life," *New Masses* (August 1927): 6.

116. Georg Lukács, *The Theory of the Novel* (Cambridge, MA: MIT Press, 1971), 41.

117. Edward Said, *Reflections on Exile and Other Essays* (Cambridge, MA: Harvard University Press, 2000), 186.

118. Smedley, *Daughter of Earth*, 272.

119. Mike Gold, "Notes of the Month," *New Masses* 6, no. 1 (June 1930): 4.

120. Qtd. in Manjapra, *M. N. Roy: Marxism and Colonial Cosmopolitanism*, 42.

121. Ibid.

122. Ibid.

123. Agnes Smedley to Florence Lennon, December 31, 1921, Florence Becker Lennon Papers.

124. "One Is Not Made of Wood," 6.

125. Foley, *Radical Representations*, vii.

126. Jon-Christian Suggs, "*Marching! Marching!* and the Idea of the Proletarian Novel," in *The Novel and the American Left: Critical Essays on Depression-Era Fiction*, ed. Janet Galligani Casey (University of Iowa Press, 2004), 152.

127. Daniel Aaron, *Writers on the Left: Episodes in American Literary Communism* (New York: Columbia University Press, 1992), 294.

128. Ibid.

129. Suggs, "Marching!" 161.

130. See Foley, *Radical Representations*, 86–128.

131. Leon Trotsky, *Literature and Revolution* (Chicago: Haymarket Books, 2005), 155.

132. Qtd. in Philip Rahv, "Proletarian Literature: A Political Autopsy," in Alan Wald, *Writing from the Left: New Essays on Radical Culture and Politics* (London: Verso, 1994), 109.

133. Ibid., 67.

134. Ibid., 68.

135. Agnes Smedley, "The Spirit of Revolt in Hindu Poetry," *Call Magazine* (June 22, 1919): 4.

136. Alice Bird, "The Bliss of a Moment," *Modern Review* (March 1920): 271–272.

137. Ibid.

138. Agnes Smedley to W.E.B. Du Bois, June 9, 1925. W.E.B. Du Bois Papers (MS 312). Special Collections and University Archives, University of Massachusetts Amherst Libraries.

139. Agnes Smedley, "The Negro Renaissance," *Modern Review* (December 1926): 659.

140. Ibid., 660.

141. Agnes Smedley, "Tendencies in Modern Chinese Literature," *Modern Review* (April 1930): 433.

142. Agnes Smedley, "Germany's Artist of Social Misery," *Modern Review* (August 1925): 148.

143. Ibid., 152–153.

144. Smedley, *Daughter of Earth*, 201.

145. Ibid., 200.

146. Ibid., 258.

147. Ibid., 220.

148. MacKinnon and MacKinnon, *Agnes Smedley*, 24. The Military Intelligence Division intercepted a statement that Smedley had produced for her lawyer. The statement mentions this meeting: "In 1915 an East Indian do not remember his name came and talked to the faculty of Normal School at Santiago California. As a member of faculty I heard the lecture 'Told of horrible conditions there, no education, no free speech and told of conditions of women.' Before that had been interested in Eastern question in Cal. Had opposed the anti-Alien Land Laws. After that met Indians in N.W. of Cal. But got little information." Office of M.I.D. to Director of Military Intelligence, January 2, 1919, MID 9771-72, RG 165.

149. While Marie's apprenticeship to Singh resembles her relationship with Lajpat Rai, Singh's physical description and Sikh identity suggest a connection to Bhagwan Singh.

150. Purnima Bose, "Transnational Resistance and Fictive Truths: Virendranath Chattopadhyaya, Agnes Smedley and the Indian Nationalist Movement," *South Asian History and Culture* 2, no. 4 (2011): 512.

151. Ibid., 516–517.

152. Smedley, *Daughter of Earth*, 219.

153. Ibid., 219.

154. Ibid., 220.

155. Ibid., 262.

156. Ibid., 263.

157. Ibid., 288.

158. Ibid., 272.

159. Ibid., 275.

160. So, *Transpacific Network*, 9.

161. Agnes Brundin, "Education of Women in India," *Hindusthanee Student* 4, no. 6 (March 1918): 1–8; Agnes Smedley, "Women and New India," *Independent Hindustan* 1, no. 1 (September 1920): 10–11; Agnes Smedley, "Sidelights on Women of India," *Call Magazine*, March 16, 1919: 4–5.

162. Smedley, "Sidelights on Women of India," 5.

163. Smedley, *Daughter of Earth*, 261.

164. Ibid., 261.

165. Ibid., 261–262.

166. Ibid., 355.

167. Ibid., 356.

168. Ibid., 276–277.

169. Ibid., 281.

170. Ibid., 281.

171. Ibid., 357.

172. Ibid.

173. Ibid., 372.

174. Ibid., 271.

175. Ibid., 296.

176. Rabinowitz, *Labor & Desire*, 12.

177. See Ramnath, *Haj to Utopia*, 91; MacKinnon and MacKinnon, *Agnes Smedley*, 42, 394; "The Case of Rita Casselis alias Rita Esther Morea," September 26, 1918, MID 10541-722/42, RG 165.

178. Price, *The Lives of Agnes Smedley*, 61–62. The way that the character Juan Diaz discredits Marie in the latter scenes of the novel, claiming she has no place in the revolutionary cause for Indian freedom, closely resembles M. N. Roy's criticisms of Smedley in his memoirs. During the meetings in Moscow, Smedley, according to Roy, wanted to speak on behalf of Virendranath Chattopadhyay, but Roy argues that "a non-Indian would not be the right person to open the Indian case." Later, Roy also described Smedley as a "fanatical hero-worshipper" who had "seemed to believe that to fall in love with famous Indian Revolutionaries would be the expression of her loyalty to India." He goes onto insinuate that Smedley had worshipped the "lonesome old man, Lajpatrai (*sic*)," then a young Indian, presumably Sailendranath Ghose, and when the latter married another American woman she eventually turned her attention to Virendranath Chattopadhay. Roy writes, "she seemed to have a grudge against me." Roy, *M. N. Roy's Memoirs*, 487.

179. Smedley, *Daughter of Earth*, 271.

180. Smedley, *Daughter of Earth*, 406.

181. Ibid., 355.

182. The exchange was republished in the booklet Agnes Smedley, *India and the Next War* (Amritsar: The Kirti Office, 1928).

183. Ibid., 15.

184. Ibid., 16–17.

185. Ibid., 17; Bill Mullen, *Un-American: W.E.B. Du Bois and the Century of World Revolution* (Philadelphia, PA: Temple University Press, 2015), 109.

186. Ibid., 21.

187. Ibid., 22–23.

188. Ibid., 35.

189. "Tributes in Brief," *People,* April 13, 1929, 11.

CHAPTER 3

1. "The India of Tagore and Kipling," *Bulletin of the Brooklyn Institute of Arts and Sciences* 24, no. 9 (November 13, 1920): 131.

2. Ibid.; "Four Lectures on 'India and Hindu Life,'" *Bulletin of the Brooklyn Institute of Arts and Sciences* 24, no. 2 (September 25, 1920): 23.

3. This was the first of four lectures that Mukerji would deliver on "India and Hindu life" that winter (likely timed to capitalize on the buzz that the real Tagore had created when he had visited the Brooklyn Museum the previous week, on November 10, 1920).

4. Dhan Gopal Mukerji to Jawaharlal Nehru, March 20, 1929, Nehru Memorial Museum and Library Archives (hereafter cited as NMML Archives).

5. J. Daniel Elam, "Republic of Anticolonial Letters: Reading Between South Asia and North America," (PhD diss, Northwestern University, 2015).

6. Two of Mukerji's children's novels, *Gay-Neck* and *Chief of the Herd,* were translated into Bangla as *Chitragreeb* and *Juthopati,* respectively, not long after their English publication. Satadru Sen additionally notes that *Chitragreeb* was listed as "recommended holiday reading" by the Bengali children's magazine publisher Hemen Ray in 1936. Rimli Bhattacharya, "Chosen Families and Self-Transformations in Dhan Gopal Mukerji's Books for Children, 1920s–1930s, *South Asia: Journal of South Asian Studies* 36, no. 1 (2013): 12; Satadru Sen, *Disciplined Natives: Race, Freedom and Confinement in Colonial India* (Delhi: Primus Books, 2012), 59.

7. Elizabeth Seeger, "Dhan Mukerji and His Books," *The Horn Book* 13, no. 4 (July–August 1937): 200–201.

8. Harold R. Isaacs, *Scratches on Our Minds: American Images of China and India* (New York: John Day Company, 1958), 241.

9. Lajpat Rai, *The United States of America: A Hindu's Impressions and a Study* (Calcutta: R. Chatterjee, 1916), 419.

10. Dhan Gopal Mukerji, *Caste and Outcast* (1923; reprint, Stanford, CA: Stanford University Press, 2002), 45.

11. Ibid., 45–46.

12. "Mukerji to Lecture on Rudyard Kipling," *Atlanta Constitution,* March 11, 1921, 6.

13. Several critics have suggested Kipling's oeuvre as the master narrative to which Mukerji responded. Harish Trivedi mentions that Mukerji seemed to be understood by readers in the United States as "an authentic indigenous counterpart to Kipling." Rimi Chatterjee argues that "Mukerji has Kipling in his mind as a kind of 'intimate enemy,'" drawing on Ashis Nandy's formulation of colonial subjectivity. Rimli Bhattacharya argues that throughout his career Mukerji was engaged in "rewriting Kipling's Indian jungle," and also examines how his writing can be historicized within the context of the Boy Scout movement in the United States and the UK. Harish Trivedi, "Reading Kipling

in India," in *The Cambridge Companion to Rudyard Kipling*, ed. Howard J. Booth (Cambridge, MA: Cambridge University Press, 2011), 191; Rimi B. Chatterjee, "Creating Boyhood on the Cusp of Two Cultures: Dhan Gopal Mukerji and Rudyard Kipling," in *Reading Children: Essays on Children's Literature*, ed. Nilanjana Gupta and Rimi B. Chatterjee (New Delhi: Orient Blackswan, 2009), 41; Rimli Bhattacharya, "Chosen Families," 10, 18.

14. "India and Its Spirit Told by Dhan Gopal Mukerji," *Nashville Tennessean*, March 12, 1921, 7.

15. Mukerji, *Caste and Outcast*, 46.

16. J. Daniel Elam, "Take Your Geography and Trace It," *Interventions*, 17, no. 4 (2015): 580–581.

17. Gordon H. Chang, "Life and Death of Dhan Gopal Mukerji," in Dhan Gopal Mukerji, *Caste and Outcast* (1923; reprint, Stanford, CA: Stanford University Press, 2002), 4. For a certain strata of young middle-class Indian men, the path to Japan for higher education was well-worn at the turn of the century. In his 1906 essay for the *Overland Monthly*, Girindra Mukerji writes, "Young men failing to obtain any decent means of livelihood, except in the over-crowded law courts, medical profession and the subordinate offices of the Government, looked upon an industrial education as their only salvation. They have begun to pour in by hundreds in Japan. Year after year, the number of Indian youths is increasing rapidly in the different parts of industrial Nippon." Girindra Mukerji, "The Hindu in America," *Overland Monthly* 51, no. 4 (April 1908): 304, *South Asian American Digital Archive*, https://www.saada.org/item/20111101-443, accessed March 10, 2018.

18. Mukerji, *Caste and Outcast*, 133.

19. Ibid.

20. Chang, "Life and Death," 4.

21. Ibid., 5.

22. Mukerji, *Caste and Outcast*, 141.

23. Ibid., 141–142.

24. Ibid., 147.

25. Ibid., 194.

26. Ibid.

27. Ibid., 195.

28. Ibid.

29. Ibid., 197.

30. Ibid., 198.

31. Shiv Narayan, "Why Emigrate?" *Modern Review* 8, no. 5 (November 1910): 532.

32. Sarangadhar Das, "Why Must We Emigrate to the United States of America," *Modern Review* 10, no. 1 (July 1911): 77.

33. M. N. Roy, *M. N. Roy's Memoirs* (Bombay: Allied Publishers Private Ltd., 1964), 22.

34. *United States v. Sailendra Nath Ghose, Agnes Smedley and others*, Arthur Pope Testimony, October 21, 1918. MID 9771-72, RG 165.

35. A. C. Bose, *Indian Revolutionaries Abroad: 1905–1927: Select Documents* (New Delhi: Northern Book Centre, 2002), 174.

36. E. M. Blanford, "In Re: Indian Revolutionists," August 31, 1917, MID 9771-72, RG 165.

37. Dhan Gopal Mukerji to Jawaharlal Nehru, October 22, 1928; Dhan Gopal Mukerji to Jawaharlal Nehru, April 8, 1929, NMML Archives.

38. Dhan Gopal Mukerji to Jawaharlal Nehru, February 2, 1929, NMML Archives.

39. Maia Ramnath, *Decolonizing Anarchism: An Antiauthoritarian History of India's Liberation Struggle* (Oakland, CA: AK Press, 2011), 79.

40. Ibid., 583.

41. Given that Indians were barred from citizenship after the *Thind* case, Ethel would have been subjected to the 1922 Cable Act, which prevented women married to aliens ineligible for naturalization from retaining their American citizenship. Rimli Bhattacharya explains that Dhan Gopal and Ethel moved to France in the fallout of the Immigration Act of 1924. Indeed, Dhan Gopal's citizenship was listed in a 1930 census as alien, and in ship manifests from 1925, 1926, 1927, Ethel's citizenship is recorded as "Great Britain" under "Alien Passengers," in spite of being born in Pennsylvania. Because their son Dhan Gopal Mukerji Jr. was born in the United States, however, he retained his citizenship through birthright. Ethel Dugan Mukerji's records on ancestry. com indicate that she filed a petition for citizenship in 1931, which she appears to have been granted by 1933. Bhattacharya, "Chosen Families," 11.

42. In Thind's brief, the terms of race, caste, and class frequently slip. At the start of the brief, Thind, Sikh by religion, is described as a "high-caste Hindu," then a "High-class Hindu." The brief then draws a distinction between the "high-class Hindu" and the "aboriginal Indian mongoloid," before comparing the difference as similar to how the "[white] American regards the negro." See Doug Coulson, *Race, Nation, and Refuge: The Rhetoric of Race in Asian American Citizenship Cases* (Albany: State University of New York Press, 2017), 60–68; Sucheta Mazumdar, "Racist Responses to Racism: The Aryan Myth and South Asians in the United States," *South Asia Bulletin* 9, no. 1 (1989): 49.

43. "Hindus Too Brunette to Vote Here," *Literary Digest* (March 10, 1923): 13, *South Asian American Digital Archive*, https://www.saada.org/item/20101210-148 accessed March 10, 2018.

44. Mabel Potter Daggett, "The Heathen Invasion," *Hampton Columbian Magazine* 27, no. 4 (October 1911): 399–411.

45. Whether by Hindu, Mukerji actually meant Sikh here is not especially clear, although he is clearer when he describes Muslim laborers.

46. Mukerji, *Caste and Outcast*, 204.

47. Ibid.

48. Chatterjee, "Creating Boyhood," 48.

49. Mukerji, "The Hindu in America," 306.

50. Das, "Why Must We Emigrate to the United States of America?," 70.

51. Balbir Singh, "Militant Bodies: Policing Race, Religion, and Violence in the U.S. Sikh Diaspora," (PhD diss., University of Washington, 2016).

52. Mukerji, *Caste and Outcast*, 205.

53. Ibid., 206.

54. Ibid., 210.

55. "American Women Victims of Hindu Mysticism," *Washington Post*, February 18, 1912, 1. The article was reprinted in a number of newspapers across the United States and Canada, including the *Vancouver World*.

56. Kirin Narayan, "Refractions of the Field at Home: American Representations of Hindu Holy Men in the 19th and 20th Centuries," *Cultural Anthropology* 8, no. 4 (1993): 478.

57. Vivek Bald, *Bengali Harlem and the Lost Histories of South Asian America* (Cambridge, MA: Harvard University Press, 2013), 17.

58. Qtd. in Sara Ann Levinsky, *A Bridge of Dreams: The Story of Paramananda, a Modern Mystic, and His Ideal of All-Conquering Love* (West Stockbridge, MA: The Lindisfarne Press, 1984), 176.

59. "American Women Victims," 1, 4.

60. Daggett, "The Heathen Invasion," 399.

61. Philip Deslippe, "The American Yoga Scare of 1927," *South Asian American Digital Archive*, https://www.saada.org/tides/article/20150910-4457, accessed March 10, 2018.

62. Bald, *Bengali Harlem*, 29.

63. Mukerji, *Caste and Outcast*, 211.

64. Ibid., 212.

65. Elam, "Take Your Geography," 580.

66. Dhan Gopal Mukerji, *My Brother's Face* (New York: E. P. Dutton, 1924), 4.

67. Dhan Gopal Mukerji to John Macrae, November 3, 1928, E. P. Dutton & Company, Inc. Records, Special Collections Research Center, Syracuse University Library (hereafter cited as E.P. Dutton & Company, Inc. Records).

68. *My Brother's Face*, 4.

69. Ibid.

70. Ibid., 5.

71. Ibid.

72. Ibid.

73. Ibid., 8.

74. Ibid.

75. Ibid.

76. Dhan Gopal Mukerji, *Visit India with Me* (New York: E. P. Dutton and Co., 1929), 6.

77. Ibid., 6.

78. The suggested titles of the book were *Visit India with Mukerji*, *To India with a Hindu*, *Visit India with a Hindu*. Memorandum for Mr. Macrae, April 6, 1929, E. P. Dutton & Company, Inc. Records.

79. John Macrae to Dhan Gopal Mukerji, December 21, 1928, E. P. Dutton & Company, Inc. Records.

80. John Macrae to Dhan Gopal Mukerji, August 13, 1929, E. P. Dutton & Company, Inc. Records.

81. Ibid.

82. Dhan Gopal Mukerji to Jawaharlal Nehru, March 20, 1929, NMML Archives.

83. Mukerji, *Visit India with Me*, 125.

84. Ibid., 125.

85. Ibid., 125–126.

86. Ibid., 128.

87. Ibid., 137.

88. Ibid., 129

89. Ibid., 8–9.

90. Ibid., 8.

91. Ibid., 52.

92. Ibid., xv.

93. John Clair Minot, "Dhan Gopal Mukerji Invites Americans to Visit His India," *San Francisco Chronicle*, October 27, 1929, E. P. Dutton & Company, Inc. Records.

94. Virginia E. Shepherd, Review of *Visit India with Me*, n.d., E. P. Dutton & Company, Inc. Records.

95. Mary Gould Ogilvie, "Son of Mother India Champions His Mother," *Tulsa Daily World*, January 19, 1930, E. P. Dutton & Company, Inc. Records.

96. "India from Different Angles," *Los Angeles Times*, March 16, 1930, E. P. Dutton & Company, Inc. Records.

97. "An India's India," *Argonaut*, December 14, 1929, E. P. Dutton & Company, Inc. Records.

98. Pratt, *Imperial Eyes*, 3.

99. Ibid., 9.

100. Mukerji, *Visit India with Me*, 6.

101. Ibid., 7.

102. Mukerji, *Caste and Outcast*, 45–46.

103. Dhan Gopal Mukerji, *A Son of Mother India Answers* (New York: E. P. Dutton and Co., 1928), 13.

104. Ibid., 58.

105. Manjapra, *Age of Entanglement*, 22.

106. Qtd. in Ibid., 22.

107. Dhan Gopal Mukerji, "The Truth About Kipling's India," *Libraries* 33, no. 8 (October 1928): 400.

108. "A Voice from the Orient," *The Bronxville Review*, 24, no. 48 (December 5, 1925): 12.

109. Mukerji, *Caste and Outcast*, 45.

110. Mukerji, *My Brother's Face*, 275–276.

111. Mukerji, *Disillusioned India*, 220.

112. Chatterjee, "Creating Boyhood," 40.

113. Judith Plotz, "Kipling's Very Special Relationship: Kipling in America, America in Kipling," in *The Cambridge Companion to Rudyard Kipling*, 37.

114. Rudyard Kipling, *American Notes* (Boston: Brown and Company, 1899), 45–50.

115. Ibid., 21.

116. Even though the poem "White Man's Burden" was fairly jingoistic and straightforward in meaning, American readers, Gretchen Murphy points out, "expressed a surprising amount of confusion about its meaning." Murphy argues that "at the root of this confusion, was their ambivalence about the idea of the United States taking up a 'white' imperial mission." Gretchen Murphy, *Shadowing the White Man's Burden: U.S. Imperialism and the Problem of the Color Line* (New York: New York University Press, 2010), 23–30.

117. Judith Plotz, "Kipling's Very Special Relationship," 37.

118. Shamsul Islam, *Kipling's Law: A Study of His Philosophy of Life* (London: The Macmillan Press, 1975), 1.

119. Qtd. in Murphy, *Shadowing the White Man's Burden*, 25.

120. Saint Nihal Singh, "A Message America Gave Me for India," *Modern Review* 6, no. 4 (October 1909): 374.

121. Sohi, *Echoes of Mutiny*, 42–43.

122. Indu Bhushan De Majumdar, *America Through Hindu Eyes* (Calcutta: Thacker, Spink, & Co., 1918), xv.

123. Ibid., 49.

124. Ibid., 50.

125. Ibid., 51–54.

126. A. R. Sarath-Roy, "Rudyard Kipling Seen through Hindu Eyes," *North American Review* 199 (February 1914): 281.

127. Ibid., 274.

128. Ibid., 271.

129. H. G. Mudgal, "Foreign Affairs," *Negro World*, October 7, 1922, 4.

130. *Boys' Life* 14, no. 2 (February 1924), 61.

131. Robert Baden-Powell, *Playing the Game: A Baden-Powell Compendium*, ed. Mario Sica (London: Pan Books, 2007).

132. Robert Baden-Powell, *Scouting for Boys*, 36th ed. (London: The Scout Association, 1991), 269.

133. Joseph Bristow, *Empire Boys: Adventures in a Man's World* (London: Harper Collins, 1991), 178.

134. Robert Baden-Powell, *Aids to Scouting for N.C.Os. and Men* (London: Gale & Folden's Military Series, 1899), 7.

135. David I. Macleod, *Building Character in the American Boy: The Boy Scouts, YMCA, and Their Forerunners, 1870–1920* (Madison: The University of Wisconsin Press, 1983), 134–135.

136. Baden-Powell, *Scouting for Boys*, 3.

137. Ibid., 4.

138. Ibid., 5.

139. Ibid., 23–24.

140. Ibid., 34.

141. See chapter 4 of Phil Deloria, *Playing Indian* (New Haven, CT: Yale University Press, 1998).

142. Javed Majeed, *Autobiography, Travel, and Post-National Identity: Gandhi, Nehru, and Iqbal* (New York: Palgrave Macmillan, 2007), 18.

143. Baden-Powell, *Scouting for Boys*, 23–24.

144. Hugh Brogan, *Mowgli's Sons: Kipling and Baden-Powell's Scouts* (London: Jonathan Cape, 1987), 42.

145. Qtd. in Brogan, *Mowgli's Sons*, 43.

146. *Wolf Cub Scout Book* (New Brunswick: Boy Scouts of America, 1954), 173–174.

147. "The Boy Scout Movement in India," *United States of India* 3, no. 10 (April 1926): 1–2, *South Asian American Digital Archive*, https://www.saada.org/item/20111129 -507, accessed March 10, 2018.

148. Ibid., 1.

149. Ibid.

150. Purnima Mankekar and Akhil Gupta, "The Homeless Self: Problems of Cultural Translation in Autobiography," in Mukerji, *Caste and Outcast*, 233.

151. Ibid.

152. Ibid., 249.

153. Mukerji, *Visit India with Me*, 3–1.

154. Dhan Gopal Mukerji, *Bunny, Hound and Clown* (New York: E. P. Dutton, 1931), 13.

155. Ibid., 11–12. This theme appeared as early Mukerji's books of poetry. In the Foreword to *Sandhya*, Mukerji remarks that the poems draw their "music from my Bengali which has told upon its English structure." Dhan Gopal Mukerji, *Sandhya: Songs of Twilight* (Paul Elder and Co., 1917), v.

156. Thomas Babington Macaulay, *Speeches by Lord Macaulay: With His Minute on Indian Education*, ed. G. M. Young (Oxford, UK: Oxford University Press, 1935),

349. In *Caste and Outcast*, Mukerji lobs a more backhanded compliment against Macaulay, describing him as "the stupidest man of genius the Lord ever made," *Caste and Outcast,* 159.

157. Mukerji, *Bunny, Hound and Clown,* 18.

158. Supriya Goswami, *Colonial India in Children's Literature* (New York: Routledge, 2012), 4.

159. Sen, *Disciplined Natives,* 45.

160. Goswami, *Colonial India in Children's Literature,* 4.

161. As Rimi Chatterjee has pointed out Mukerji could only have presumed that the majority of his readers were American, given that his publisher E. P. Dutton primarily marketed books in the United States. Chatterjee, "Creating Boyhood," 44.

162. Mukerji makes a series of interesting statements in this article: "As I went on studying America I was struck by the fact that the American adult had very little repose, and that he also did not have in his life anything like the daily life in a Hindu home. If there is anything that distinguishes a home in India it is its sense of repose. I believe, however, that if Americans study how we create serenity in India they will be able to know serenity here in America." Dhan Gopal Mukerji, "Why I Write in English About Hindu Life," *The Sufi Quarterly,* E. P. Dutton & Company, Inc. Records.

163. Mukerji, *Bunny, Hound and Clown,* 19.

164. Jacqueline Rose, *The Case of Peter Pan or the Impossibility of Children's Fiction* (London: The Macmillan Press Ltd., 1984), 2.

165. Goswami, *Colonial India in Children's Literature,* 108.

166. Bhattacharya, "Chosen Families," 11–12.

167. Ibid., 12.

168. Ibid., 22.

169. Dhan Gopal Mukerji, *Gay-Neck: The Story of a Pigeon* (New York: Dutton Children's Books, 1927), 180.

170. Dhan Gopal Mukerji, *Hari, the Jungle Lad* (New York: E. P. Dutton & Co., 1924), 16.

171. Katrine Hvidt Bie, "Mukerji's 'Gay Neck' Beautiful Odyssey of a Pigeon's Life," *Brooklyn Times,* July 9, 1925, E. P. Dutton & Company, Inc. Records.

172. As Kenneth B. Kidd argues in *Making American Boys,* two discourses shaped the "ideological and practical work of boy education and supervision in America." The first was boyology, what Kidd describes as the "descriptive and prescriptive writing on boyhood," preoccupied with "formal and informal middle-class character building or boy work." The other, Kidd argues was the genre of the "feral tale," which often imagined childhood characters (though not exclusively children) reared outside of civilization or "mainstream human culture." Kenneth B. Kidd, *Making American Boys: Boyology and the Feral Tale* (Minneapolis: University of Minnesota, 2004), 1–2.

173. Dhan Gopal Mukerji, *The Secret Listeners of the East* (New York: E. P. Dutton and Co., 1926), 1, 5.

174. Ibid., 171.

175. Ibid., 13.

176. Ibid., 171.

177. Ibid., 168.

178. *New York Herald,* June 25, 1926, E. P. Dutton & Company, Inc. Records.

179. "The Secret Listeners of the East," *Outlook,* June 2, 1926, E. P. Dutton & Company, Inc. Records.

180. Norman E. Mack, "Glamorous Adventure," *Buffalo Sunday Times*, April 25, 1926, E. P. Dutton & Company, Inc. Records.

181. "The Secret Listeners of the East," *Independent*, April 24, 1926, E. P. Dutton & Company, Inc. Records.

CHAPTER 4

1. W.E.B. Du Bois to Dhan Gopal Mukerji, November 7, 1927, W.E.B. Du Bois Papers (MS 312). Special Collections and University of Massachusetts Amherst Libraries (hereafter cited as W.E.B. Du Bois Papers).

2. Ibid.

3. W.E.B. Du Bois to Lala Lajpat Rai, November 9, 1927, W.E.B. Du Bois Papers.

4. W.E.B. Du Bois to Dhan Gopal Mukerji, October 29, 1927, W.E.B. Du Bois Papers.

5. Dhan Gopal Mukerji to W.E.B. Du Bois, November 4, 1927, W.E.B. Du Bois Papers.

6. Ibid.

7. At one point, Matthew asks his wife Sara if he had ever heard the Ippolitov-Ivanov's *Caucasian Sketches*, which famously concludes with the "March of the Sardar." W.E.B. Du Bois, *Dark Princess: A Romance* (1928; reprint, Jackson: University Press of Mississippi, 1995), 137.

8. Madhumita Lahiri, "World Romance: Genre, Internationalism, and W.E.B. Du Bois," *Callaloo* 33, no. 2 (Spring 2010): 546.

9. W.E.B. Du Bois to Harcourt, Brace and Company, October 15, 1927, W.E.B. Du Bois Papers.

10. Harcourt, Brace and Company to W.E.B. Du Bois, October 14, 1927, W.E.B. Du Bois Papers.

11. Shawn Michelle Smith, *Photography on the Color Line: W.E.B. Du Bois, Race, and Visual Culture* (Durham, NC: Duke University Press, 2004), 5.

12. Du Bois, *The Souls of Black Folk*, 3.

13. Ibid.

14. Ibid.

15. W.E.B. Du Bois, "Criteria of Negro Art," in Winston Napier, *African American Literary Theory: A Reader* (New York: New York University Press, 2000), 18.

16. George S. Schuyler to W.E.B. Du Bois, October 11, 1928, W.E.B. Du Bois Papers.

17. Alain Locke, "The Negro Intellectual," *New York Herald Tribune Books*, May 20, 1928, 12.

18. "The Literary Procession," *New York Age*, June 23, 1928, 4.

19. "Race Discrimination," *New York Times Book Review*, May 13, 1928, 22.

20. Lahiri, "World Romance," 546.

21. Dohra Ahmad, *Landscapes of Hope: Anti-Colonial Utopianism in America* (New York: Oxford University Press, 2009), 151.

22. Du Bois, *Dark Princess*, 109.

23. Ibid., 3.

24. Ibid., 5.

25. Ibid., 14.

26. Ibid., 3.

27. Ibid., 5.

28. I draw on Brent Hayes Edwards's discussion of *The Autobiography of an Ex-Colored Man* here, in which he notes how the novel, which also traces a transatlantic

journey, serves as a "reminder that the 'color line' must be comprehended in its subtle 'facets' (and in international waters)." Edwards, *The Practice of Diaspora*, 42.

29. Du Bois, *Dark Princess*, 3.

30. Ibid., 7.

31. Ibid.

32. Samuel Doku argues that the allusion to leviathan also refers to Hobbes's theory of sovereign power; in Du Bois's rendering, however, the reference comes to stand in for a critique of "Western hegemonic and imperialistic conditions in American and European democratic politics." The immediate allusion to Humboldt University, I might also suggest, connects back to Matthew's anger toward the University of Manhattan. The promise of education, into which Du Bois invested so much time and energy, continued to produce sites of knowledge production that were shaped by racism. Samuel O. Doku, *Cosmopolitanism in the Fictive Imagination of W.E.B. Du Bois: Toward the Humanization of a Revolutionary Art* (London: Lexington Books, 2015), 58.

33. Du Bois, *Dark Princess*, 8.

34. Ibid. Italics mine.

35. Ibid., 16.

36. The council of "darker nations" has several correlatives, as both Dohra Ahmad and Bill Mullen have suggested, including the Universal Race Congress of 1911 and the Berlin Committee. Another organization that might have served as inspiration was the League of Oppressed Peoples, which involved many people associated with the India Home Rule League, including Lajpat Rai, Dudley Field Malone, Arthur Pope, J. T. Sunderland, and Ananda Coomaraswamy. Du Bois had agreed to become a sponsor of the league in 1919. Arthur Upham Pope to W.E.B. Du Bois, November 10, 1919, W.E.B. Du Bois Papers.

37. Homi Bhabha, *The Location of Culture* (1994; reprint, London: Routledge Classics, 2004), 125.

38. Du Bois, *Dark Princess*, 24.

39. Ibid., 22.

40. Ibid., 21.

41. Ibid., 22; Bill Mullen notes that this was likely an allusion to Claude McKay's speech to the Comintern in 1922 published as "Negro v. Ameriki" in Russia, which argued for the distinctive nature of the Black American experience and its potential contribution to the Comintern cause. Bill Mullen, *Un-American: W.E.B. Du Bois and the Century of World Revolution* (Philadelphia, PA: Temple University Press, 2015), 68.

42. Du Bois, *Dark Princess*, 29.

43. Ibid., 34.

44. Ibid., 8.

45. Sanda Mayzaw Lwin, "Romance with a Message: W.E.B. Du Bois's *Dark Princess* and the Problem of the Color Line," in *Strange Affinities: The Gender and Sexual Politics of Comparative Racialization,* ed. Grace Kyungwon Hong and Roderick A. Ferguson (Durham, NC: Duke University Press, 2005), 186.

46. Ibid., 186.

47. Frantz Fanon, *Black Skin, White Masks* (1952), trans. Charles Lam Markmann (New York: Grove Press, 1967), 109.

48. Arna Bontemps, "The Awakening: A Memoir," in *Remembering the Harlem Renaissance*, ed. Cary D. Wintz (New York: Garland Publishing, 1996), 245.

49. Smedley corresponded with Du Bois and requested information and photographs in preparation for her essay "The Negro Renaissance," published in *Modern Review.*

Her letter to Du Bois begins by introducing herself as a "former member of the Civic Club, and an American woman who was actively engaged in the work connected with the movement for the independence of India." They had met, she wrote, five years earlier in 1920. Agnes Smedley to W.E.B. Du Bois, June 9, 1925; Letter from K.D. Shastri to W.E.B. Du Bois, January 22, 1918, W.E.B. Du Bois Papers.

50. "Exploitation of Asia as Menace to Peace," *New York Evening Post,* September 22, 1914, 14.

51. Ibid.

52. Ibid.

53. Ibid.

54. Ibid.

55. W.E.B. Du Bois, "The African Roots of War," *Atlantic Monthly* 115, no. 5 (May 1915): 708. For further discussion of this essay, see Kenneth Robert Janken, *Rayford W. Logan and the Dilemma of the African American Intellectual* (Amherst: University of Massachusetts Press, 1993), 34–35; Ann Stoler, "On Degrees of Imperial Sovereignty" *Public Culture* 18, no. 1 (2006): 126; Amy Kaplan, *The Anarchy of Empire in the Making of U.S. Culture* (Cambridge, MA: Harvard University Press, 2005), 171–172.

56. Du Bois, "The African Roots of War," 709.

57. Ibid., 712.

58. Agnes Smedley, *Daughter of Earth* (1929; reprint, New York: Feminist Press, 1987), 272.

59. "A Manifesto of the Indian National Party," March 1916, W.E.B. Du Bois Papers; Agnes Smedley, "Women and New India" (San Francisco: Hindusthan Gadar Party, 1920), W.E.B. Du Bois Papers; "How to Form a Regular Branch of the Friends of Freedom for India, ca. 1920," W.E.B. Du Bois Papers.

60. "Notes and News," *Independent Hindustan* 1, no. 5 (January 1921): 113, *South Asian American Digital Archive,* https://www.saada.org/item/20120806-1019, accessed March 10, 2018.

61. Banarsidas Chaturvedi to W.E.B. Du Bois, September 15, 1925, W.E.B. Du Bois Papers.

62. Banarsidas Chaturvedi to W.E.B. Du Bois, November 9, 1924, W.E.B. Du Bois Papers.

63. Banarsidas Chaturvedi to W.E.B. Du Bois, September 15, 1925, W.E.B. Du Bois Papers.

64. W.E.B. Du Bois, "To the People of India," October 15, 1925, W.E.B. Du Bois Papers.

65. W.E.B. Du Bois, "The Color Line Belts the World," *W.E.B. Du Bois on Asia,* 33; "To the Nations of the World," in *The Oxford W.E.B. Du Bois Reader,* ed. Eric J. Sundquist (New York: Oxford University Press, 1996), 625.

66. W.E.B. Du Bois, *Black Reconstruction in America,* 1860–1880 (1935; reprint, New York: The Free Press, 1998), 704.

67. W.E.B. Du Bois, "Socialism and the Negro," *Crisis* 22, no. 6 (October 1921): 246–247.

68. K. Paramu Pillai to W.E.B. Du Bois, June 10, 1908. W.E.B. Du Bois Papers.

69. Gustav Spiller, ed., *Papers on Inter-Racial Problems Communicated to the First Universal Race Congress* (London: P. S. King and Son, 1911), xiii.

70. Ibid., 1.

71. Mary White Ovington, "Review of *Dark Princess*," *Chicago Bee,* August 4, 1928; qtd. in Homi Bhabha, "Global Minoritarian Literature," in *Shades of the Planet:*

American Literature as World Literature, ed. Wai Chee Dimock and Lawrence Buell (Princeton, NJ: Princeton University Press, 2007), 186.

72. Bhabha, "Global Minoritarian Literature," 187.

73. Lahiri, "World Romance," 541–542.

74. Nico Slate, *Colored Cosmopolitanism: The Shared Struggle for Freedom in the United States and India* (Cambridge, MA: Harvard University Press, 2012), 97; Bill Mullen also suggests that the character Matthew is based on Smedley and Harry Haywood, the Communist Party USA leader who was recruited after his work as a train porter in Chicago. Mullen, *Un-American*, 111.

75. Vermonja Alston, "Cosmopolitan Fantasies, Aesthetics, and Bodily Value: W.E.B. Du Bois's *Dark Princess* and the Trans/Gendering of Kautilya," *Journal of Transnational American Studies* 3, no. 1 (2011): 19.

76. Ibid.

77. W.E.B. Du Bois to Dhan Gopal Mukerji, October 29, 1927. W.E.B. Du Bois Papers.

78. See Gerald Horne, *The End of Empires: African Americans and India* (Philadelphia, PA: Temple University Press, 2008); Nico Slate, *Colored Cosmopolitanism*; Bill Mullen and Fred Ho, ed., Afro-Asia: Revolutionary Political and Cultural Connections Between African Americans and *Asian Americans* (Durham, NC: Duke University Press, 2008); Vijay Prashad, *Everybody Was Kung-Fu Fighting: Afro-Asian Connections and the Myth of Cultural Purity* (Boston: Beacon Press, 2001).

79. Richard Wright, *The Color Curtain: A Report on the Bandung Conference* (1956; reprint, Jackson: University Press of Mississippi, 1994).

80. B. R. Ambedkar to W.E.B. Du Bois, ca. July 1946, W.E.B. Du Bois Papers.

81. Vivek Bald, *Bengali Harlem and the Lost Histories of South Asian America* (Cambridge, MA: Harvard University Press, 2013).

82. Drawing on the scholarship of Nico Slate and Vijay Prashad, the activist and community historian Anirvan Chatterjee, who cofounded the Berkeley South Asian Radical History Walking Tour with Barnali Ghose, has curated a website that highlights the history of South Asian and African American solidarity. *The Secret History of South Asian and African American Solidarity*, http://blackdesisecrethistory.org, accessed March 10, 2018.

83. Pranav Jani, "Bihar, California, and the U.S. Midwest: the early radicalization of Jayaprakash Narayan," *Postcolonial Studies* 16, no. 2 (2013): 161–162.

84. Tizarat Gill and Manan Desai, "H. G. Mudgal, Harlem Editor," *South Asian American Digital Archive*, https://www.saada.org/tides/article/hg-mudgal-harlem-editor, accessed March 10, 2018.

85. H. G. Mudgal, "The Temper of the Times," *Negro World*, January 3, 1931, 4.

86. Herbert Parson to W.E.B. Du Bois, September 25, 1917, W.E.B. Du Bois Papers.

87. "Connection Between Hindus and Radical Elements," MID 9771-B-58, RG 165.

88. James Weldon Johnson, "Views and Reviews," *New York Age*, October 22, 1921, 4.

89. James Weldon Johnson, "Views and Reviews," *New York Age*, December 24, 1921, 4.

90. Syud Hossain, "The Affairs of India," *Crisis* 24, no. 2 (June 1922): 82; "The Woes of India," *Crisis* 22, no. 1 (May 1921): 27.

91. See "India's Saint," *Crisis* 22, no. 3 (July 1921): 124–125; "The Boycott in India," *Crisis* 22, no. 6 (October 1921): 270–272; "Gandhi and India," *Crisis* 23, no. 5 (March 1922): 203–207; "An Open Letter from Gandhi," *Crisis* 22, no. 4 (August 1921): 170.

92. Blanche Watson, "'Saint' Gandhi: The Greatest Man in the World," *Brownies' Book* 2, no. 12 (December 1921): 344.

93. W.E.B. Du Bois, "As the Crow Flies," *Brownies' Book* 2, no. 12 (December 1921): 345.

94. Vijay Prashad, *The Karma of Brown Folk* (Minneapolis: University of Minnesota, 2000), 174.

95. Ibid., 174–175.

96. Alston, "Cosmopolitan Fantasies," 18.

97. Prashad, *The Karma of Brown Folk*, 175.

98. Tamara Bhalla, "The True Romance of W.E.B. Du Bois's *Dark Princess*," *S&F Online* 14, no. 3 (2018).

99. Alys Eve Weinbaum, "Interracial Romance and Black Internationalism," in *Next to the Color Line: Gender, Sexuality, and W.E.B. Du Bois*, ed. Susan Gillman and Alys Weinbaum (Minneapolis: University of Minnesota Press, 2007), 101.

100. Kenneth W. Warren, "An Inevitable Drift? Oligarchy, Du Bois, and the Politics of Race between the Wars," *boundary 2* 27, no. 3 (2000): 153–154.

101. Smedley, *Daughter of Earth*, 281.

102. Prashad, *The Karma of Brown Folk*, 175.

103. Du Bois, *Dark Princess*, 227.

104. Ibid.

105. Ibid.

106. Ibid.

107. Ibid.

108. Ibid.

109. Ahmad, *Landscapes of Hope*, 159.

110. Early Modernists have linked the Indian boy in *A Midsummer Night's Dream* to nascent British imperial interests in Asia and the Americas. Beyond these subtle hints, *Dark Princess* adapts a central theme that runs through Shakespeare's play, namely, the escape from a world of irrational laws. The play moves between two different contrasting worlds: the opening setting of Athens, codified by law and hierarchies in which desires can lead to death sentences, and the woods, where those rules are suspended, unlikely relationships are fostered, and hierarchies are overturned (if only temporarily). In the liminal setting of the magical woods, Hermia lives as a kind of Athenian exile. All around her hierarchies collapse, characters deemed homely are rendered beautiful, and social relations are reworked until they culminate in the exiled lovers' marriage. See Ania Loomba, "The Great Indian Vanishing Trick—Colonialism, Property, and the Family in *A Midsummer Night's Dream*," in *A Feminist Companion to Shakespeare*, 2nd ed., ed. Dympna Callaghan (West Sussex: John Wiley and Sons, 2016), 179–205; Henry Buchanan, "'India' and the Golden Age in *A Midsummer Night's Dream*," in *Shakespeare Survey, Volume 65*, ed. Peter Holland (Cambridge, MA: Cambridge University Press, 2012), 58–68.

111. Du Bois, *Dark Princess*, 227.

112. The chapter drew heavily from the work of historian J. A. Rogers, a former Pullman Porter whose 1917 *From "Superman" to Man* presented a debate between a porter and a white Southern politician. The first volume of Rogers's series *Sex and Race* contained a chapter titled "Who Were the First Inhabitants of India?" which shared many of the same quotations as Du Bois's subsequent essay. J. A. Rogers, *Sex and Race, Volume 1: Negro-Caucasian Mixing in All Ages and All Lands—The Old World* (St. Petersburg, FL: Helga M. Rogers, 1968).

113. W.E.B. Du Bois, *The World and Africa: An Inquiry into the Party Which Africa Has Played in World History* (New York: Viking Press, 1947), 176–177.

114. Thomas Trautmann, *Aryans and British India* (Berkeley: University of California Press, 1997), 4.

115. Ibid., 195.

116. Ibid., 212–213.

117. Later translations would express doubt that the word *vrsasipra* referred to nose at all, and may have referred to cheek, lip, or jaw. Ibid., 212.

118. Ibid., 211.

119. Ibid.

120. Ibid., 214.

121. Du Bois, "The Clash of Colour," 114.

122. Alys Eve Weinbaum, "Reproducing Racial Globality: W.E.B. Du Bois and the Sexual Politics of Black Internationalism," *Social Text* 67, vol. 19, no. 2 (Summer 2001): 31.

123. Alston, "Cosmopolitan Fantasies," 9.

124. Du Bois, *The World and Africa*, 177.

125. Ibid., 177–178.

126. Du Bois, *Dark Princess*, 228.

127. Ibid., 219.

128. Lahiri, "World Romance," 544.

129. Du Bois, *Dark Princess*, 220.

130. Rebecka Rutledge Fisher, "The Anatomy of a Symbol: Reading W.E.B. Du Bois's *Dark Princess: A Romance*," *CR: The New Centennial Review* 6, no. 3 (Winter 2006): 115.

131. Du Bois, *Dark Princess*, 221.

132. Lisa Lowe, *The Intimacies of Four Continents* (Durham, NC: Duke University Press, 2015).

133. Du Bois, *Dark Princess*, 20.

134. Ibid., 11.

135. Ibid., 278.

136. Ibid., 279.

137. Ibid., 282.

138. Ibid.

139. Ibid., 286.

140. Elam, "Take Your Geography and Trace It," 576.

141. Amor Kohli, "But That's Just Mad! Reading the Utopian Impulse in *Dark Princess* and *Black Empire*," *African Identities* 7, no. 2 (2009): 165.

142. Ibid.

143. Du Bois, *Dark Princess*, 311.

144. Paul Gilroy, *The Black Atlantic: Modernity and Double Consciousness* (Cambridge, MA: Harvard University Press, 1993), 126.

145. Du Bois, "The Clash of Colour," 113.

146. Ibid.

147. Ibid.

148. Ibid.

149. Ibid., 112.

150. W.E.B. Du Bois, "Criteria of Negro Art," *African American Literary Theory*, 21.

151. Letter from W.E.B. Du Bois to Harcourt, Brace, and Company, November 29, 1927, W.E.B. Du Bois Papers.

CHAPTER 5

1. Katherine Mayo, *Mother India* (New York: Harcourt, Brace and Company, 1927), 3–4.

2. Ibid., 7.

3. Dinshah P. Ghadiali, *American Sex Problems* (Malaga: Spectro-Chrome Institute, 1929), Frontispiece.

4. Ibid., 2.

5. Ibid., 3.

6. These Indian writers' emphasis on the physical and abject recalls Achille Mbembe's description of "elements of the obscene, vulgar, and grotesque [. . .] intrinsic to all systems of domination and to the means by which those systems are confirmed or deconstructed." Following Mbembe, we can trace how through the deployment of the grotesque, these *tu quoque* rejoinders similarly served to lay bare the very terms of the imperialist discourse exemplified in Mayo's writings. Achille Mbembe, "The Banality of Power and the Aesthetics of Vulgarity in the Postcolony," trans. Janet Roitman, *Public Culture* 4, no. 2 (1992): 1–2.

7. Irene Cleaton and Allen Cleaton, *Books and Battles: American Literature, 1920–1930* (New York: Houghton Mifflin, 1937), 209.

8. Claire Jean Kim coins the term "racial triangulation" to discuss the ways by which Asian Americans have historically been racialized in relation to African Americans and whites, and how this triangulation "reinforce[s] White racial power, insulating it from minority encroachment or challenge." My use of the term "racial triangulation" is indebted to this formulation, but differs in that it describes a process by which different racialized or caste-marked subjects within a colonial society are triangulated in order to justify Euro-American imperialist projects. Claire Jean Kim, "The Racial Triangulation of Asian Americans," *Politics & Society* 27, no. 1 (1999): 129.

9. Paul Teed, in particular, emphasizes the debate on American identity and memory catalyzed by the *Mother India* controversy. Teed especially follows responses by American intellectuals, including J. T. Sunderland, an acquaintance of Lajpat Rai who eventually served as the president of the India Home Rule League in New York. Paul Teed, "Race Against Memory: Katherine Mayo, Jabez Sunderland, and Indian Independence," *American Studies* 44. no. 1–2 (2003): 35–57.

10. Mrinalini Sinha, *Specters of Mother India: The Global Restructuring of an Empire* (Durham, NC: Duke University Press, 2007).

11. K. L. Gauba, *Friends and Foes: An Autobiography* (New Delhi: Indian Book Co., 1974), 80.

12. Christina A. Joseph and Anandam P. Kavoori, "Colonial Discourse and the Writings of Katherine Mayo," *American Journalism* 24, no. 3 (2007): 58.

13. See Katherine Mayo, *Justice to All: The Story of the Pennsylvania State Police* (1917; reprint, Boston: Houghton Mifflin Company, 1920), 53, 141, 209; Katherine Mayo, *The Standard-Bearers: True Stories of Heroes of Law and Order* (Boston: Houghton Mifflin Company, 1918); Katherine Mayo, *Mounted Justice: True Stories of the Pennsylvania State Police* (Boston: Houghton Mifflin Company, 1922).

14. Sinha, *Specters of Mother India*, 70.

15. Ibid., 68.

16. Ibid.

17. Katherine Mayo, "Big Mary," *Atlantic Monthly* 107 (January 1911): 112.

18. Ibid., 113.

19. Ibid., 115.

20. Katherine Mayo, "My Law and Thine," *Atlantic Monthly* 109 (February 1912): 239.

21. Ibid., 244.

22. Joseph and Kavoori, "Colonial Discourse," 60.

23. Deepa Kumar, "Imperialist Feminism," *International Socialist Review* 102 (Fall 2016): 56–70.

24. Katherine Mayo, *The Isles of Fear: The Truth about the Philippines* (New York: Harcourt, Brace and Company, 1925), 94.

25. William Jennings Bryan, *Republic or Empire?* (Chicago: Independence Company, 1899), 22.

26. As Paul Teed argues, Mayo attempted to reclaim the American Revolution analogy from anticolonialists in both India and the Philippines, recasting the historical memory and legacy of the revolution through a shared Anglo-Saxon "racial experience." Teed, "Race Against Memory," 42–44.

27. Mayo, *The Isles of Fear*, 11.

28. Ibid., 212.

29. Ibid.; Teed, "Race Against Memory," 43.

30. Ibid., 9.

31. Ibid., 10.

32. Nicholas Roosevelt, "America's Blundering Devotion to the Philippines," *New York Times*, April 5, 1924, BR3.

33. Qtd. in Manoranjan Jha, *Katherine Mayo and India* (New Delhi: People's Publishing House, 1971), 21.

34. Mayo, *The Isles of Fear*, 13.

35. Mayo, *Mother India*, 240.

36. Ibid., 192.

37. Ibid., 146.

38. Mayo, *The Isles of Fear*, 10.

39. Ibid., 46.

40. Even Mayo's organizational ties were linked to promoting good relations between the British and Americans: in 1920, Mayo cofounded the British Apprentice Club in New York, to provide hospitality to cadets of the British armed forces while their ships were docked in the city. See Teed, "Race Against Memory," 36; Sinha, *Specters of Mother India*, 71.

41. Mayo, *Mother India*, 32.

42. Jha, *Katherine Mayo and India*, 52.

43. For a detailed account of Bagai's life, see chapter four, "Obstacles This Way, Blockades That Way" in Erica Lee and Judy Yung, *Angel Island: Immigrant Gateway to America* (New York: Oxford University Press, 2010).

44. "Here's Letter to the World from Suicide," *San Francisco Examiner*, March 17, 1928, Box 5, Folder 18, South Asians in North America Collection.

45. Royal S. Copeland. *"Hindus Are White": A Plea for Fair Play to Americans* (New York: Hindu Citizenship Committee, 1927), Box 4, Folder 4, South Asians in North America Collection.

46. Sinha, *Specters of Mother India*, 1–3.

47. Qtd. in Jha, *Katherine Mayo and India*, 63.

48. "'Mother India' is Unforgettable; Its Horror Lives On," *Chicago Daily Tribune*, December 31, 1927, 8; P. W. Wilson, "India Is Her Own Worst Enemy," *New York Times*, June 5, 1927, BR1; M. F. Cummings, "Shall India Break Her Bonds?" *Los Angeles Times*, June 19, 1927, 30.

49. Anupama Arora, "'Neighborhood Assets' or 'Neighborhood Nuisances?' National Anxieties in Katherine Mayo's *Mother India*," *Women's Studies* 37, no. 2 (2008): 131–155; Asha Nadkarni, "'World-Menace': National Reproduction and Public Health in Katherine Mayo's *Mother India*," *American Quarterly* 60, no. 3 (2008): 805–827.

50. Copeland, "Hindus Are White," 14.

51. W.E.B. Du Bois, "As the Crow Flies," *Crisis* 34, no. 9 (November 1927): 293.

52. Agnes Smedley, "Bootlickers' Handbook of India," *New Masses* 3, no. 7 (November 1927): 26.

53. Ibid.

54. "Gandhi Gives View of Miss Mayo's Book," *New York Times*, October 9, 1927, E3.

55. Sinha, *Specters of Mother India*, 103.

56. Charles P. Driscoll, "The World and All," *Brownsville Herald*, November 25, 1928, 4.

57. *The United States of India* 5, nos. 6–8 (December-January-February 1928), *South Asian American Digital Archive*, https://www.saada.org/item/20111212-545, accessed January 2, 2017; The Pacific Coast Khalsa Diwan Society—better known as the Stockton Sikh Temple—published a more measured response by future Congressman Dalip Singh Saund, who framed his critique of Mayo as a simple attempt to "answer the various questions that commonly arise in the minds of the American people regarding the cultural and political problems of India." The book, incidentally, was dedicated to Bhagat Singh Thind. Dalip Singh Saund, *My Mother India* (Los Angeles: Wetzel Publish Co., 1930), n.p.

58. "Calls U.S. Woman Earth's Most Dangerous Animal," *Chicago Daily Tribune*, September 11, 1927, 5.

59. "Book by Miss Mayo Rouses Hindu India," *New York Times*, October 6, 1927, 6.

60. "Hindus Here Burn Miss Mayo's Book," *New York Times*, January 22, 1928, 49.

61. "Confessions," *Chicago Daily Tribune*, August 6, 1927, 10.

62. "Wants Book by a Foreigner Criticizing Our National Life," *New York Times*, April 16, 1928, 26.

63. John Riddelhi, "A Step-Son of Mother India's Aunt Answers: A Parody Investigation of America in Miss Mayo's Best Manner," *Vanity Fair* (August 1928): 67.

64. Wyndham Lewis, "Mother India," *Enemy: A Review of Art and Literature* 2 (1927): xiv.

65. Ibid., xvii.

66. "Chickens Come Home to Roost," *New York Times*, August 20, 1929, 21.

67. Linda Hutcheon, *A Theory of Parody: The Teachings of Twentieth-Century Art Forms* (New York: Methuen, 1985), 6.

68. Ibid., 32.

69. Linda Hutcheon, *The Politics of Postmodernism*, 2nd ed. (London: Routledge, 2002), 97.

70. Homi Bhabha, *The Location of Culture* (London: Routledge Classics, 2004), 122.

71. C. S. Ranga Iyer, *Father India* (London: Selwyn & Blount, 1927), 29.

72. Ibid., 33.

73. Gauba, *Friends and Foes*, 71.

74. Ibid., 82.

75. Also included in his list of sources Judge Lindsey's *Companionate Marriage*, Edith Hooker's *Laws of Sex*, Woolston's *Prostitution in the United States*, Viscount Bryce's *Modern Democracies*, *Federal Reports as to Chicago Riots*, and magazines such as *Literary Digest*, *Time and Tide*, and *Current History*.

76. Gauba, *Friends and Foes*, 85.

77. Sherwood Eddy, *Challenge of the East* (New York: Farrar & Rinehart, 1931), 61.

78. Frank Swinnerton, "U.S. Customs Bars Entry of 'Uncle Sham' from India," *Chicago Daily Tribune*, August 17, 1929, 8.

79. Interestingly, Gauba explains that a passage relating to "the preference for Negroes by white women in America" was excised for the U.S. edition. His U.S. publisher Claude Kendall would go on to publish salacious murder mysteries such as Gladys St. John Loe's *Smoking Altars* (1936), Tiffany Thayer's *Thirteen Women* (1930), and Frank Walford's *Twisted Clay* (1933), a book that was banned in Canada and Australia for its lurid themes, including patricide, lesbianism, and suicide. See Curtis Evans, "Murder of the Publisher: Who Killed Claude Kendall?" *The Passing Tramp* (May 15, 2013): http://thepassingtramp.blogspot.com/2013/05/the-controversies-of-claudekendall.html.

80. Bailey Millard, "East Is East, West Is West," *Los Angeles Times*, October 4, 1931, 4.

81. Qtd. in Gauba, *Friends and Foes*, 86.

82. K. L. Gauba, *Uncle Sham: Being the Strange Tale of a Civilisation Run Amok* (Lahore: Times Publishing Co., 1927), 11.

83. Mayo, *Mother India*, 27; Sinha, *Specters of Mother India*, 62.

84. Mayo, *Mother India*, 28.

85. Ibid., 122.

86. Victor Mendoza, *Metroimperial Intimacies: Fantasy, Racial-Sexual Governance, and the Philippines in U.S. Imperialism, 1899–1913* (Durham, NC: Duke University Press, 2015), 28–29.

87. Ibid., 29.

88. Smedley, "Bootlickers' Handbook of India," 27.

89. Gauba, *Uncle Sham*, 6.

90. Ibid., 72.

91. Ibid.

92. Gauba, *Uncle Sham*, 41.

93. Ibid., 46.

94. Ibid.

95. Ibid., 35. Italics mine.

96. George Schuyler, "Views and Reviews," *Pittsburgh Courier*, December 7, 1929, 12.

97. Ibid., 12.

98. "Imitation of Life," *Afro-American*, February 16, 1935, 4.

99. Ralph Brewing, "'Uncle Sham' Bares Sex Secret of United States," *Afro-American*, April 5, 1930, 11.

100. Ibid., 11.

101. Gauba, *Uncle Sham*, 6.

102. Ghadiali, *American Sex Problems*, 77.

103. Ibid., 78.

104. Ibid., 84.

105. Mukerji, *A Son of Mother India Answers*, 9.

106. Ibid., 9–10.

107. Ibid., 9. For more on the racial implications of "white slave" discourse and the corresponding Mann Act, see Jessica R. Pliley, *Policing Sexuality: The Mann Act and the Making of the FBI* (Cambridge, MA: Harvard University Press, 2014).

108. Ibid., 10.

109. Dhan Gopal Mukerji, *Visit India with Me* (New York: E. P. Dutton and Co., 1929), 160.

110. To give a snapshot of violence against Dalit communities in India, Kamalakar Duvvuru reports that nearly 40,000 caste-related crimes against Scheduled Castes were recorded in 2013, including instances of sexual assault, beatings, and lynchings by upper-caste members. In a disturbing echo of the public spectacles of violence during Jim Crow, lynchings of Dalits persist in the present, with the additional horror of these events being broadcast through social media. Duvvuru explains, "Lynching is the high caste's way of forcibly reminding Dalits of their inferiority," and such crimes are committed by upper-caste members with relative impunity. Kamalakar Duvvuru, "Lynching: Public Celebration of Painful Experience of the Marginalised," *Countercurrents* (September 3, 2014): https://www.countercurrents.org/duvvuru030914.htm, accessed March 10, 2018.

111. Ibid., 160–161.

112. Lajpat Rai, *Unhappy India: Being a Reply to Miss Katherine Mayo's 'Mother India.'* (Calcutta: Banna Publishing Co., 1928), xiv–xv.

113. Mayo, *Mother India*, 4.

114. Rai, *Unhappy India*, 1–2.

115. Lajpat Rai, *The United States of America: A Hindu's Impressions and a Study* (Calcutta: R. Chatterjee, 1916), 389.

116. Rai, *Unhappy India*, ix.

117. Mayo, *Mother India*, 176–177.

118. Sinha, *Specters of Mother India*, 105. In *Un/Common Cultures*, Kamala Visweswaran also details the relationship between Ambedkar, Du Bois, and Lajpat Rai, pointing to the different ways in which the writers formulated comparisons between caste and race. Kamala Visweswaran, *Un/Common Cultures: Racism and the Rearticulation of Cultural Difference* (Durham: Duke University Press, 2010), 151–159.

119. Rai, *Unhappy India*, 124.

120. Ibid., 122.

121. Ibid., xviii.

122. Ibid., 141.

123. Amy Kaplan, *The Anarchy of Empire in the Making of U.S. Culture* (Cambridge, MA: Harvard University Press, 2005), 202.

124. W.E.B. Du Bois, *Darkwater: Voices from Within the Veil* (New York: Harcourt, Brace and Howe, 1920), 95.

125. Rai, *Unhappy India*, xv.

126. Ibid., 136.

127. Ibid., 141.

128. Nadkarni, "World-Menace," 807.

129. Rai, *Unhappy India*, 240.

130. Slate, *Colored Cosmopolitanism*, 61.

131. Qtd. in Visweswaran, *Un/Common Cultures*, 155–156.

132. Ibid., 156.

133. Sudhindra Bose, *Mother America: Realities of American Life as Seen by an Indian* (Baroda: Bhatt, 1934), frontispiece.

134. Ibid., 70.

135. Ibid., 71.

136. Ibid., 75.

137. Ibid., 4.

138. Ibid., 5.

139. Ibid., 6.

140. Ibid.
141. Ibid., 10.
142. Ibid., 46.
143. Ibid., 43.
144. Ibid., 116.
145. Ibid., 48.
146. Sugata Bose and Kris Manjapra, *Cosmopolitan Thought Zones: South Asia and the Global Circulation of Ideas* (New York: Palgrave Macmillan, 2010), 1.

AFTERWORD

1. Mrinalini Sinha, *Specters of Mother India: The Global Restructuring of an Empire* (Durham, NC: Duke University Press, 2007), 103.
2. Dhan Gopal Mukerji to Jawaharlal Nehru, April 16, 1929, NMML Archives.
3. Dhan Gopal Mukerji to Jawaharlal Nehru, November 17, 1929, NMML Archives.
4. Dhan Gopal Mukerji to Jawaharlal Nehru, April 8, 1929, NMML Archives.
5. In spite of the hostility of the U.S. government to Indian radicals, the Gadar Party did reconstitute itself after the Hindu–German conspiracy trial, and California remained an important node of activity for Gadar Party radicals into the 1920s and 1930s. As Maia Ramnath has described it, the postwar Gadar had effectively become "Gadar 2.0" and much more ideologically in sync with Communism. Maia Ramnath, *Haj to Utopia: How the Ghadar Movement Charted Global Radicalism and Attempted to Overthrow the British Empire* (Berkeley: University of California Press, 2011), 136–151.
6. Dhan Gopal Mukerji to Jawaharlal Nehru, May 4, 1936. NMML Archives.
7. Seema Sohi, "From 1917 to 2017: Immigration, Exclusion, and 'National Security,'" *South Asian American Digital Archive*, https://www.saada.org/tides/article/1917-2017, accessed March 10, 2018.
8. In his sharp critique of what he dubs "the Indian ideology," Perry Anderson argues that the violence of the Indian state and inequalities of its democracy are not "recent maladies of a once healthy system" but "descend from its original composition," pointing specifically to the failures of the Indian National Congress and the nationalist movement. Perry Anderson, *The Indian Ideology* (London: Verso Books, 2013), 181.
9. Pankaj Mishra, "India at 70, and the Passing of Another Illusion," *New York Times,* August 11, 2017, https://www.nytimes.com/2017/08/11/opinion/india-70-partition-pankaj-mishra.html, accessed March 10, 2018.
10. Amitava Kumar, *Immigrant, Montana* (New York: Alfred A. Knopf Company, 2018), 199.
11. Ibid., 200.
12. Sucheta Mazumdar, "Racist Responses to Racism: The Aryan Myth and South Asians in the United States," *South Asia Bulletin* 9, no. 1 (1989): 47–55.
13. Vanita Reddy and Anantha Sudhakar, "Introduction: Feminist and Queer Afro-Asian Formations," *S&F Online* 14, no. 3 (2018).
14. Ibid.
15. See Nayan Shah, *Stranger Intimacy: Contesting Race, Sexuality and the Law in the North American West* (Berkeley: University of California Press, 2012); Karen Leonard, *Making Ethnic Choices: California's Punjabi Mexican Americans* (Philadelphia, PA: Temple University Press, 1992).

Index

Manan Desai is an Assistant Professor in the Department of American Culture and the Program in Asian/Pacific Islander American Studies at the University of Michigan. He serves on the Academic Council of the South Asian American Digital Archive.

Jere Takahashi, *Nisei/Sansei: Shifting Japanese American Identities and Politics*

Velina Hasu Houston, ed., *But Still, Like Air, I'll Rise: New Asian American Plays*

Josephine Lee, *Performing Asian America: Race and Ethnicity on the Contemporary Stage*

Deepika Bahri and Mary Vasudeva, eds., *Between the Lines: South Asians and Postcoloniality*

E. San Juan Jr., *The Philippine Temptation: Dialectics of Philippines–U.S. Literary Relations*

Carlos Bulosan and E. San Juan Jr., eds., *The Cry and the Dedication*

Carlos Bulosan and E. San Juan Jr., eds., *On Becoming Filipino: Selected Writings of Carlos Bulosan*

Vicente L. Rafael, ed., *Discrepant Histories: Translocal Essays on Filipino Cultures*

Yen Le Espiritu, *Filipino American Lives*

Paul Ong, Edna Bonacich, and Lucie Cheng, eds., *The New Asian Immigration in Los Angeles and Global Restructuring*

Chris Friday, *Organizing Asian American Labor: The Pacific Coast Canned-Salmon Industry, 1870–1942*

Sucheng Chan, ed., *Hmong Means Free: Life in Laos and America*

Timothy P. Fong, *The First Suburban Chinatown: The Remaking of Monterey Park, California*

William Wei, *The Asian American Movement*

Yen Le Espiritu, *Asian American Panethnicity*

Velina Hasu Houston, ed., *The Politics of Life*

Renqiu Yu, *To Save China, To Save Ourselves: The Chinese Hand Laundry Alliance of New York*

Shirley Geok-lin Lim and Amy Ling, eds., *Reading the Literatures of Asian America*

Karen Isaksen Leonard, *Making Ethnic Choices: California's Punjabi Mexican Americans*

Gary Y. Okihiro, *Cane Fires: The Anti-Japanese Movement in Hawaii, 1865–1945*

Sucheng Chan, *Entry Denied: Exclusion and the Chinese Community in America, 1882–1943*